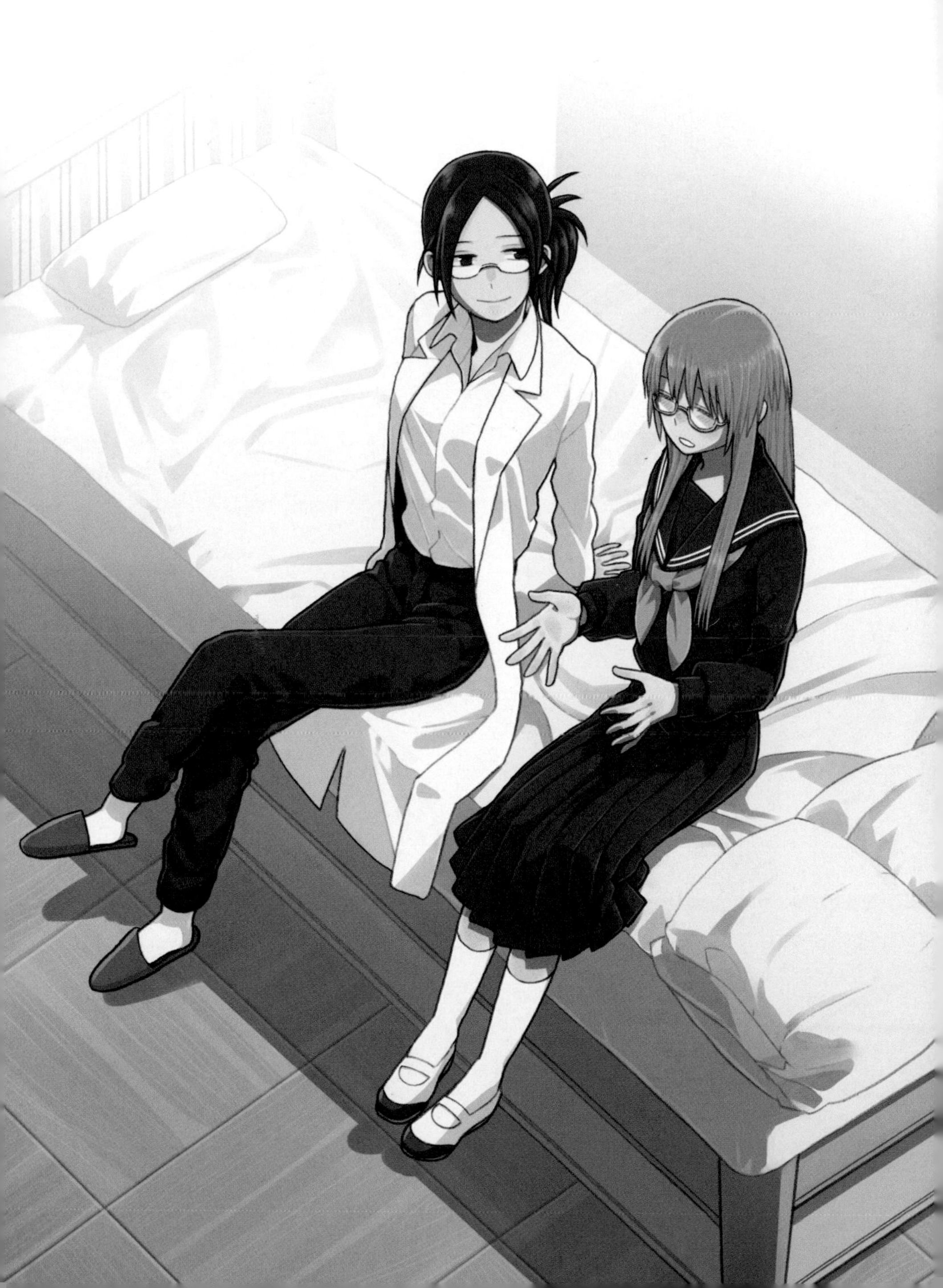

Contents

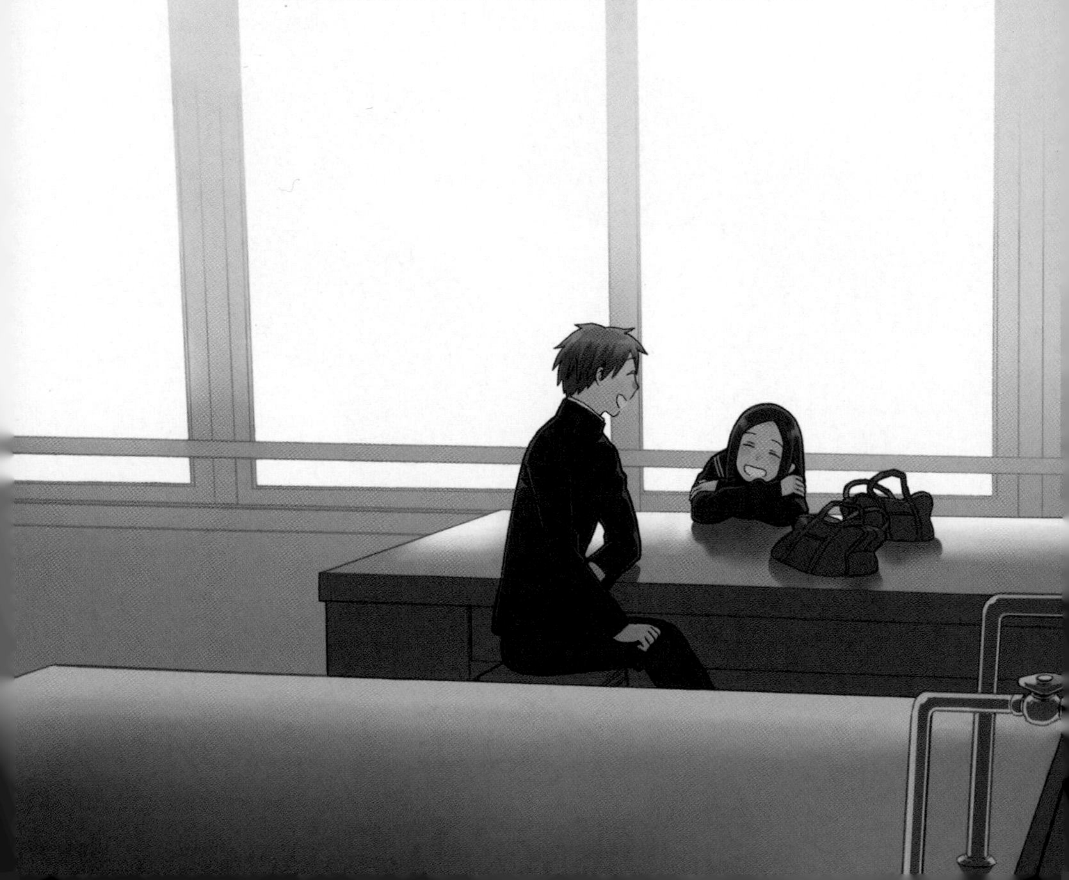

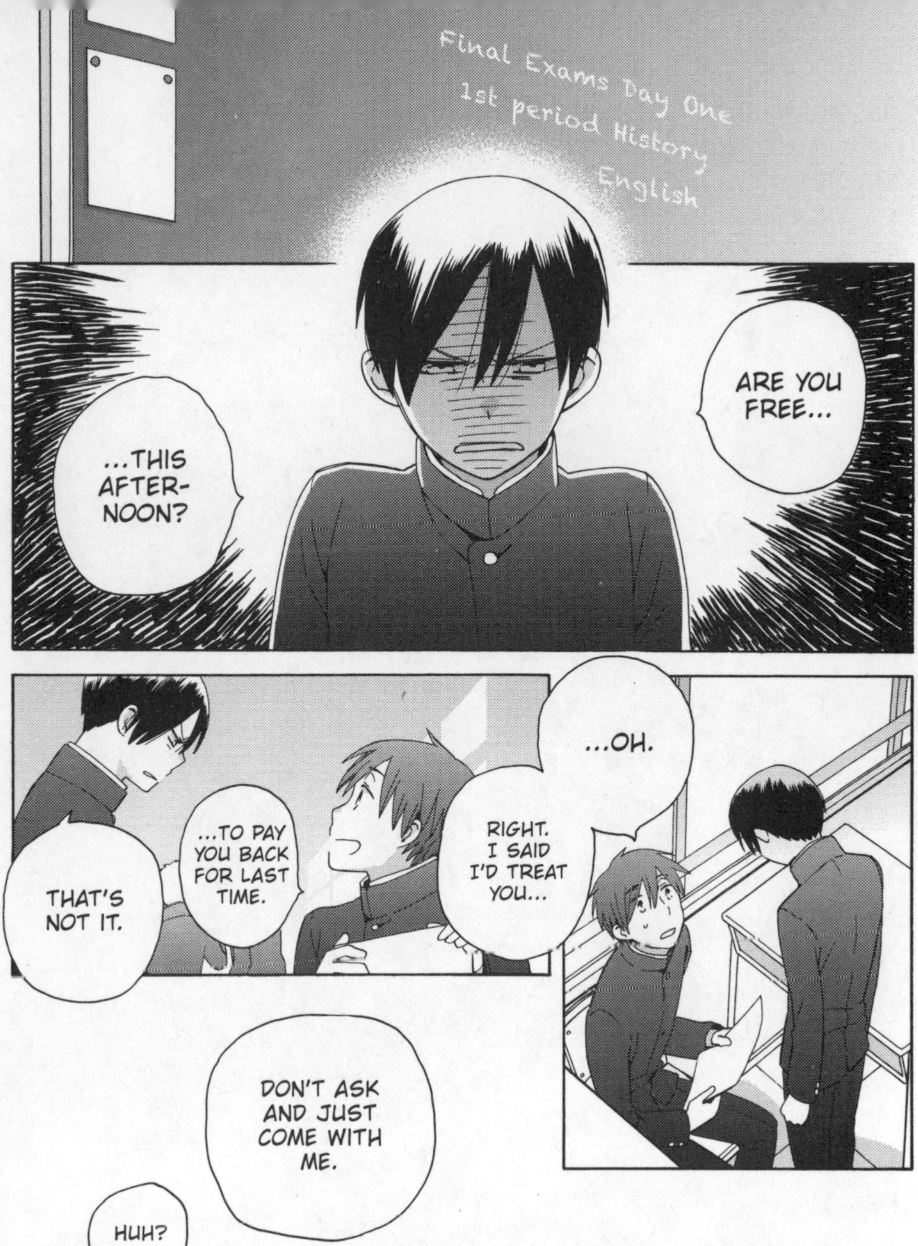
Final Exams Day One
1st period History
English
ARE YOU FREE...
...THIS AFTER-NOON?
...OH.
RIGHT. I SAID I'D TREAT YOU...
...TO PAY YOU BACK FOR LAST TIME.
THAT'S NOT IT.
DON'T ASK AND JUST COME WITH ME.
HUH?

Love at Fourteen

[Intermission 57]

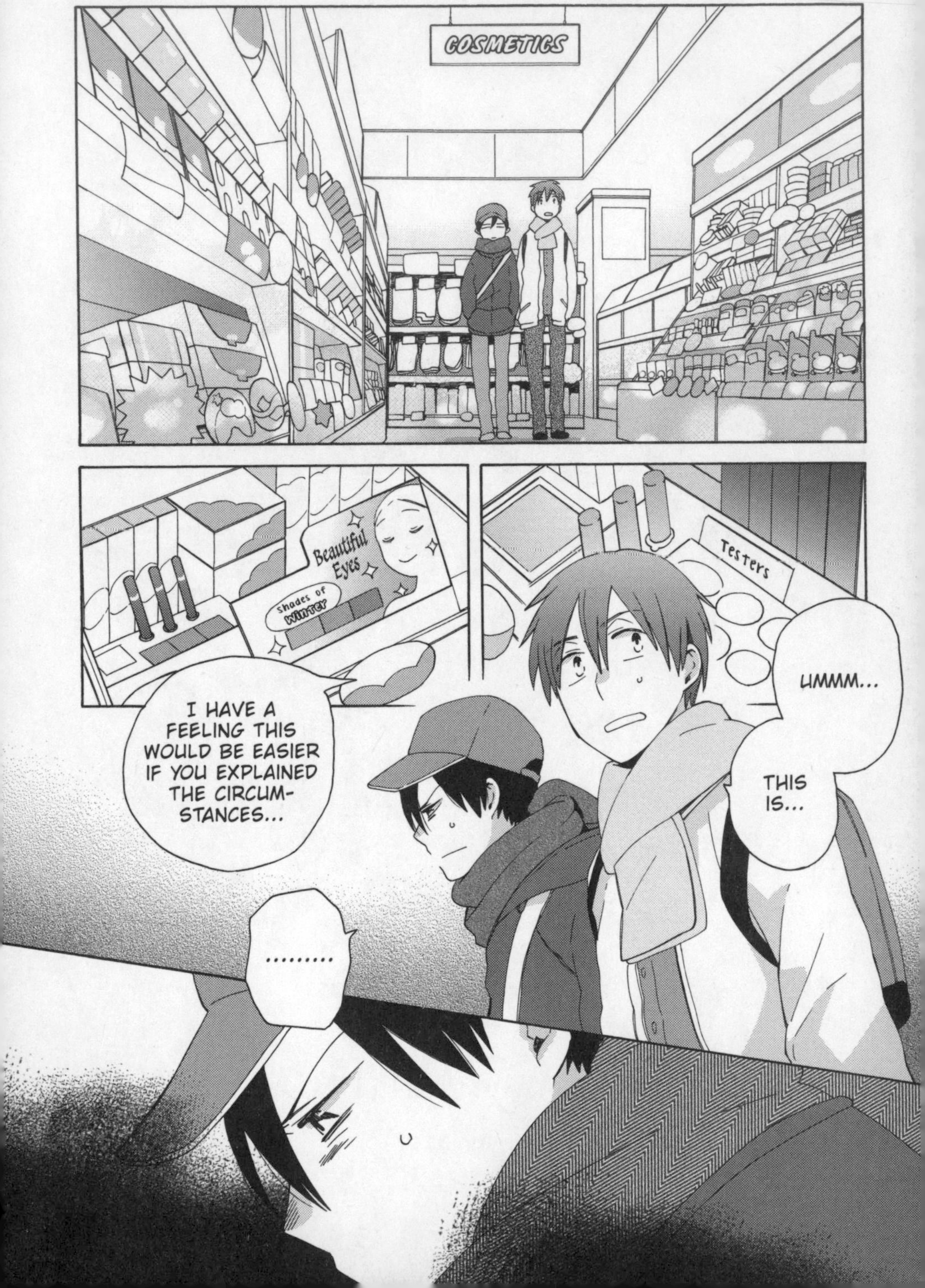

COSMETICS
Testers
UMMM...
THIS IS...
Beautiful Eyes
Shades of Winter
I HAVE A FEELING THIS WOULD BE EASIER IF YOU EXPLAINED THE CIRCUM-STANCES...
....

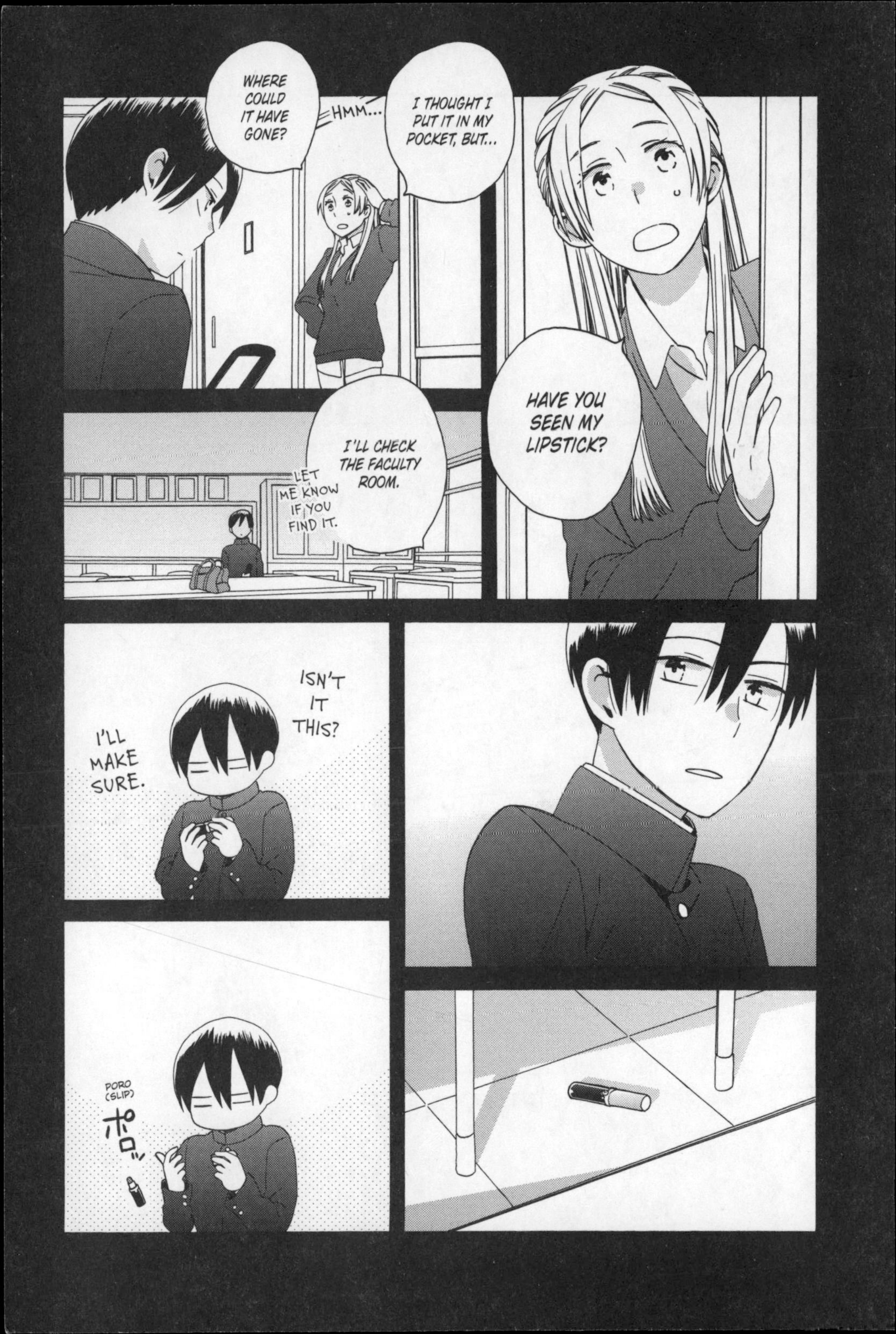
HAVE YOU SEEN MY LIPSTICK?
I THOUGHT I PUT IT IN MY POCKET, BUT...
HMM...
WHERE COULD IT HAVE GONE?
I'LL CHECK THE FACULTY ROOM.
LET ME KNOW IF YOU FIND IT.
ISN'T IT THIS?
I'LL MAKE SURE.
PORO (SLIP)
ポロッ

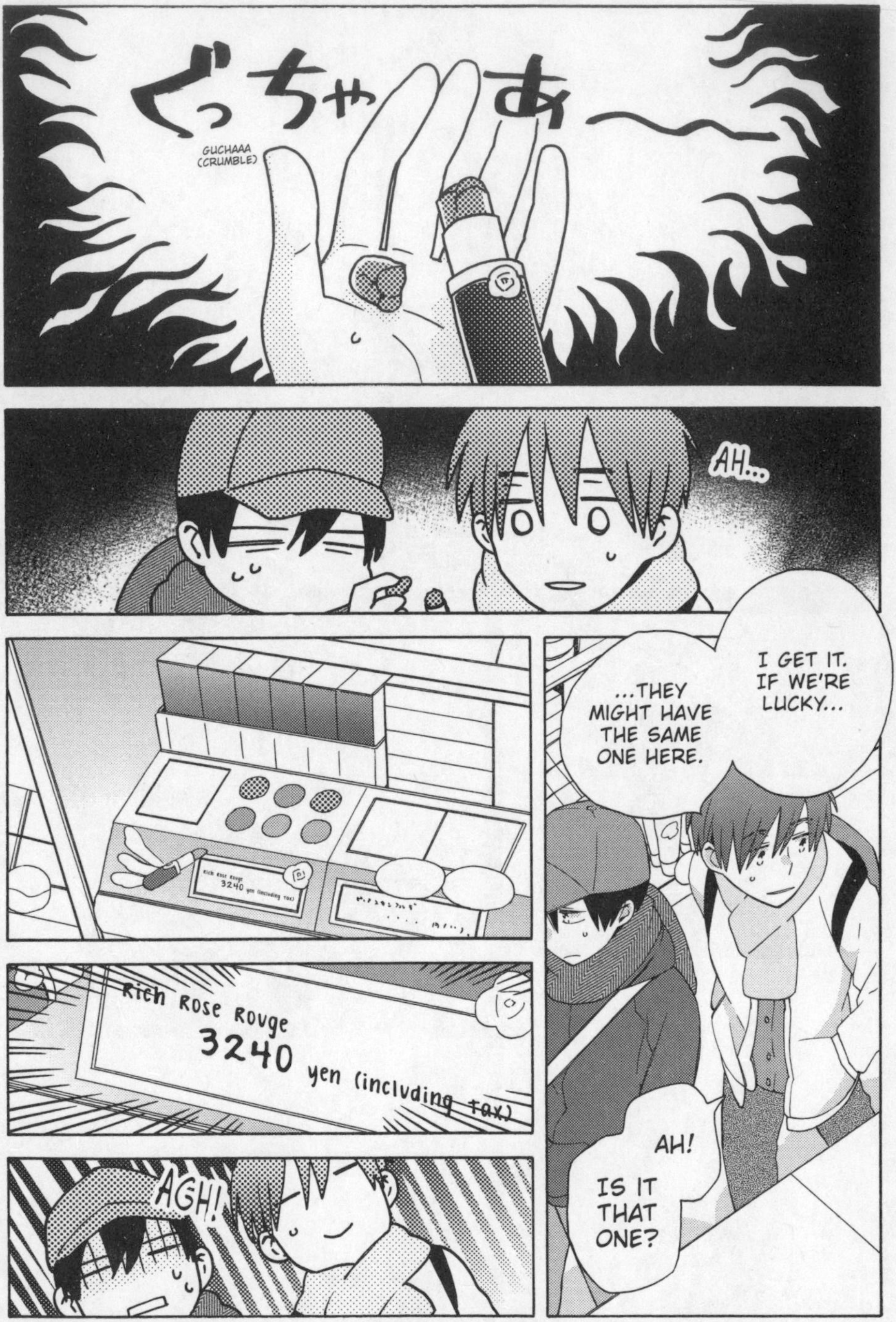
ぐっちゃあ~
GUCHAAA (CRUMBLE)
AH...
I GET IT. IF WE'RE LUCKY...
...THEY MIGHT HAVE THE SAME ONE HERE.
AH!
IS IT THAT ONE?
Rich Rose Rouge 3240 yen (including tax)
Rich Rose Rouge
3240 yen (including tax)
AGH!

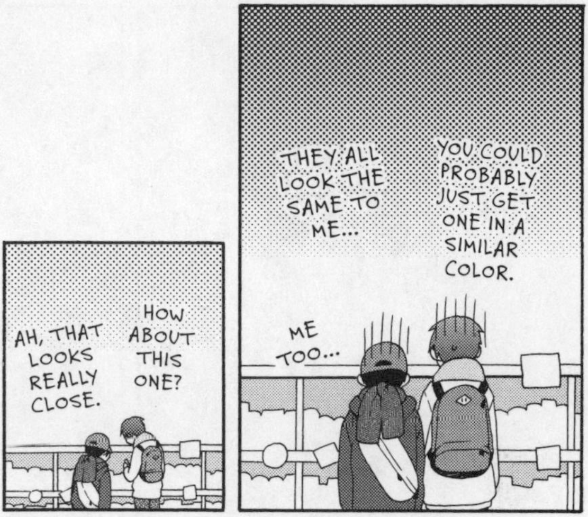
YOU COULD PROBABLY JUST GET ONE IN A SIMILAR COLOR.
THEY ALL LOOK THE SAME TO ME...
ME TOO...
HOW ABOUT THIS ONE?
AH, THAT LOOKS REALLY CLOSE.

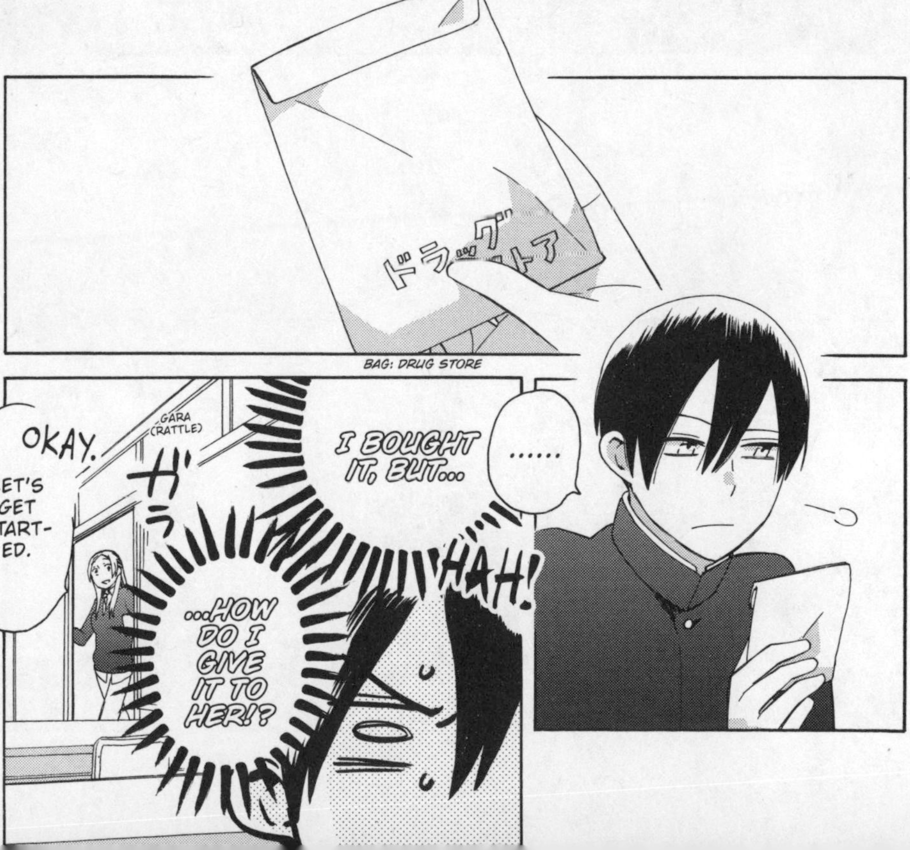
BAG: DRUG STORE
......
I BOUGHT IT, BUT...
...HOW DO I GIVE IT TO HER!?
HAH!
ガラ
GARA (RATTLE)
OKAY.
LET'S GET START-ED.

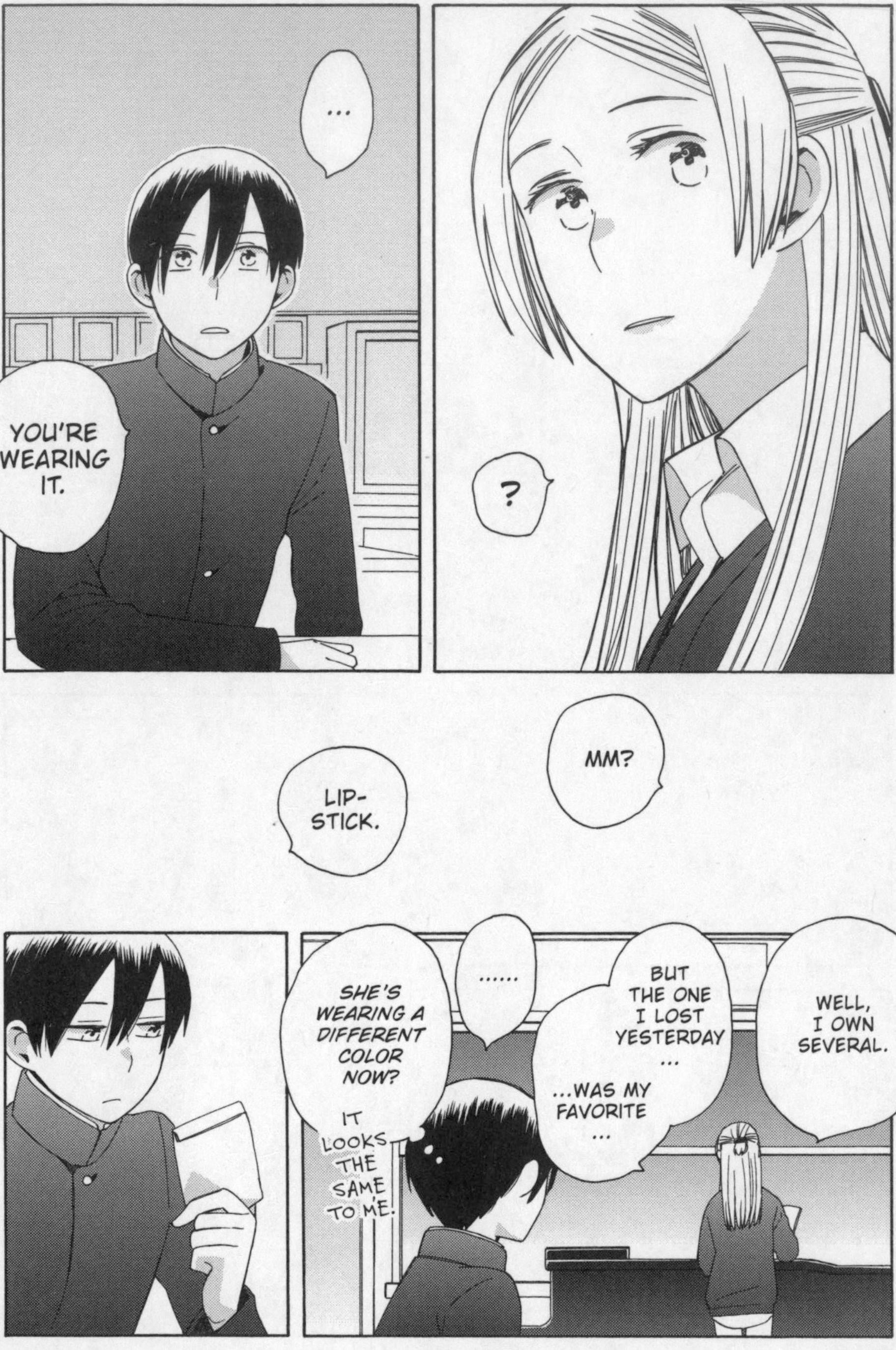
?
...
YOU'RE WEARING IT.
MM?
LIP-STICK.
WELL, I OWN SEVERAL.
BUT THE ONE I LOST YESTERDAY ...
...WAS MY FAVORITE ...
......
SHE'S WEARING A DIFFERENT COLOR NOW?
IT LOOKS THE SAME TO ME.

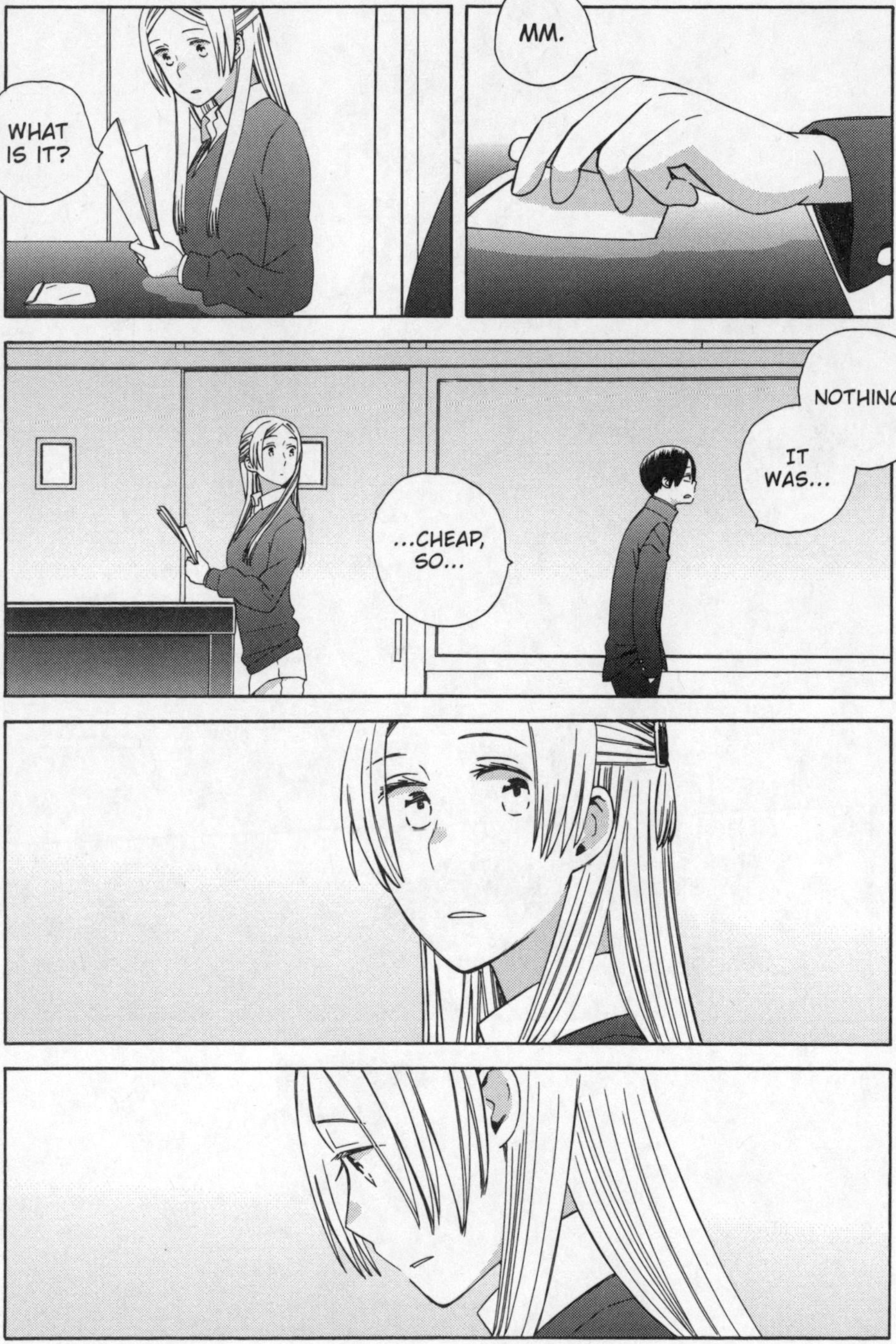
MM.
WHAT IS IT?
NOTHING.
IT WAS...
...CHEAP, SO...

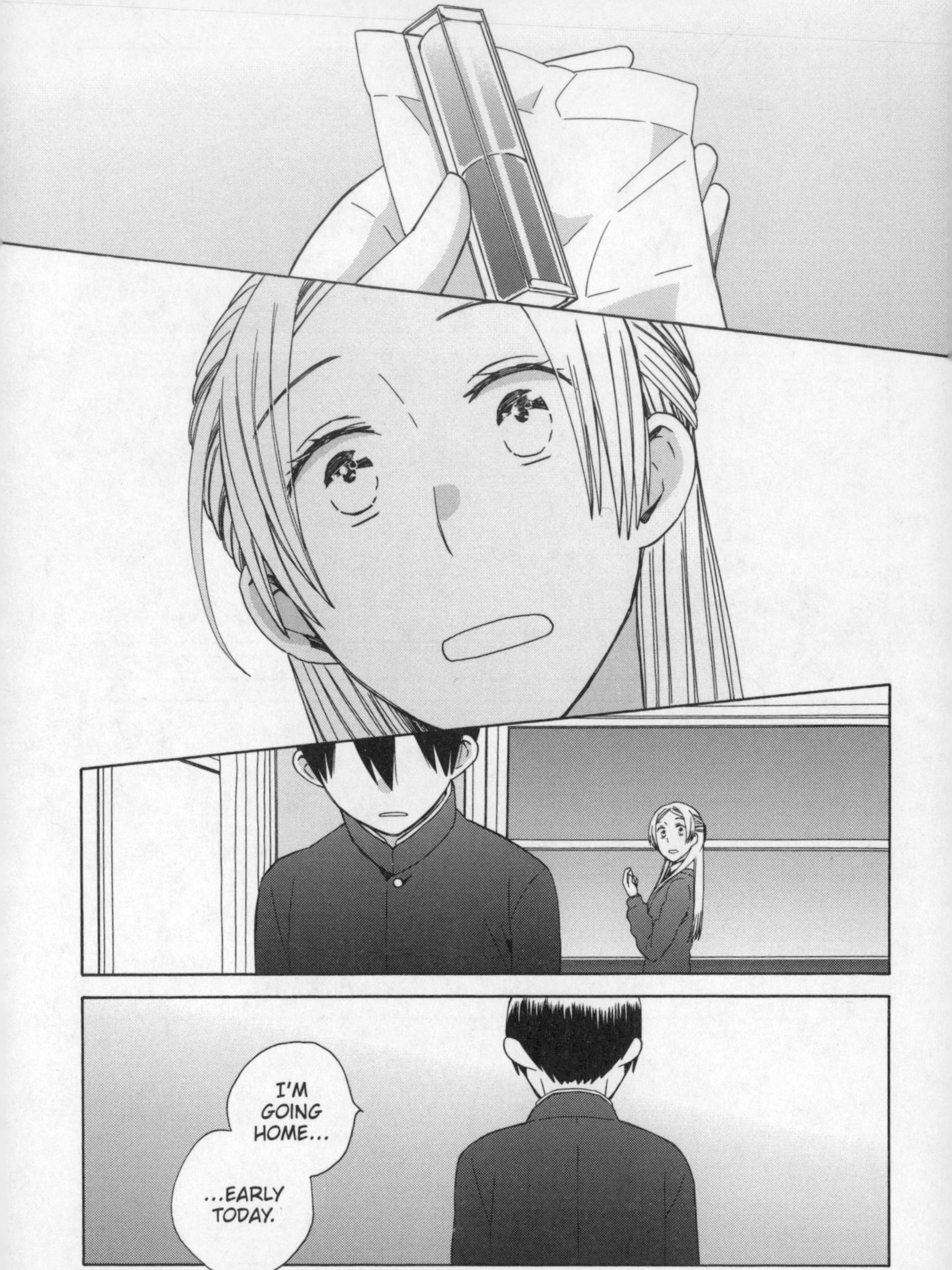
I'M GOING HOME...
...EARLY TODAY.

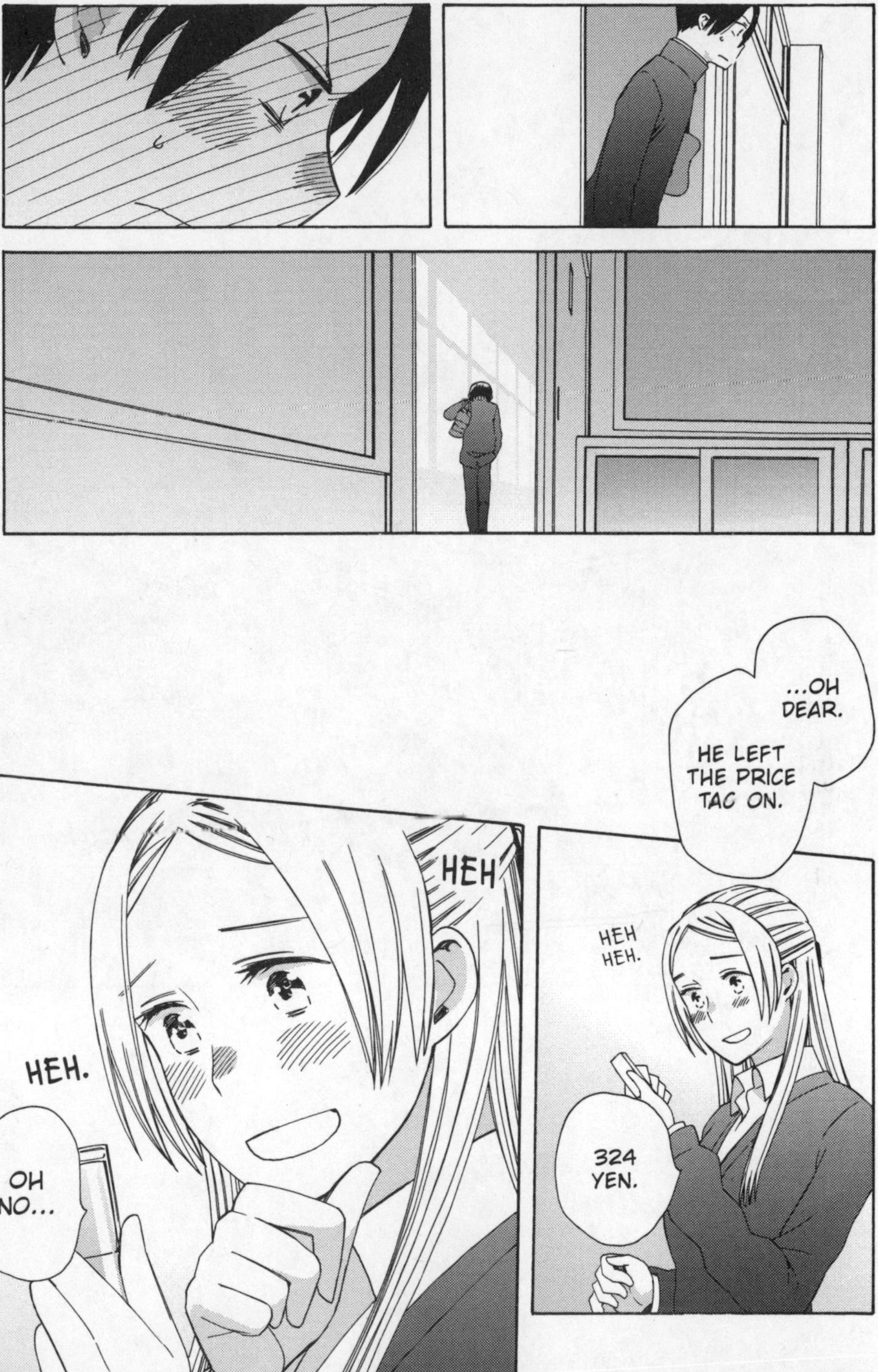
...OH DEAR.
HE LEFT THE PRICE TAC ON.
HEH HEH.
324 YEN.
HEH
HEH.
OH NO...

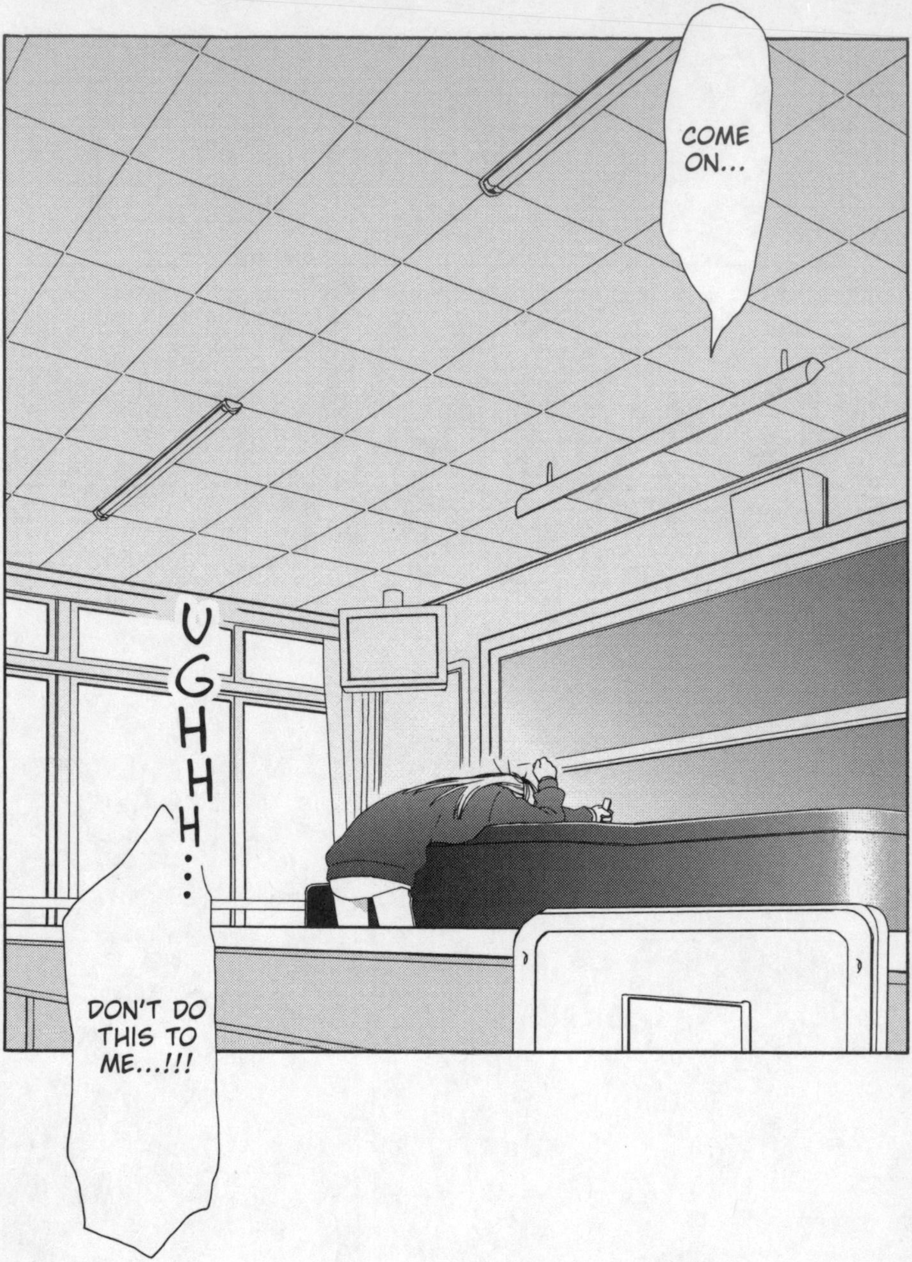
COME ON...
UGHHH...
DON'T DO THIS TO ME...!!!

Fin

Love at Fourteen

[Chapter 42]

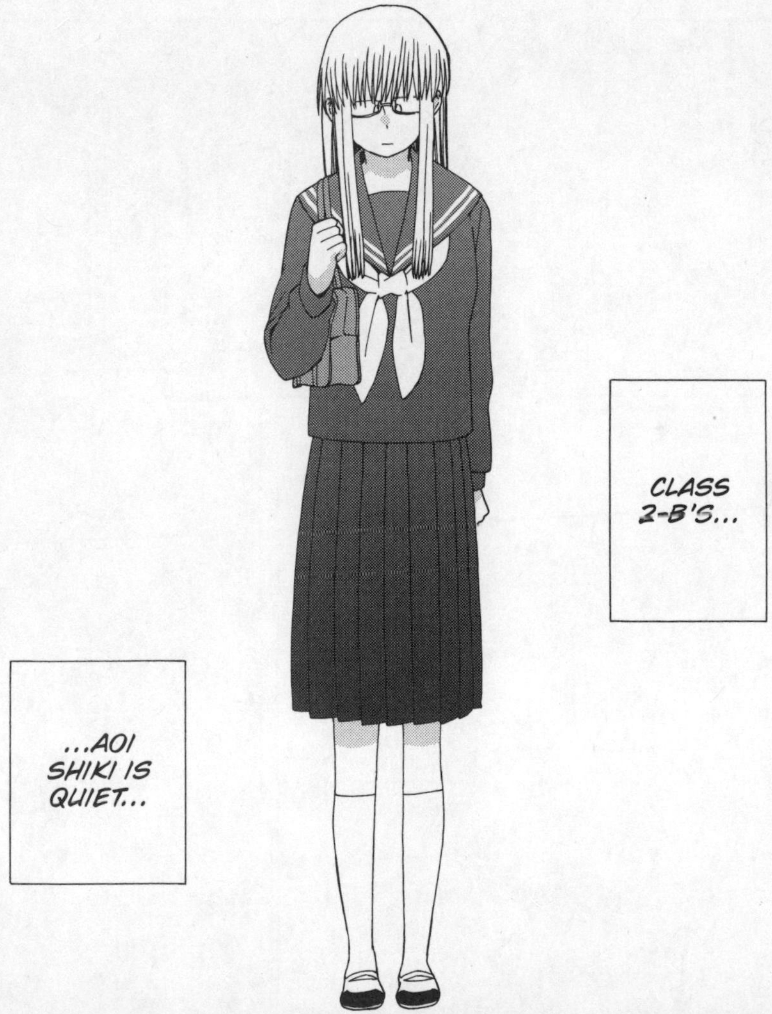
CLASS 2-B'S...
...AOI SHIKI IS QUIET...

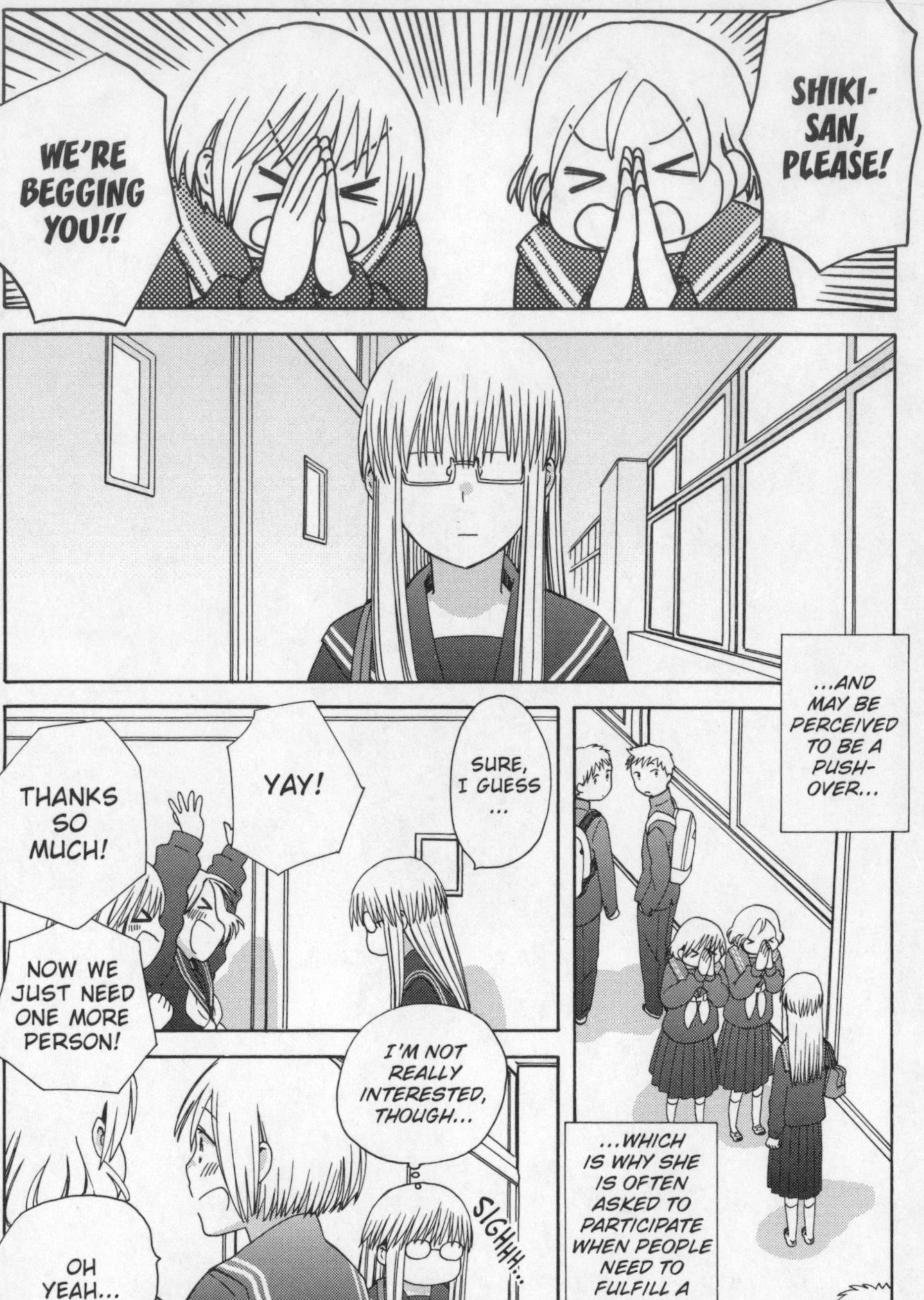
SHIKI-SAN, PLEASE!
WE'RE BEGGING YOU!!
...AND MAY BE PERCEIVED TO BE A PUSH-OVER...
...WHICH IS WHY SHE IS OFTEN ASKED TO PARTICIPATE WHEN PEOPLE NEED TO FULFILL A HEAD COUNT.
SURE, I GUESS ...
YAY!
THANKS SO MUCH!
NOW WE JUST NEED ONE MORE PERSON!
I'M NOT REALLY INTERESTED, THOUGH...
SIGHHH...
OH YEAH...

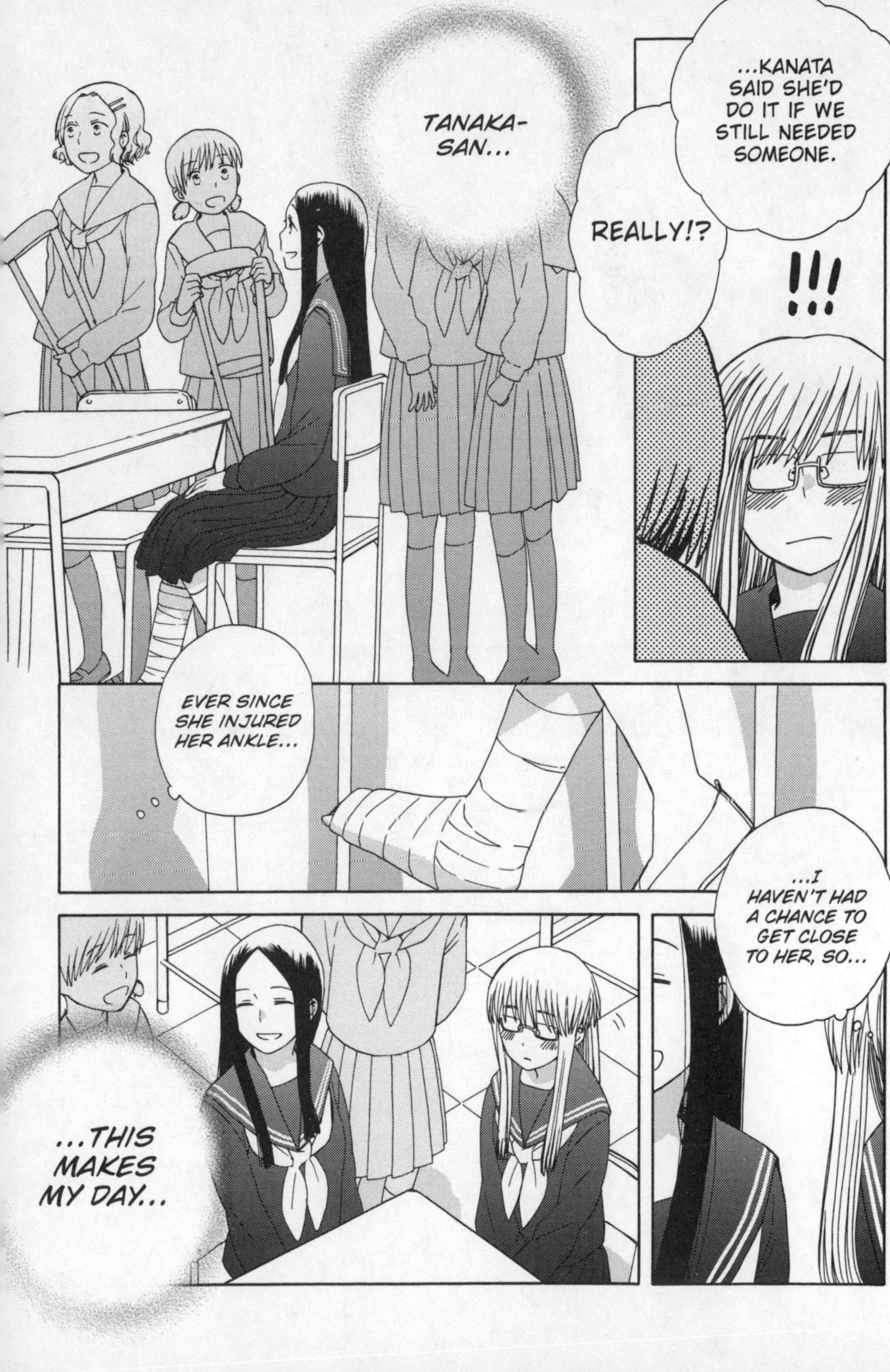
...KANATA SAID SHE'D DO IT IF WE STILL NEEDED SOMEONE.
REALLY!?
!!!
TANAKA-SAN...
EVER SINCE SHE INJURED HER ANKLE...
...I HAVEN'T HAD A CHANCE TO GET CLOSE TO HER, SO...
...THIS MAKES MY DAY...

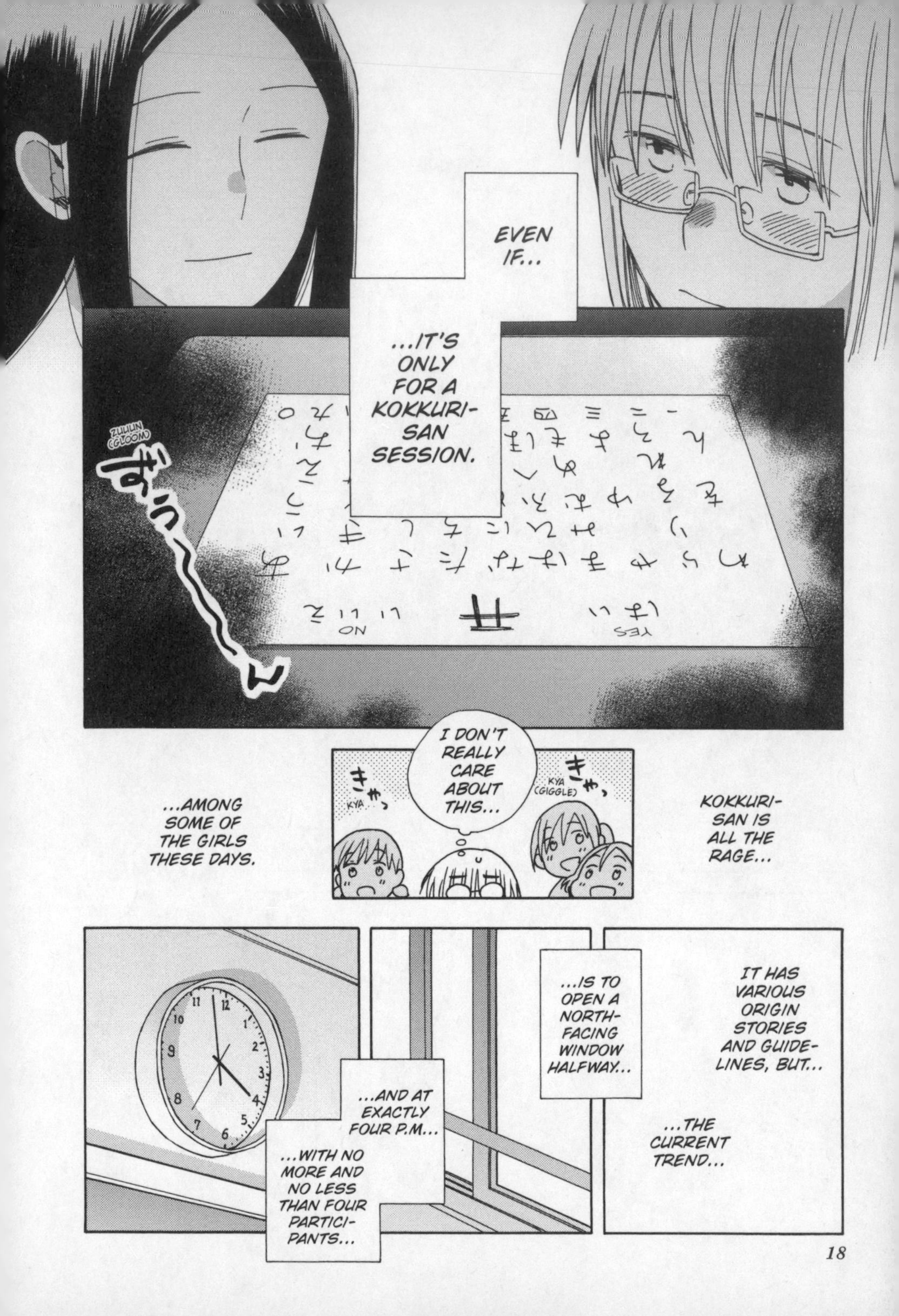

EVEN IF...
...IT'S ONLY FOR A KOKKURI-SAN SESSION.
ZUUUN (GLOOM)
YES
NO
KOKKURI-SAN IS ALL THE RAGE...
KYA (GIGGLE)
I DON'T REALLY CARE ABOUT THIS...
KYA
...AMONG SOME OF THE GIRLS THESE DAYS.
IT HAS VARIOUS ORIGIN STORIES AND GUIDE-LINES, BUT...
...THE CURRENT TREND...
...IS TO OPEN A NORTH-FACING WINDOW HALFWAY...
...AND AT EXACTLY FOUR P.M...
...WITH NO MORE AND NO LESS THAN FOUR PARTICI-PANTS...

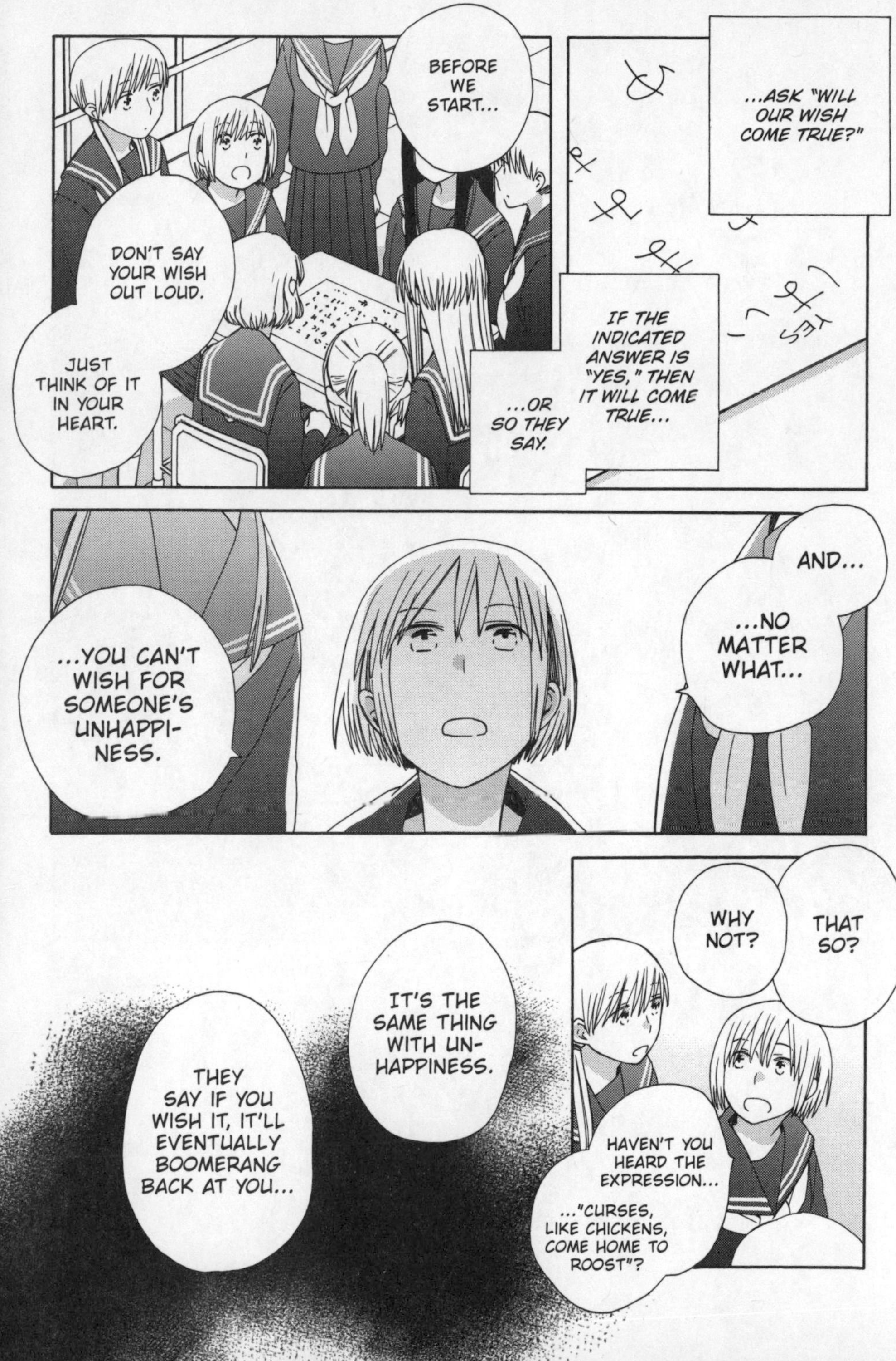
...ASK "WILL OUR WISH COME TRUE?"
IF THE INDICATED ANSWER IS "YES," THEN IT WILL COME TRUE...
...OR SO THEY SAY.
BEFORE WE START...
DON'T SAY YOUR WISH OUT LOUD.
JUST THINK OF IT IN YOUR HEART.
AND...
...NO MATTER WHAT...
...YOU CAN'T WISH FOR SOMEONE'S UNHAPPI-NESS.
THAT SO?
WHY NOT?
HAVEN'T YOU HEARD THE EXPRESSION...
..."CURSES, LIKE CHICKENS, COME HOME TO ROOST"?
IT'S THE SAME THING WITH UN-HAPPINESS.
THEY SAY IF YOU WISH IT, IT'LL EVENTUALLY BOOMERANG BACK AT YOU...

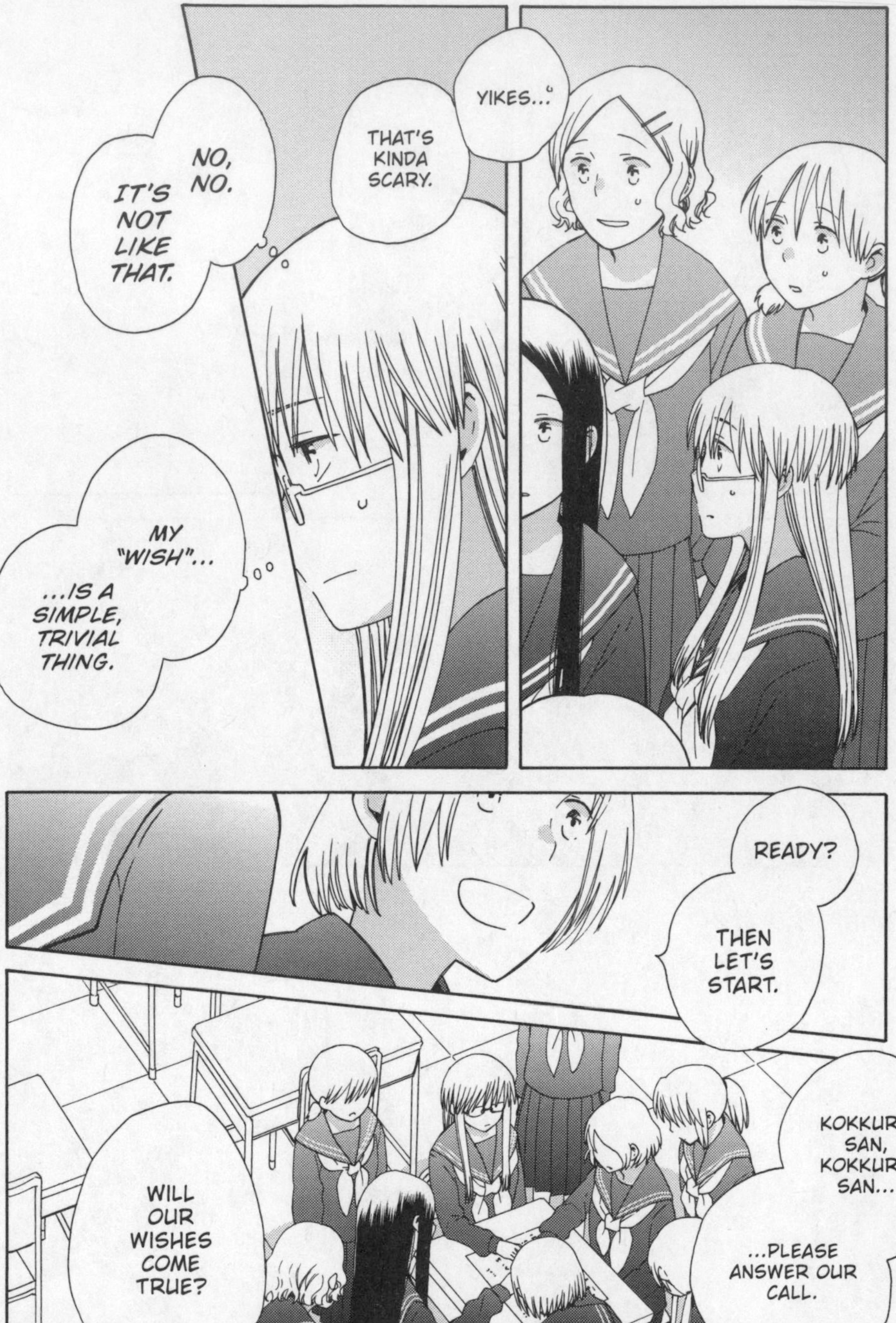
YIKES...
THAT'S KINDA SCARY.
NO, NO.
IT'S NOT LIKE THAT.
MY "WISH"...
...IS A SIMPLE, TRIVIAL THING.
READY?
THEN LET'S START.
KOKKURI-SAN, KOKKURI-SAN...
...PLEASE ANSWER OUR CALL.
WILL OUR WISHES COME TRUE?

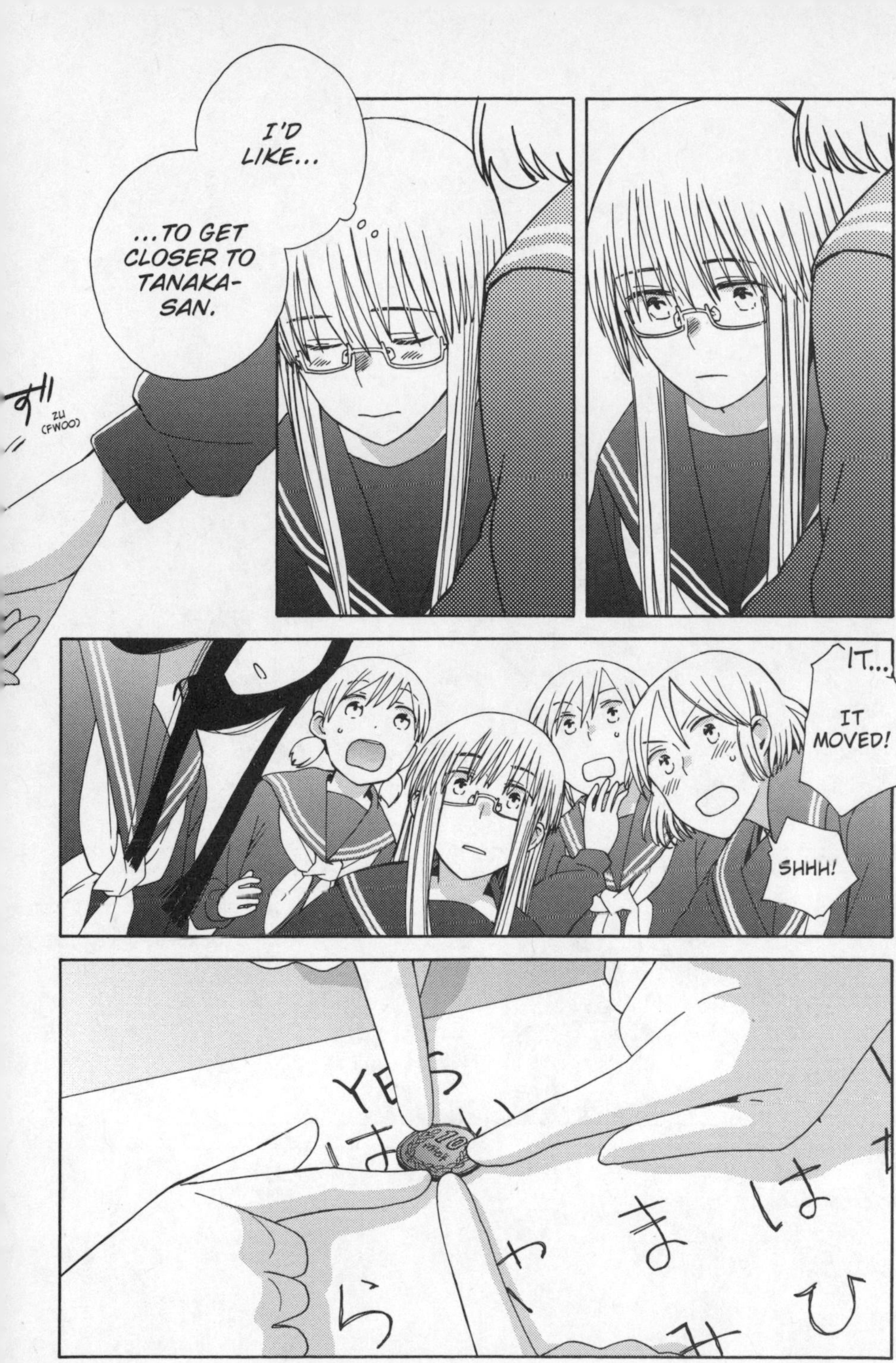
I'D LIKE...
...TO GET CLOSER TO TANAKA-SAN.
ずい
ZU (FWOO)
IT...
IT MOVED!
SHHH!
YES
はい

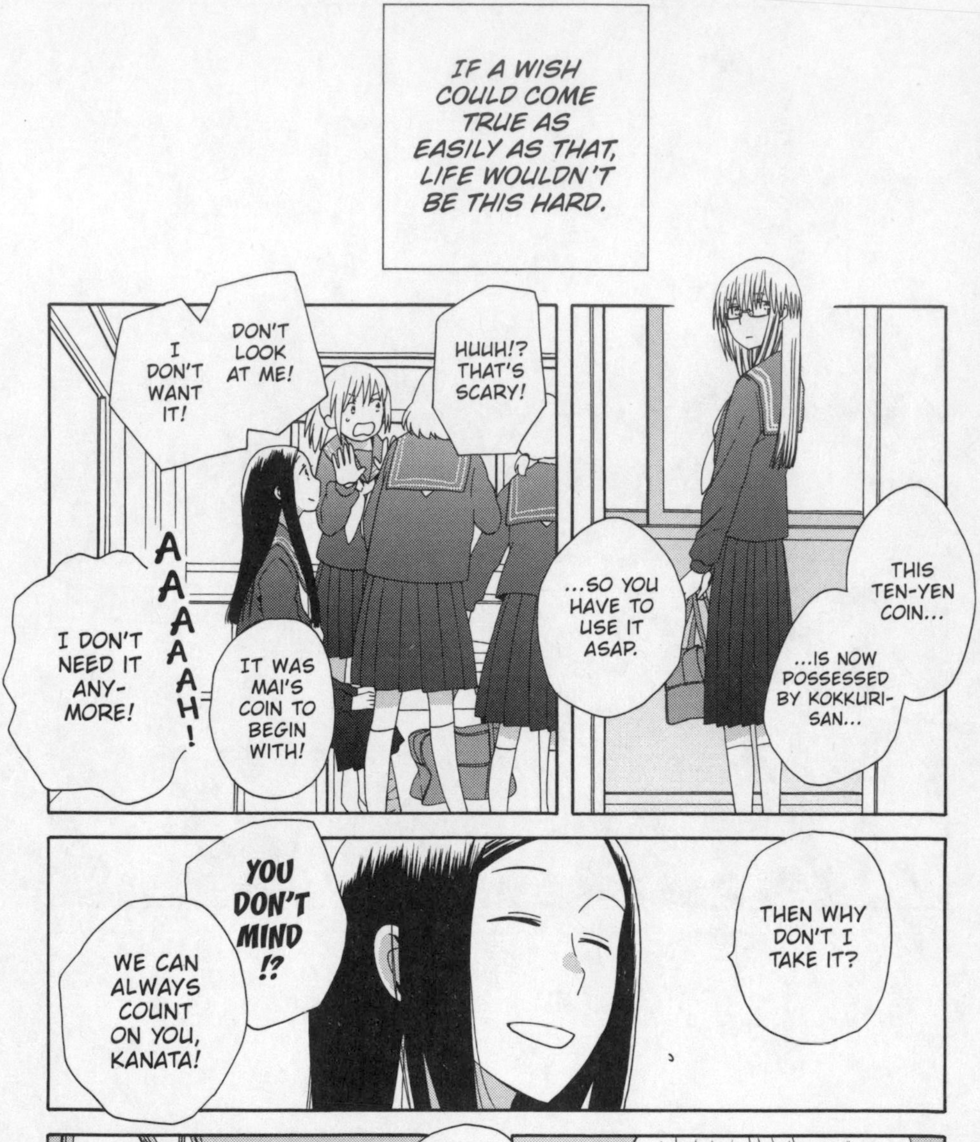
IF A WISH COULD COME TRUE AS EASILY AS THAT, LIFE WOULDN'T BE THIS HARD.
THIS TEN-YEN COIN...
...IS NOW POSSESSED BY KOKKURI-SAN...
...SO YOU HAVE TO USE IT ASAP.
HUUH!? THAT'S SCARY!
DON'T LOOK AT ME!
I DON'T WANT IT!
IT WAS MAI'S COIN TO BEGIN WITH!
AAAAAH!
I DON'T NEED IT ANY-MORE!
THEN WHY DON'T I TAKE IT?
YOU DON'T MIND!?
WE CAN ALWAYS COUNT ON YOU, KANATA!
I ONLY GOT TO BE NEXT TO HER...
...FOR A MOMENT.
NOW I'M DE-PRESSED.

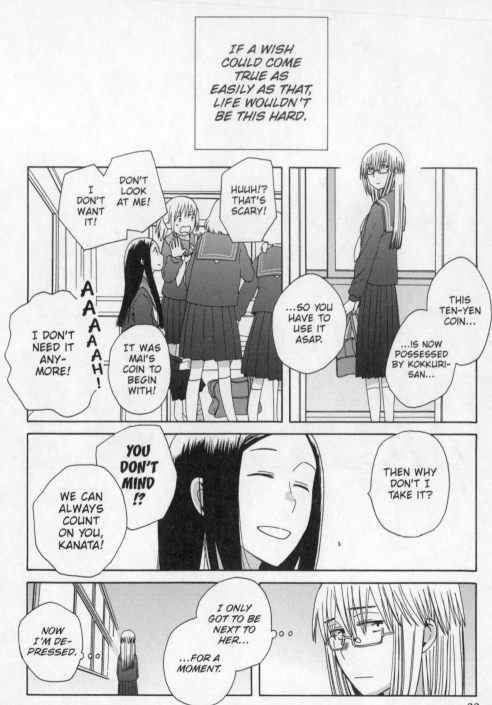

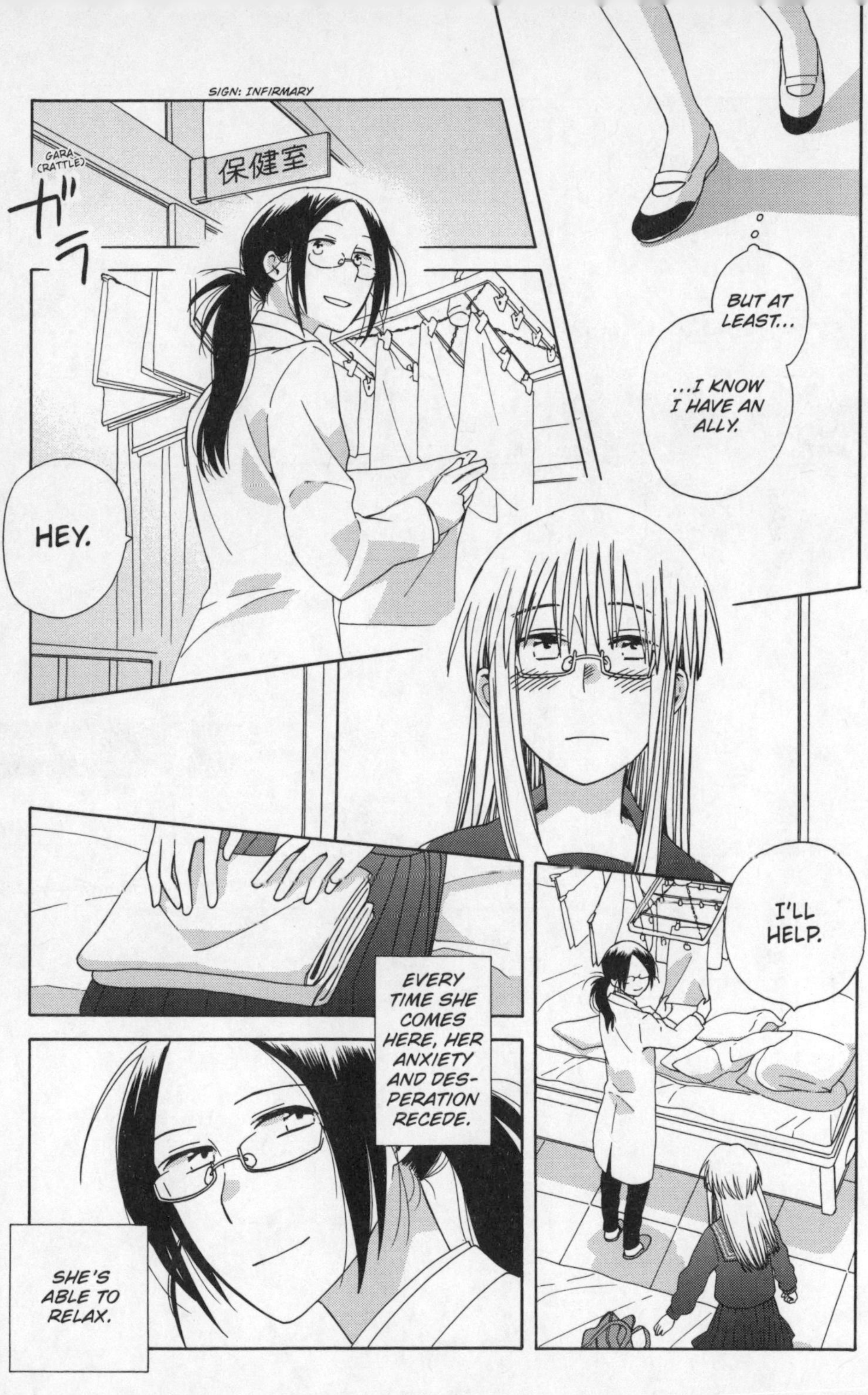
BUT AT LEAST...
...I KNOW I HAVE AN ALLY.
SIGN: INFIRMARY
保健室
ガラ
GARA (RATTLE)
HEY.
I'LL HELP.
EVERY TIME SHE COMES HERE, HER ANXIETY AND DESPERATION RECEDE.
SHE'S ABLE TO RELAX.

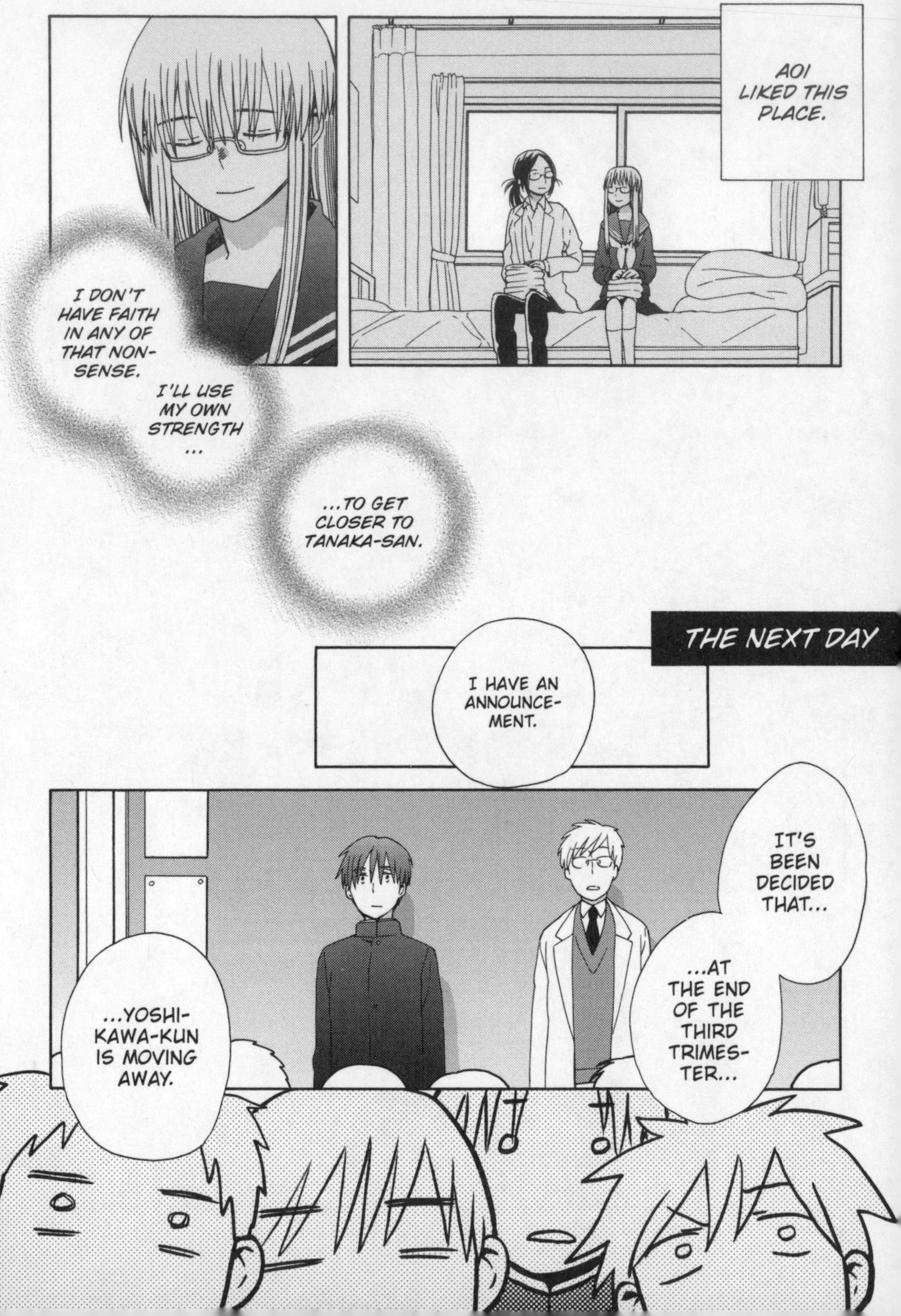
AOI LIKED THIS PLACE.
I DON'T HAVE FAITH IN ANY OF THAT NON-SENSE.
I'LL USE MY OWN STRENGTH ...
...TO GET CLOSER TO TANAKA-SAN.
THE NEXT DAY
I HAVE AN ANNOUNCE-MENT.
IT'S BEEN DECIDED THAT...
...AT THE END OF THE THIRD TRIMES-TER...
...YOSHI-KAWA-KUN IS MOVING AWAY.

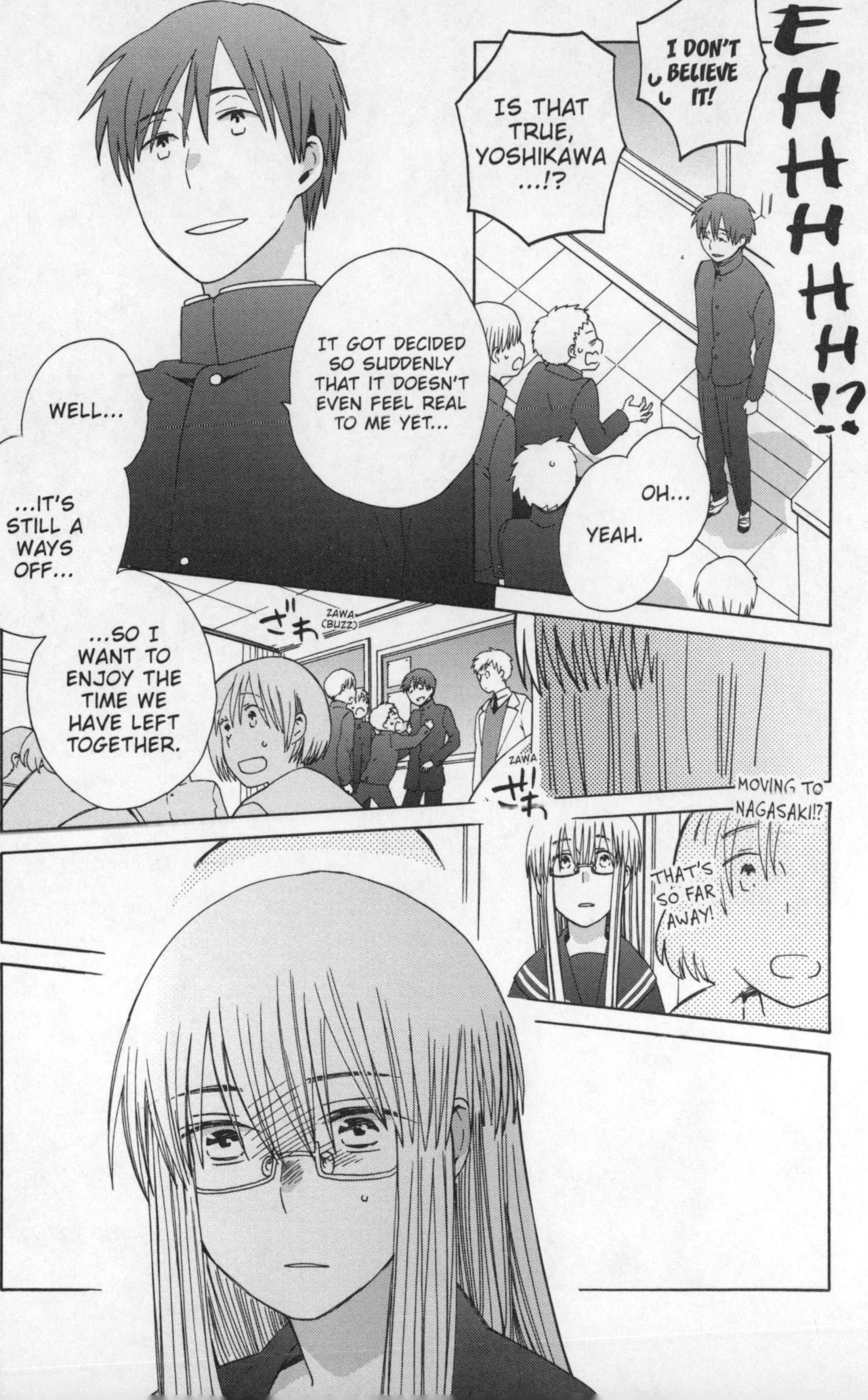
EHHHHH!?
I DON'T BELIEVE IT!
IS THAT TRUE, YOSHIKAWA ...!?
OH... YEAH.
IT GOT DECIDED SO SUDDENLY THAT IT DOESN'T EVEN FEEL REAL TO ME YET...
WELL...
...IT'S STILL A WAYS OFF...
...SO I WANT TO ENJOY THE TIME WE HAVE LEFT TOGETHER.
ざわ ZAWA (BUZZ)
ざわ ZAWA
MOVING TO NAGASAKI!?
THAT'S SO FAR AWAY!

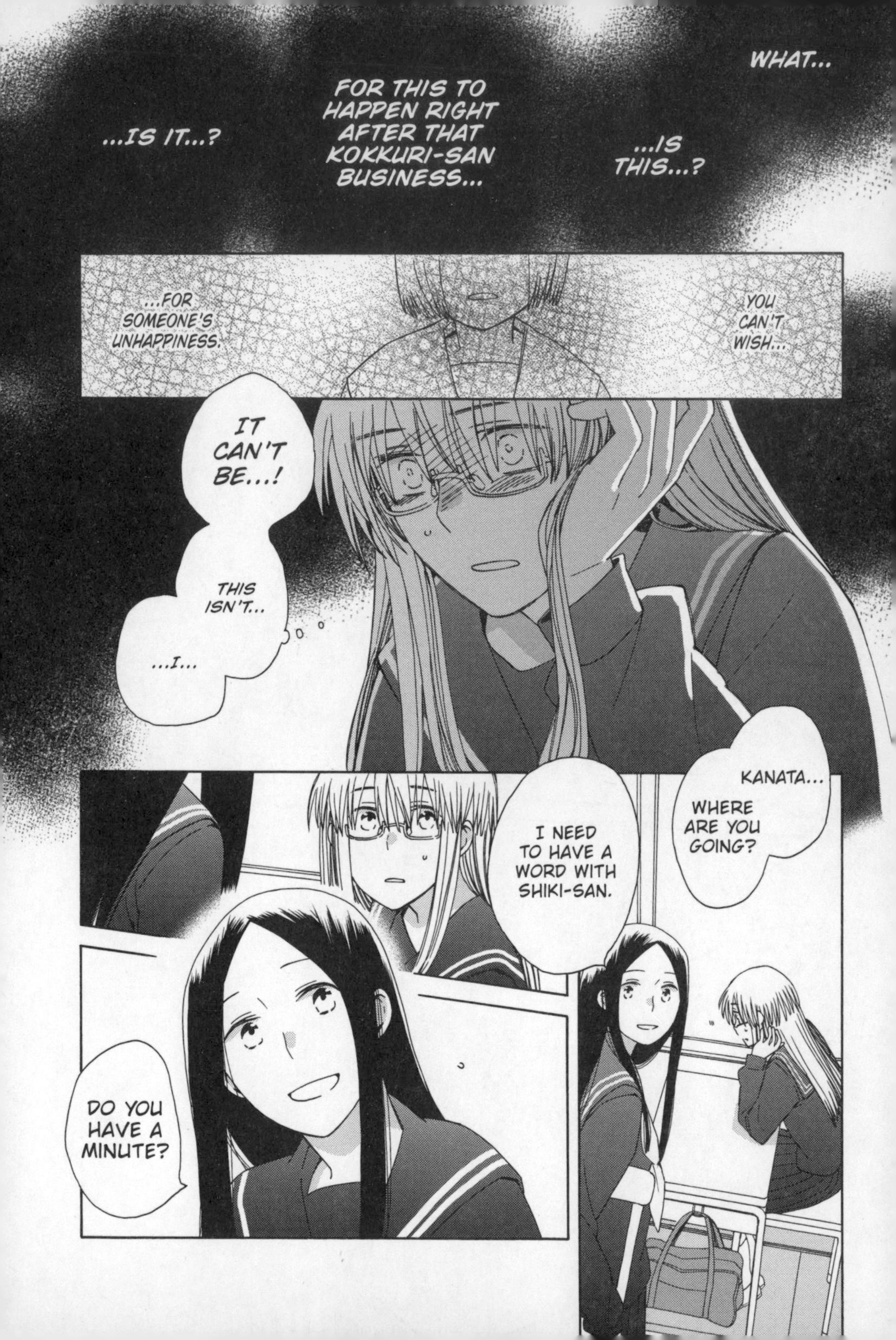
WHAT...
...IS THIS...?
FOR THIS TO HAPPEN RIGHT AFTER THAT KOKKURI-SAN BUSINESS...
...IS IT...?
YOU CAN'T WISH...
...FOR SOMEONE'S UNHAPPINESS.
IT CAN'T BE...!
THIS ISN'T...
...I...
KANATA...
WHERE ARE YOU GOING?
I NEED TO HAVE A WORD WITH SHIKI-SAN.
DO YOU HAVE A MINUTE?

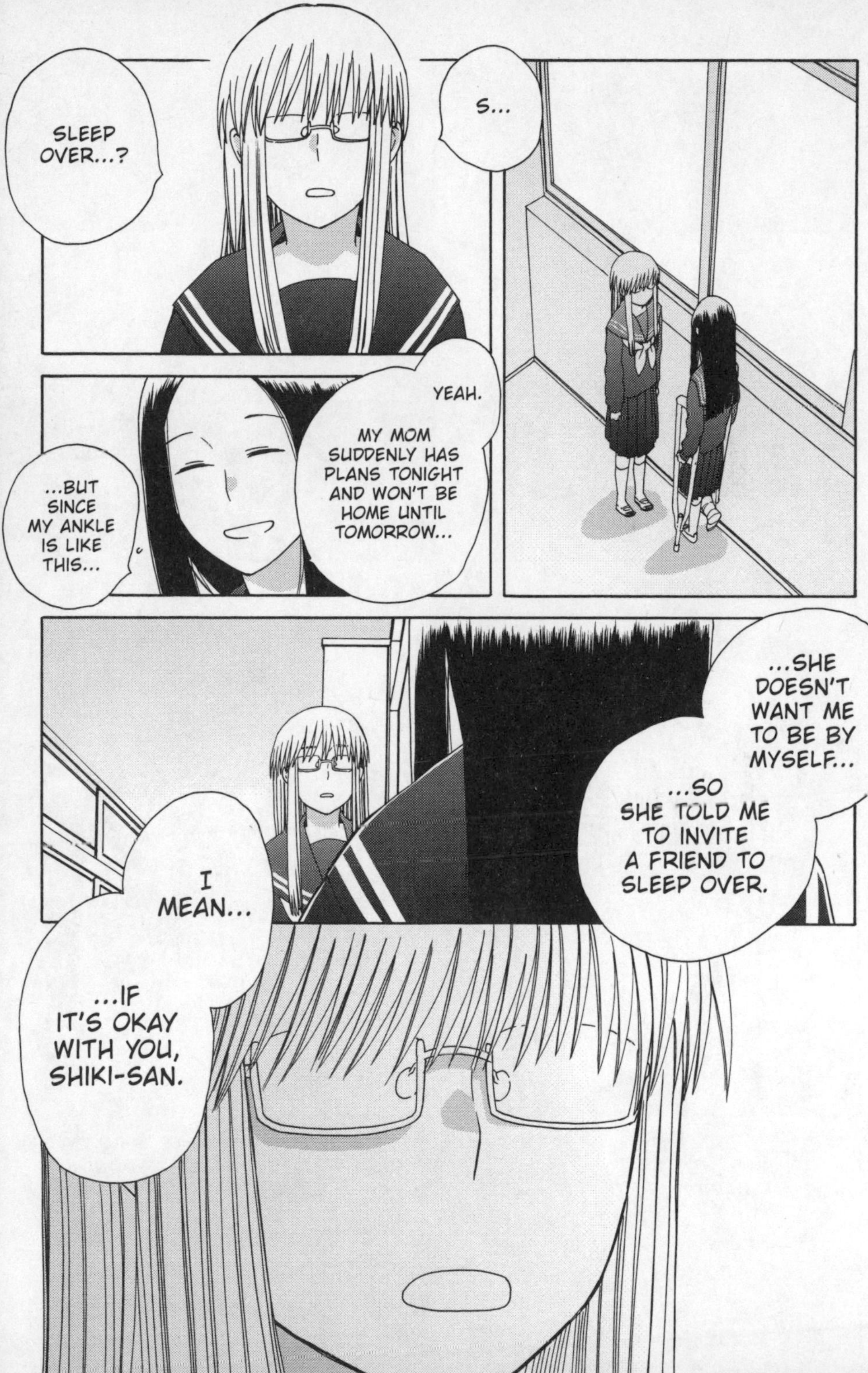
S...
SLEEP OVER...?
YEAH.
MY MOM SUDDENLY HAS PLANS TONIGHT AND WON'T BE HOME UNTIL TOMORROW...
...BUT SINCE MY ANKLE IS LIKE THIS...
...SHE DOESN'T WANT ME TO BE BY MYSELF...
...SO SHE TOLD ME TO INVITE A FRIEND TO SLEEP OVER.
I MEAN...
...IF IT'S OKAY WITH YOU, SHIKI-SAN.

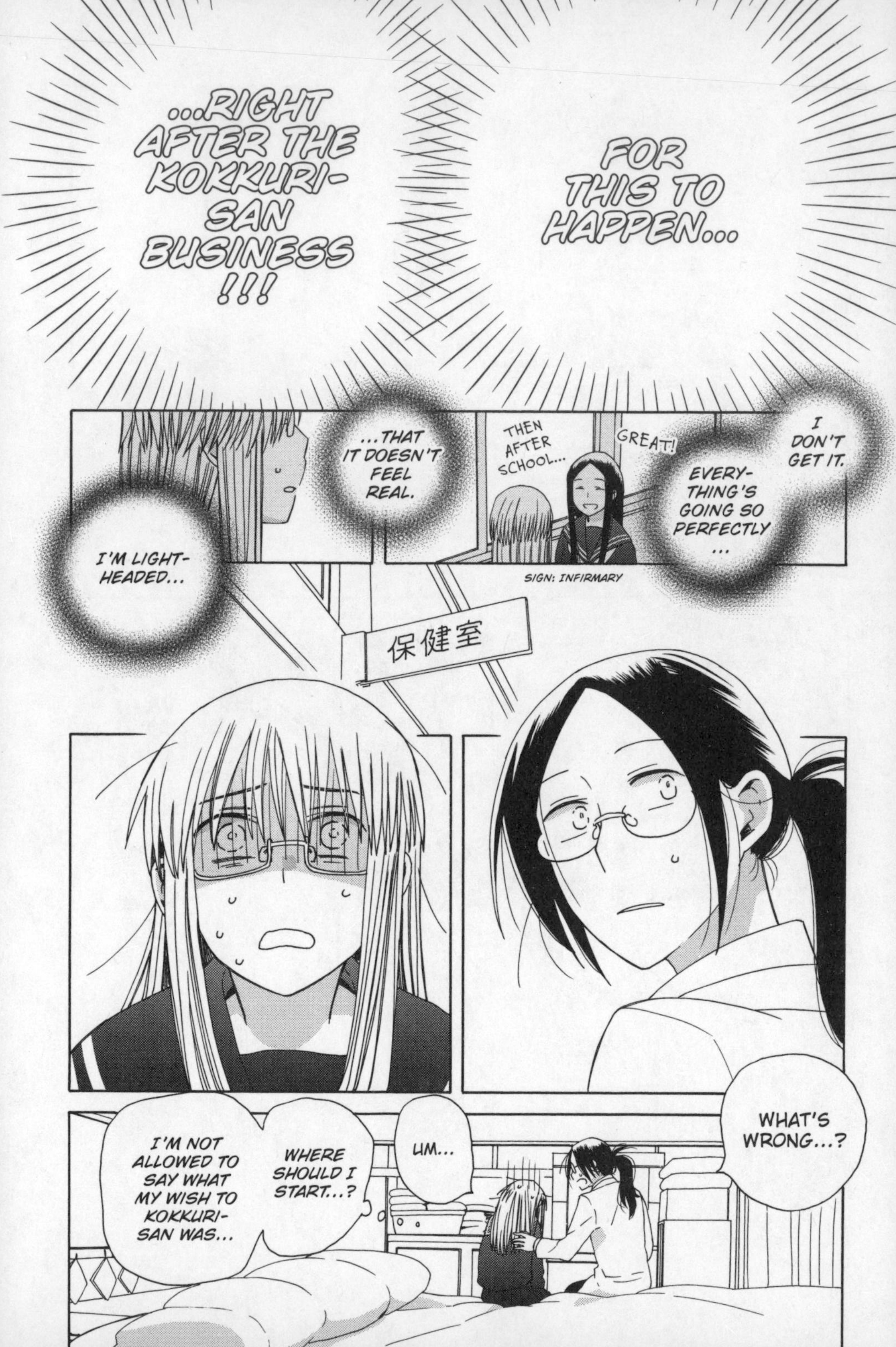
FOR THIS TO HAPPEN...
...RIGHT AFTER THE KOKKURI-SAN BUSINESS!!!
I DON'T GET IT.
EVERYTHING'S GOING SO PERFECTLY...
GREAT!
THEN AFTER SCHOOL...
...THAT IT DOESN'T FEEL REAL.
I'M LIGHT-HEADED...
SIGN: INFIRMARY
保健室
WHAT'S WRONG...?
UM...
WHERE SHOULD I START...?
I'M NOT ALLOWED TO SAY WHAT MY WISH TO KOKKURI-SAN WAS...

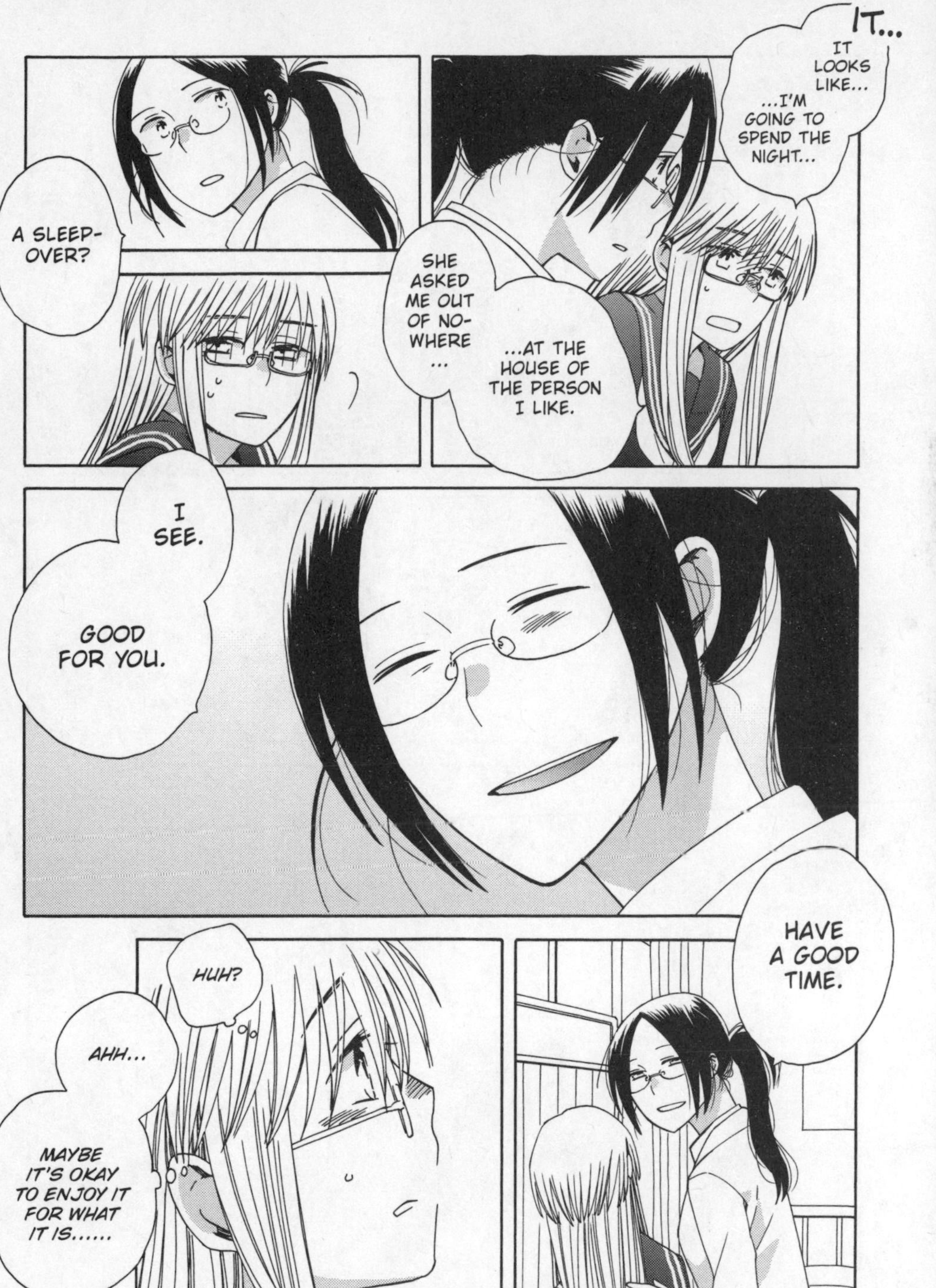
IT...
IT LOOKS LIKE... ...I'M GOING TO SPEND THE NIGHT...
...AT THE HOUSE OF THE PERSON I LIKE.
A SLEEP-OVER?
SHE ASKED ME OUT OF NO-WHERE ...
I SEE.
GOOD FOR YOU.
HAVE A GOOD TIME.
HUH?
AHH...
MAYBE IT'S OKAY TO ENJOY IT FOR WHAT IT IS......

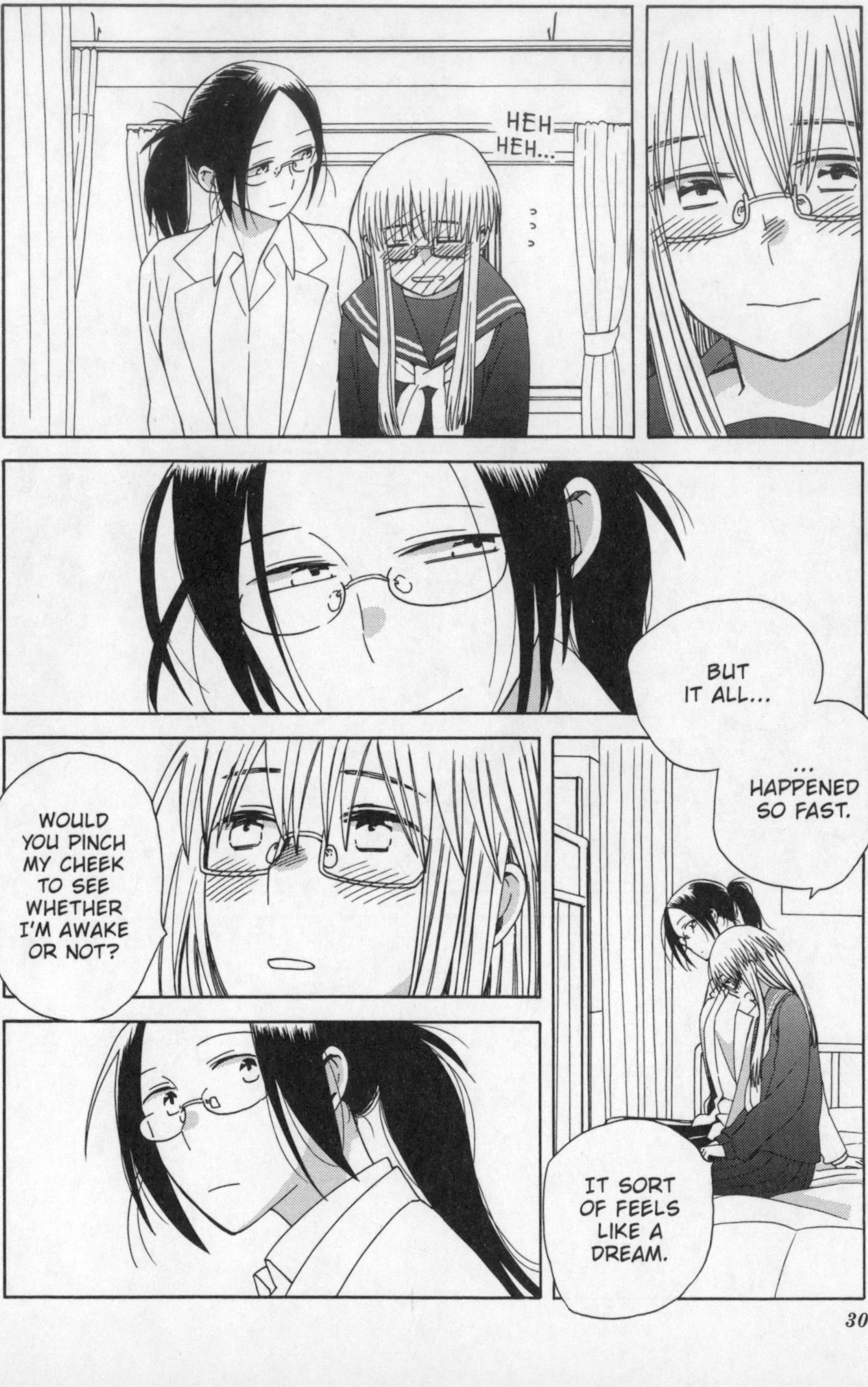
HEH HEH...
BUT IT ALL...
... HAPPENED SO FAST.
IT SORT OF FEELS LIKE A DREAM.
WOULD YOU PINCH MY CHEEK TO SEE WHETHER I'M AWAKE OR NOT?

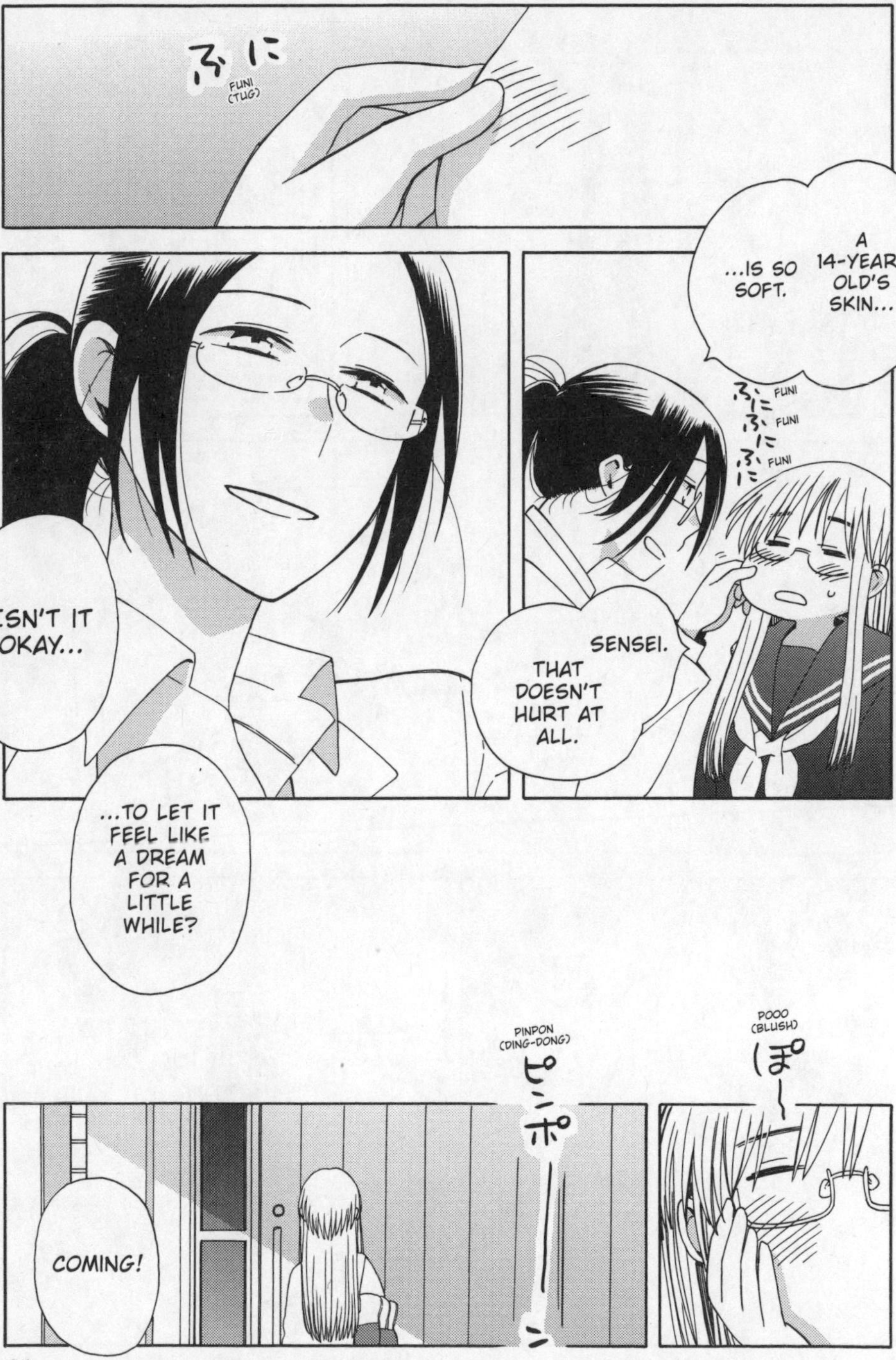
ふに
FUNI (TUG)
A 14-YEAR-OLD'S SKIN...
...IS SO SOFT.
ふにふにふに
FUNI FUNI FUNI
SENSEI.
THAT DOESN'T HURT AT ALL.
ISN'T IT OKAY...
...TO LET IT FEEL LIKE A DREAM FOR A LITTLE WHILE?
ぽ～
POOO (BLUSH)
ピンポーン
PINPON (DING-DONG)
COMING!

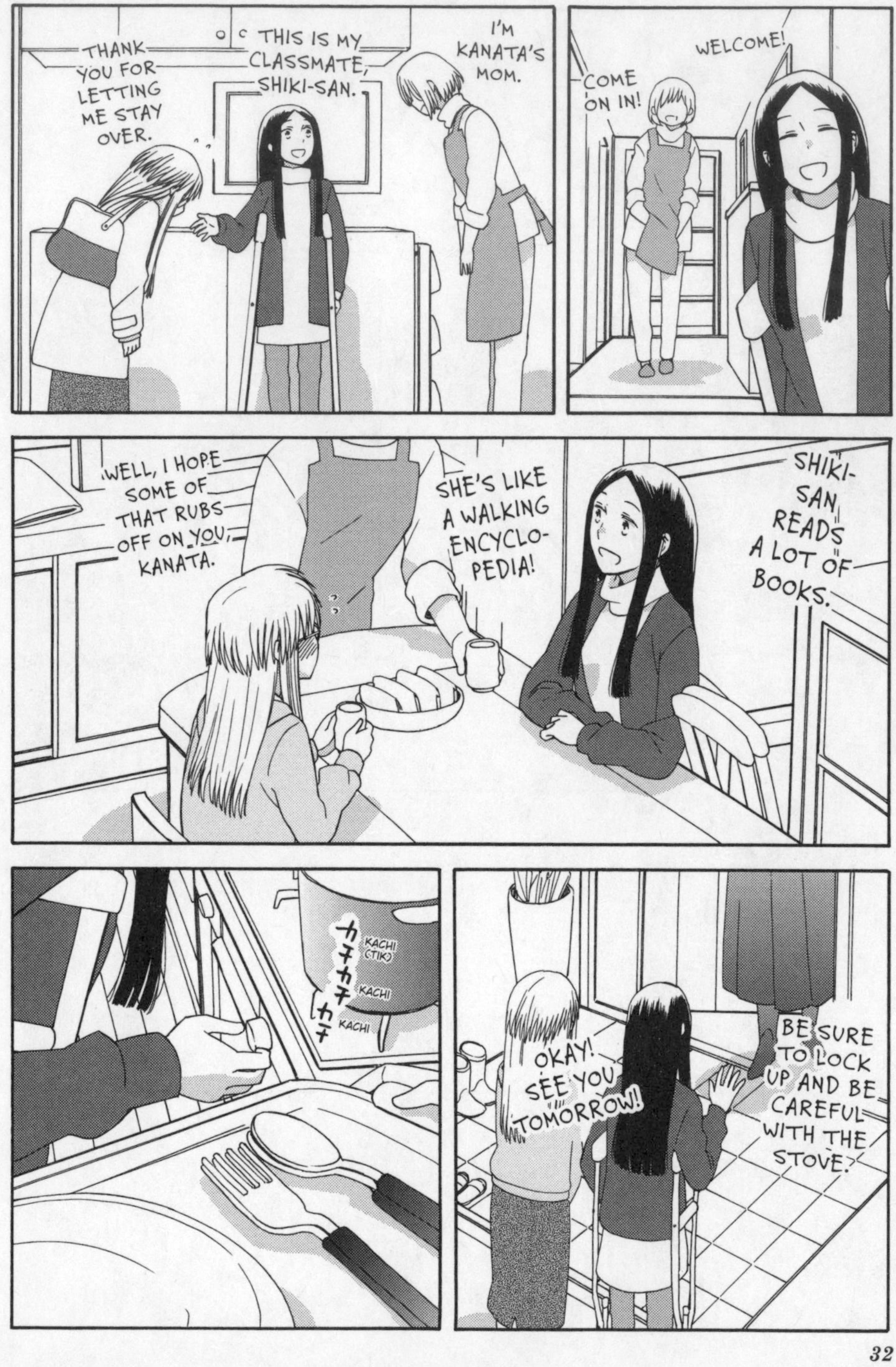
WELCOME!
COME ON IN!
I'M KANATA'S MOM.
THIS IS MY CLASSMATE, SHIKI-SAN.
THANK YOU FOR LETTING ME STAY OVER.
SHIKI-SAN READS A LOT OF BOOKS.
SHE'S LIKE A WALKING ENCYCLOPEDIA!
WELL, I HOPE SOME OF THAT RUBS OFF ON YOU, KANATA.
BE SURE TO LOCK UP AND BE CAREFUL WITH THE STOVE.
OKAY! SEE YOU TOMORROW!
カチ KACHI (TIK)
カチ KACHI
カチ KACHI

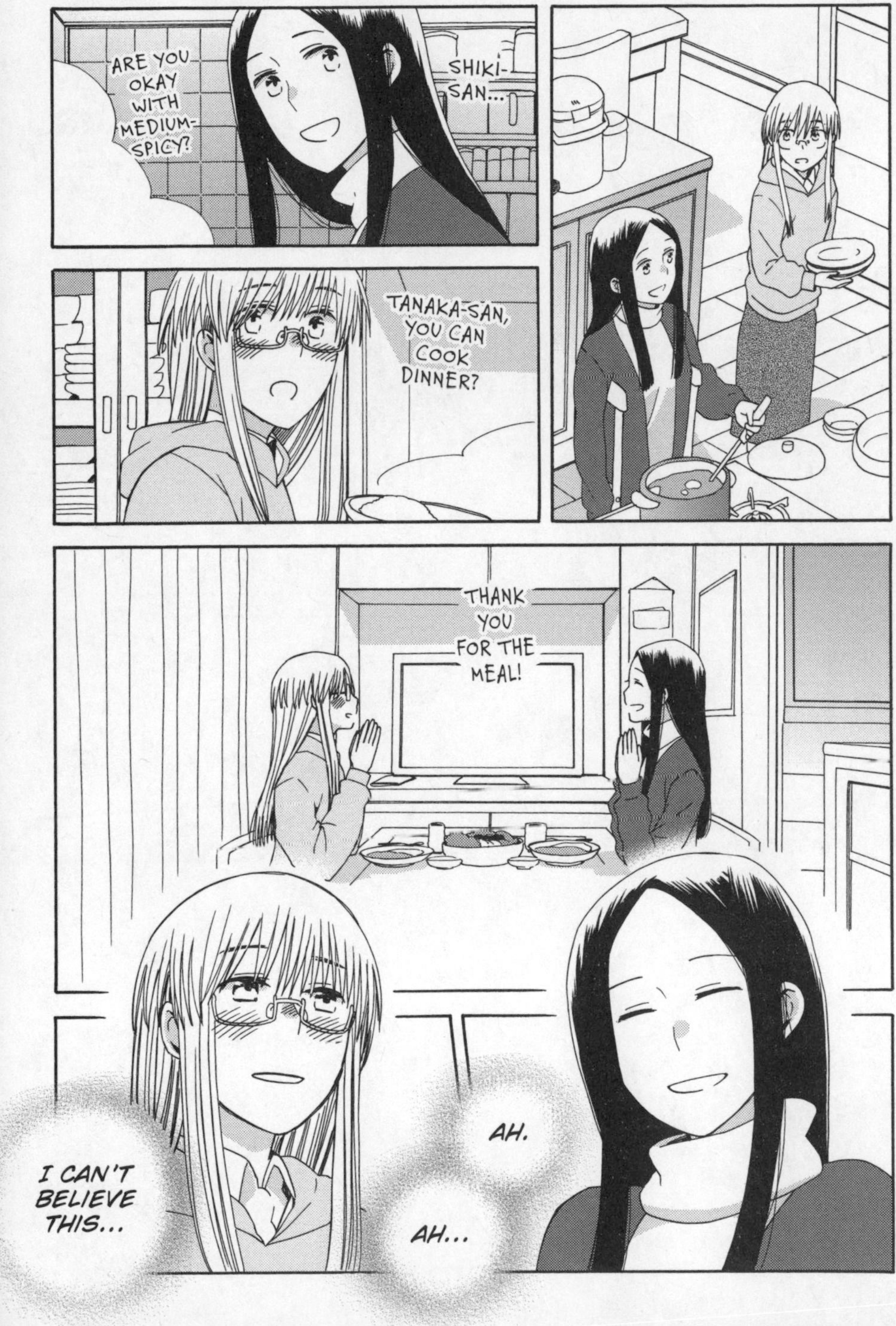
SHIKI-SAN...
ARE YOU OKAY WITH MEDIUM-SPICY?
TANAKA-SAN, YOU CAN COOK DINNER?
THANK YOU FOR THE MEAL!
AH.
AH...
I CAN'T BELIEVE THIS...

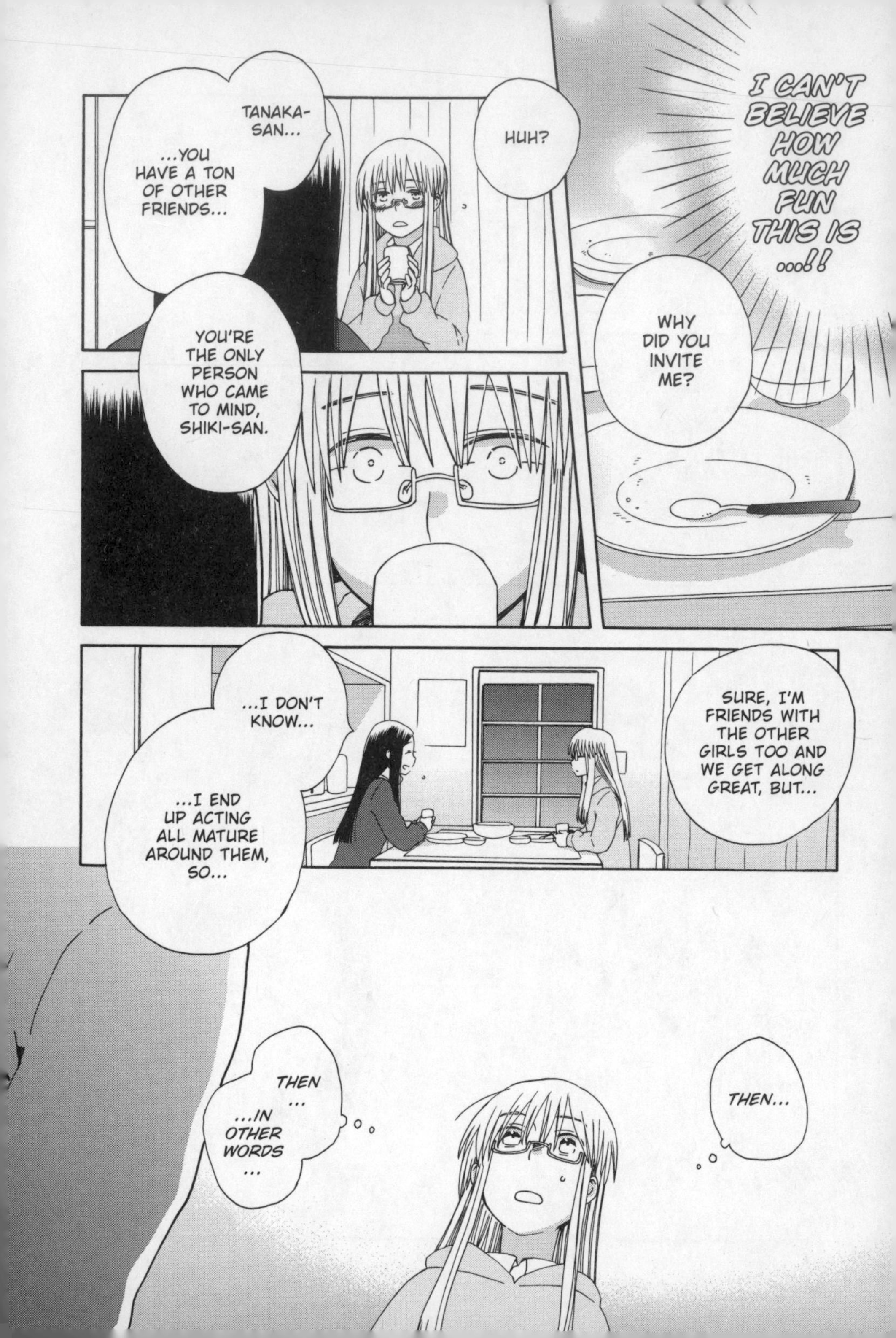
I CAN'T BELIEVE HOW MUCH FUN THIS IS ...!!
WHY DID YOU INVITE ME?
HUH?
TANAKA-SAN...
...YOU HAVE A TON OF OTHER FRIENDS...
YOU'RE THE ONLY PERSON WHO CAME TO MIND, SHIKI-SAN.
SURE, I'M FRIENDS WITH THE OTHER GIRLS TOO AND WE GET ALONG GREAT, BUT...
...I DON'T KNOW...
...I END UP ACTING ALL MATURE AROUND THEM, SO...
THEN...
THEN ... ...IN OTHER WORDS ...

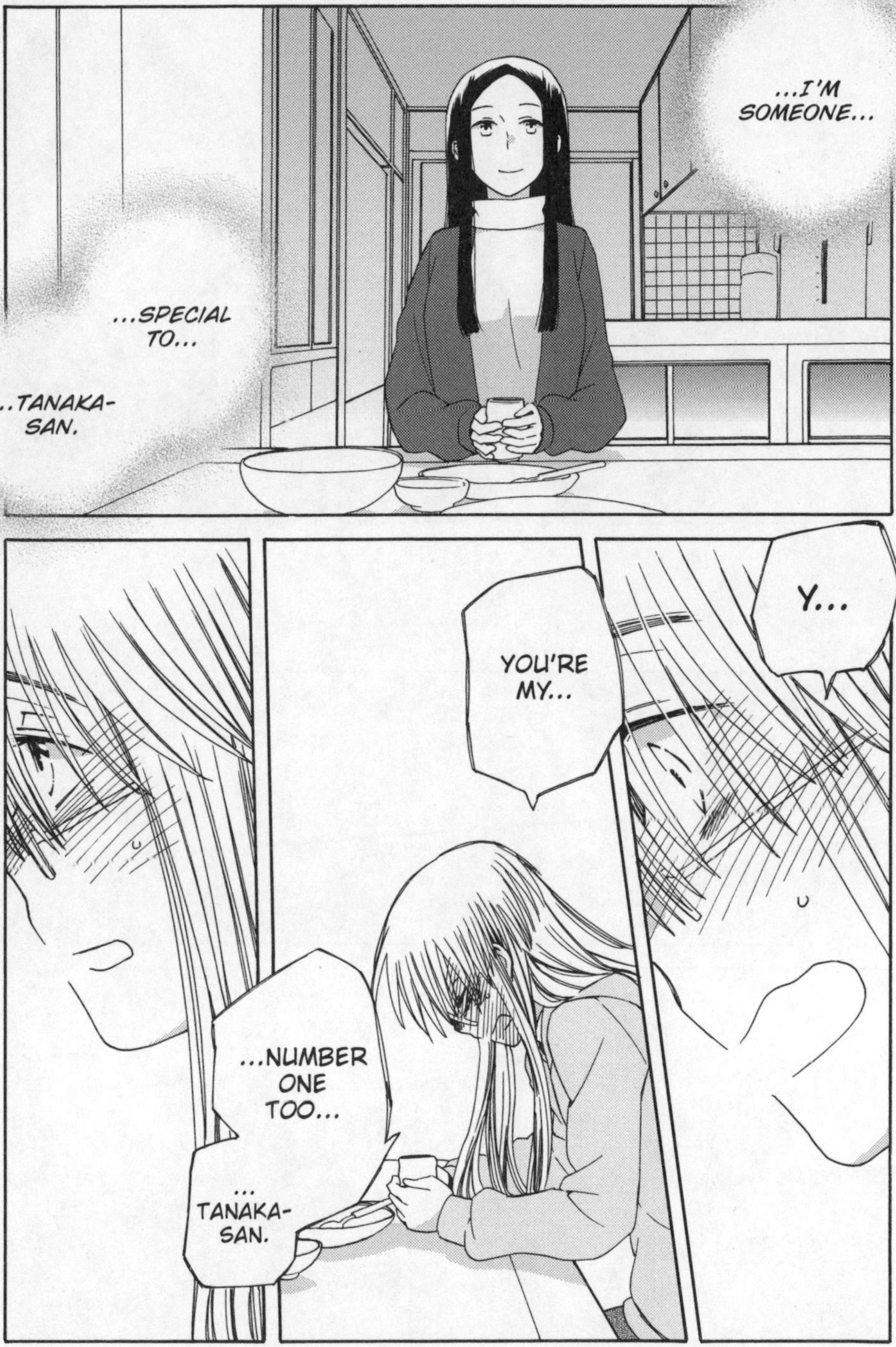
...I'M SOMEONE...
...SPECIAL TO...
...TANAKA-SAN.
Y...
YOU'RE MY...
...NUMBER ONE TOO...
...TANAKA-SAN.

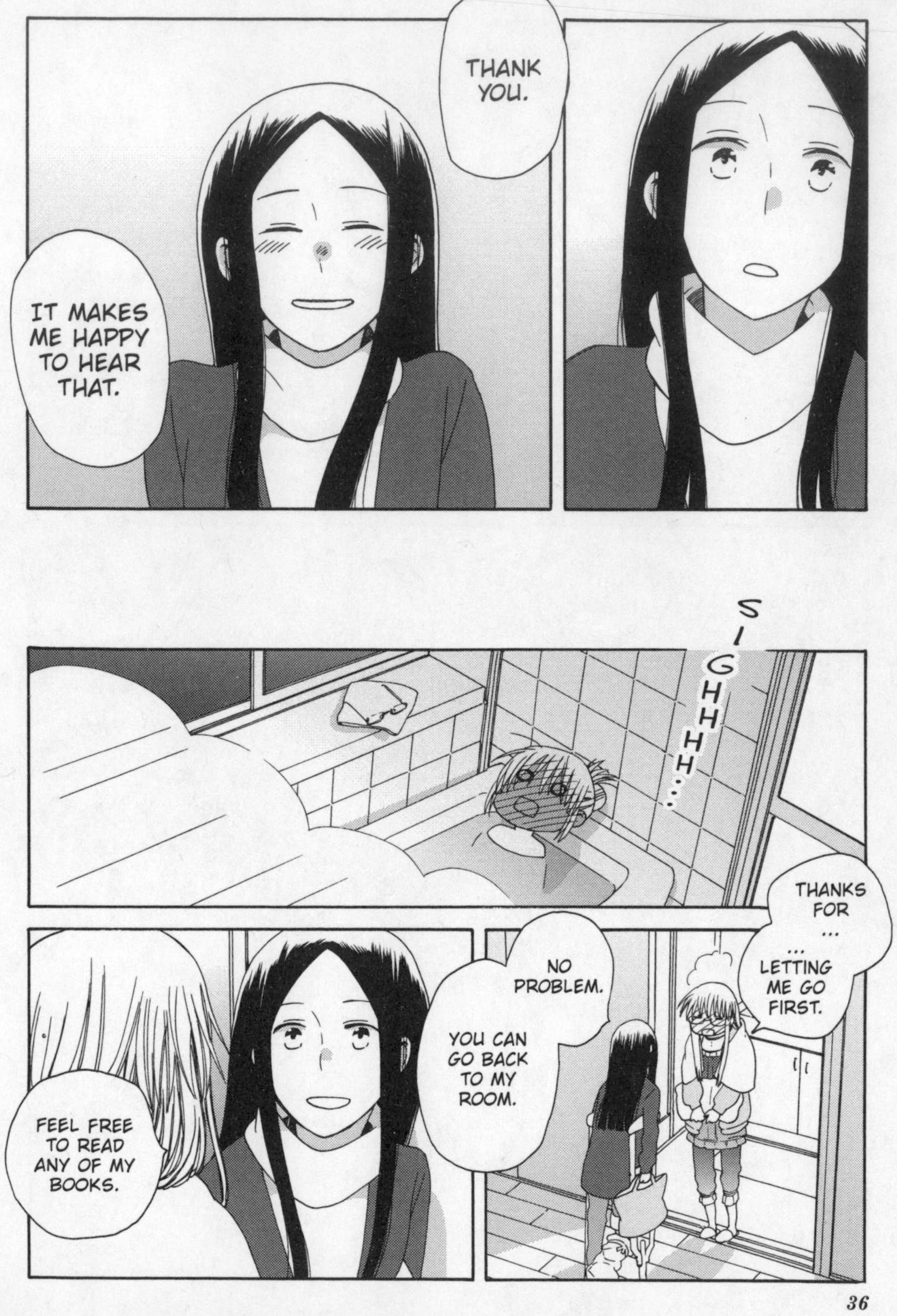
THANK YOU.
IT MAKES ME HAPPY TO HEAR THAT.
SIGHHHH...
THANKS FOR ...
... LETTING ME GO FIRST.
NO PROBLEM.
YOU CAN GO BACK TO MY ROOM.
FEEL FREE TO READ ANY OF MY BOOKS.

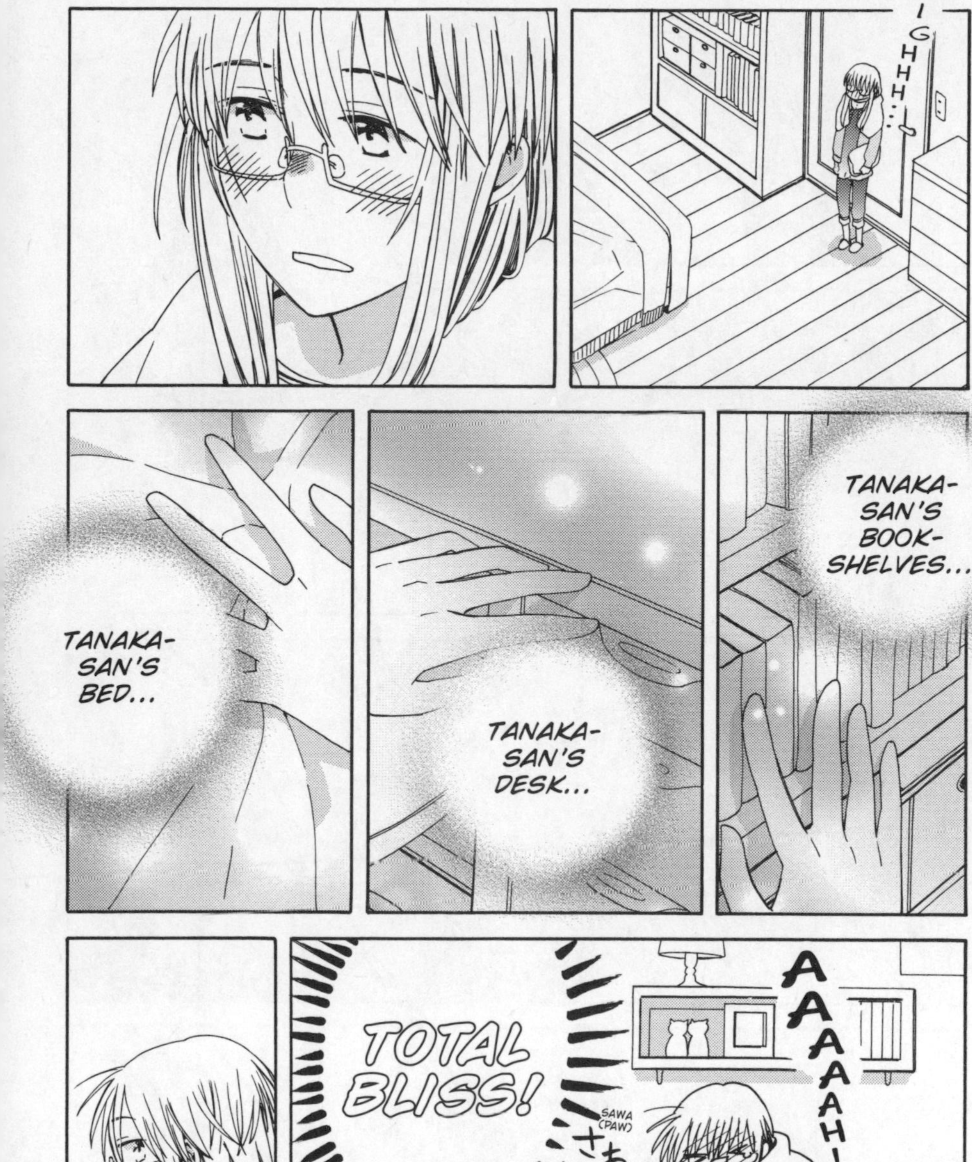
SIGHHH...
TANAKA-SAN'S BOOKSHELVES...
TANAKA-SAN'S DESK...
TANAKA-SAN'S BED...
AAAAAAH!
TOTAL BLISS!
さわ
SAWA (PAW)
さわ
SAWA
さわ
SAWA

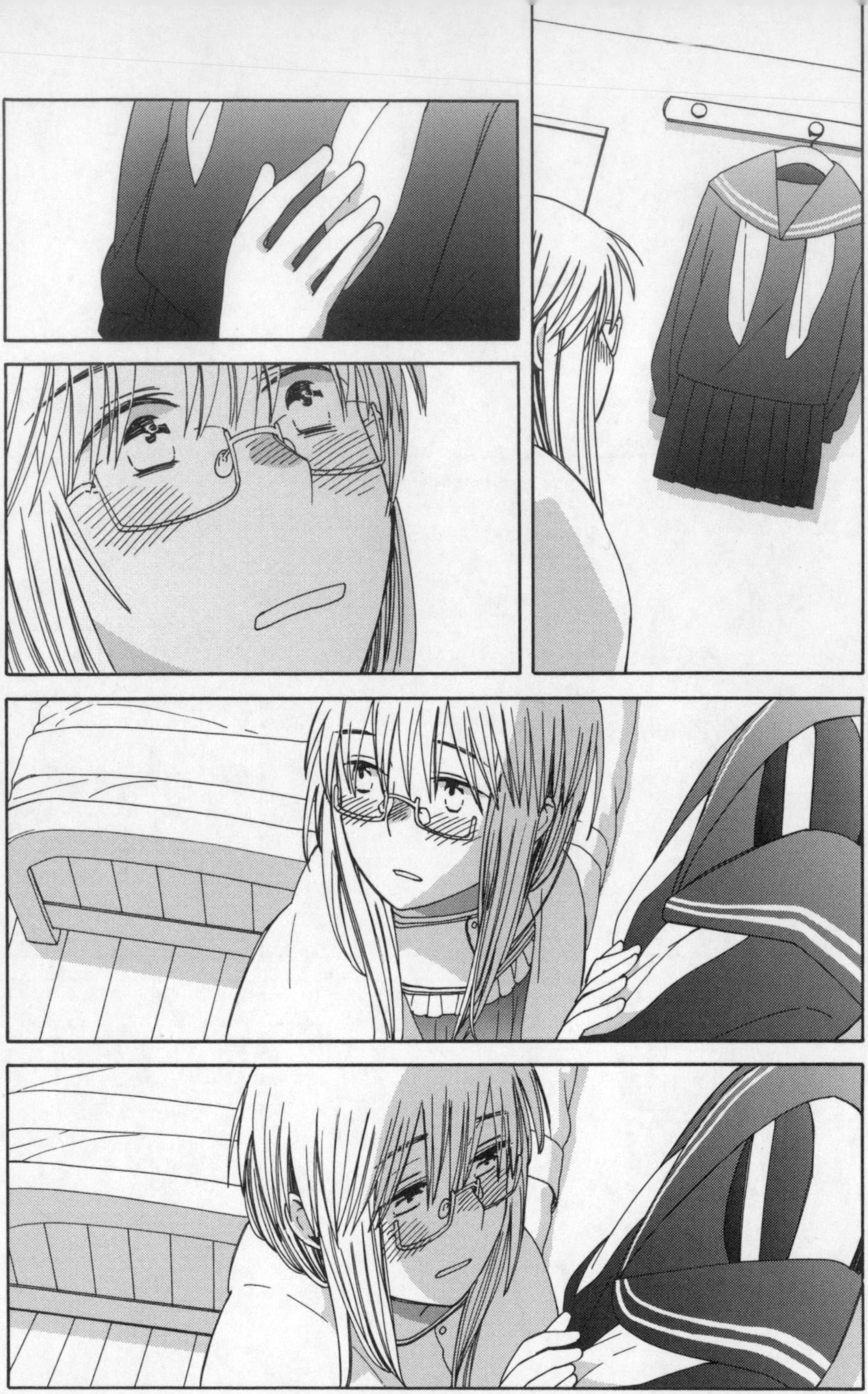

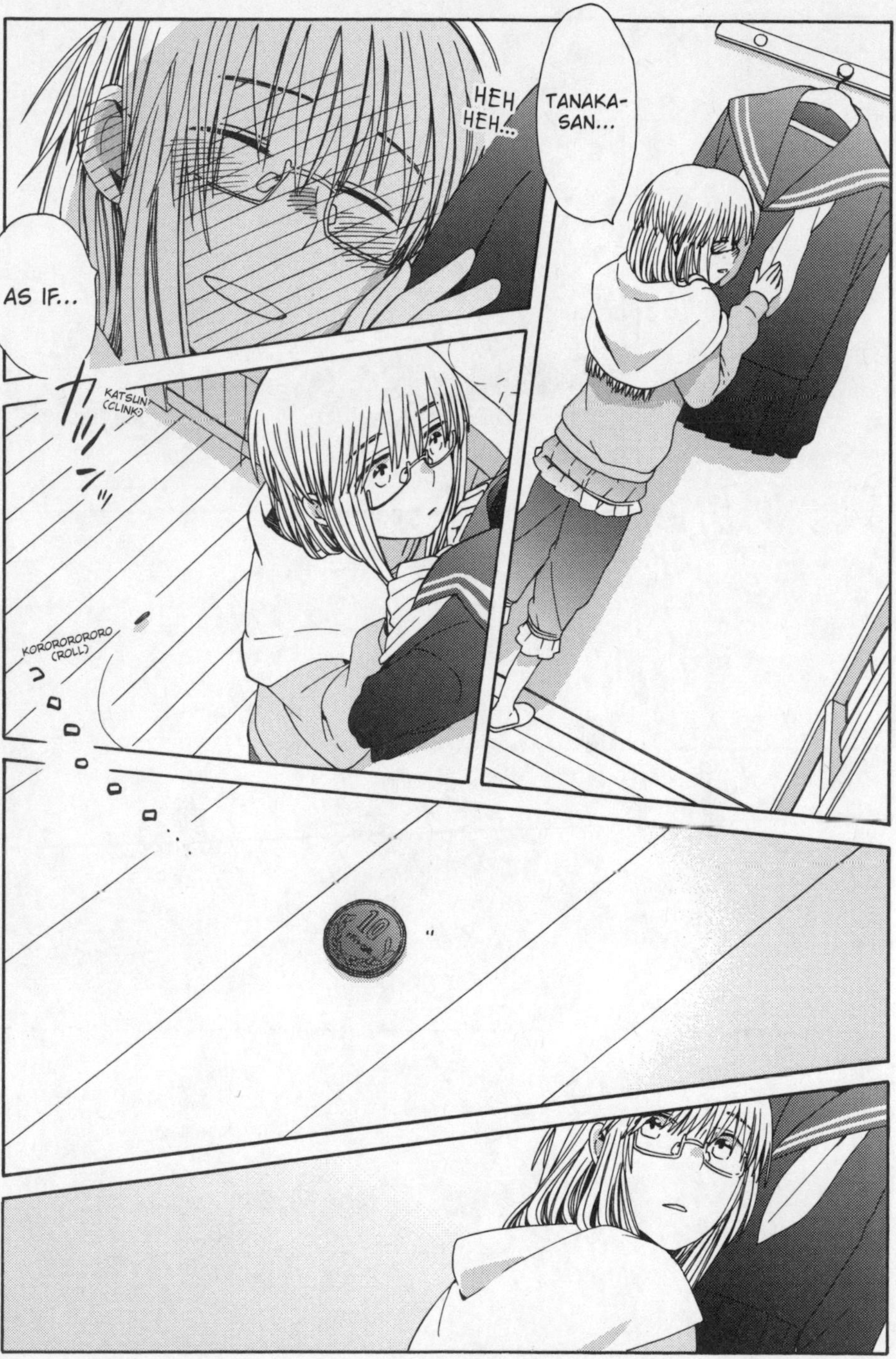
TANAKA-SAN...
HEH HEH...
AS IF...
KATSUN (CLINK)
KORORORORO (ROLL)

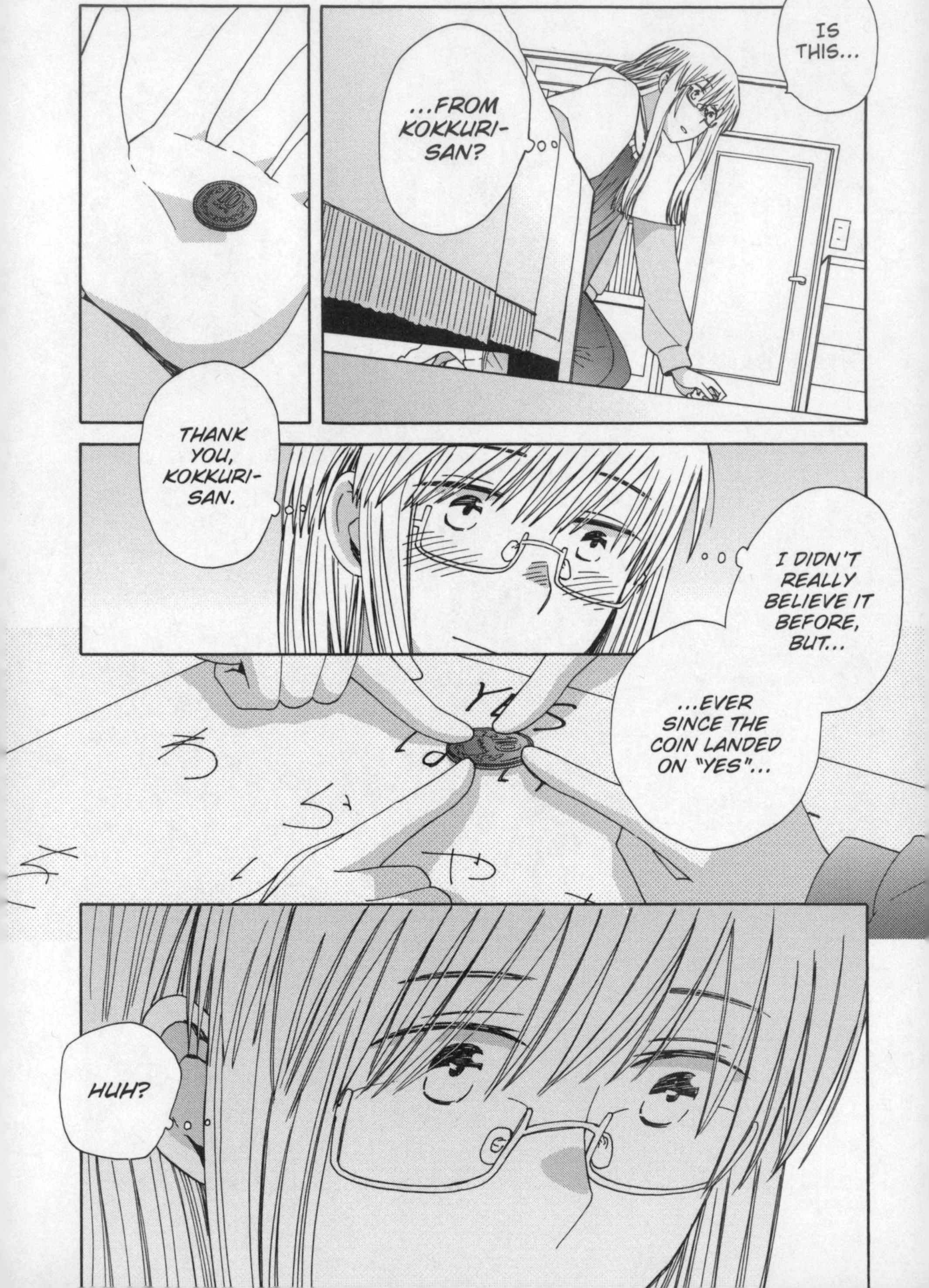
IS THIS...
...FROM KOKKURI-SAN?
THANK YOU, KOKKURI-SAN.
I DIDN'T REALLY BELIEVE IT BEFORE, BUT...
...EVER SINCE THE COIN LANDED ON "YES"...
YES
HUH?

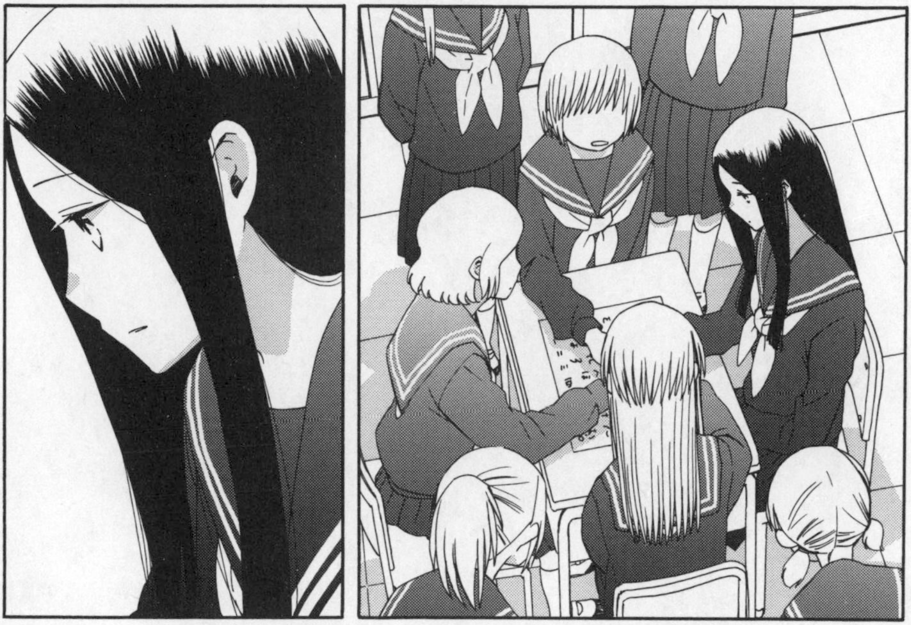

WHAT DID TANAKA-SAN WISH FOR?

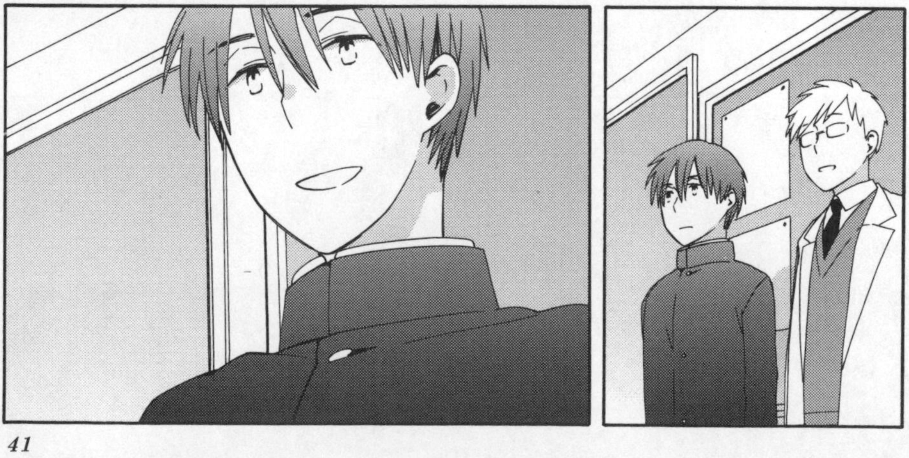

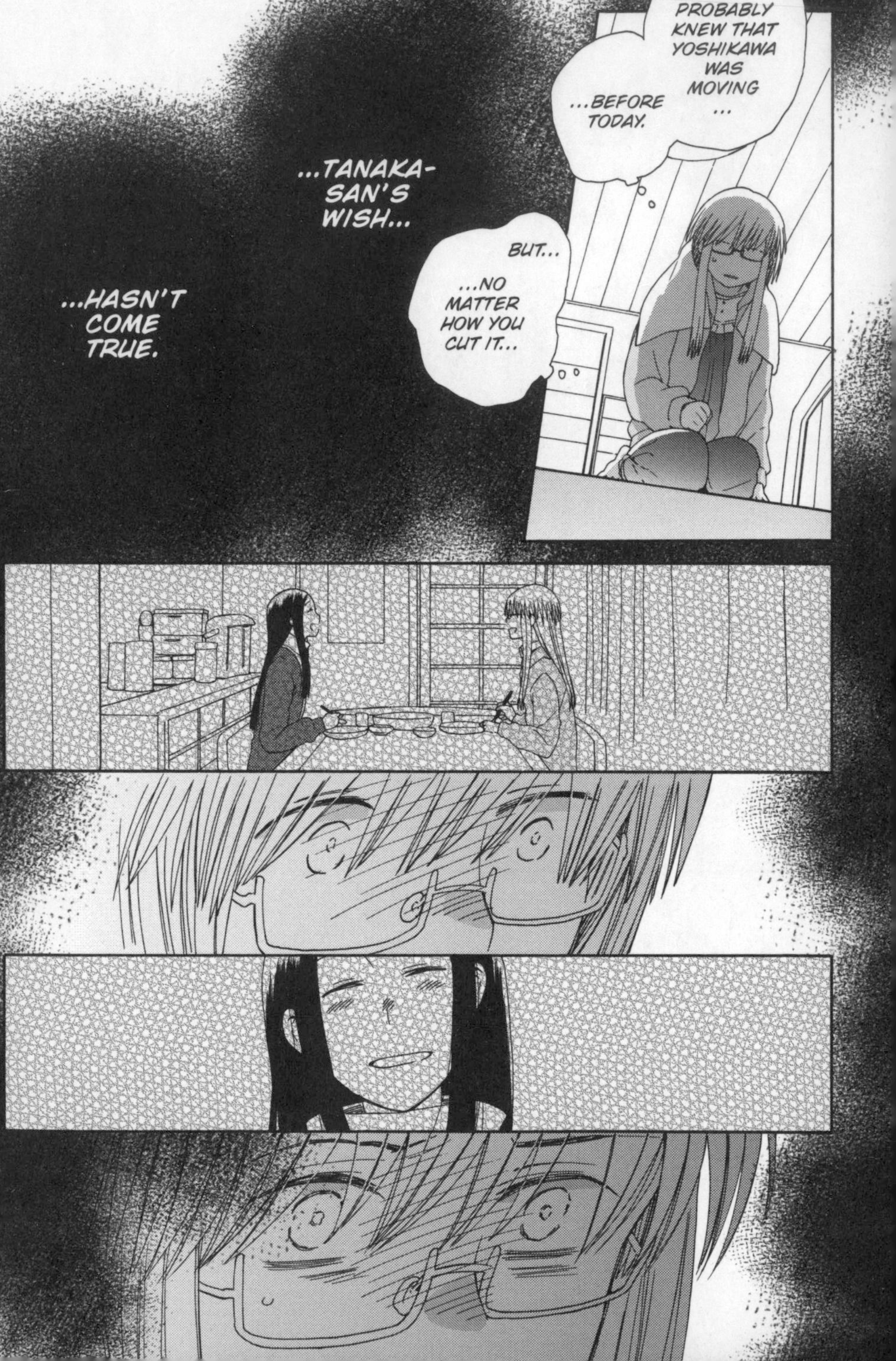
SHE PROBABLY KNEW THAT YOSHIKAWA WAS MOVING ...
...BEFORE TODAY.
BUT...
...NO MATTER HOW YOU CUT IT...
...TANAKA-SAN'S WISH...
...HASN'T COME TRUE.

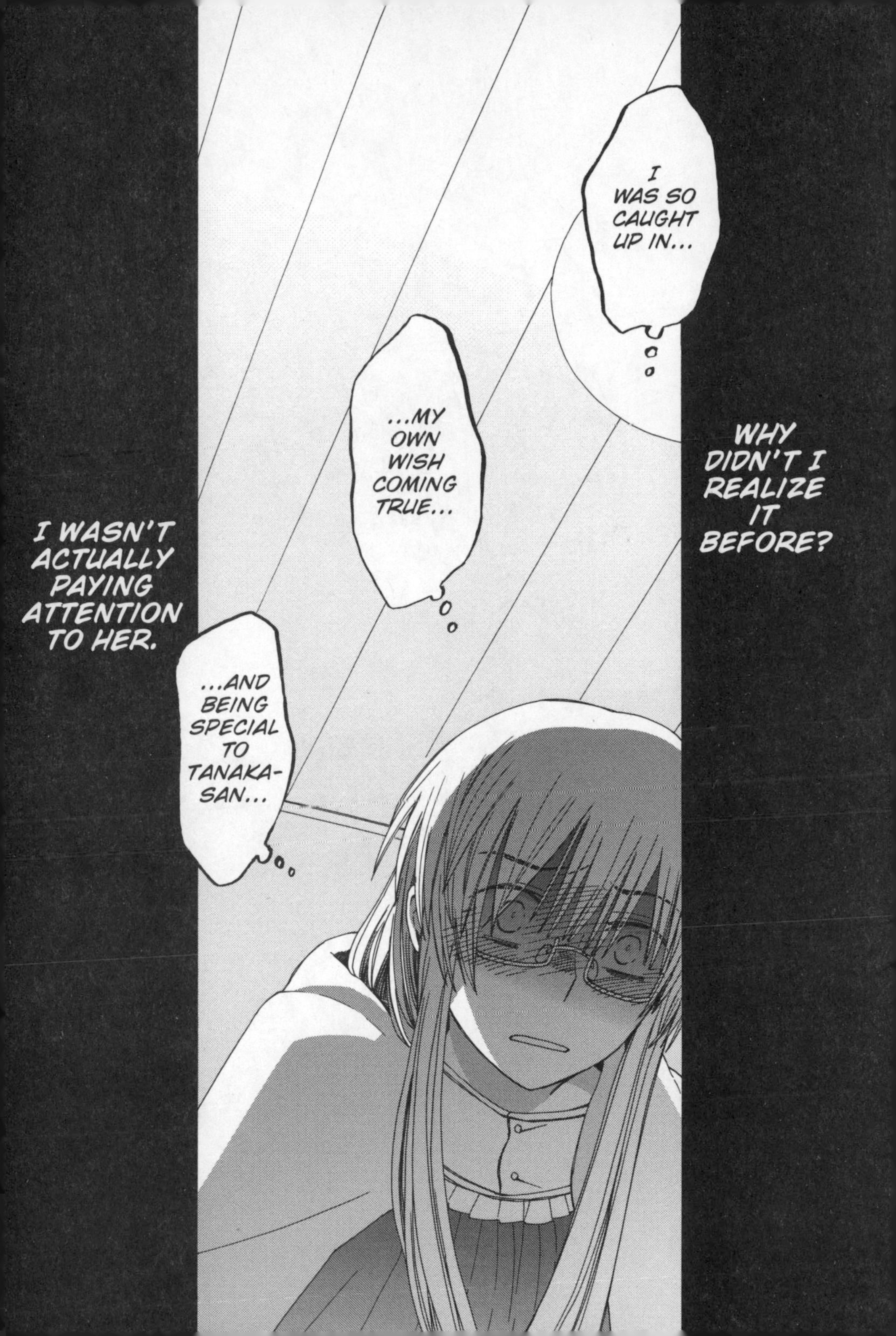
WHY DIDN'T I REALIZE IT BEFORE?
I WAS SO CAUGHT UP IN...
...MY OWN WISH COMING TRUE...
...AND BEING SPECIAL TO TANAKA-SAN...
I WASN'T ACTUALLY PAYING ATTENTION TO HER.

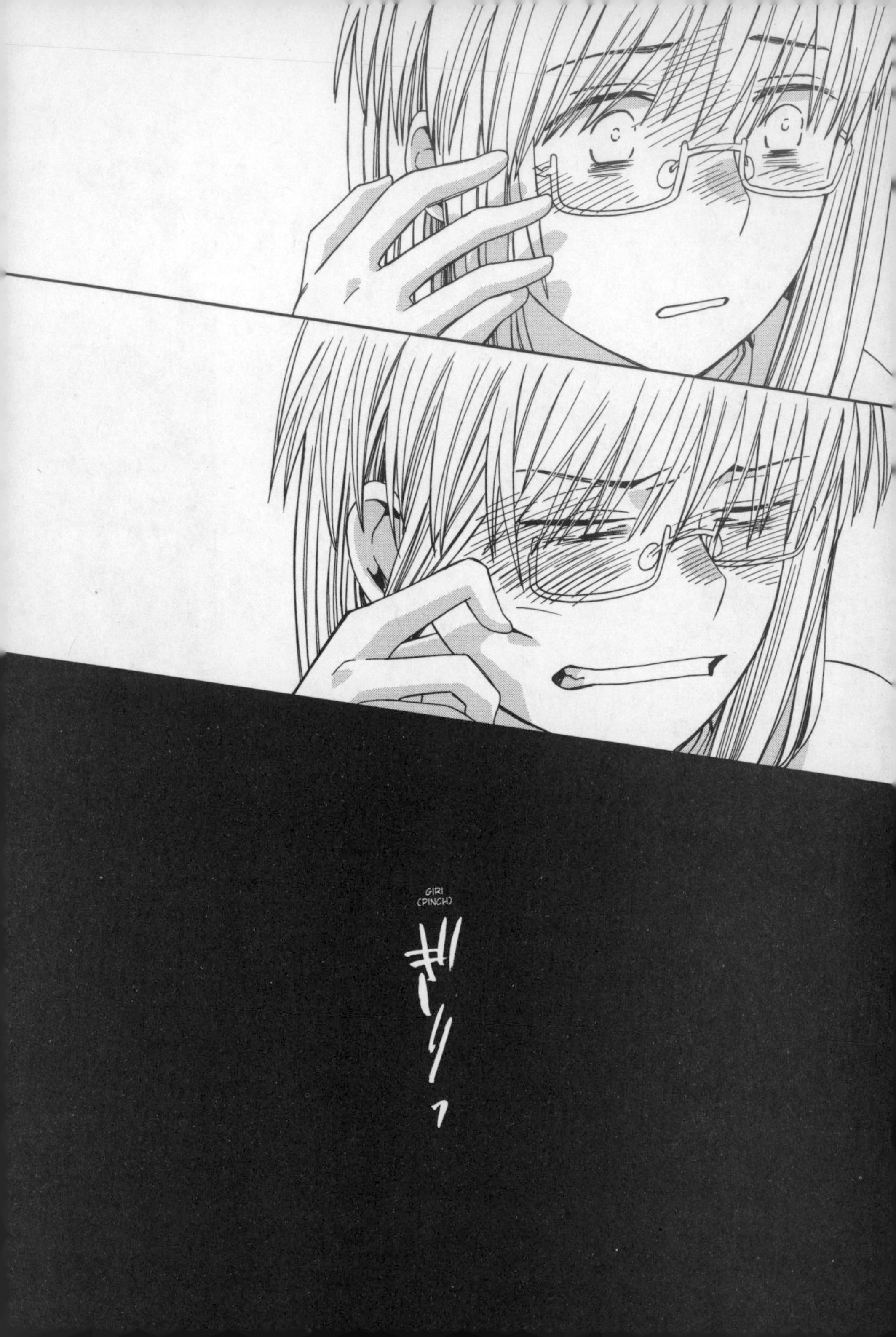
GIRI
(PINCH)
ぎりっ

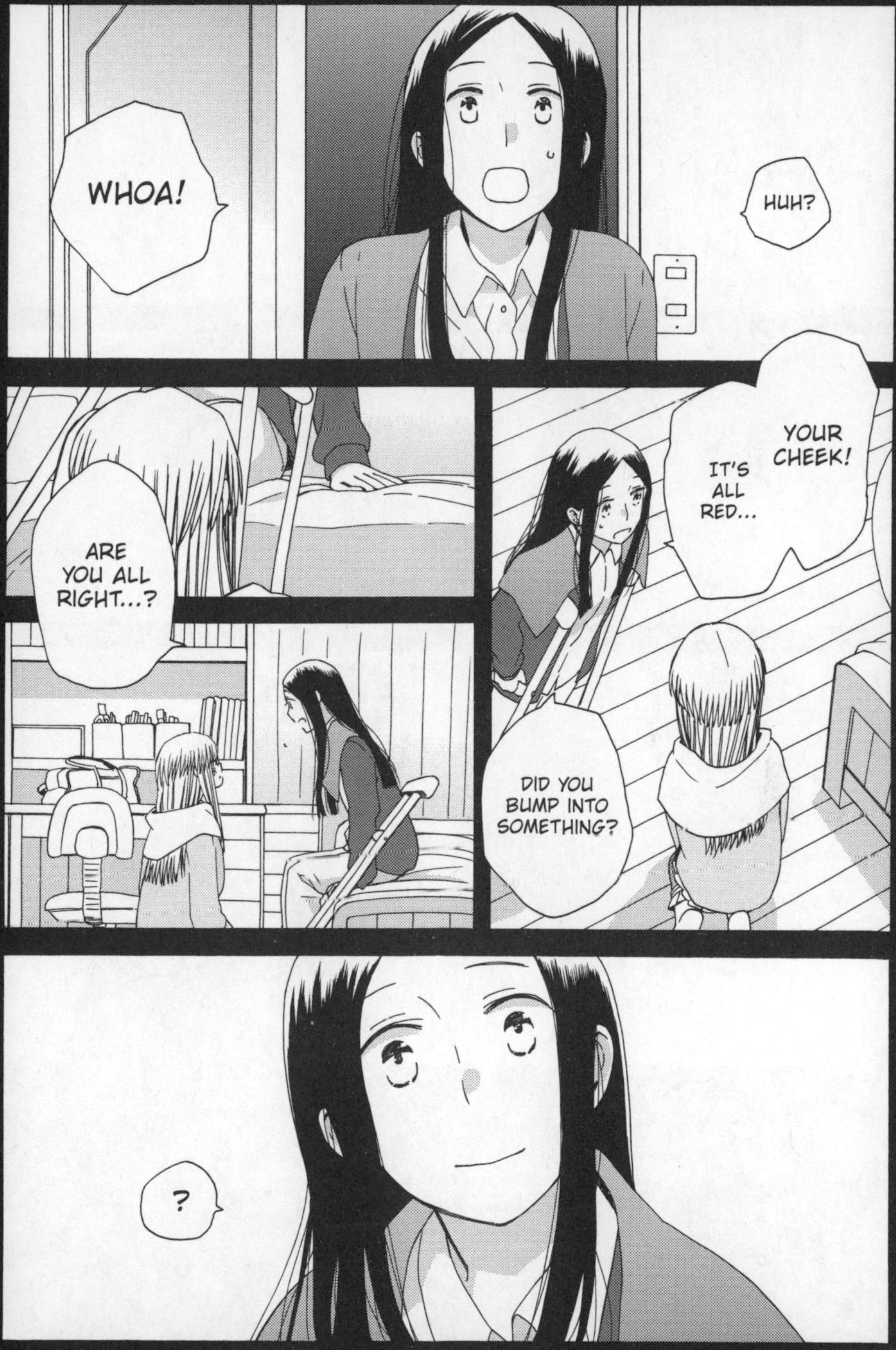
HUH?
WHOA!
YOUR CHEEK! IT'S ALL RED...
DID YOU BUMP INTO SOMETHING?
ARE YOU ALL RIGHT...?
?

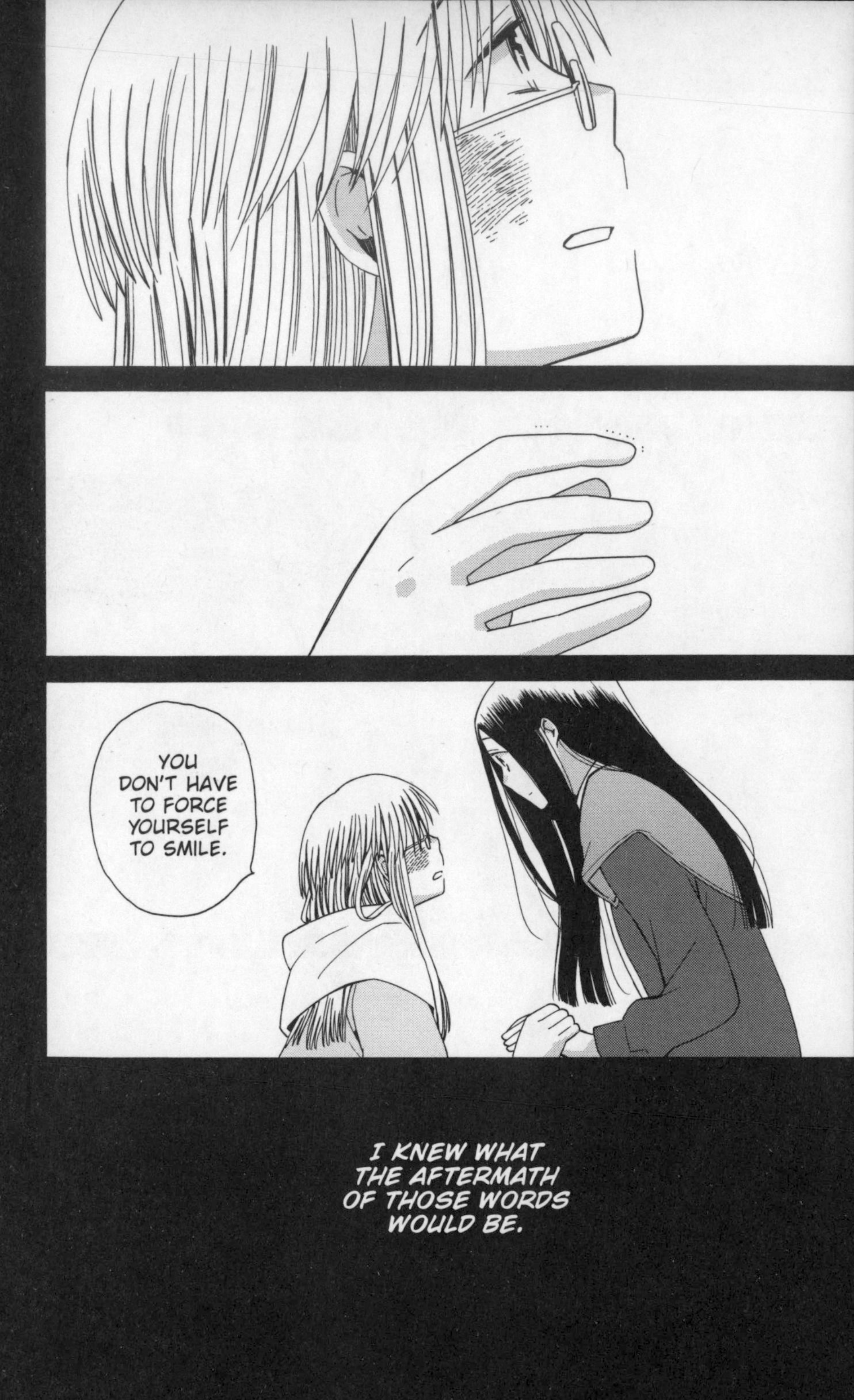
YOU DON'T HAVE TO FORCE YOURSELF TO SMILE.
I KNEW WHAT THE AFTERMATH OF THOSE WORDS WOULD BE.

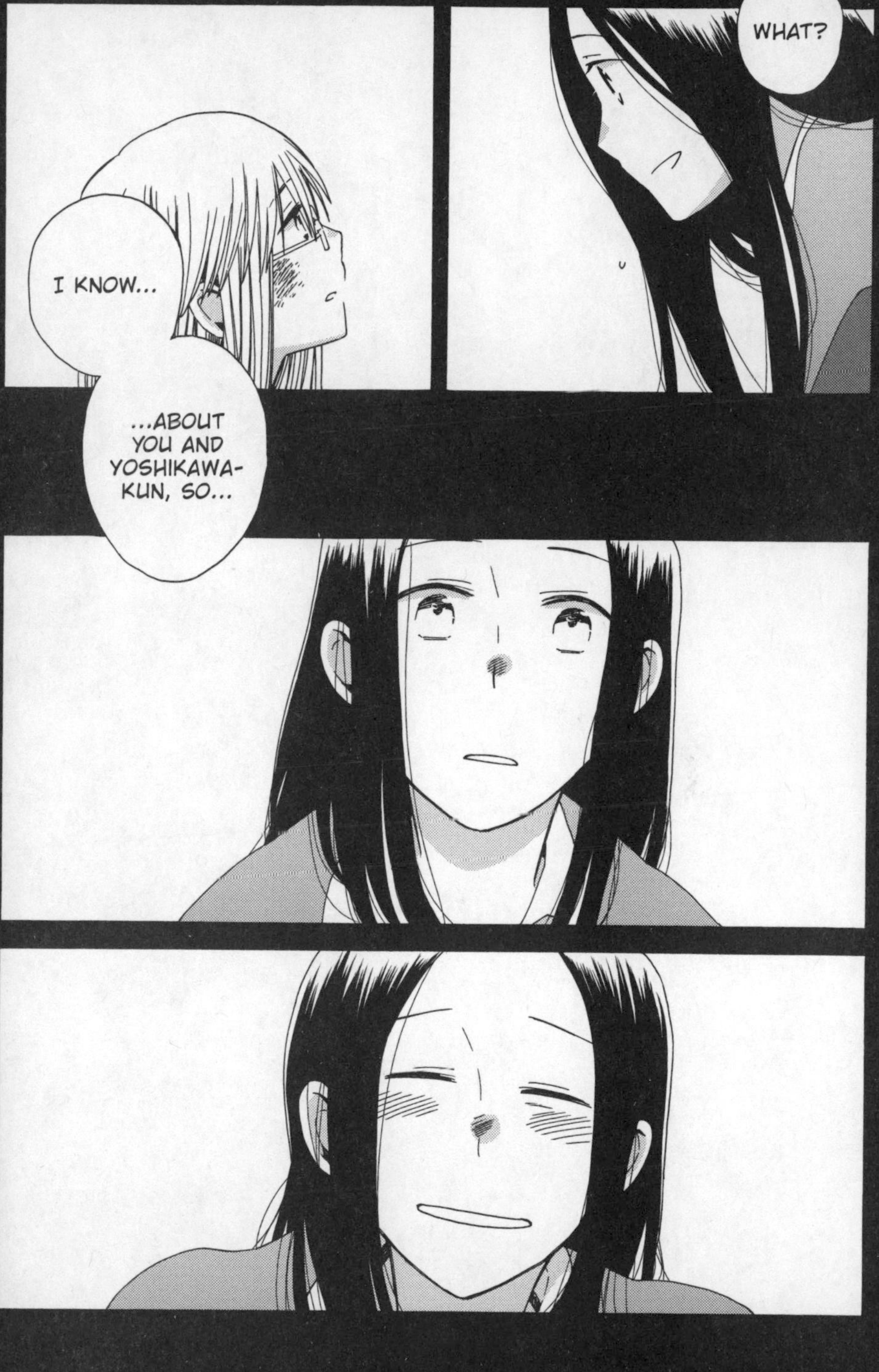
WHAT?
I KNOW...
...ABOUT YOU AND YOSHIKAWA-KUN, SO...

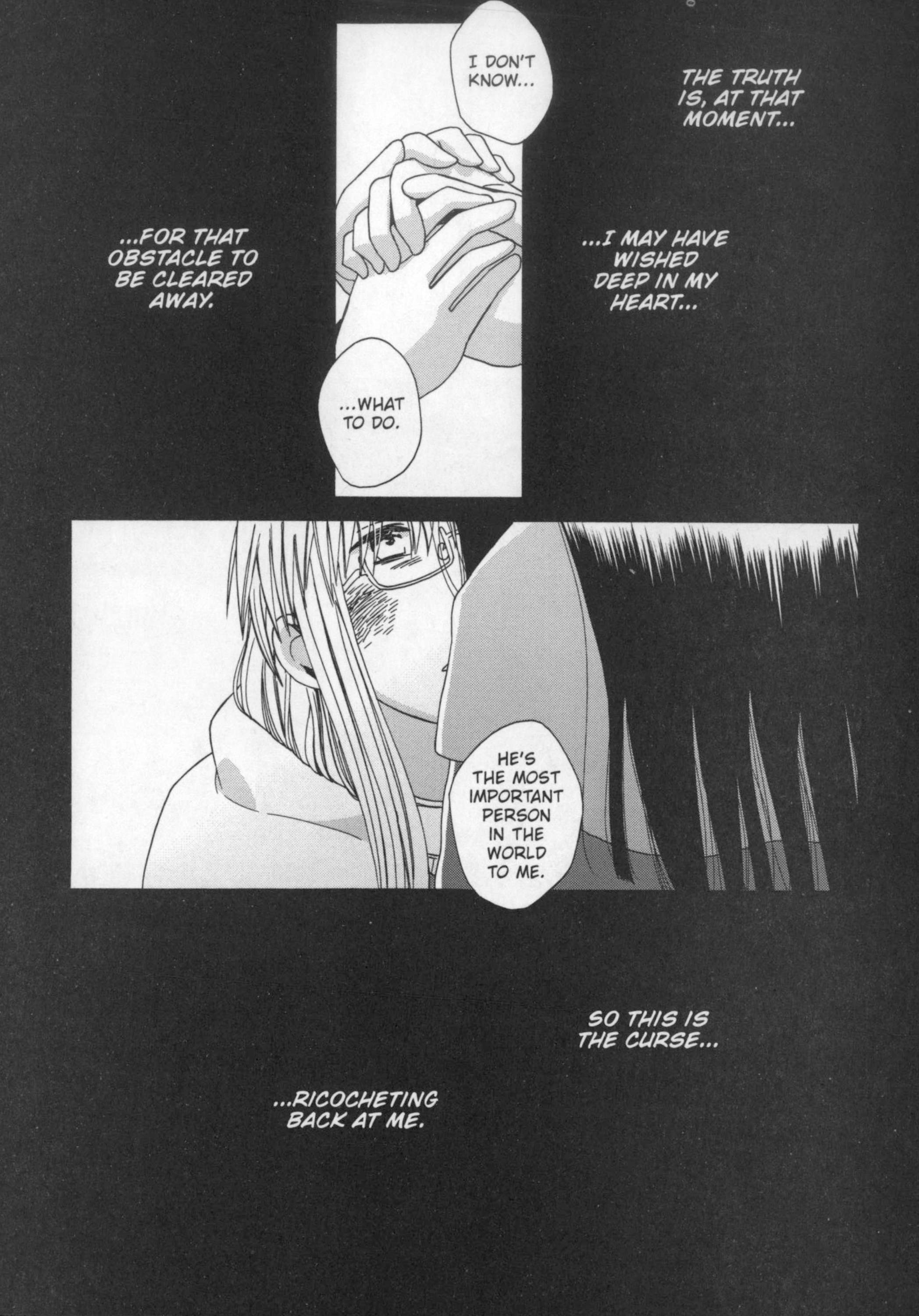
THE TRUTH IS, AT THAT MOMENT...
I DON'T KNOW...
...I MAY HAVE WISHED DEEP IN MY HEART...
...FOR THAT OBSTACLE TO BE CLEARED AWAY.
...WHAT TO DO.
HE'S THE MOST IMPORTANT PERSON IN THE WORLD TO ME.
SO THIS IS THE CURSE...
...RICOCHETING BACK AT ME.

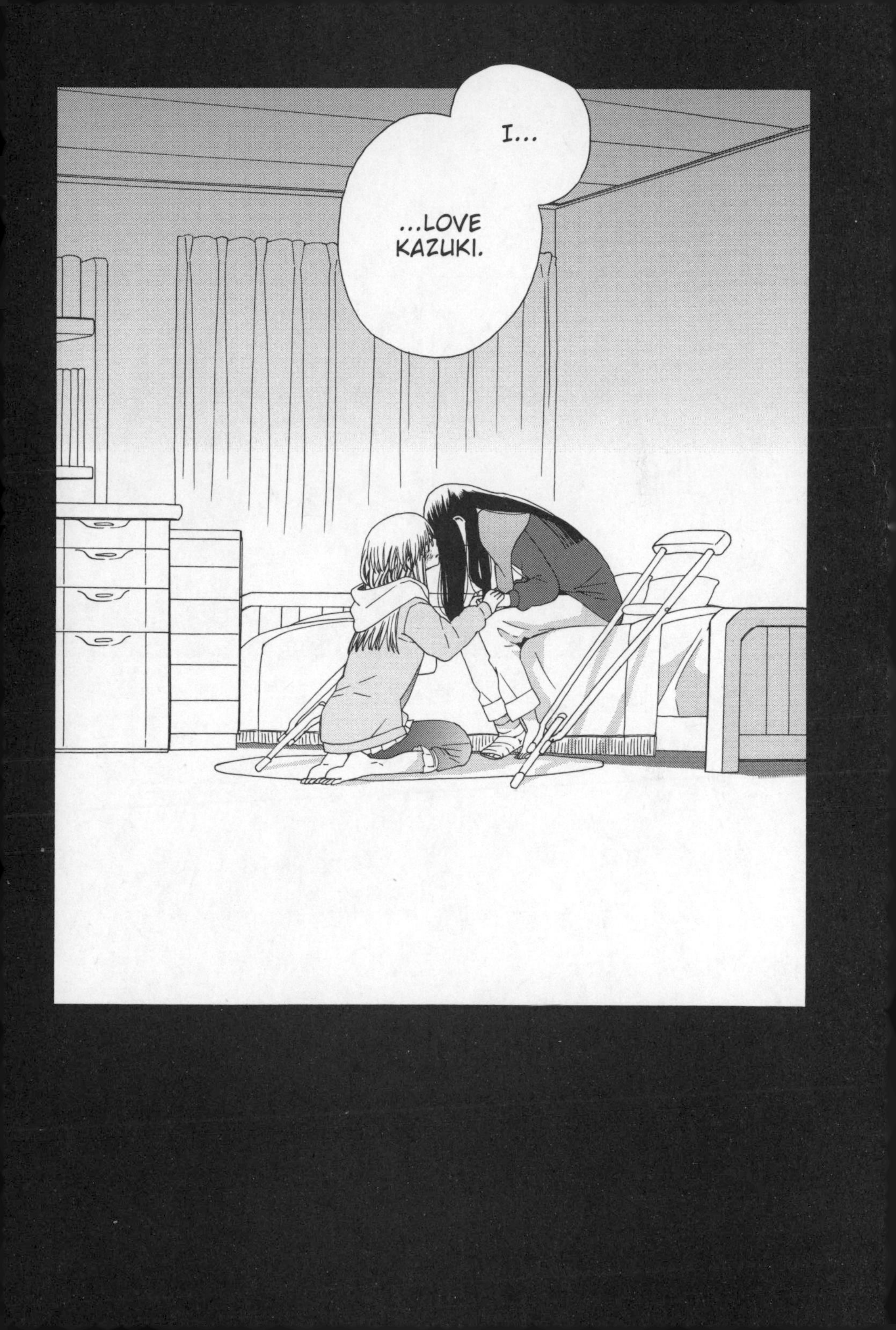
I...
...LOVE KAZUKI.

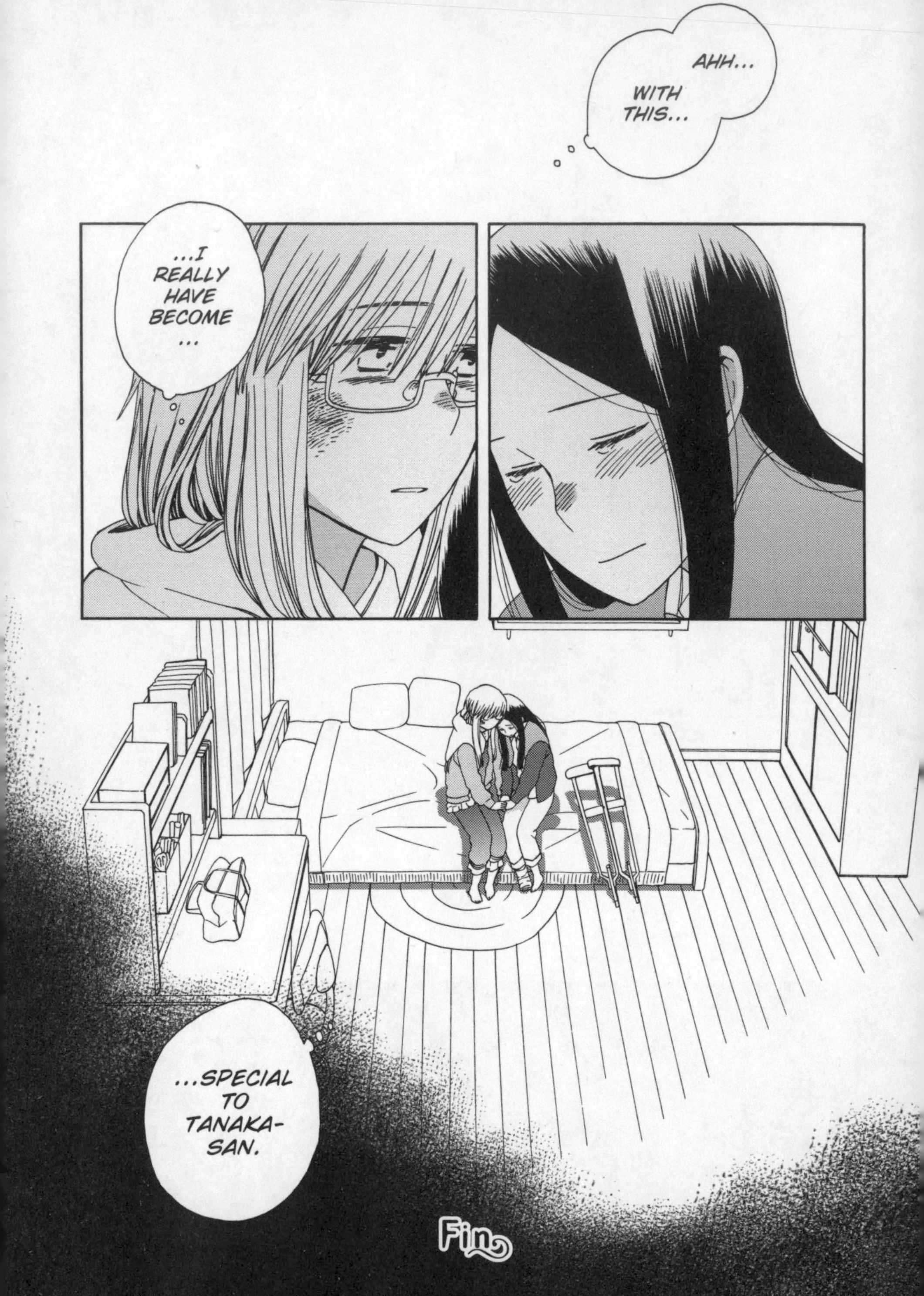
AHH... WITH THIS...
...I REALLY HAVE BECOME ...
...SPECIAL TO TANAKA-SAN.
Fin

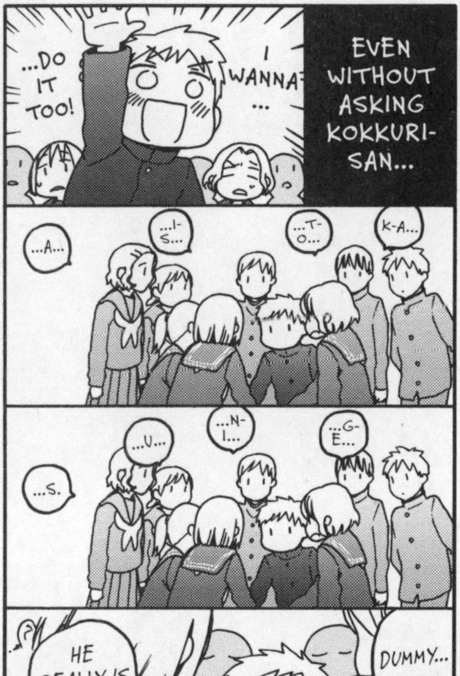
EVEN WITHOUT ASKING KOKKURI-SAN...
I WANNA-...
...DO IT TOO!
K-A...
...T-O...
...I-S...
...A...
...G-E...
...N-I...
...U...
...S.
DUMMY...
SO STUPID ...
WHAT CAN I SAY?
HE REALLY IS DUMB...

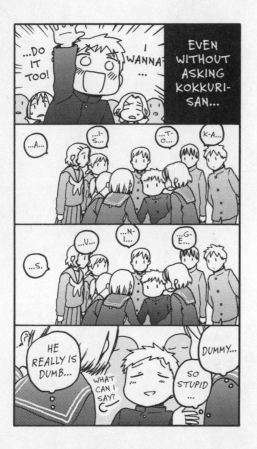

Love at Fourteen

Fuka Mizutani

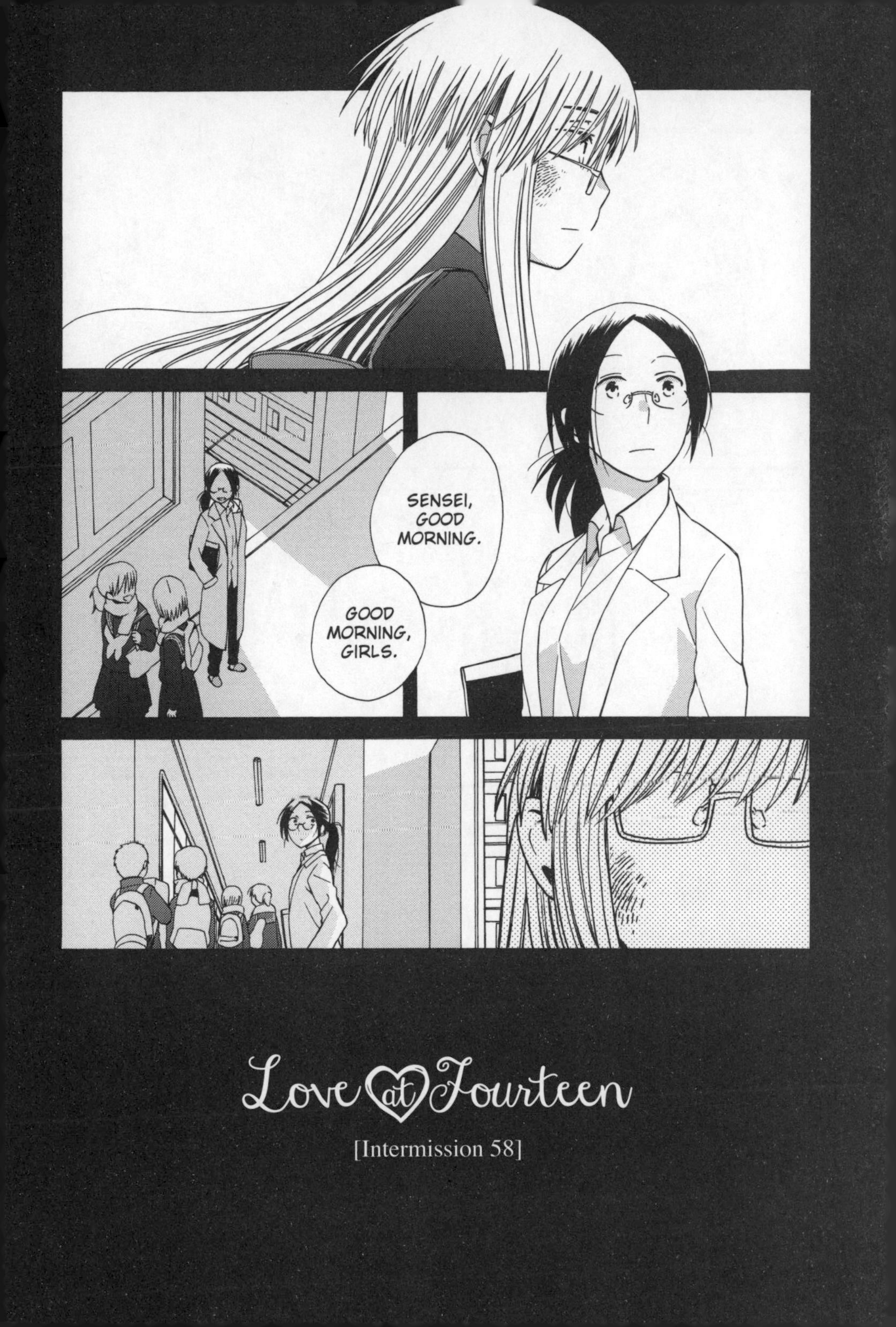
SENSEI, GOOD MORNING.
GOOD MORNING, GIRLS.

Love at Fourteen

[Intermission 58]

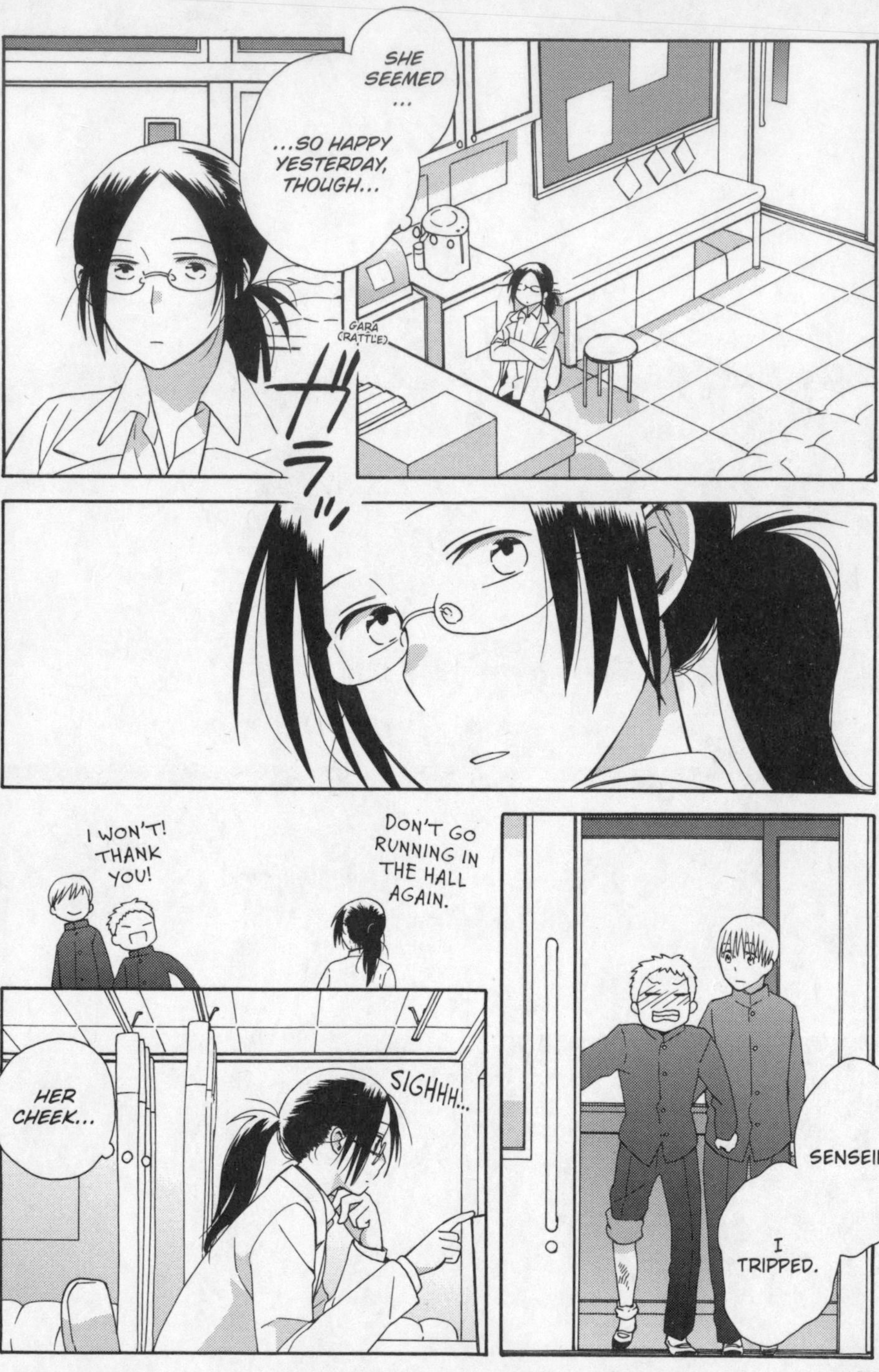
SHE SEEMED ... ...SO HAPPY YESTERDAY, THOUGH...
GARA (RATTLE)
SENSEIII!
I TRIPPED.
DON'T GO RUNNING IN THE HALL AGAIN.
I WON'T! THANK YOU!
SIGHHH...
HER CHEEK...

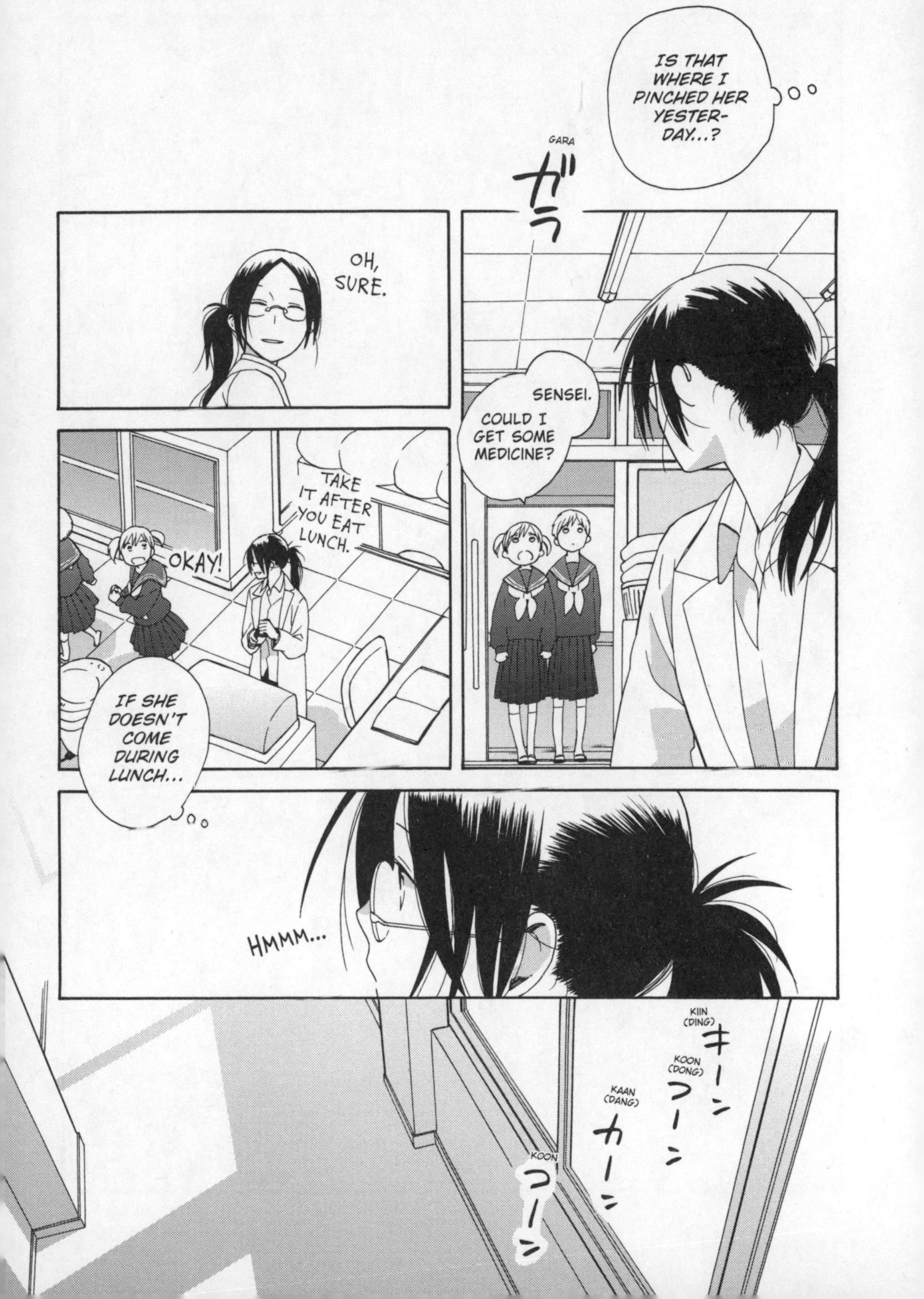
IS THAT WHERE I PINCHED HER YESTER-DAY...?
GARA
ガラ
SENSEI.
COULD I GET SOME MEDICINE?
OH, SURE.
TAKE IT AFTER YOU EAT LUNCH.
OKAY!
IF SHE DOESN'T COME DURING LUNCH...
HMMM...
KIIN (DING)
キーン
KOON (DONG)
コーン
KAAN (DANG)
カーン
KOON
コーン

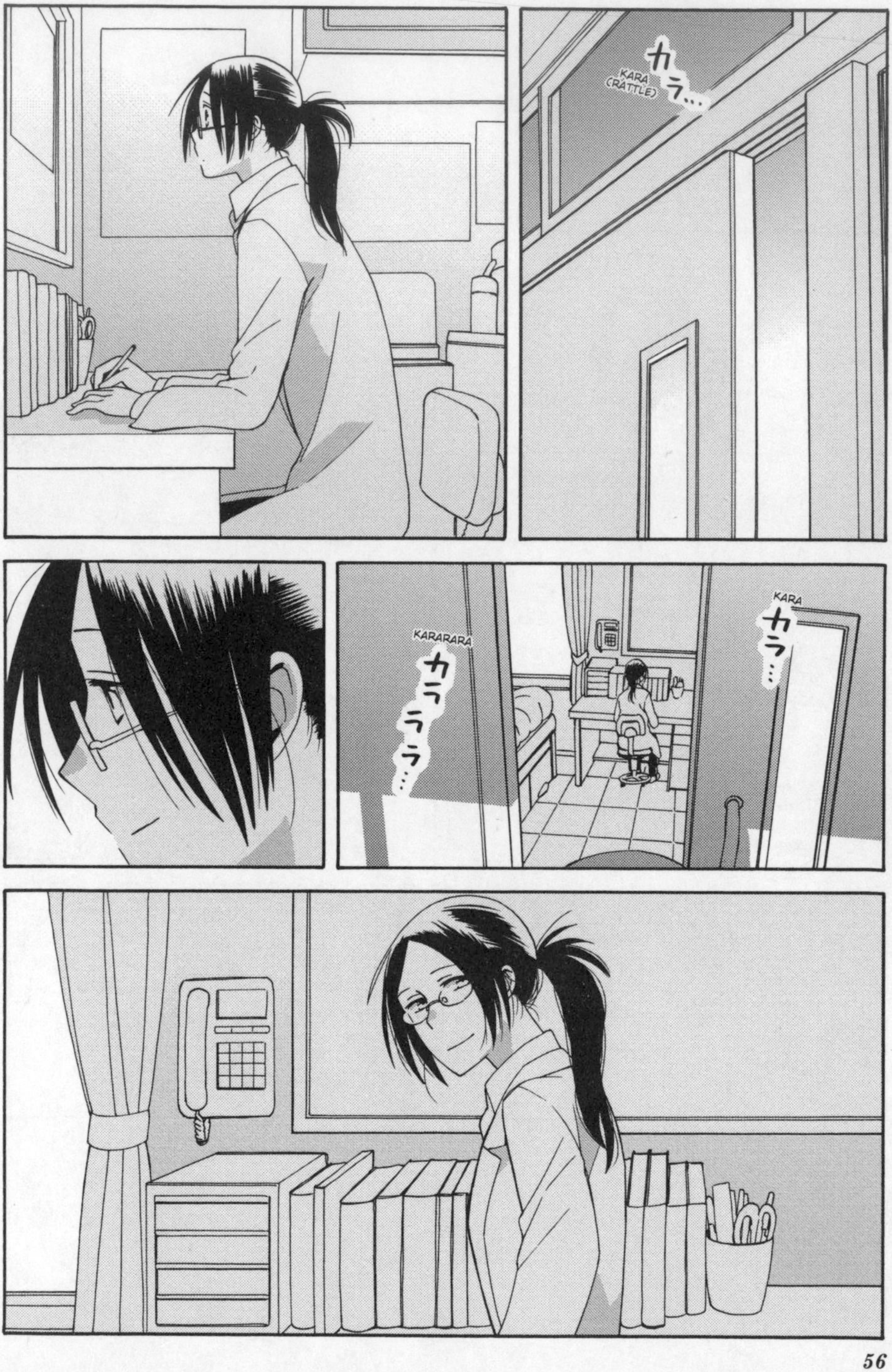
カラ…
KARA (RATTLE)
カラ…
KARA
カラララ…
KARARARA

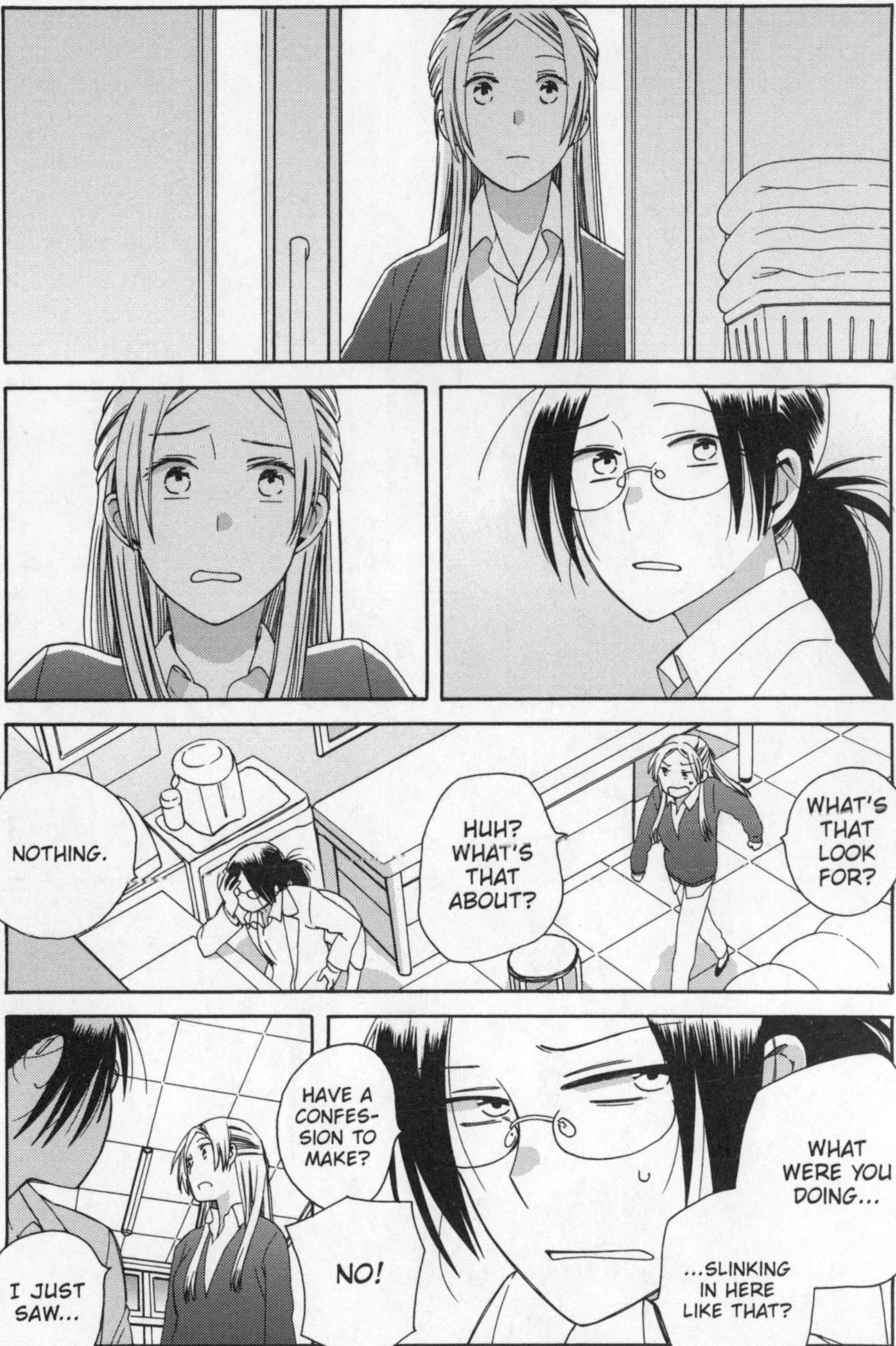
WHAT'S THAT LOOK FOR?
HUH? WHAT'S THAT ABOUT?
NOTHING.
WHAT WERE YOU DOING...
...SLINKING IN HERE LIKE THAT?
HAVE A CONFESSION TO MAKE?
NO!
I JUST SAW...

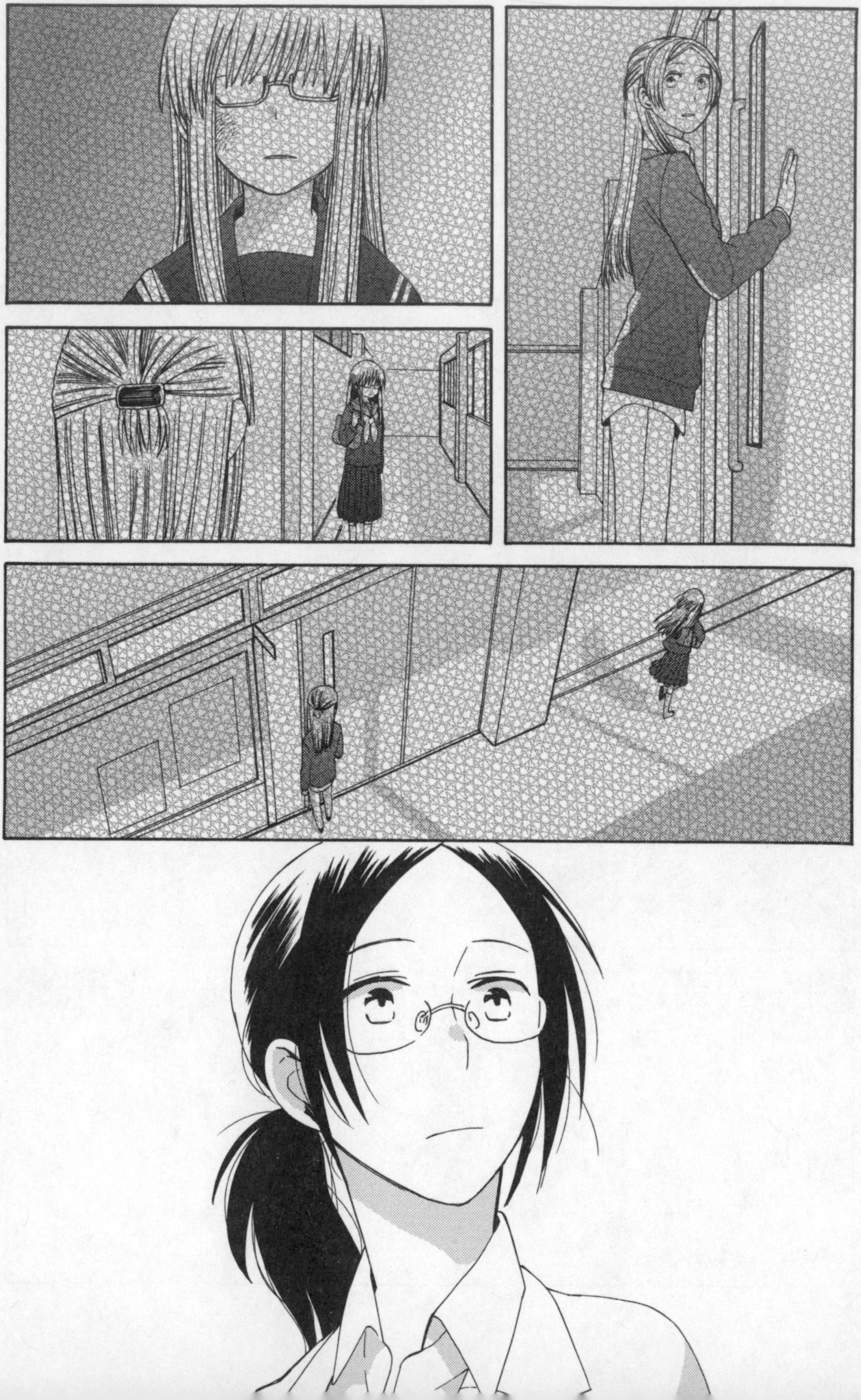

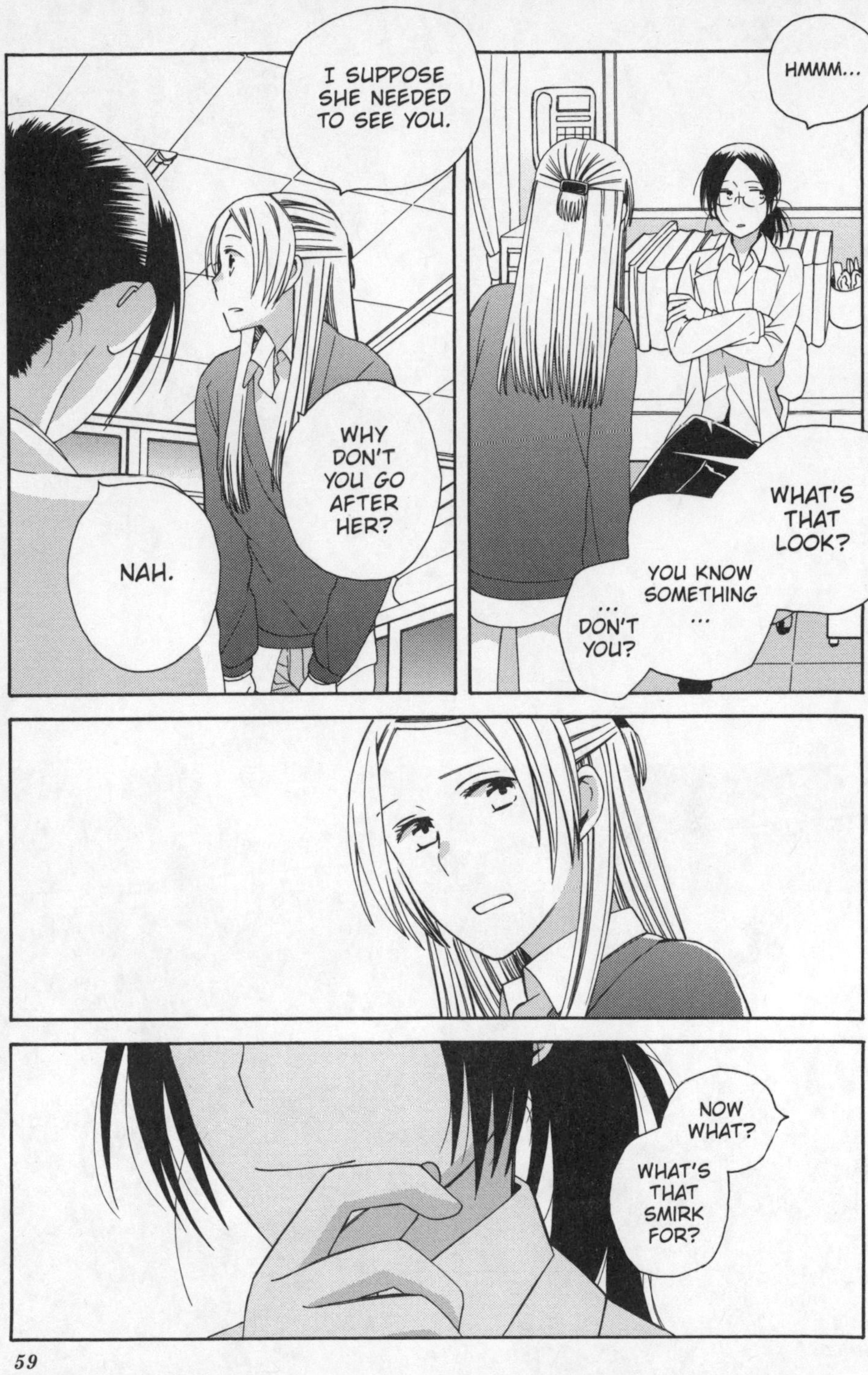
HMMM...
WHAT'S THAT LOOK?
YOU KNOW SOMETHING...
...DON'T YOU?
I SUPPOSE SHE NEEDED TO SEE YOU.
WHY DON'T YOU GO AFTER HER?
NAH.
NOW WHAT?
WHAT'S THAT SMIRK FOR?

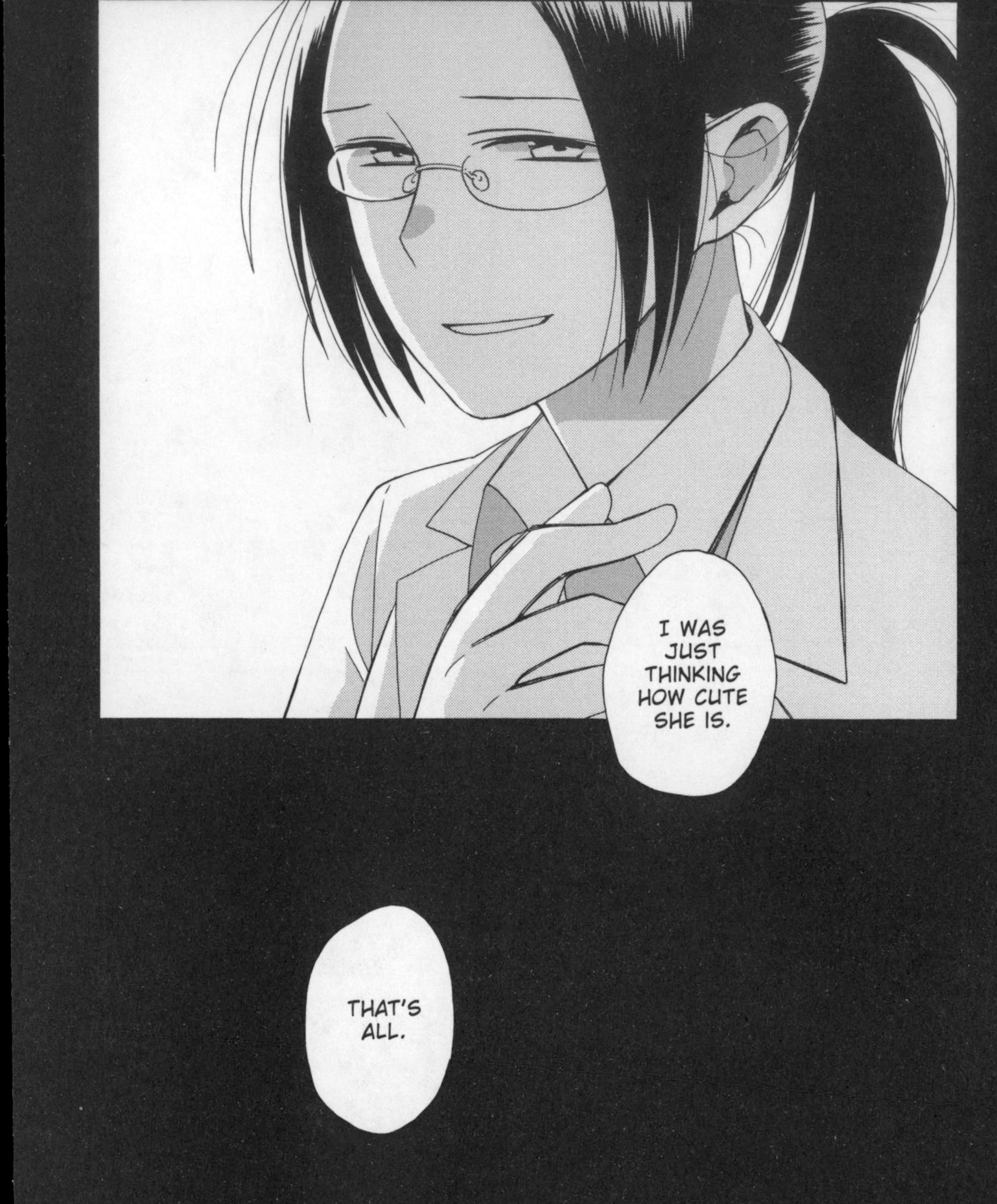
I WAS JUST THINKING HOW CUTE SHE IS.
THAT'S ALL.

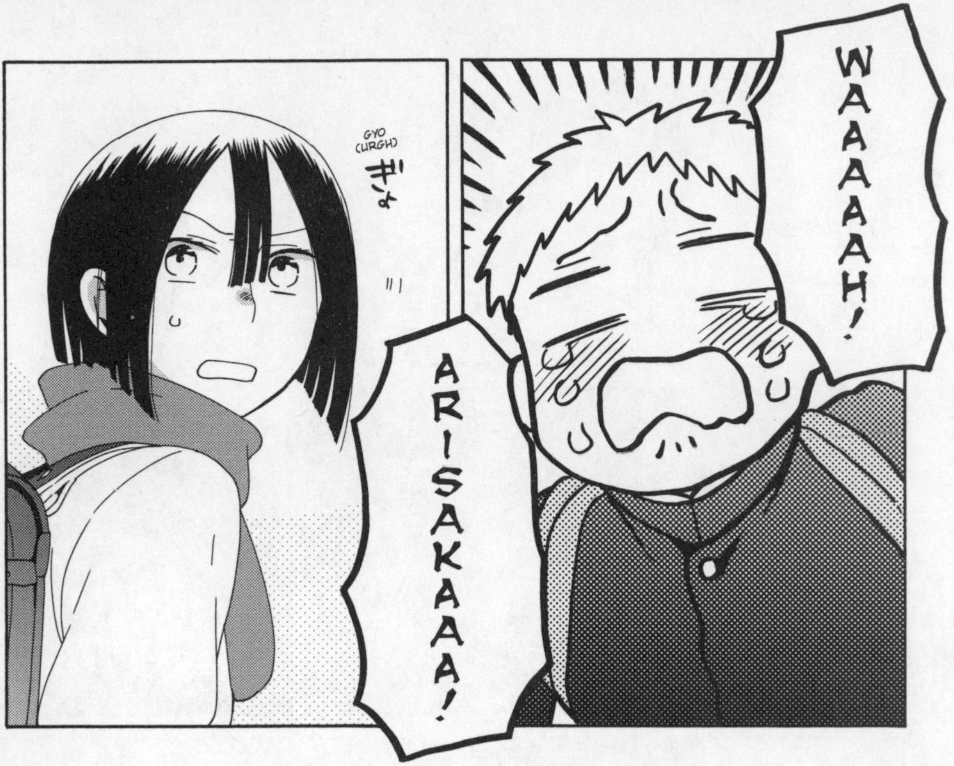
WAAAAAH!
ARISAKAAA!
GYO (URGH)
ぎょ

Love at Fourteen

[Intermission 59]

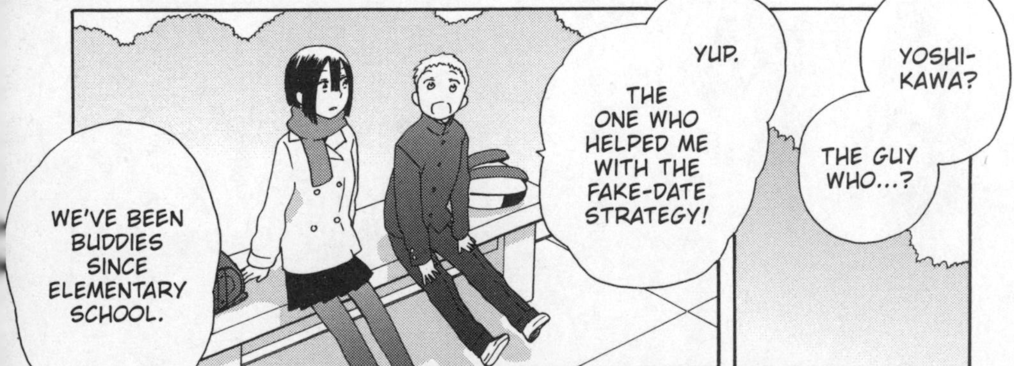
YOSHI-KAWA?
THE GUY WHO...?
YUP.
THE ONE WHO HELPED ME WITH THE FAKE-DATE STRATEGY!
WE'VE BEEN BUDDIES SINCE ELEMENTARY SCHOOL.

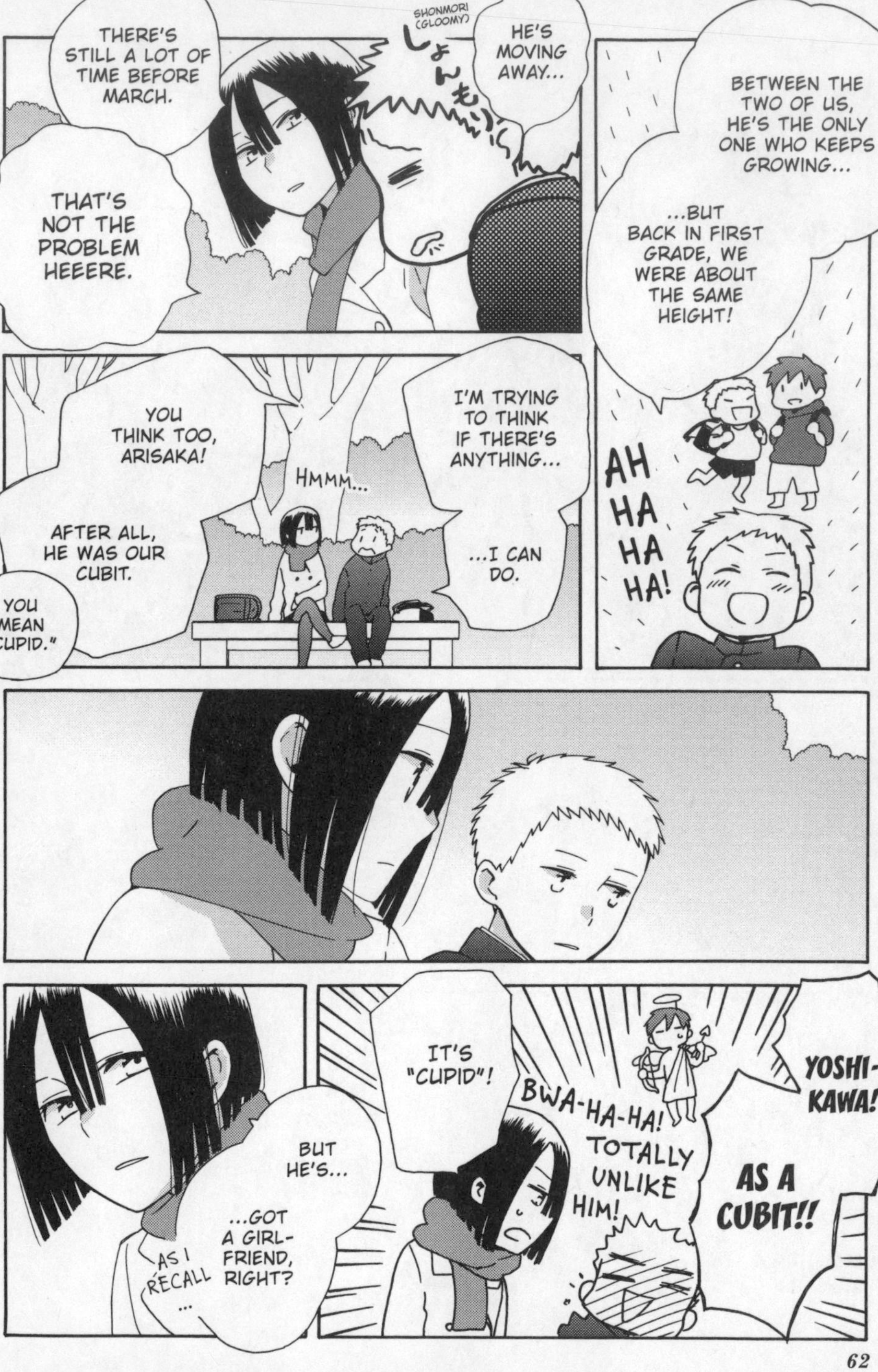
BETWEEN THE TWO OF US, HE'S THE ONLY ONE WHO KEEPS GROWING...
...BUT BACK IN FIRST GRADE, WE WERE ABOUT THE SAME HEIGHT!
AH HA HA HA!
HE'S MOVING AWAY...
SHONMORI (GLOOMY)
しょんもり
THERE'S STILL A LOT OF TIME BEFORE MARCH.
THAT'S NOT THE PROBLEM HEEERE.
I'M TRYING TO THINK IF THERE'S ANYTHING...
...I CAN DO.
HMMM...
YOU THINK TOO, ARISAKA!
AFTER ALL, HE WAS OUR CUBIT.
YOU MEAN "CUPID."
YOSHI-KAWA!
AS A CUBIT!!
IT'S "CUPID"!
BWA-HA-HA! TOTALLY UNLIKE HIM!
BUT HE'S...
...GOT A GIRL-FRIEND, RIGHT?
AS I RECALL...

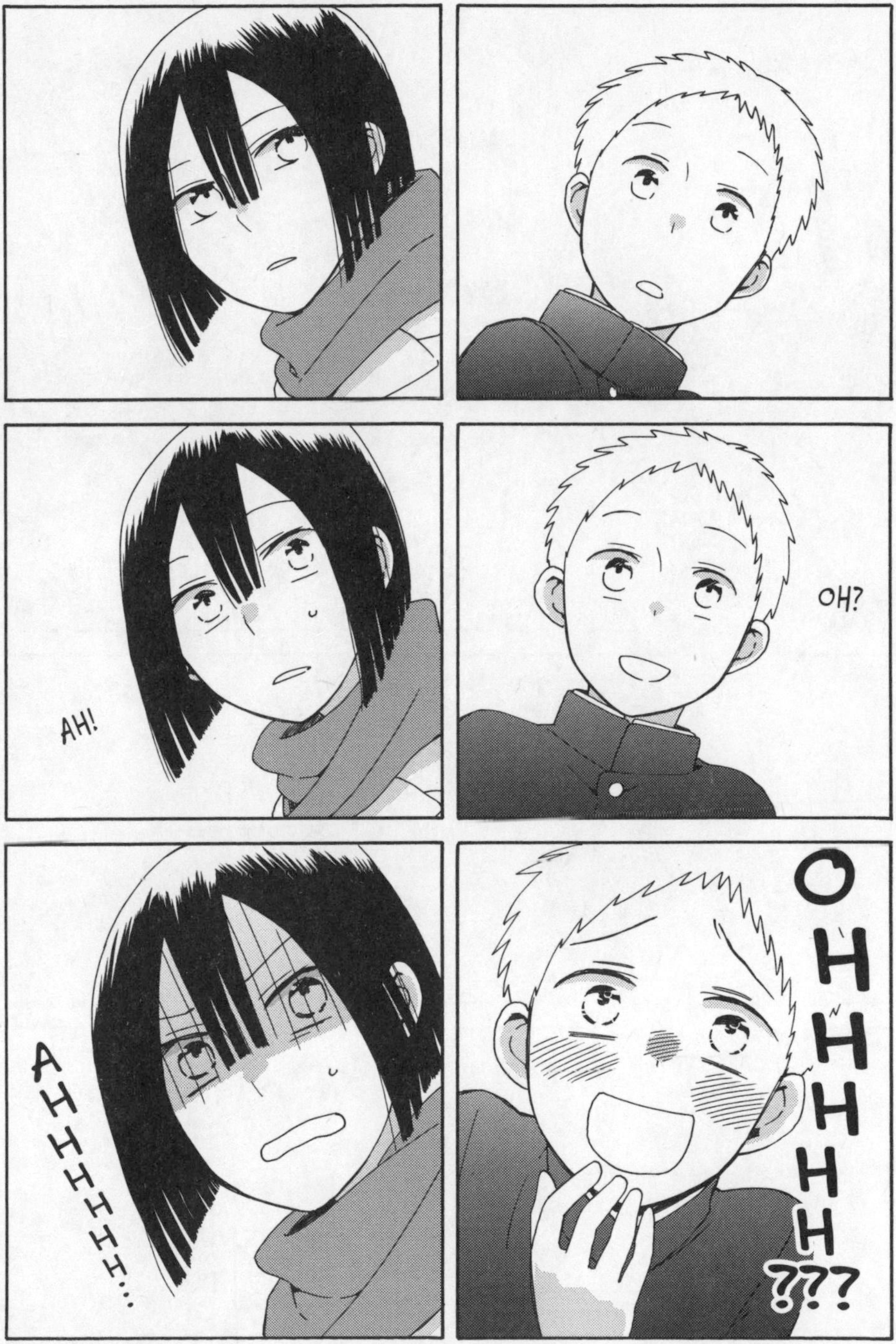
OH?
AH!
OHHHHH???
AHHHHH...

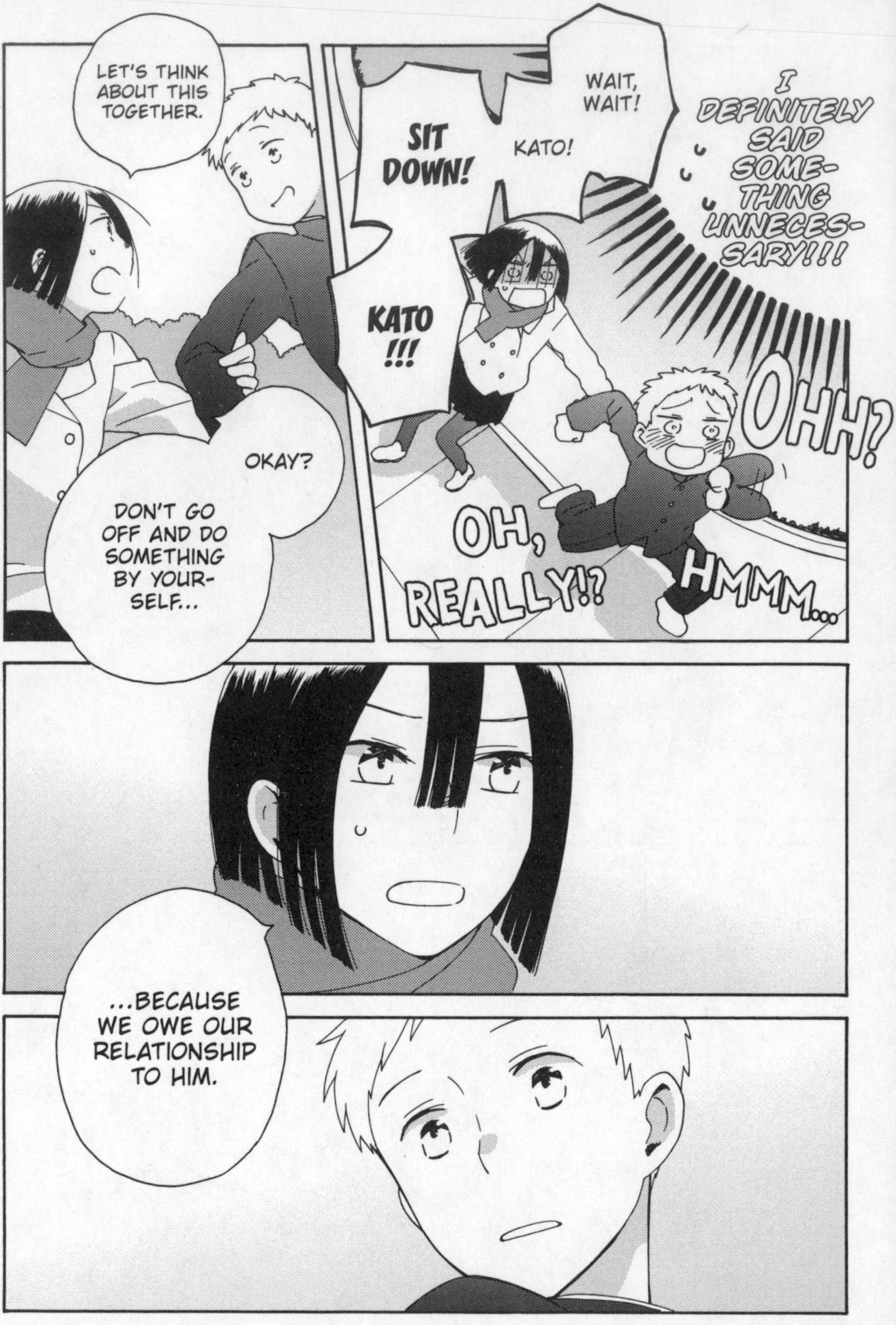
I DEFINITELY SAID SOME-THING UNNECES-SARY!!!
WAIT, WAIT!
KATO!
SIT DOWN!
KATO !!!
OHH?
HMMM...
OH, REALLY!?
LET'S THINK ABOUT THIS TOGETHER.
DON'T GO OFF AND DO SOMETHING BY YOUR-SELF...
OKAY?
...BECAUSE WE OWE OUR RELATIONSHIP TO HIM.

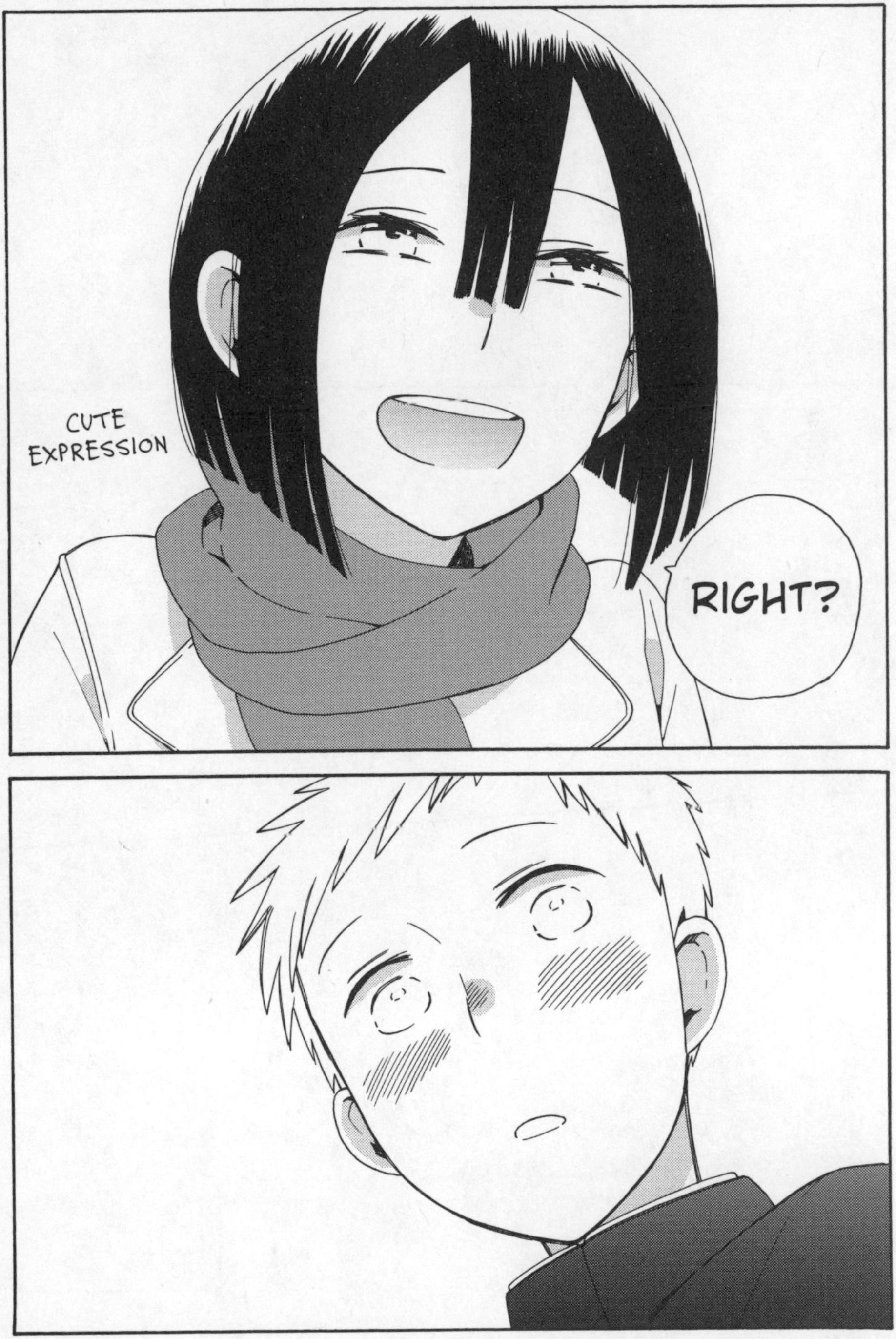
RIGHT?
CUTE EXPRESSION

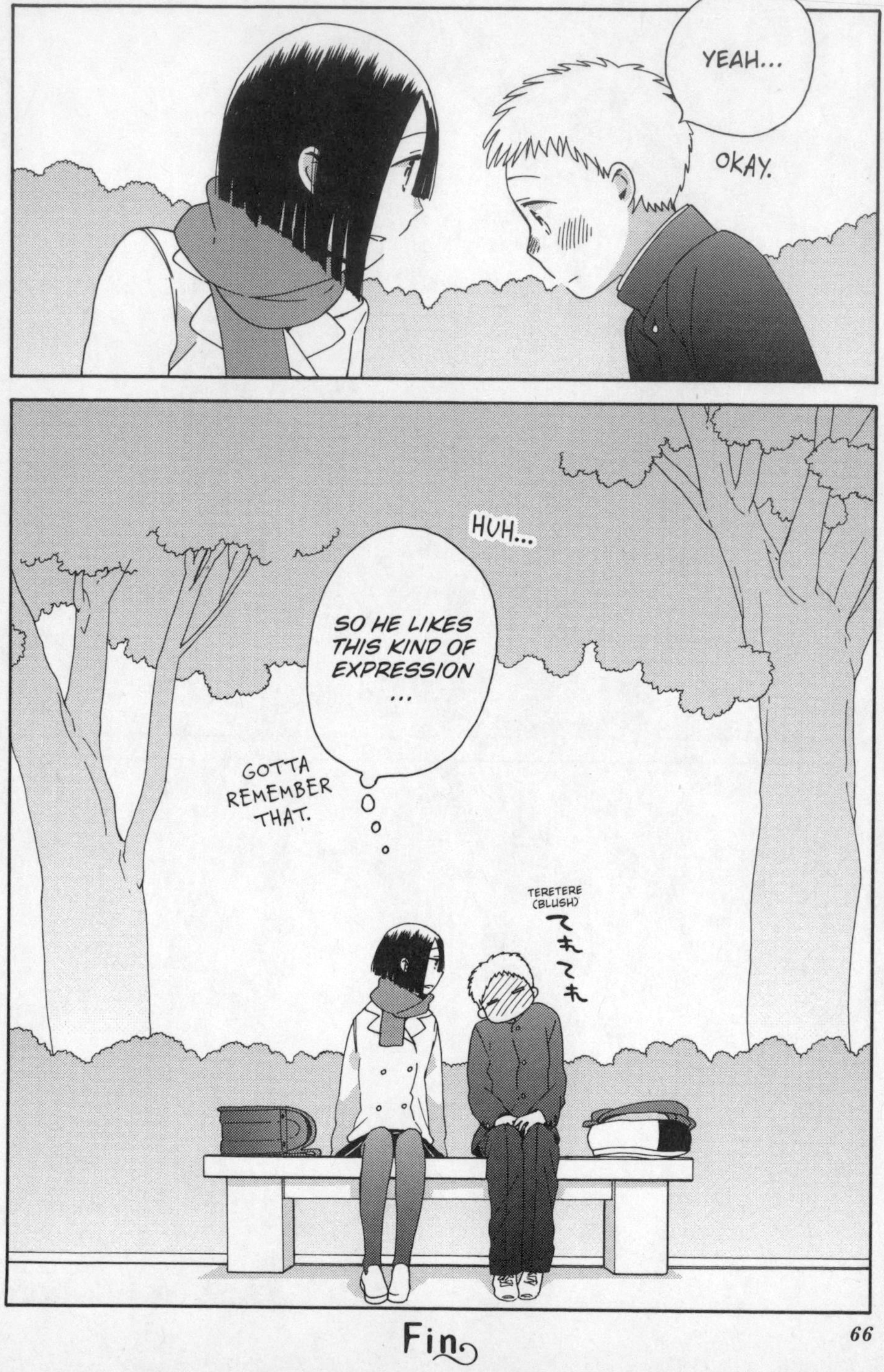
YEAH...
OKAY.
HUH...
SO HE LIKES THIS KIND OF EXPRESSION ...
GOTTA REMEMBER THAT.
TERETERE (BLUSH)
てれてれ

Fin

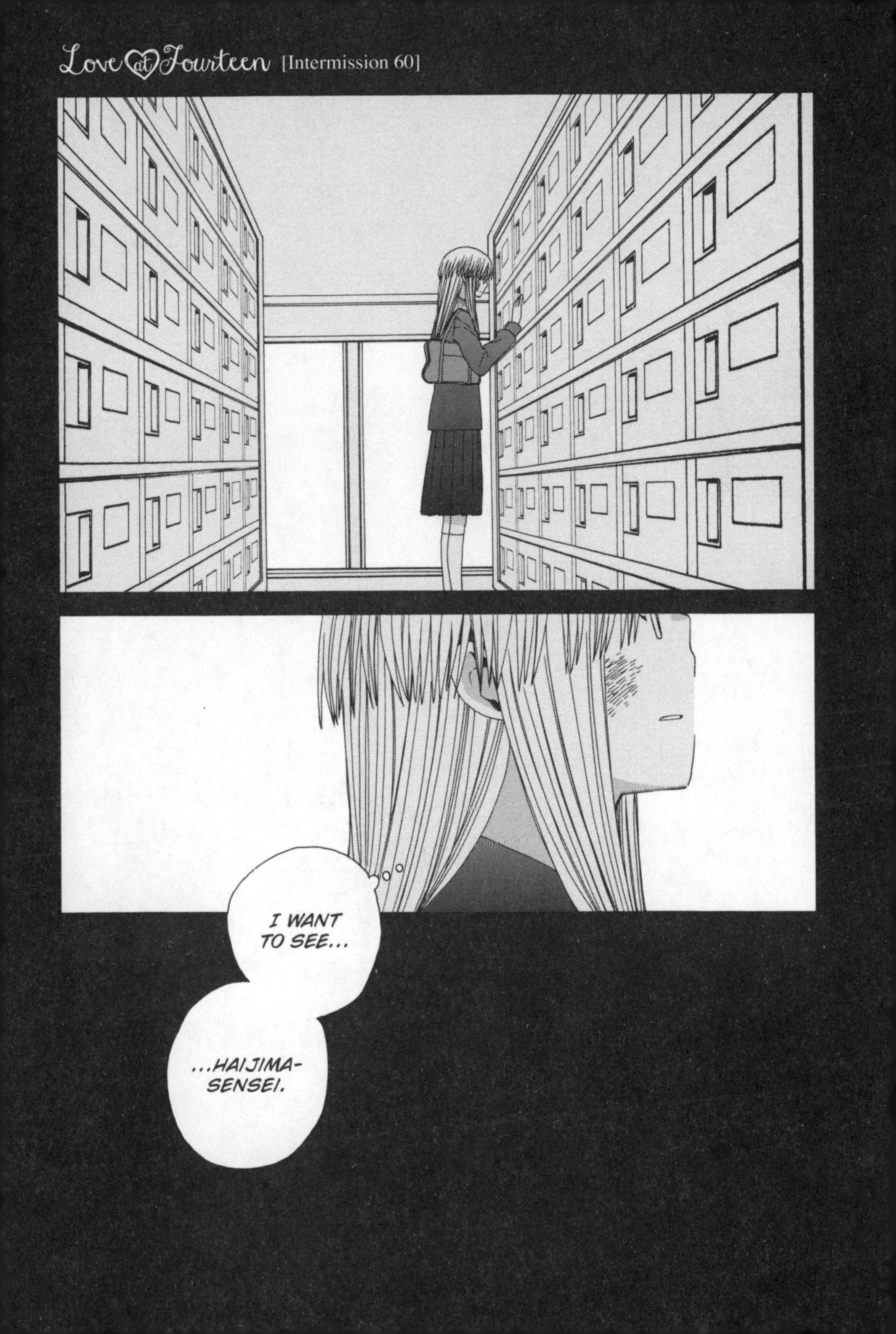
I WANT TO SEE...
...HAIJIMA-SENSEI.

Love at Fourteen

[Intermission 60]

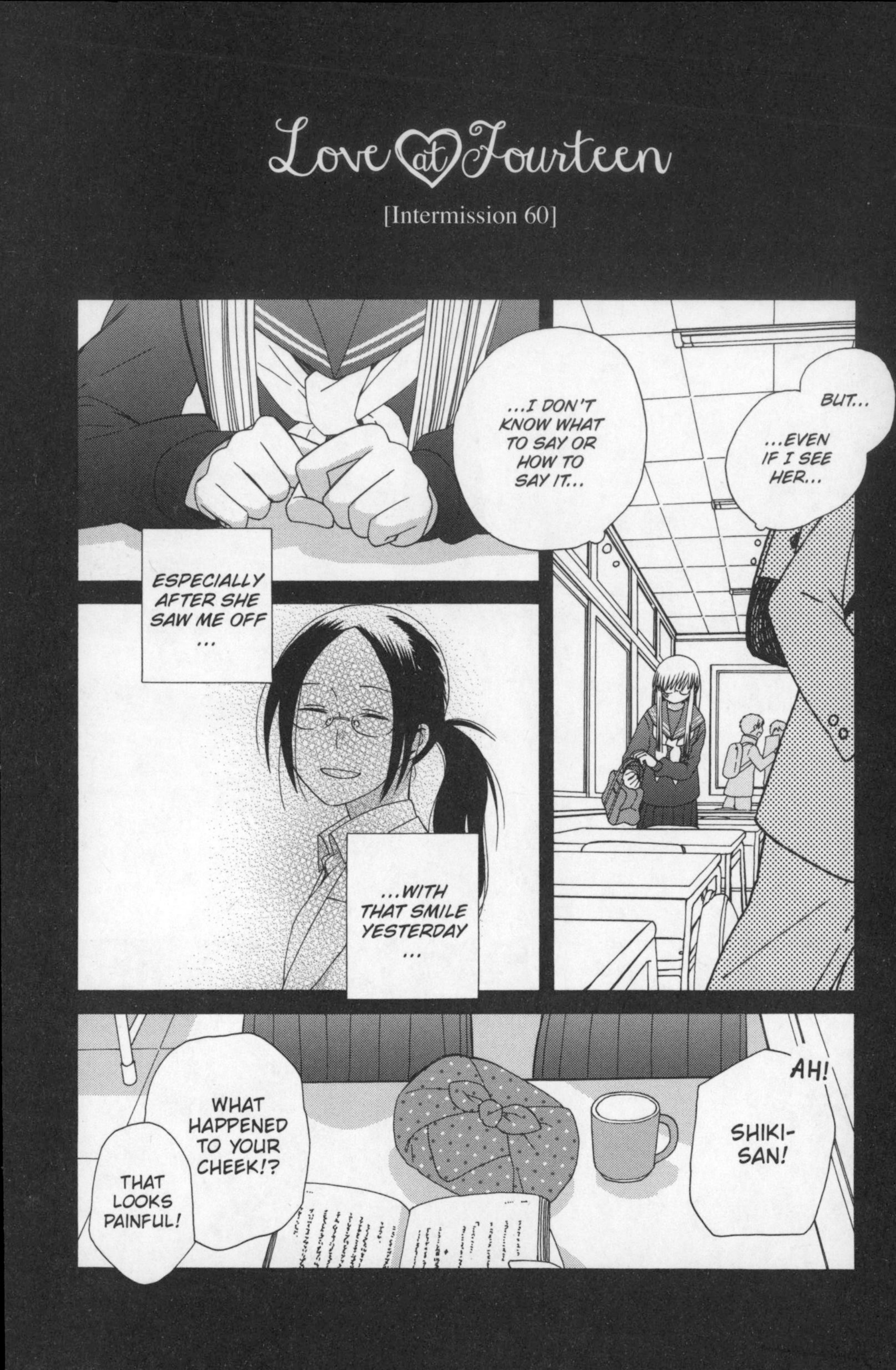
BUT...
...EVEN IF I SEE HER...
...I DON'T KNOW WHAT TO SAY OR HOW TO SAY IT...
ESPECIALLY AFTER SHE SAW ME OFF ...
...WITH THAT SMILE YESTERDAY ...
AH!
SHIKI-SAN!
WHAT HAPPENED TO YOUR CHEEK!?
THAT LOOKS PAINFUL!

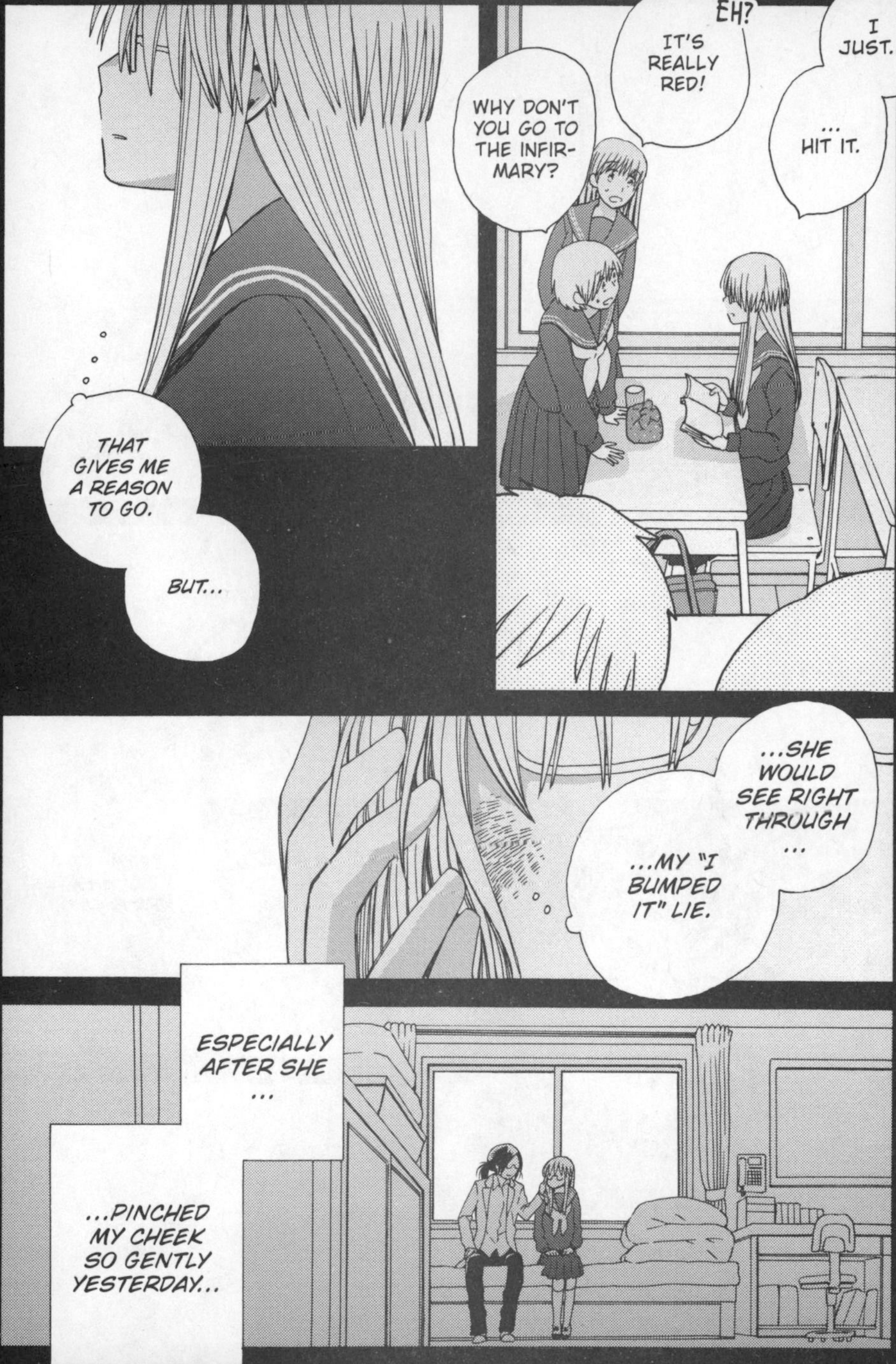
I JUST...
... HIT IT.
EH?
IT'S REALLY RED!
WHY DON'T YOU GO TO THE INFIRMARY?
THAT GIVES ME A REASON TO GO.
BUT...
...SHE WOULD SEE RIGHT THROUGH ...
...MY "I BUMPED IT" LIE.
ESPECIALLY AFTER SHE ...
...PINCHED MY CHEEK SO GENTLY YESTERDAY...

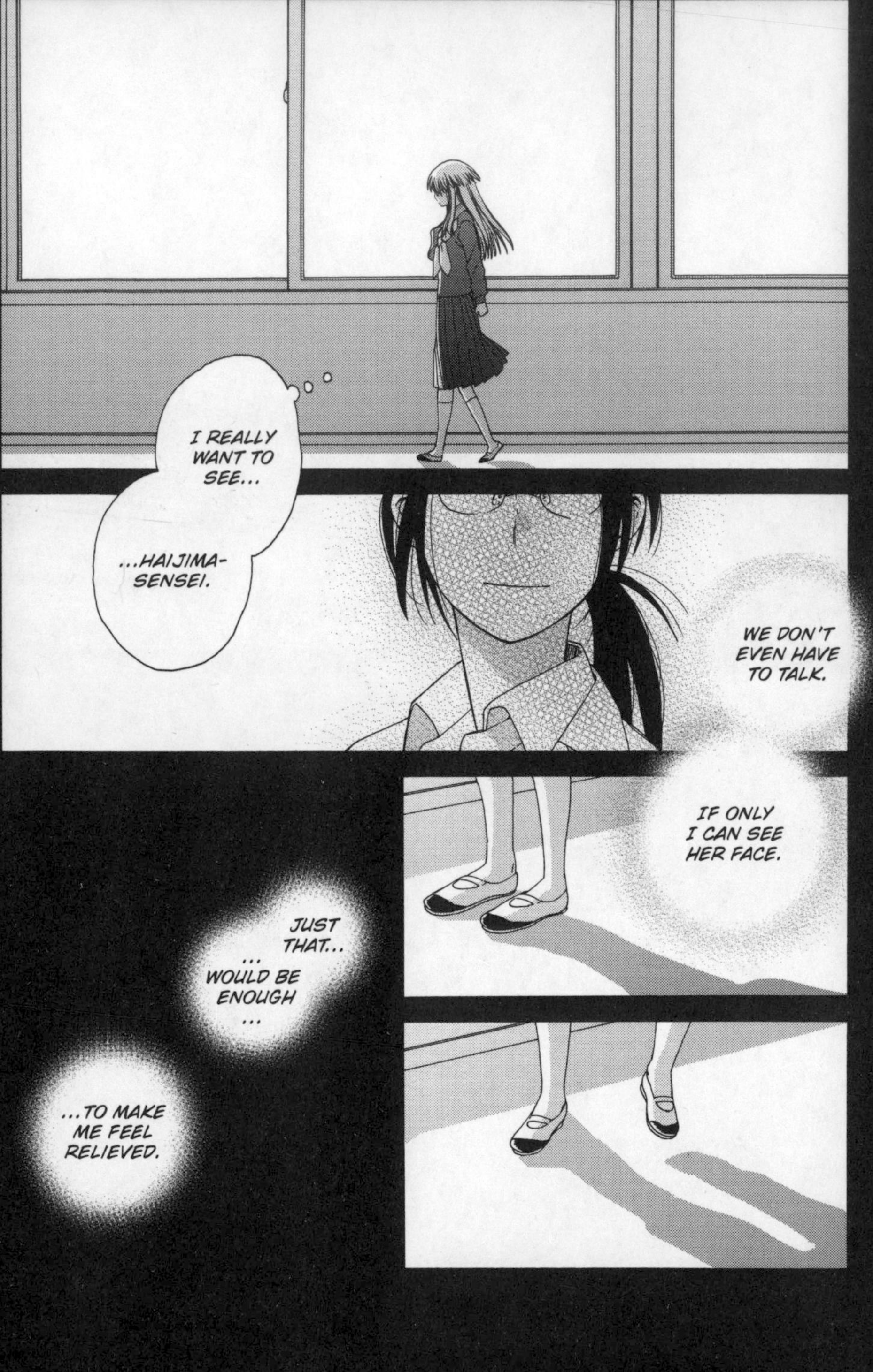
I REALLY WANT TO SEE...
...HAIJIMA-SENSEI.
WE DON'T EVEN HAVE TO TALK.
IF ONLY I CAN SEE HER FACE.
JUST THAT...
...WOULD BE ENOUGH...
...TO MAKE ME FEEL RELIEVED.

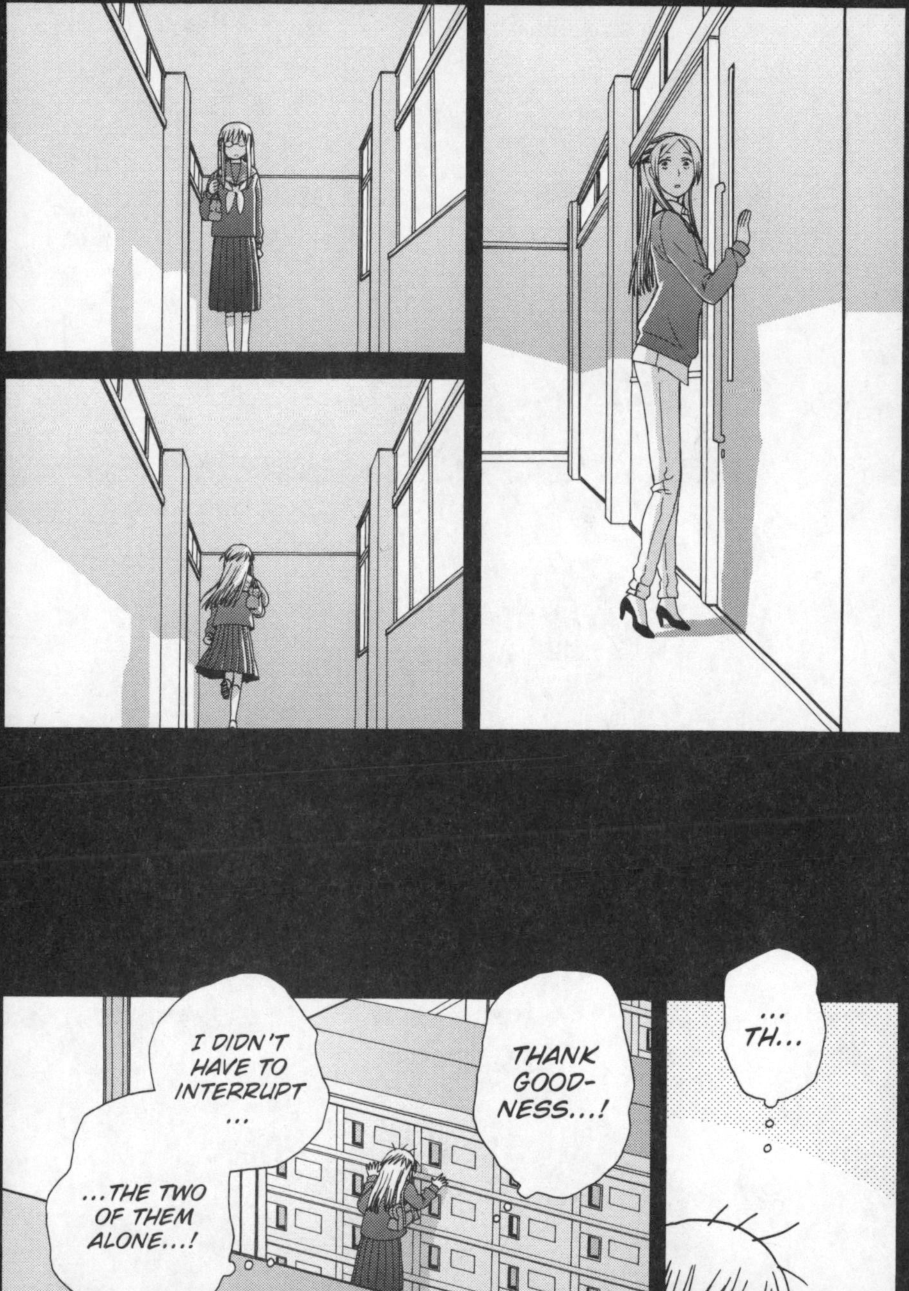
...TH...
THANK GOOD-NESS...!
I DIDN'T HAVE TO INTERRUPT...
...THE TWO OF THEM ALONE...!

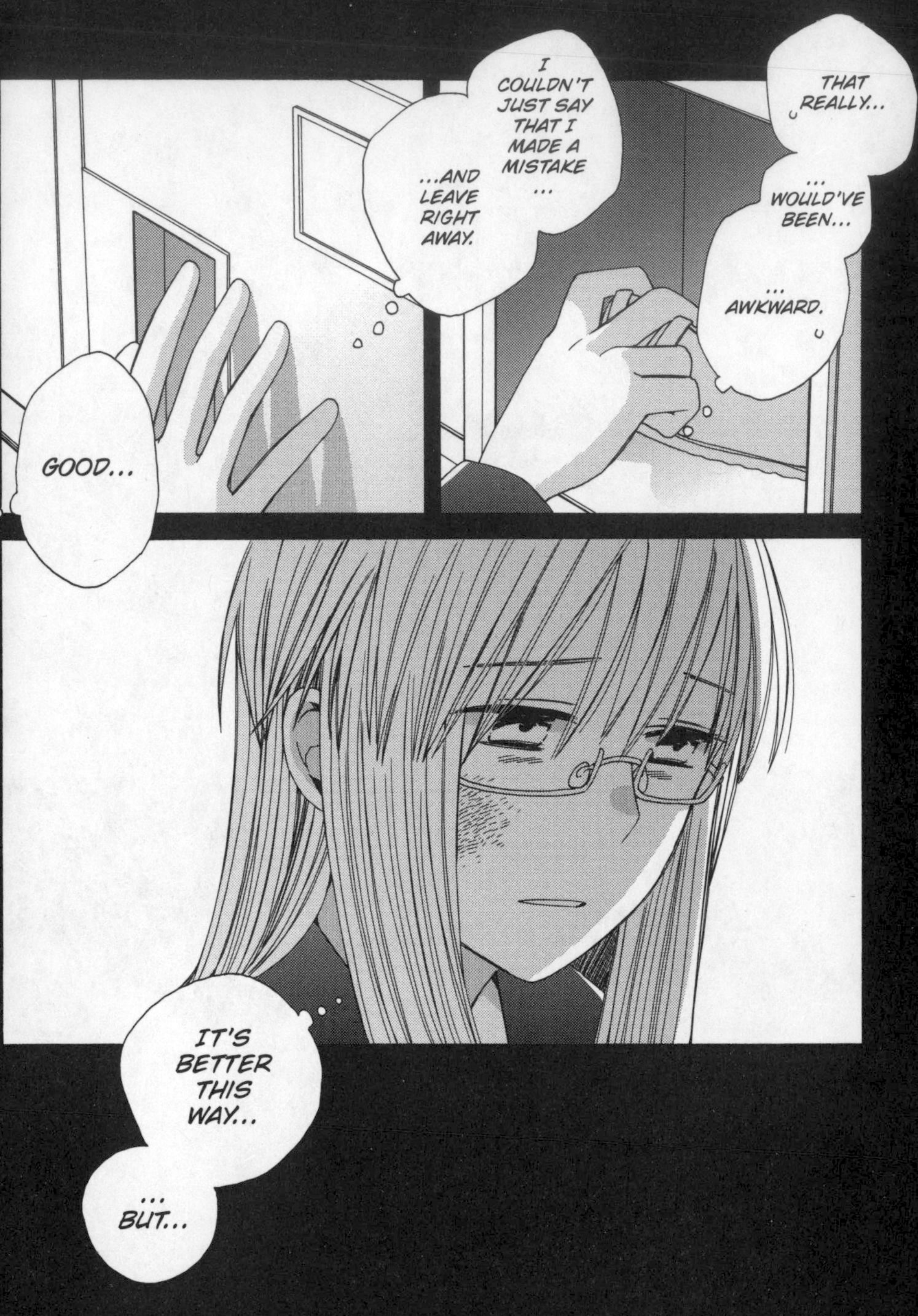
I COULDN'T JUST SAY THAT I MADE A MISTAKE ...
...AND LEAVE RIGHT AWAY.
THAT REALLY...
...WOULD'VE BEEN...
...AWKWARD.
GOOD...
IT'S BETTER THIS WAY...
...BUT...

Love at Fourteen

Fuka Mizutani

Love at Fourteen

[Chapter 43]

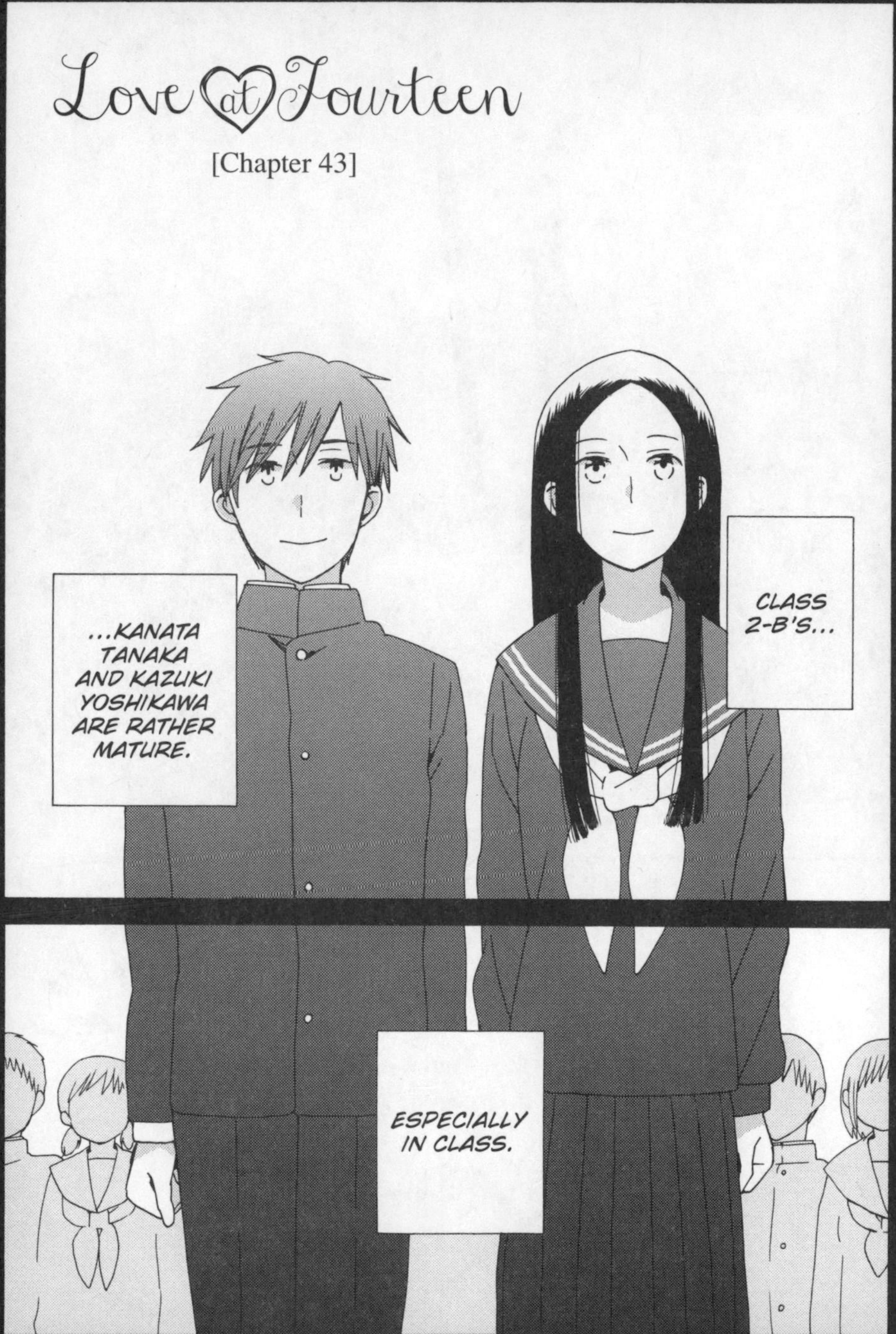
CLASS 2-B'S...
...KANATA TANAKA AND KAZUKI YOSHIKAWA ARE RATHER MATURE.
ESPECIALLY IN CLASS.

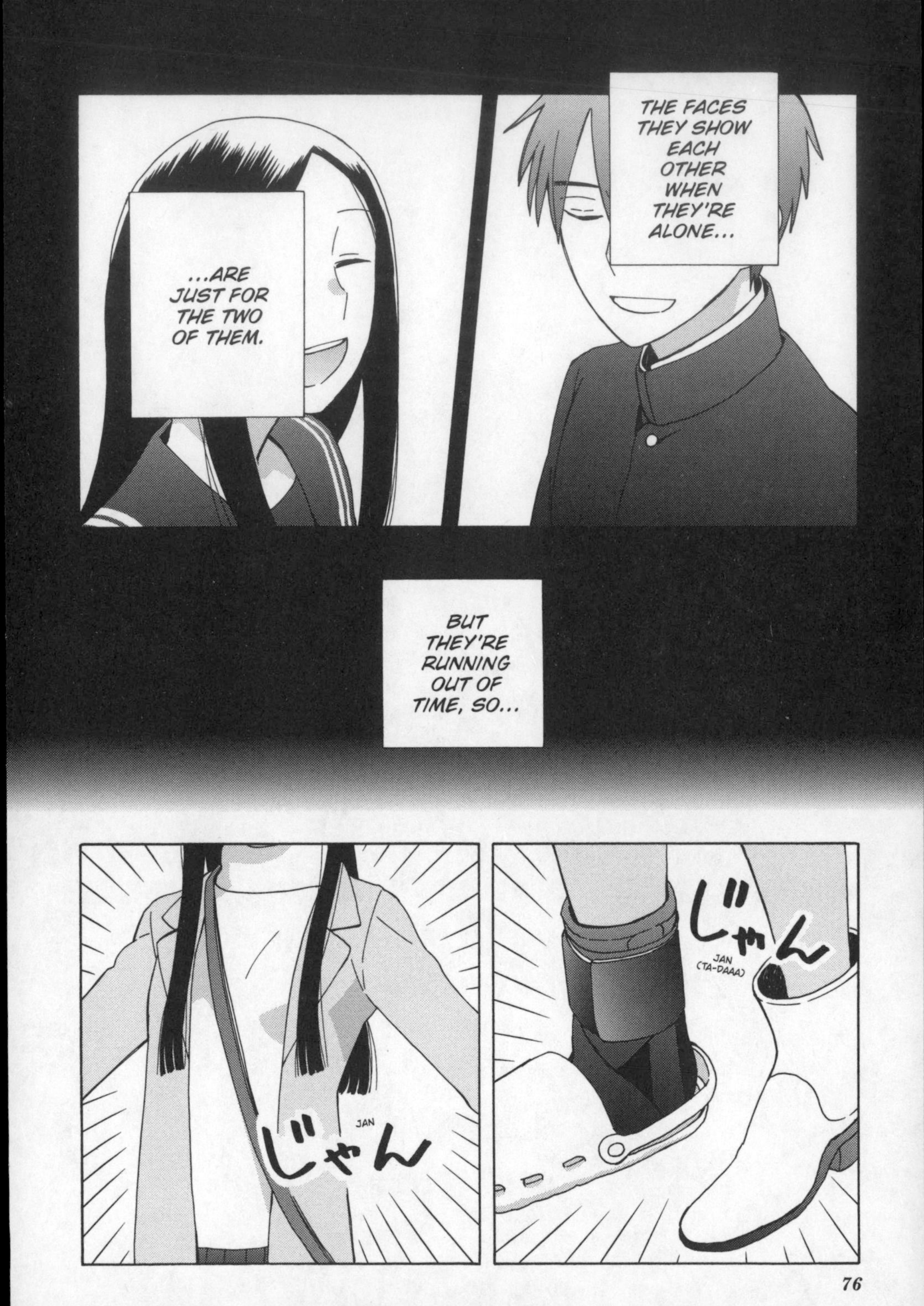
THE FACES THEY SHOW EACH OTHER WHEN THEY'RE ALONE...
...ARE JUST FOR THE TWO OF THEM.
BUT THEY'RE RUNNING OUT OF TIME, SO...
じゃん
JAN (TA-DAAA)
じゃん
JAN

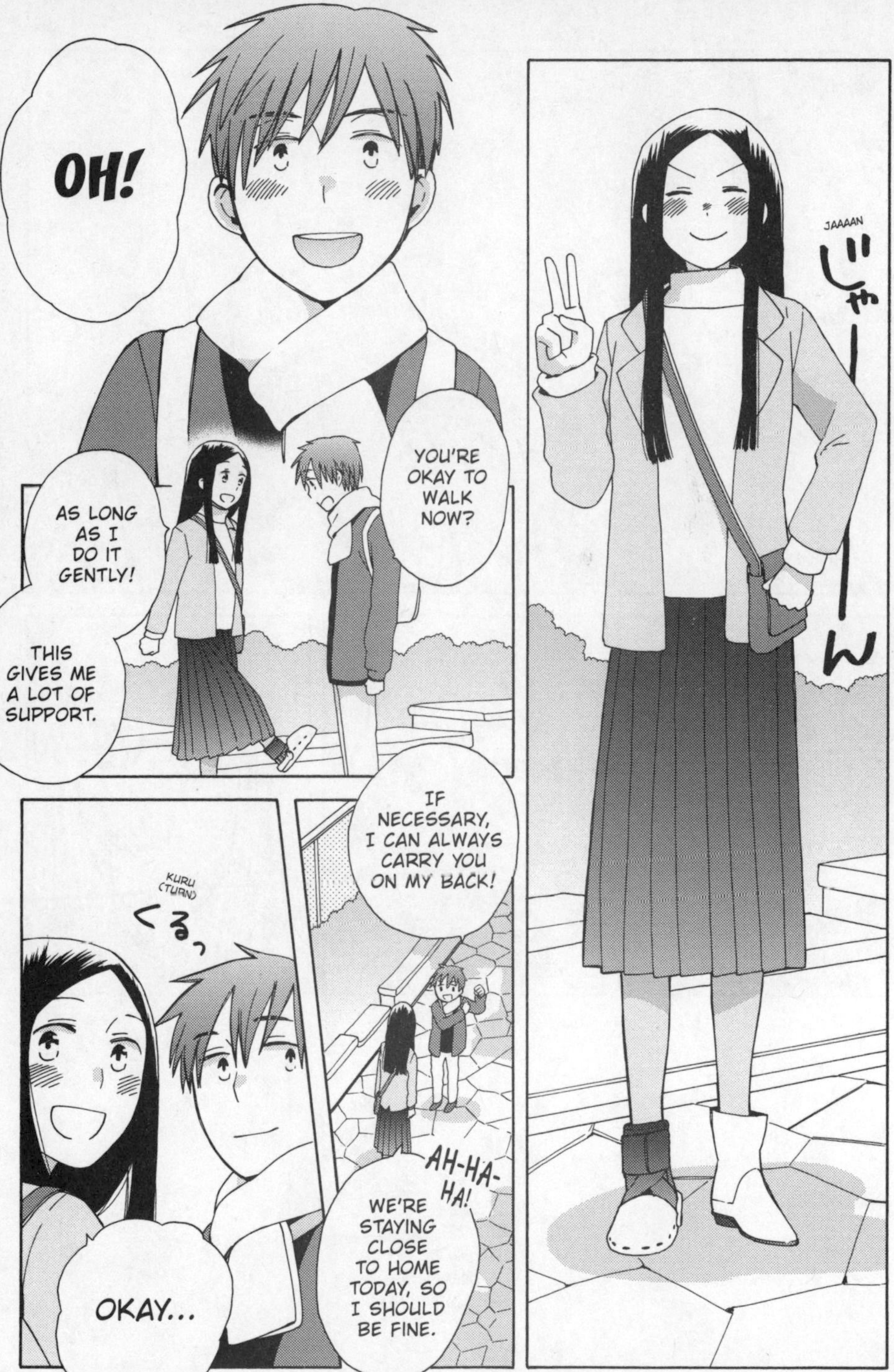
JAAAAN
じゃーーん
OH!
YOU'RE OKAY TO WALK NOW?
AS LONG AS I DO IT GENTLY!
THIS GIVES ME A LOT OF SUPPORT.
IF NECESSARY, I CAN ALWAYS CARRY YOU ON MY BACK!
AH-HA-HA!
WE'RE STAYING CLOSE TO HOME TODAY, SO I SHOULD BE FINE.
KURU (TURN)
くるっ
OKAY...

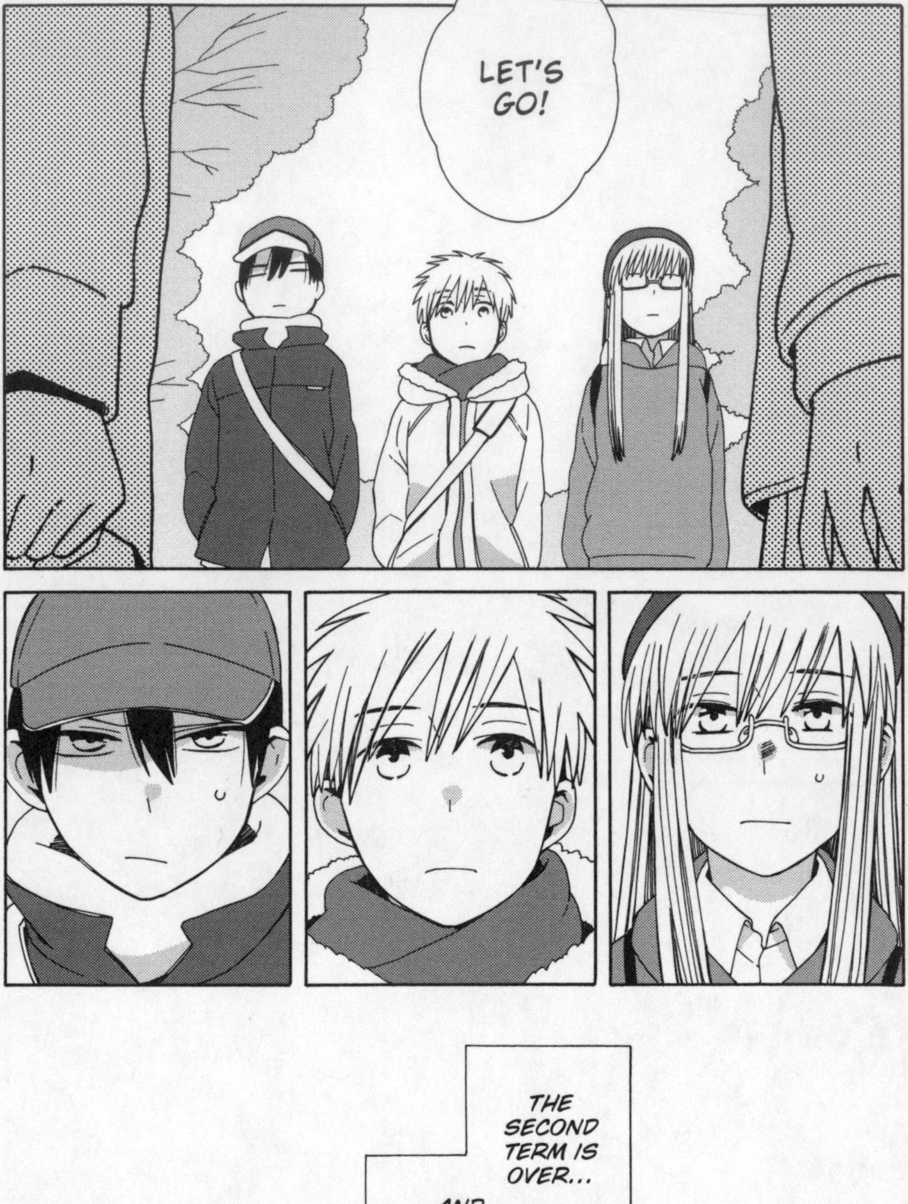
LET'S GO!
THE SECOND TERM IS OVER...
...AND WINTER BREAK HAS BEGUN.

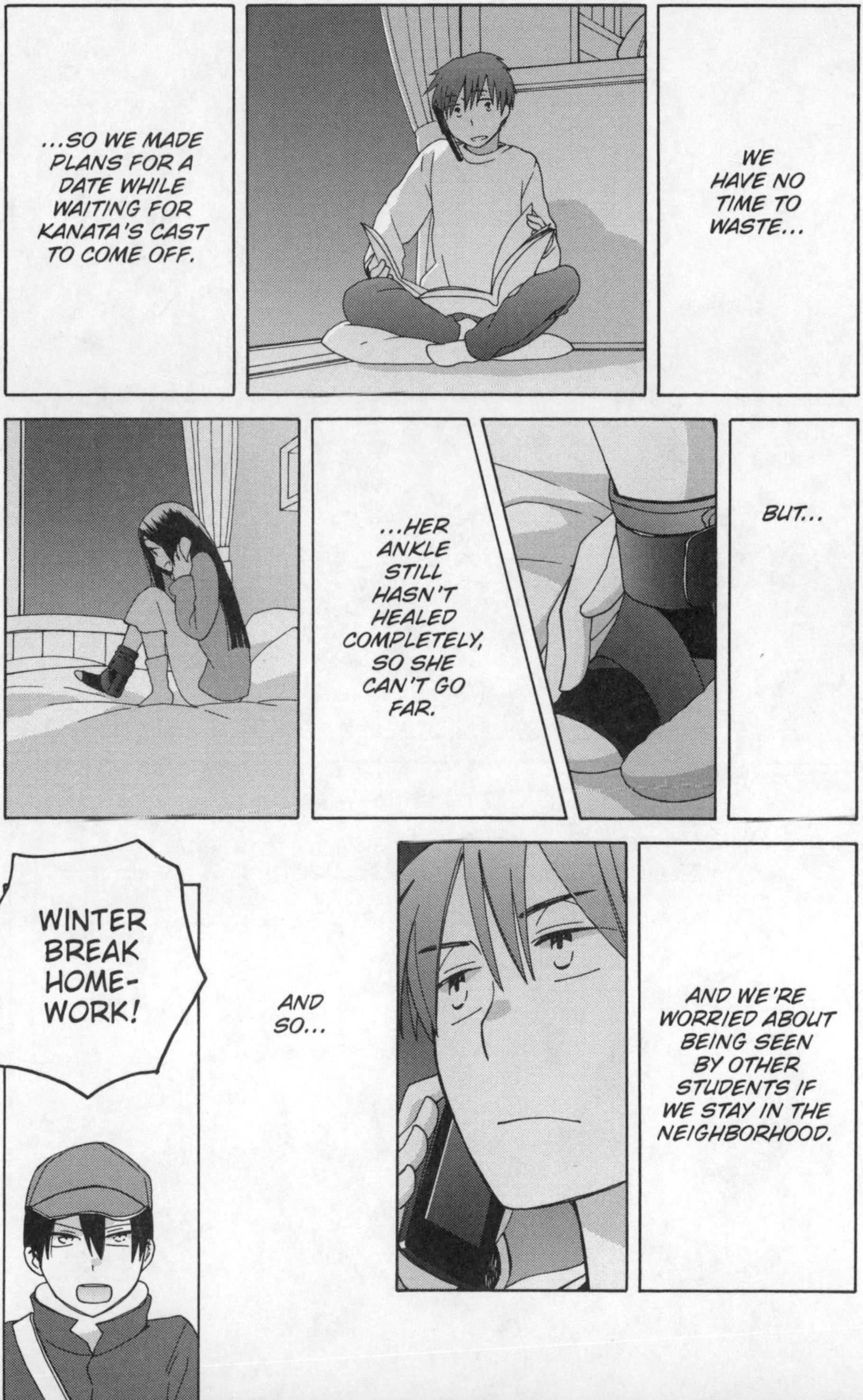
WE HAVE NO TIME TO WASTE...
...SO WE MADE PLANS FOR A DATE WHILE WAITING FOR KANATA'S CAST TO COME OFF.
BUT...
...HER ANKLE STILL HASN'T HEALED COMPLETELY, SO SHE CAN'T GO FAR.
AND WE'RE WORRIED ABOUT BEING SEEN BY OTHER STUDENTS IF WE STAY IN THE NEIGHBORHOOD.
AND SO...
WINTER BREAK HOME-WORK!

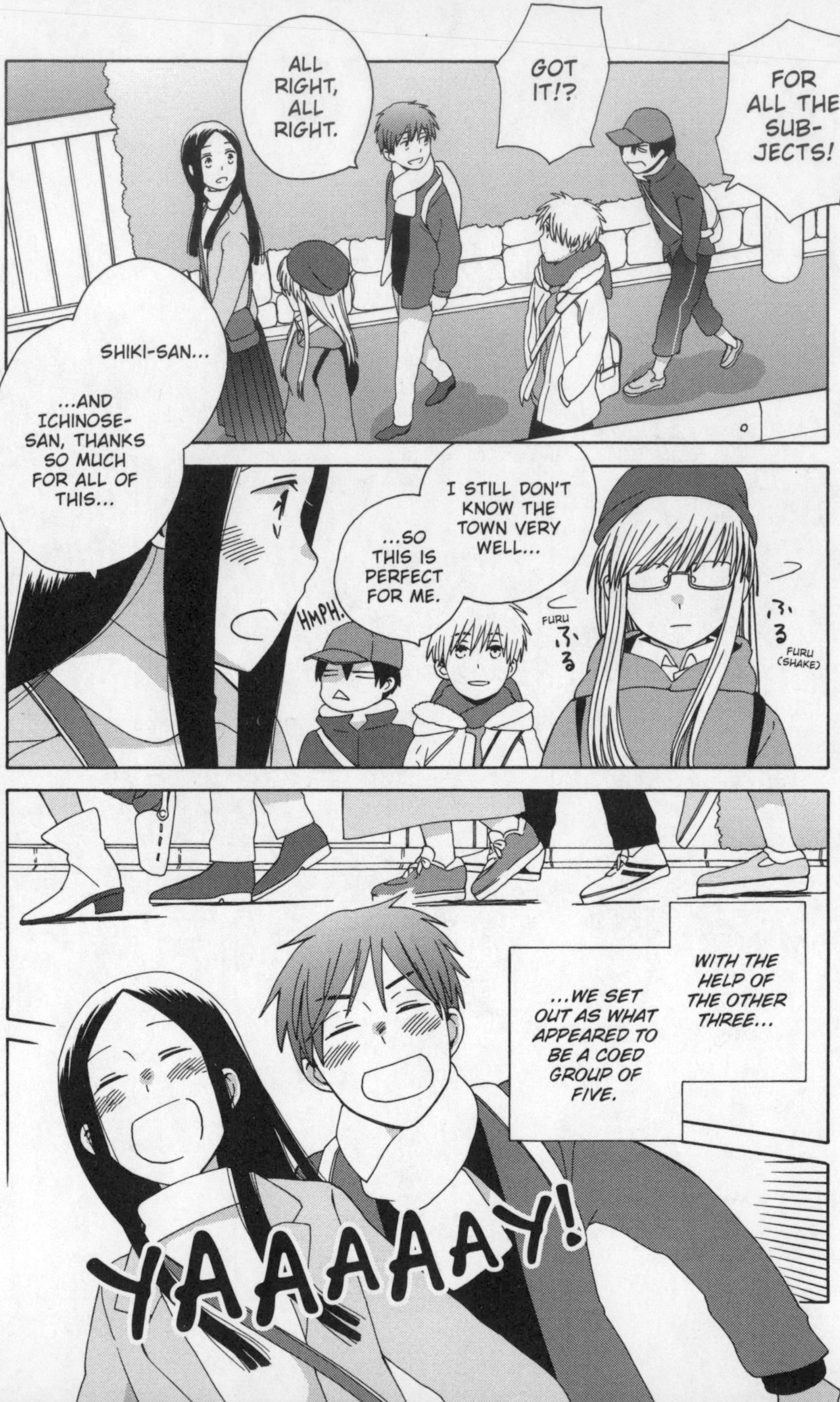
FOR ALL THE SUB-JECTS!
GOT IT!?
ALL RIGHT, ALL RIGHT.
SHIKI-SAN...
...AND ICHINOSE-SAN, THANKS SO MUCH FOR ALL OF THIS...
FURU ふる (SHAKE)
FURU ふる
I STILL DON'T KNOW THE TOWN VERY WELL...
...SO THIS IS PERFECT FOR ME.
HMPH.
WITH THE HELP OF THE OTHER THREE...
...WE SET OUT AS WHAT APPEARED TO BE A COED GROUP OF FIVE.
YAAAAAAY!

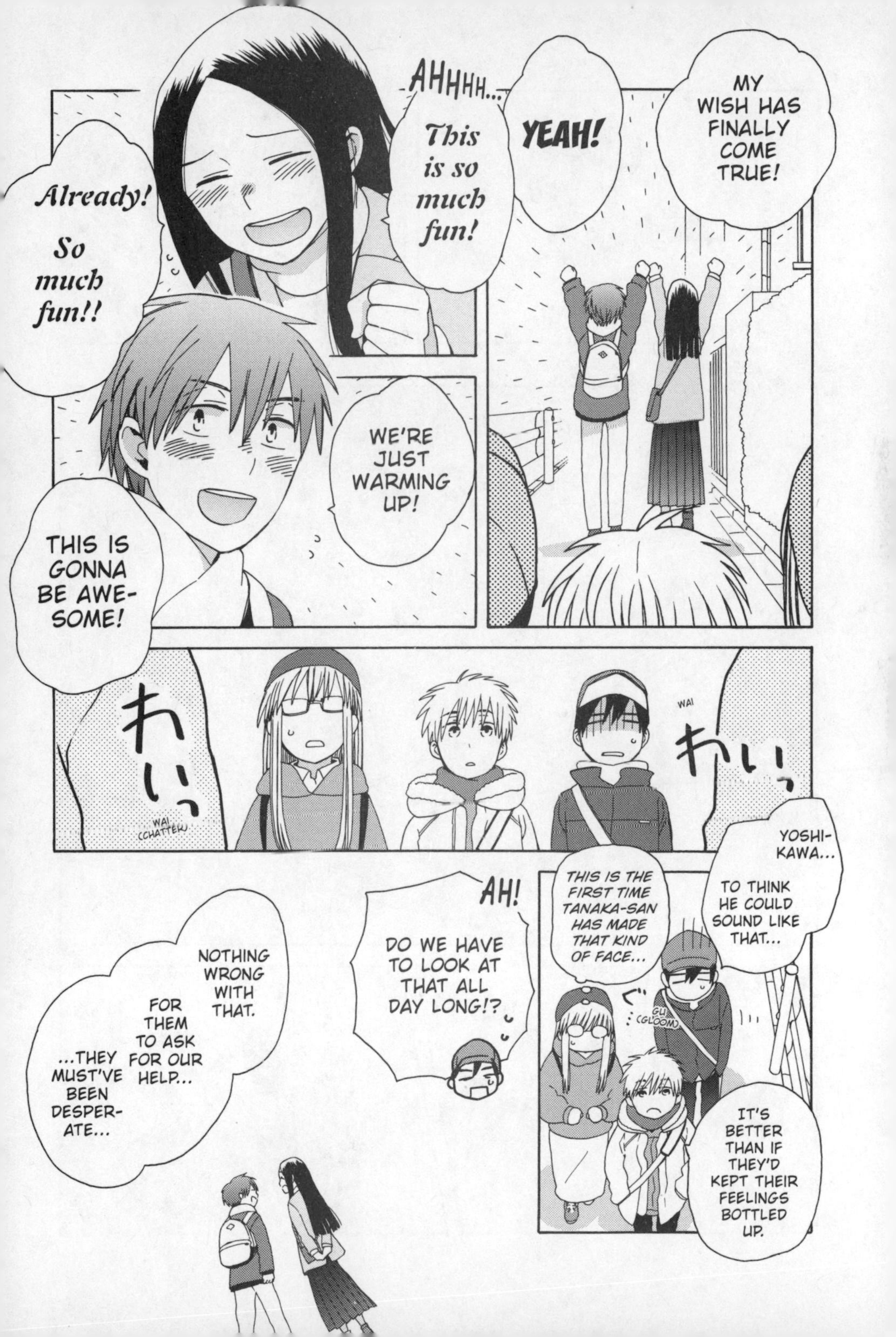
MY WISH HAS FINALLY COME TRUE!
YEAH!
AHHHH...
This is so much fun!
Already!
So much fun!!
WE'RE JUST WARMING UP!
THIS IS GONNA BE AWESOME!
WAI
わいっ
わいっ
WAI (CHATTER)
YOSHIKAWA...
TO THINK HE COULD SOUND LIKE THAT...
THIS IS THE FIRST TIME TANAKA-SAN HAS MADE THAT KIND OF FACE...
GU (GLOOM)
IT'S BETTER THAN IF THEY'D KEPT THEIR FEELINGS BOTTLED UP.
AH!
DO WE HAVE TO LOOK AT THAT ALL DAY LONG!?
NOTHING WRONG WITH THAT.
FOR THEM TO ASK FOR OUR HELP...
...THEY MUST'VE BEEN DESPERATE...

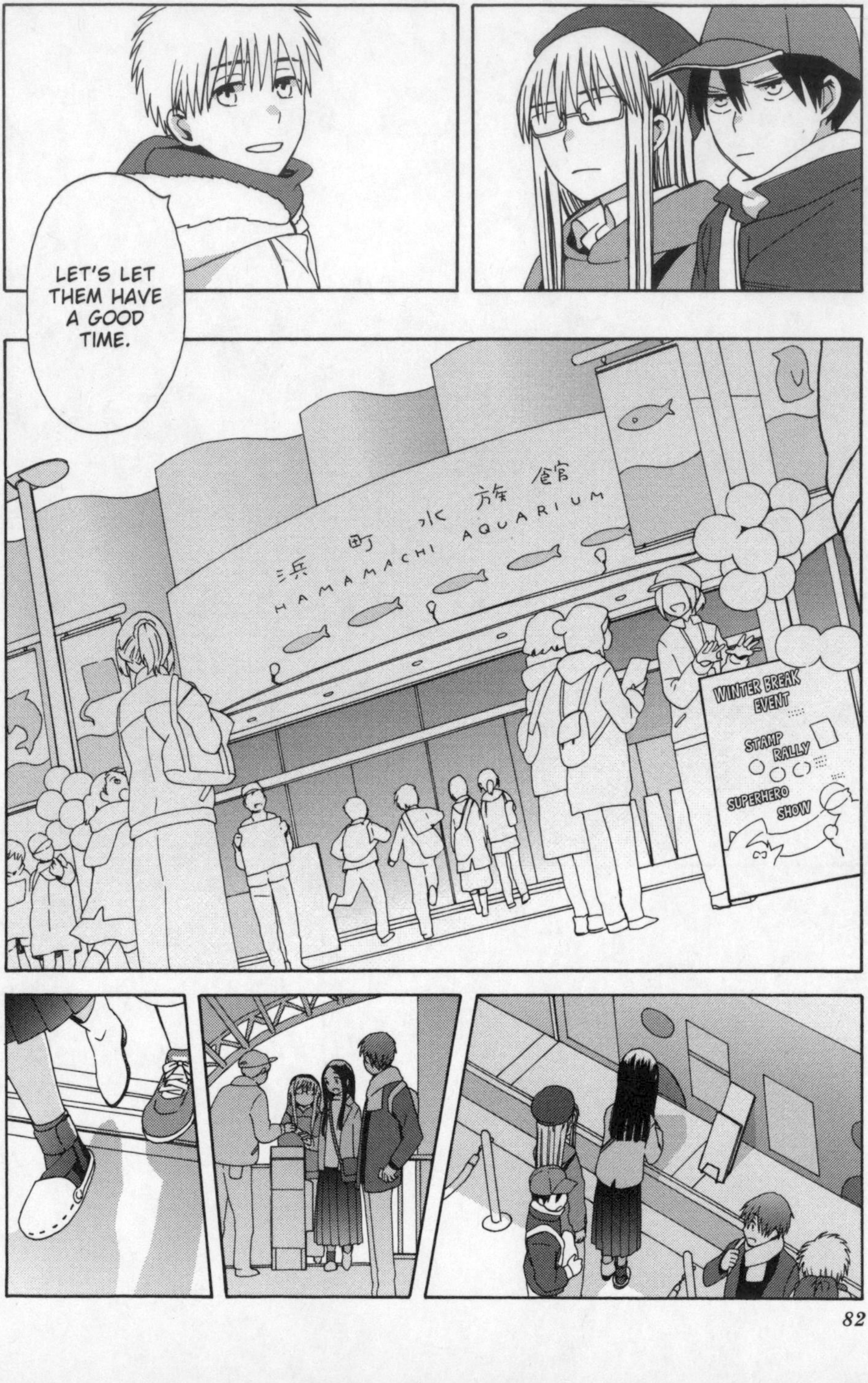
LET'S LET THEM HAVE A GOOD TIME.
浜町水族館
HAMAMACHI AQUARIUM
WINTER BREAK EVENT
STAMP RALLY
SUPERHERO SHOW

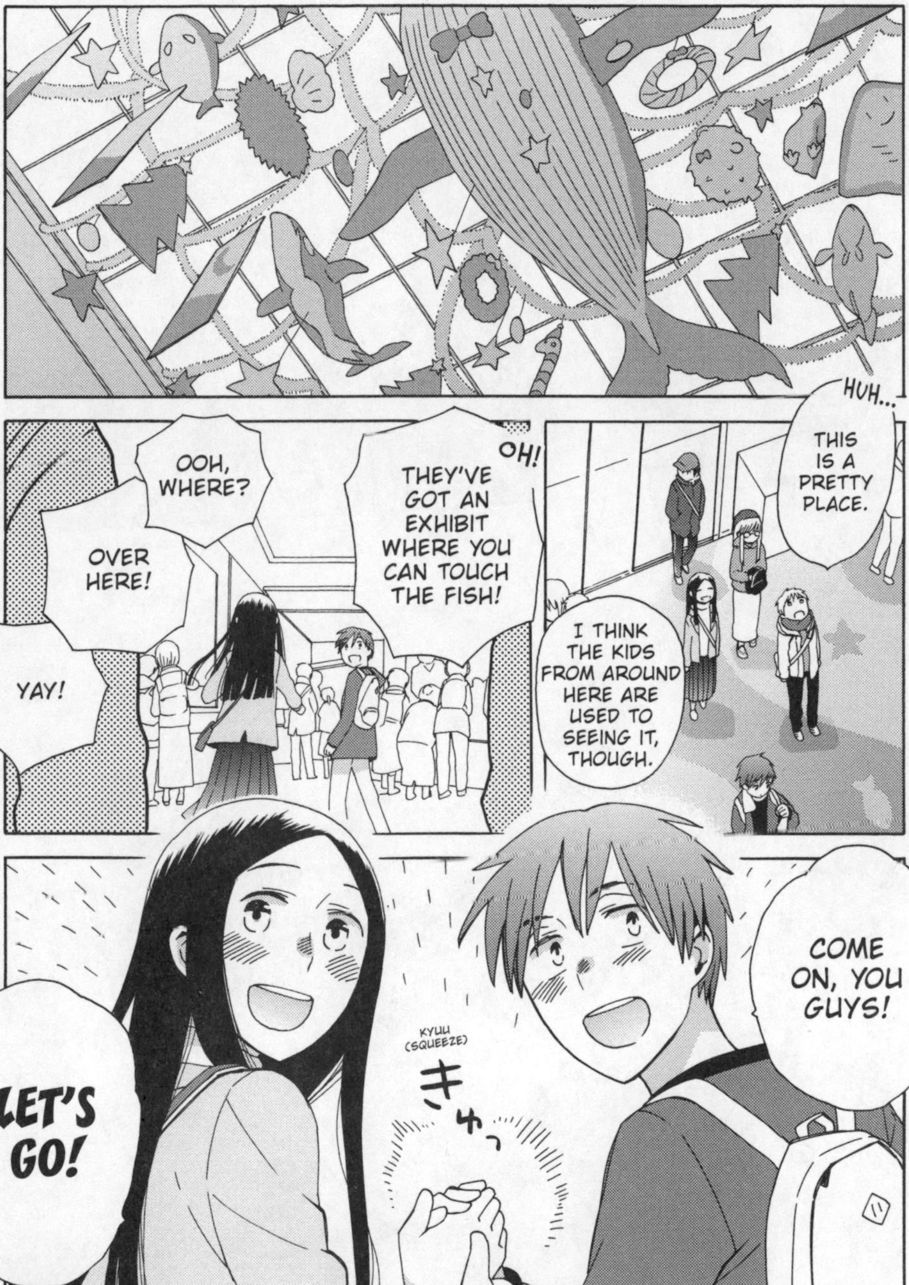
HUH...
THIS IS A PRETTY PLACE.
I THINK THE KIDS FROM AROUND HERE ARE USED TO SEEING IT, THOUGH.
OH!
THEY'VE GOT AN EXHIBIT WHERE YOU CAN TOUCH THE FISH!
OOH, WHERE?
OVER HERE!
YAY!
COME ON, YOU GUYS!
KYUU (SQUEEZE)
きゅっ
LET'S GO!

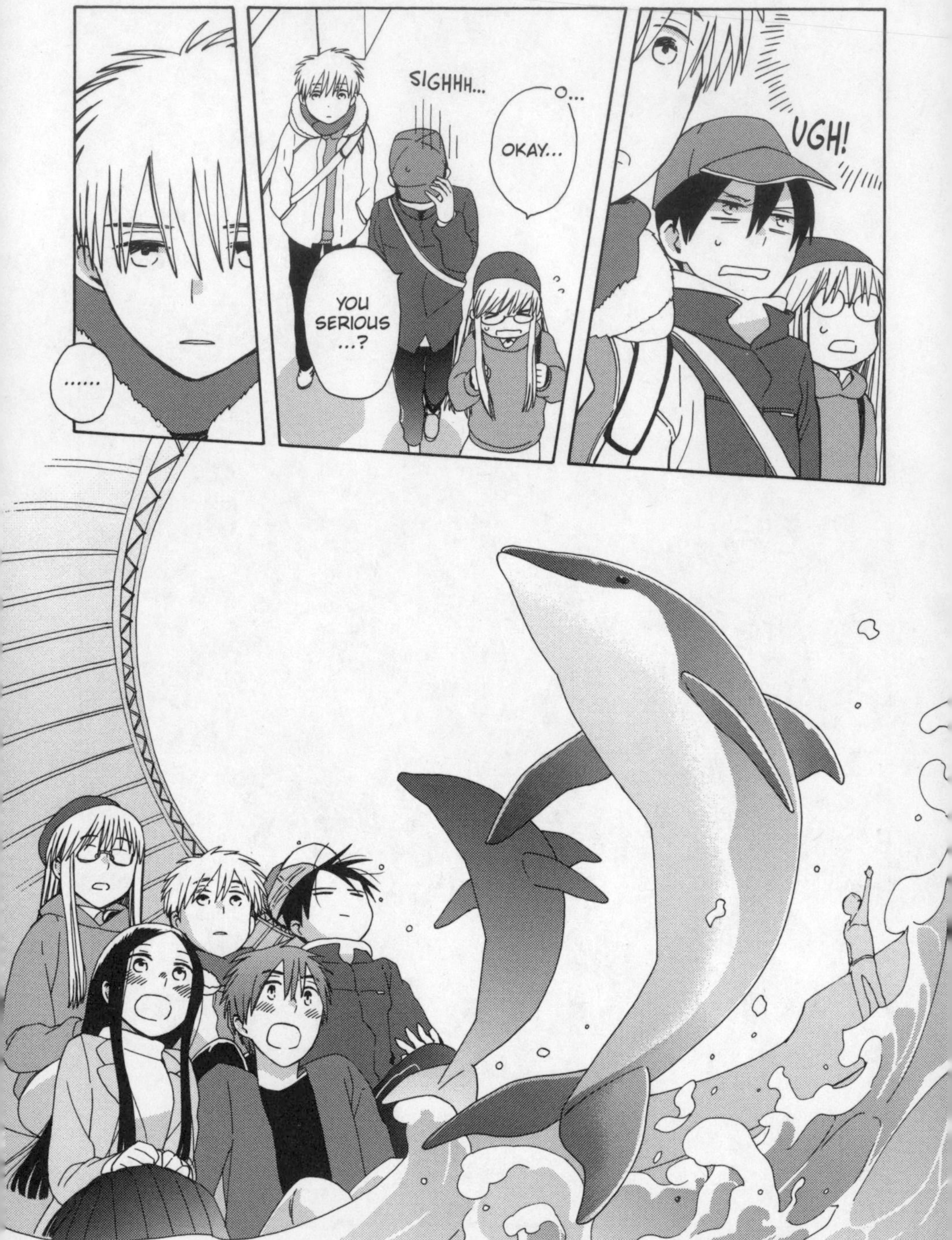
UGH!
O...
OKAY...
SIGHHH...
YOU SERIOUS ...?
......

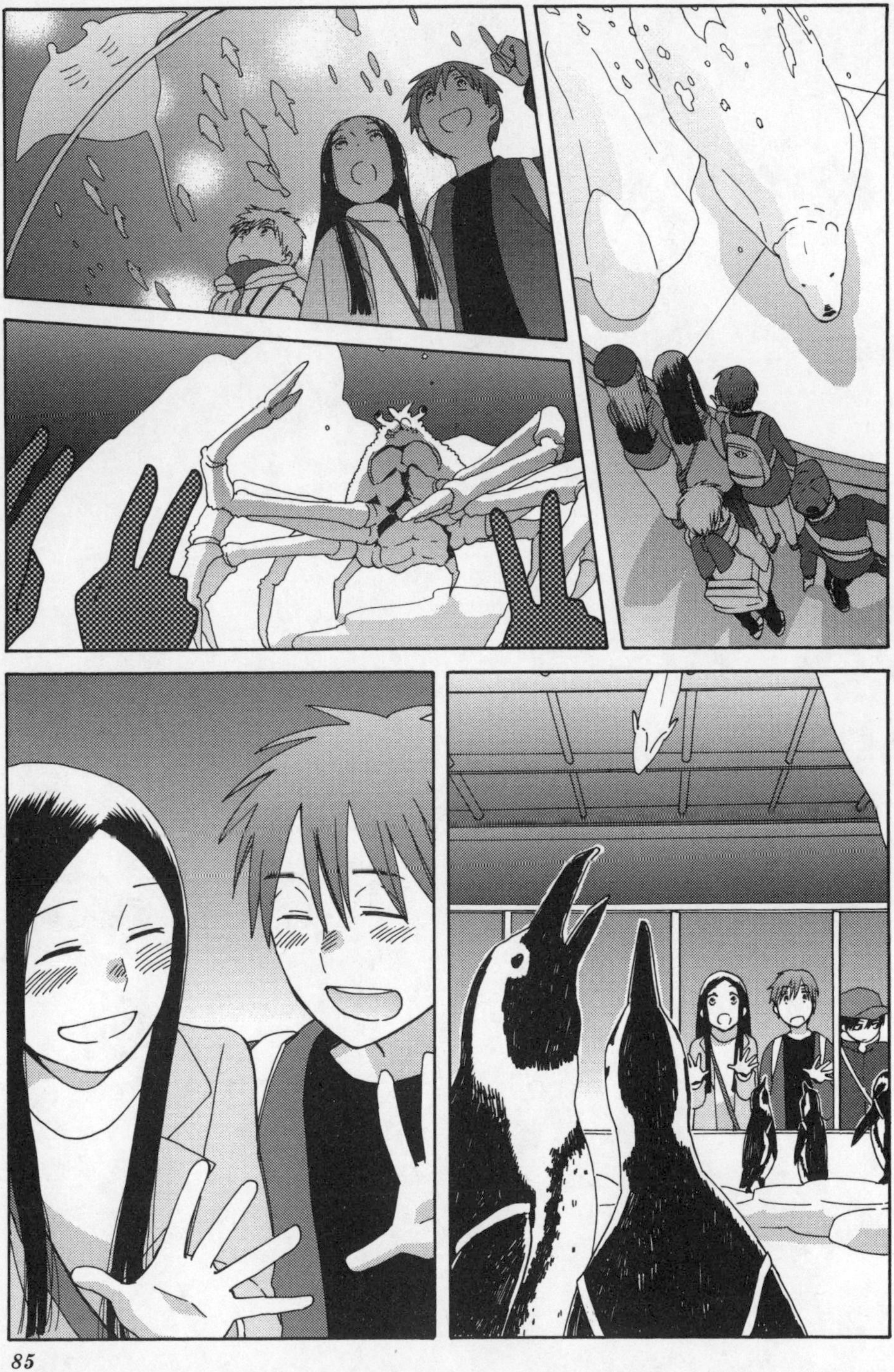

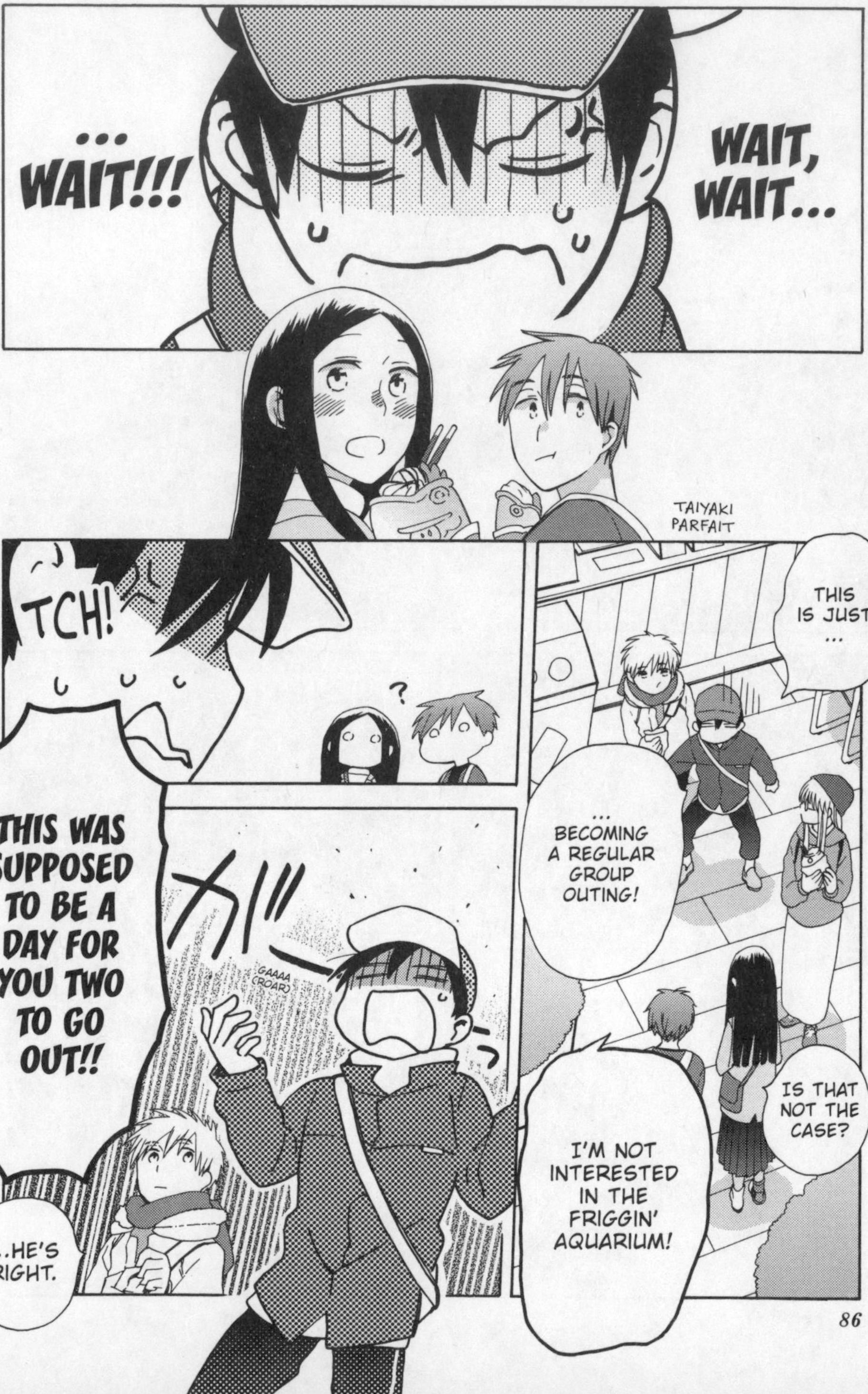

WAIT, WAIT...
...WAIT!!!
TAIYAKI PARFAIT
THIS IS JUST ...
... BECOMING A REGULAR GROUP OUTING!
IS THAT NOT THE CASE?
TCH!
?
THIS WAS SUPPOSED TO BE A DAY FOR YOU TWO TO GO OUT!!
GAAAA (ROAR)
I'M NOT INTERESTED IN THE FRIGGIN' AQUARIUM!
...HE'S RIGHT.

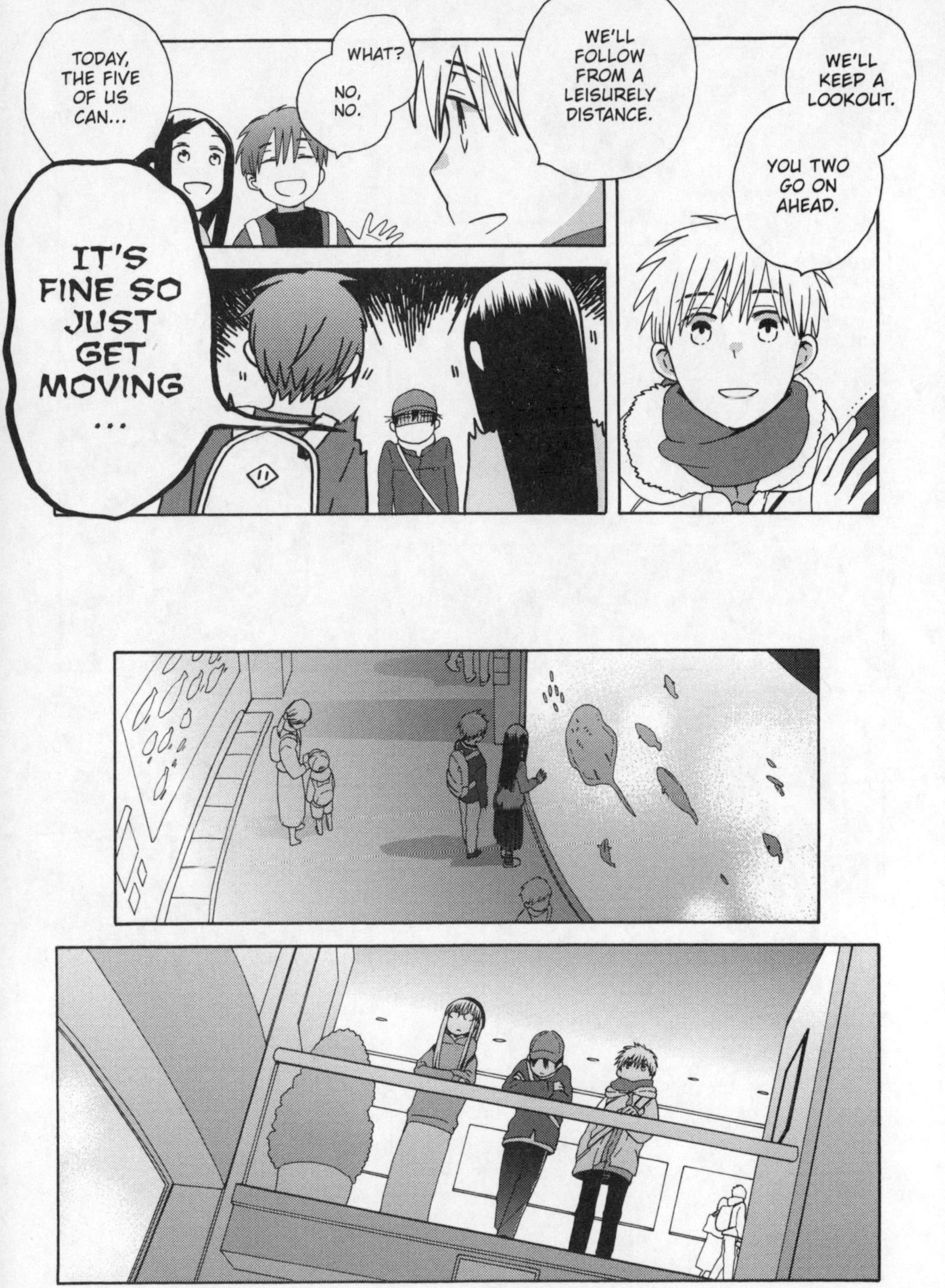

WE'LL KEEP A LOOKOUT.
YOU TWO GO ON AHEAD.
WE'LL FOLLOW FROM A LEISURELY DISTANCE.
WHAT?
NO, NO.
TODAY, THE FIVE OF US CAN...
IT'S FINE SO JUST GET MOVING...

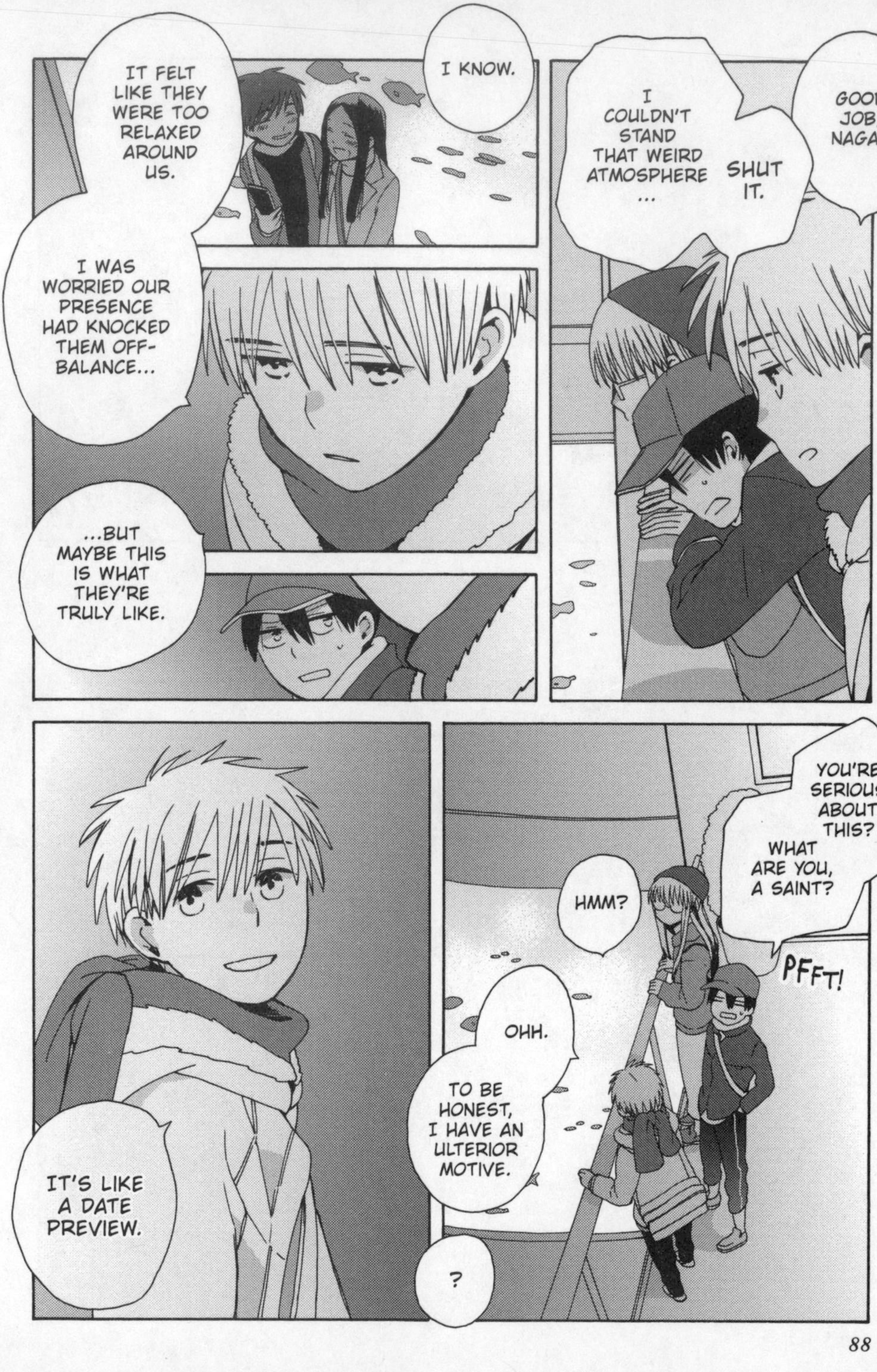
GOOD JOB, NAGAI.
I COULDN'T STAND THAT WEIRD ATMOSPHERE ...
SHUT IT.
I KNOW.
IT FELT LIKE THEY WERE TOO RELAXED AROUND US.
I WAS WORRIED OUR PRESENCE HAD KNOCKED THEM OFF-BALANCE...
...BUT MAYBE THIS IS WHAT THEY'RE TRULY LIKE.
YOU'RE SERIOUS ABOUT THIS?
WHAT ARE YOU, A SAINT?
HMM?
PFFT!
OHH.
TO BE HONEST, I HAVE AN ULTERIOR MOTIVE.
?
IT'S LIKE A DATE PREVIEW.

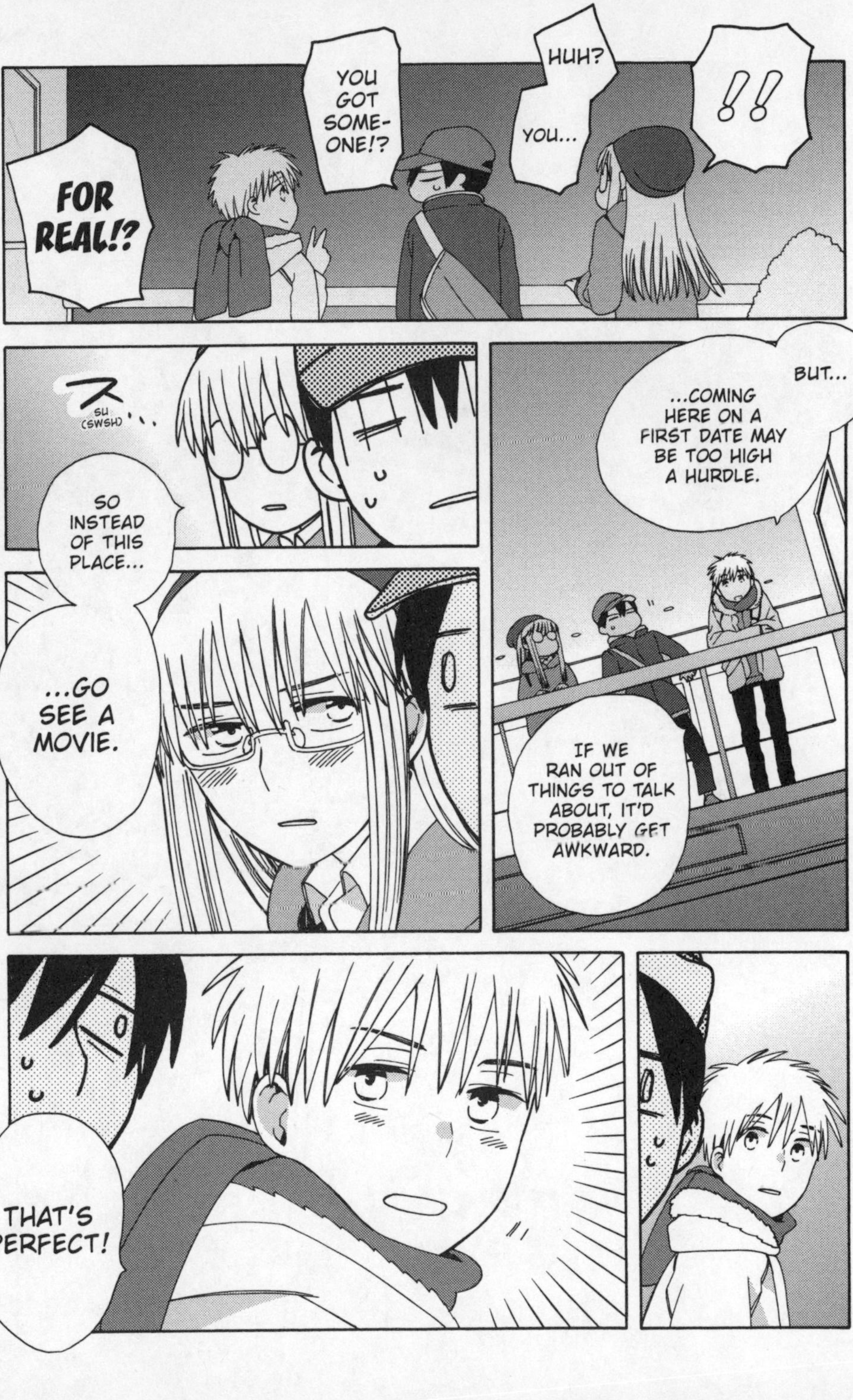
!!
HUH?
YOU...
YOU GOT SOME-ONE!?
FOR REAL!?
BUT...
...COMING HERE ON A FIRST DATE MAY BE TOO HIGH A HURDLE.
IF WE RAN OUT OF THINGS TO TALK ABOUT, IT'D PROBABLY GET AWKWARD.
ス
SU (SWSH)
SO INSTEAD OF THIS PLACE...
...GO SEE A MOVIE.
THAT'S PERFECT!

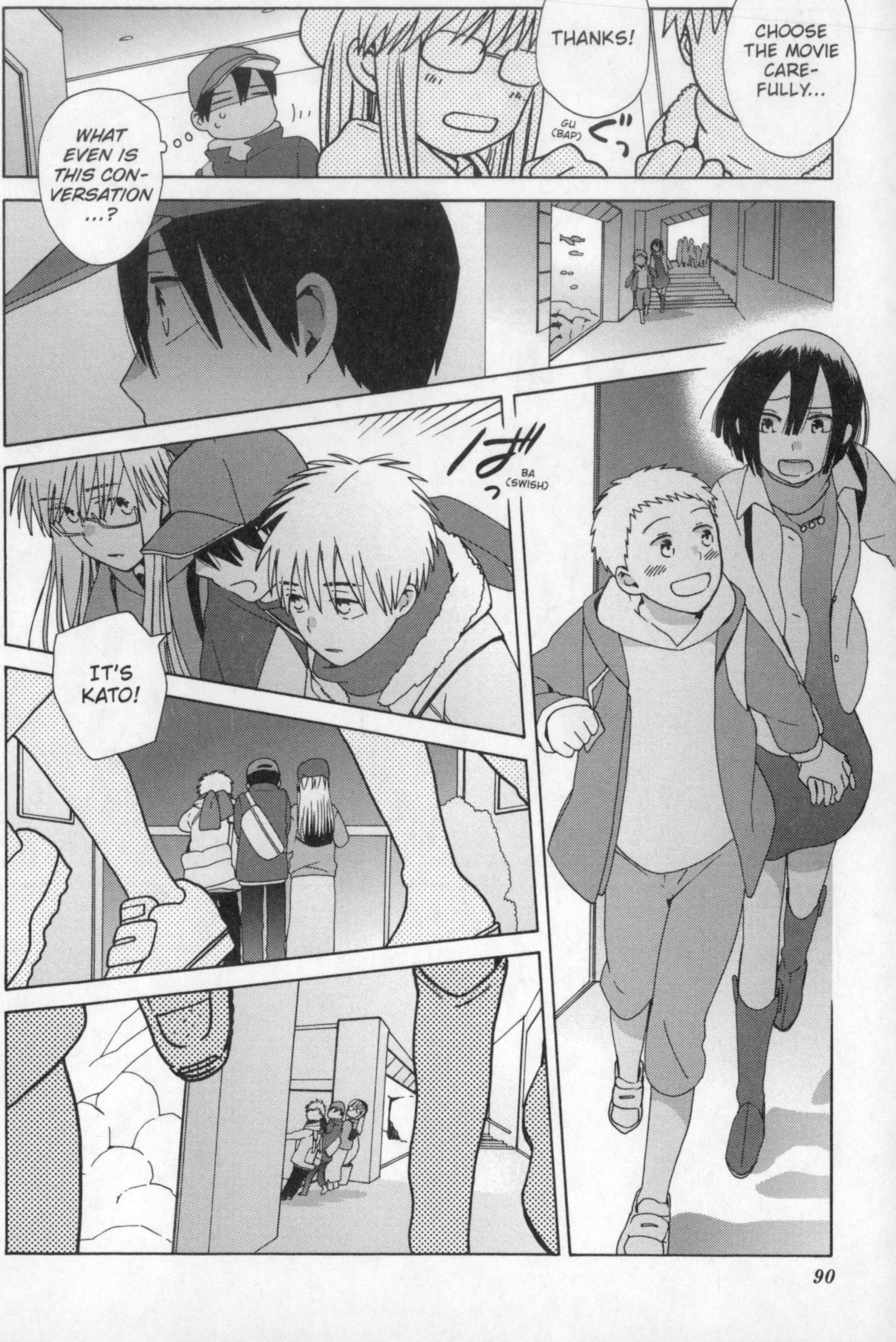
CHOOSE THE MOVIE CARE-FULLY...
THANKS!
ぐっ
GU (BAP)
WHAT EVEN IS THIS CON-VERSATION ...?
ばっ
BA (SWISH)
IT'S KATO!

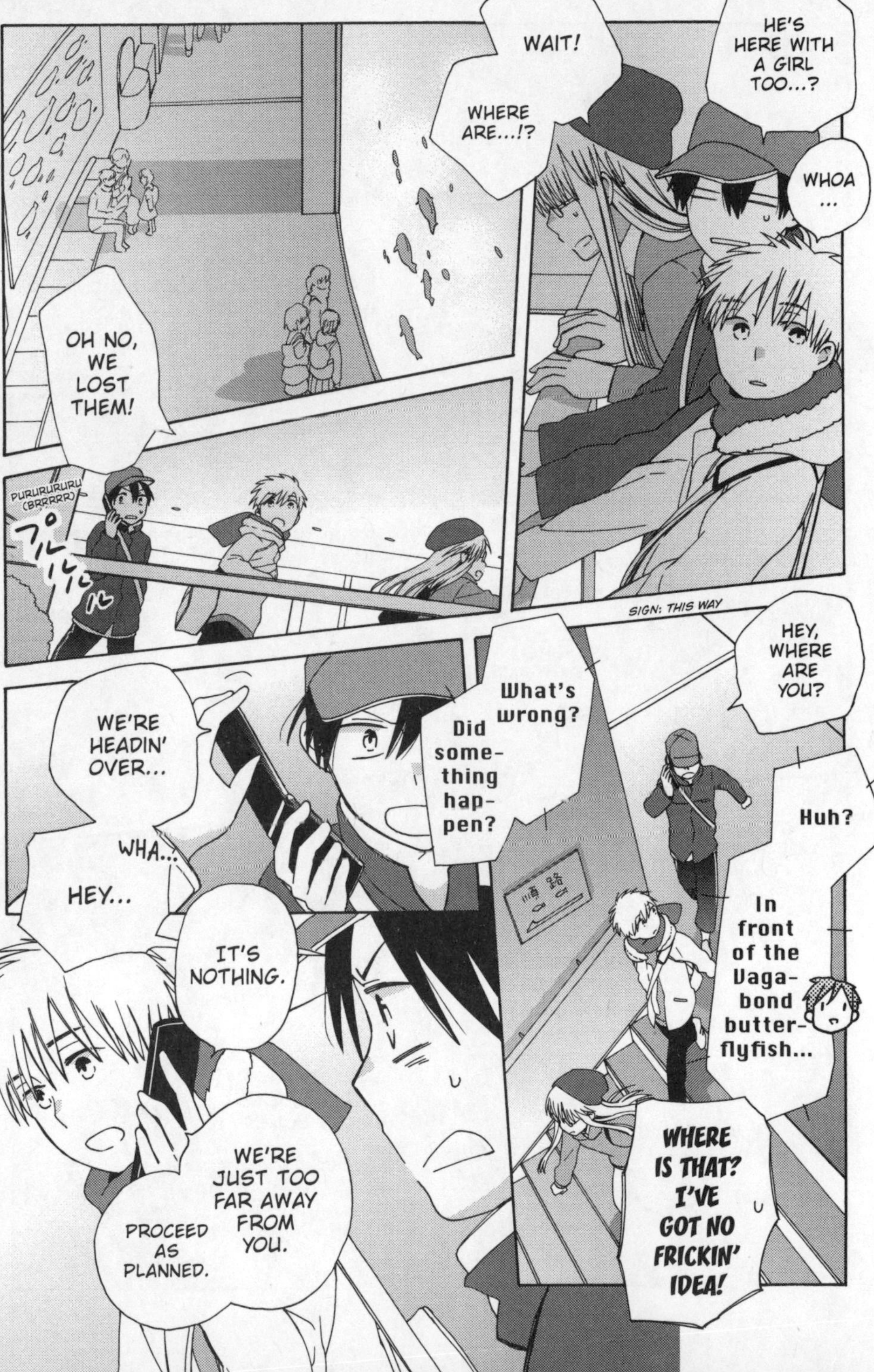
HE'S HERE WITH A GIRL TOO...?
WAIT!
WHOA ...
WHERE ARE...!?
OH NO, WE LOST THEM!
PURURURURU (BRRRRR)
プルルル
SIGN: THIS WAY
HEY, WHERE ARE YOU?
Huh?
In front of the Vagabond butterflyfish...
WHERE IS THAT? I'VE GOT NO FRICKIN' IDEA!
順路
What's wrong? Did something happen?
WE'RE HEADIN' OVER...
WHA...
HEY...
IT'S NOTHING.
WE'RE JUST TOO FAR AWAY FROM YOU.
PROCEED AS PLANNED.

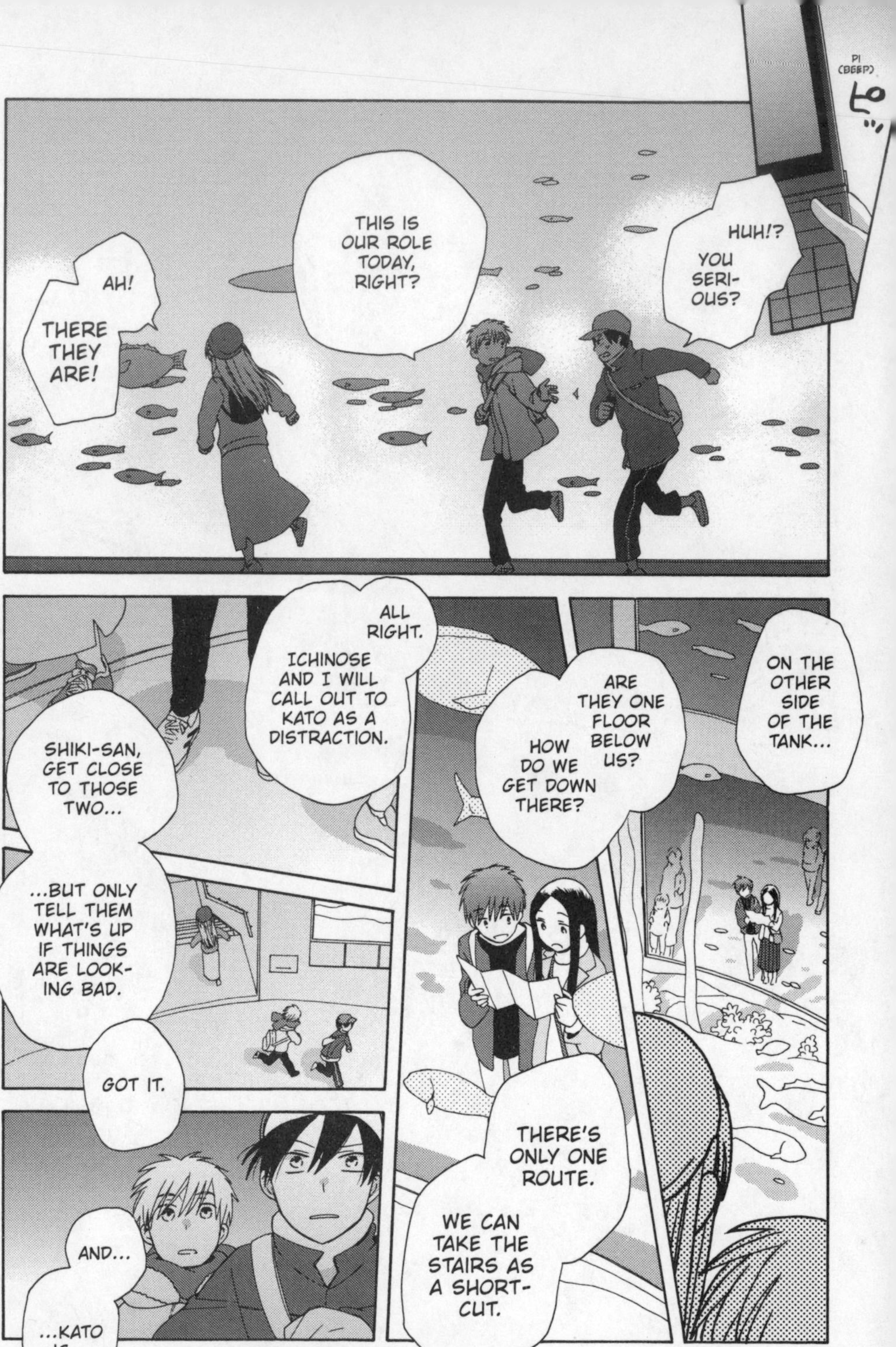
PI (BEEP)
HUH!? YOU SERIOUS?
THIS IS OUR ROLE TODAY, RIGHT?
AH! THERE THEY ARE!
ON THE OTHER SIDE OF THE TANK...
ARE THEY ONE FLOOR BELOW US? HOW DO WE GET DOWN THERE?
THERE'S ONLY ONE ROUTE. WE CAN TAKE THE STAIRS AS A SHORTCUT.
ALL RIGHT. ICHINOSE AND I WILL CALL OUT TO KATO AS A DISTRACTION.
SHIKI-SAN, GET CLOSE TO THOSE TWO...
...BUT ONLY TELL THEM WHAT'S UP IF THINGS ARE LOOKING BAD.
GOT IT.
AND...
...KATO IS...

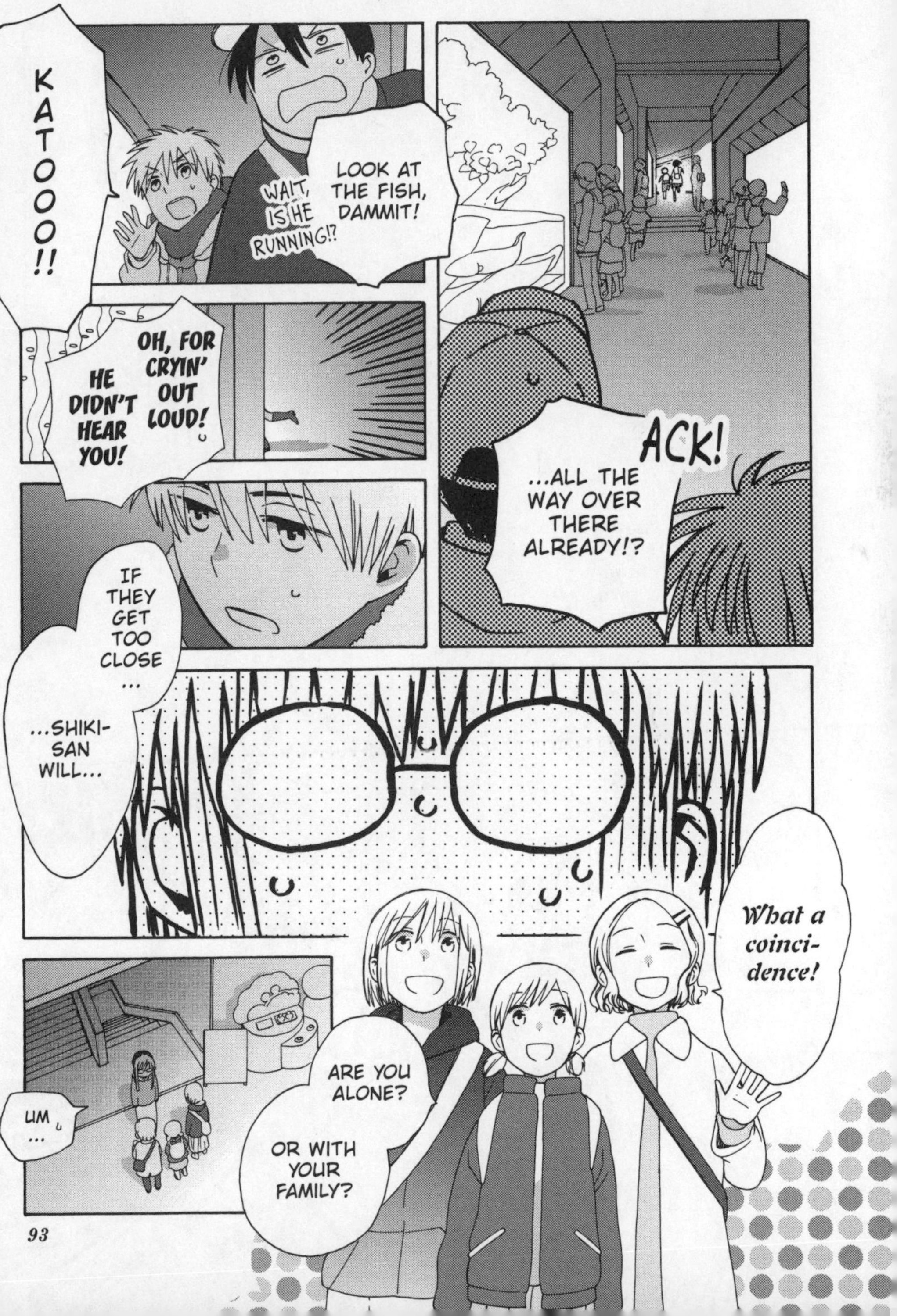
ACK!
...ALL THE WAY OVER THERE ALREADY!?
KATOOOO!!
LOOK AT THE FISH, DAMMIT!
WAIT, IS HE RUNNING!?
OH, FOR CRYIN' OUT LOUD!
HE DIDN'T HEAR YOU!
IF THEY GET TOO CLOSE...
...SHIKI-SAN WILL...
What a coinci-dence!
ARE YOU ALONE?
OR WITH YOUR FAMILY?
UM...

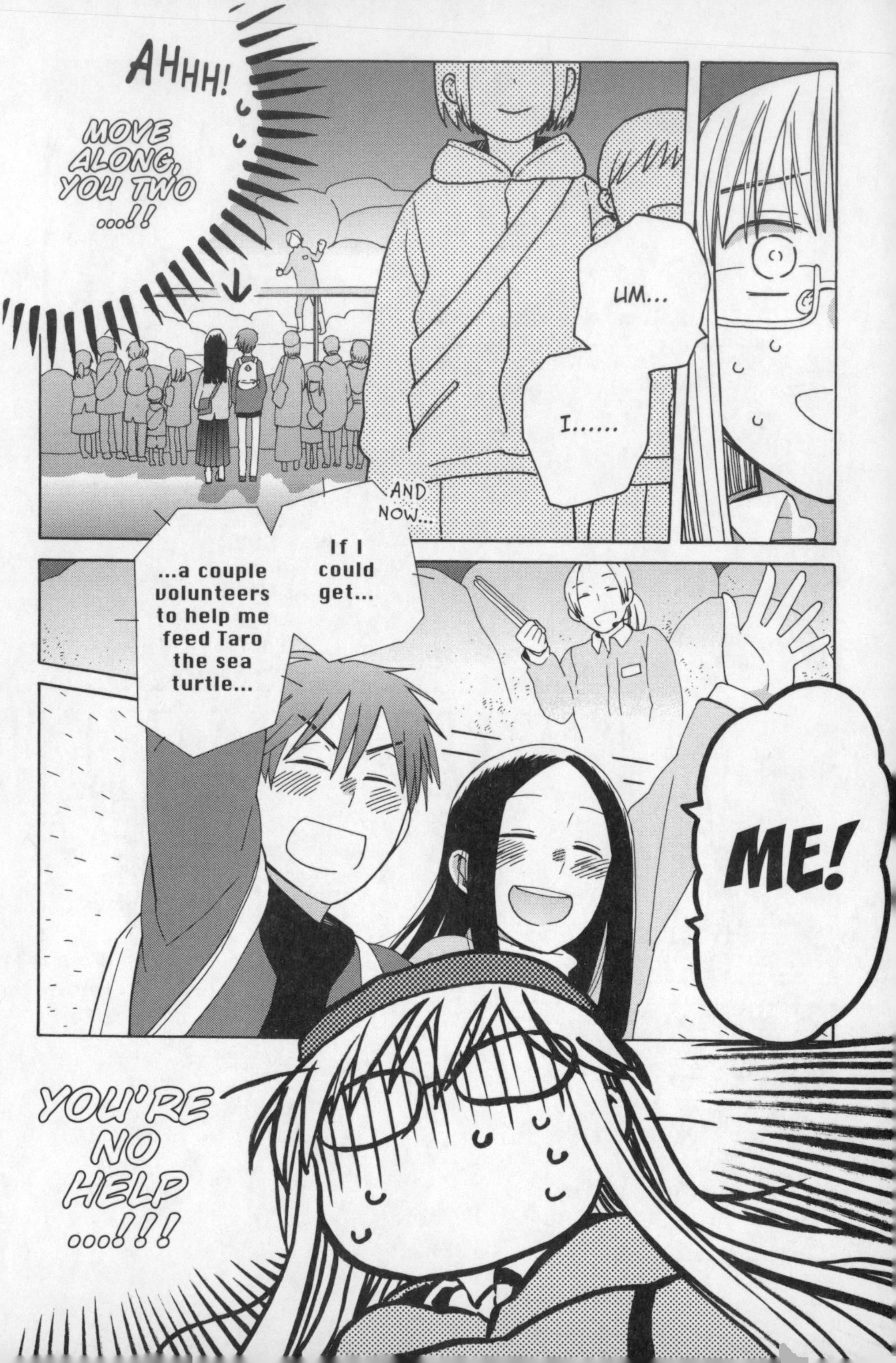
UM...
I......
AHHH!
MOVE ALONG, YOU TWO ...!!
AND NOW...
If I could get...
...a couple volunteers to help me feed Taro the sea turtle...
ME!
YOU'RE NO HELP ...!!!

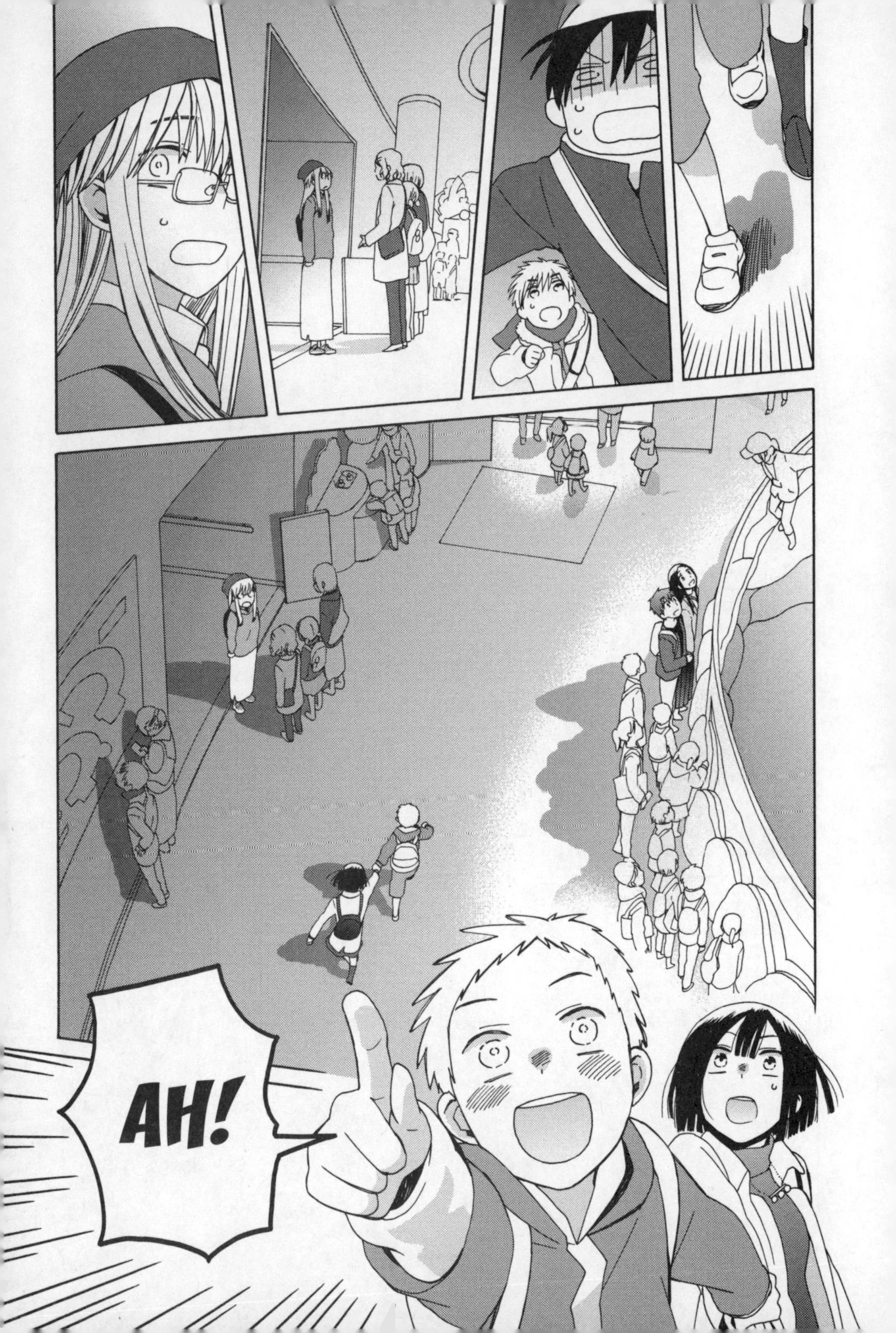
AH!

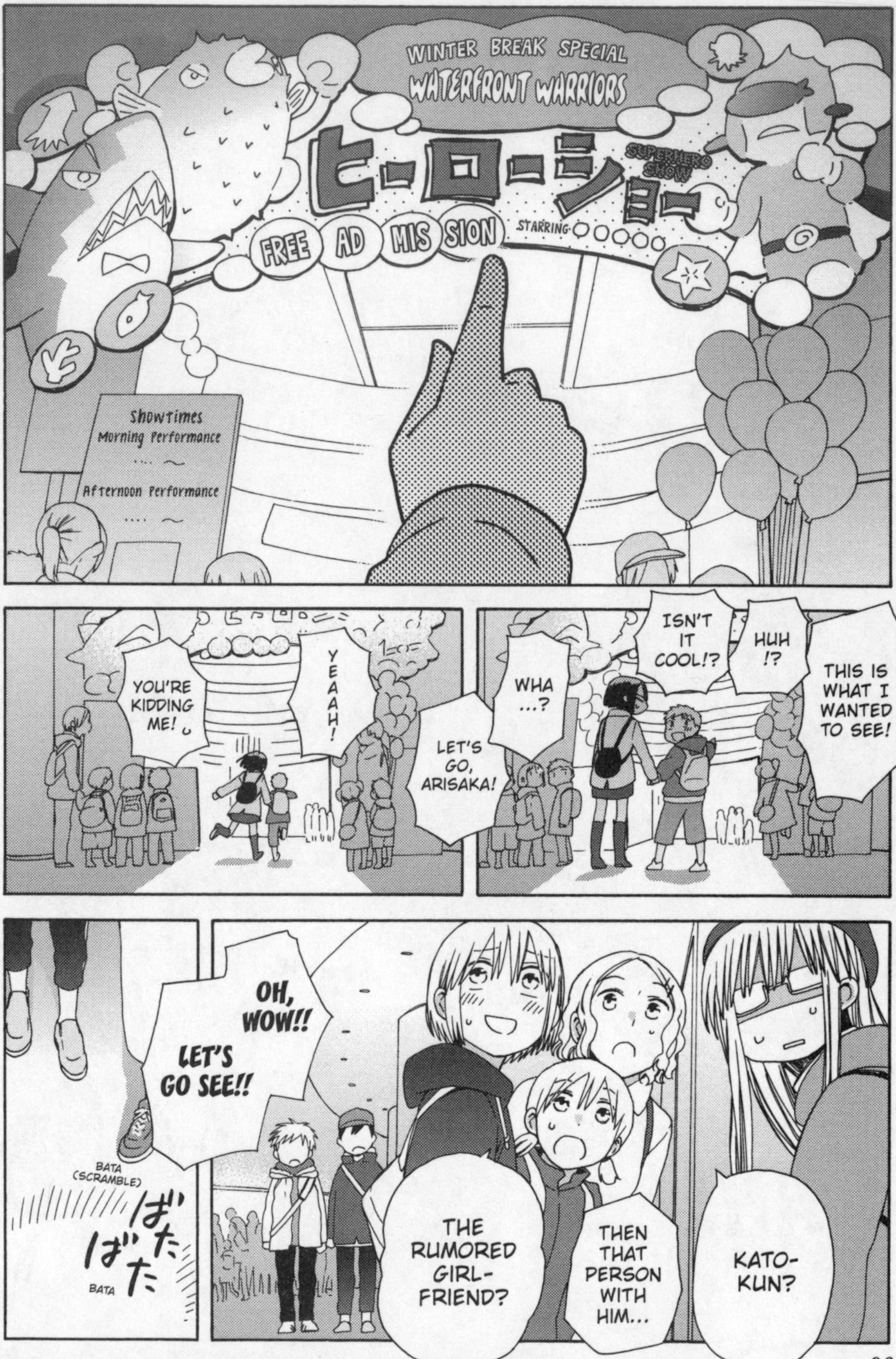
WINTER BREAK SPECIAL
WATERFRONT WARRIORS
ヒーローショー
SUPERHERO SHOW
FREE AD MIS SION
STARRING ○○○○○
Showtimes
Morning Performance
.... ~
Afternoon Performance
.... ~
THIS IS WHAT I WANTED TO SEE!
HUH!?
ISN'T IT COOL!?
WHA...?
LET'S GO, ARISAKA!
YEAAAH!
YOU'RE KIDDING ME!
KATO-KUN?
THEN THAT PERSON WITH HIM...
THE RUMORED GIRL-FRIEND?
OH, WOW!!
LET'S GO SEE!!
BATA (SCRAMBLE)
ばたばた
BATA

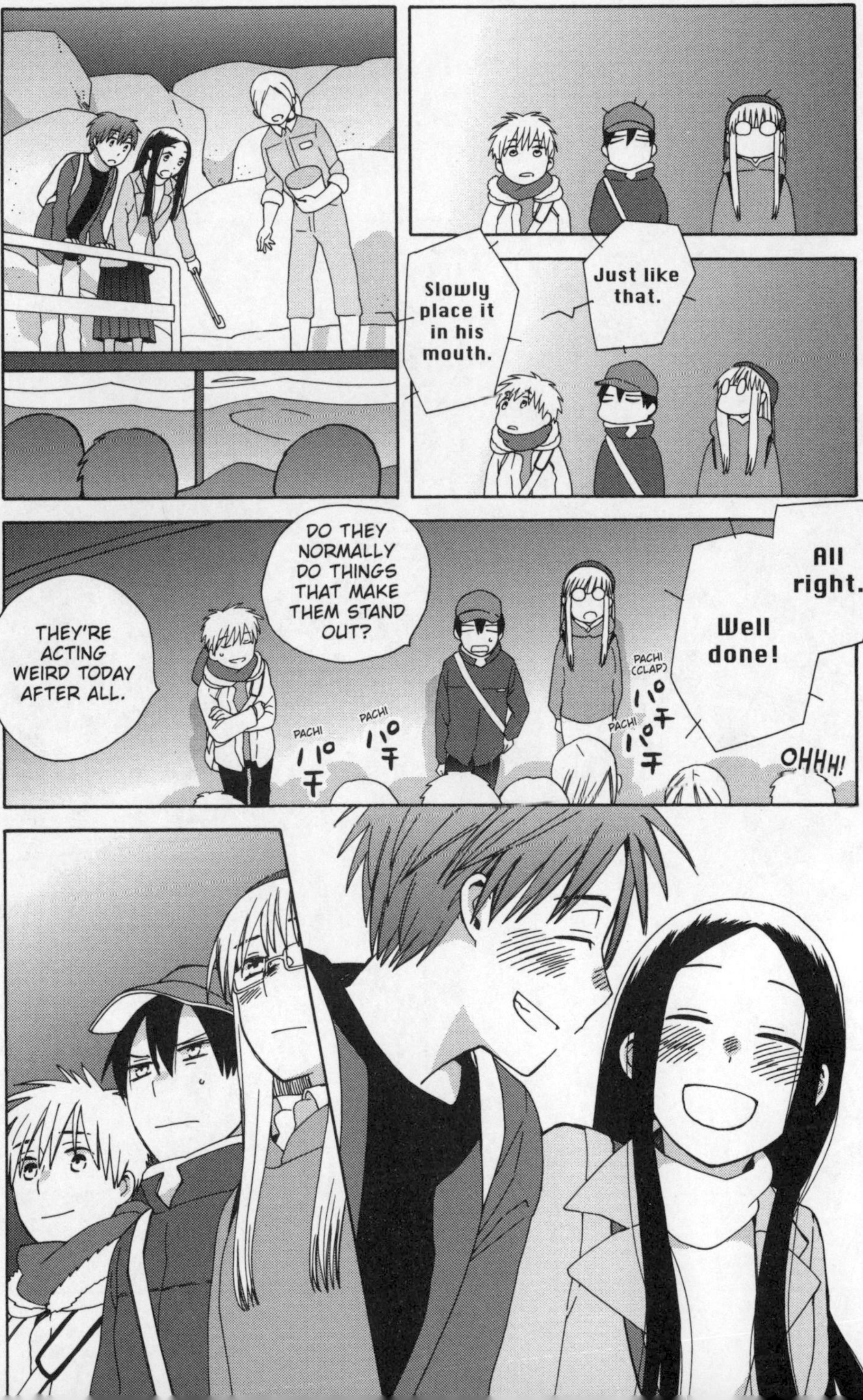
Slowly place it in his mouth.
Just like that.
All right.
Well done!
OHHH!
PACHI (CLAP)
パチ
PACHI
パチ
DO THEY NORMALLY DO THINGS THAT MAKE THEM STAND OUT?
PACHI
パチ
PACHI
パチ
THEY'RE ACTING WEIRD TODAY AFTER ALL.

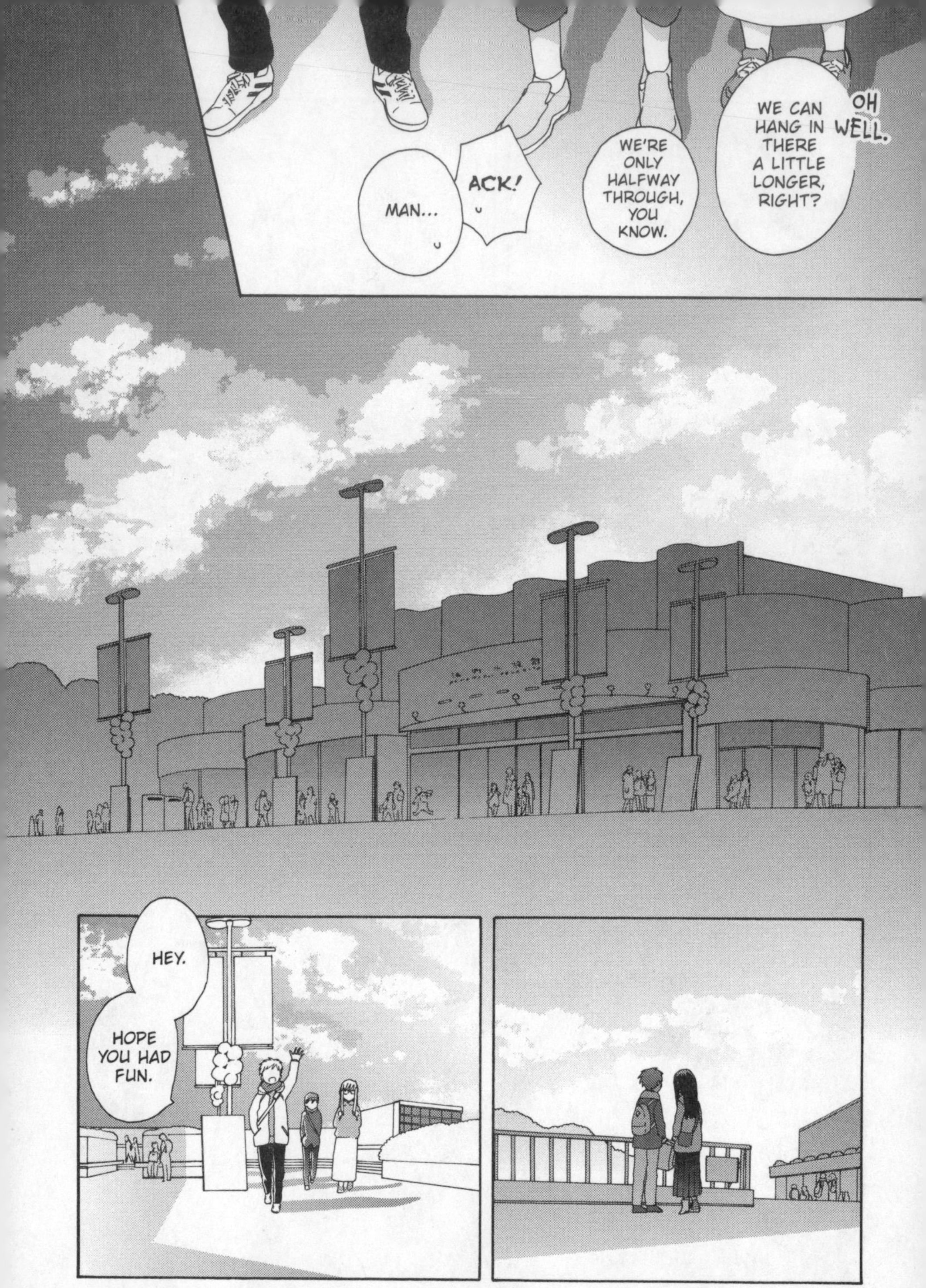
OH WELL.
WE CAN HANG IN THERE A LITTLE LONGER, RIGHT?
WE'RE ONLY HALFWAY THROUGH, YOU KNOW.
ACK!
MAN...
HEY.
HOPE YOU HAD FUN.

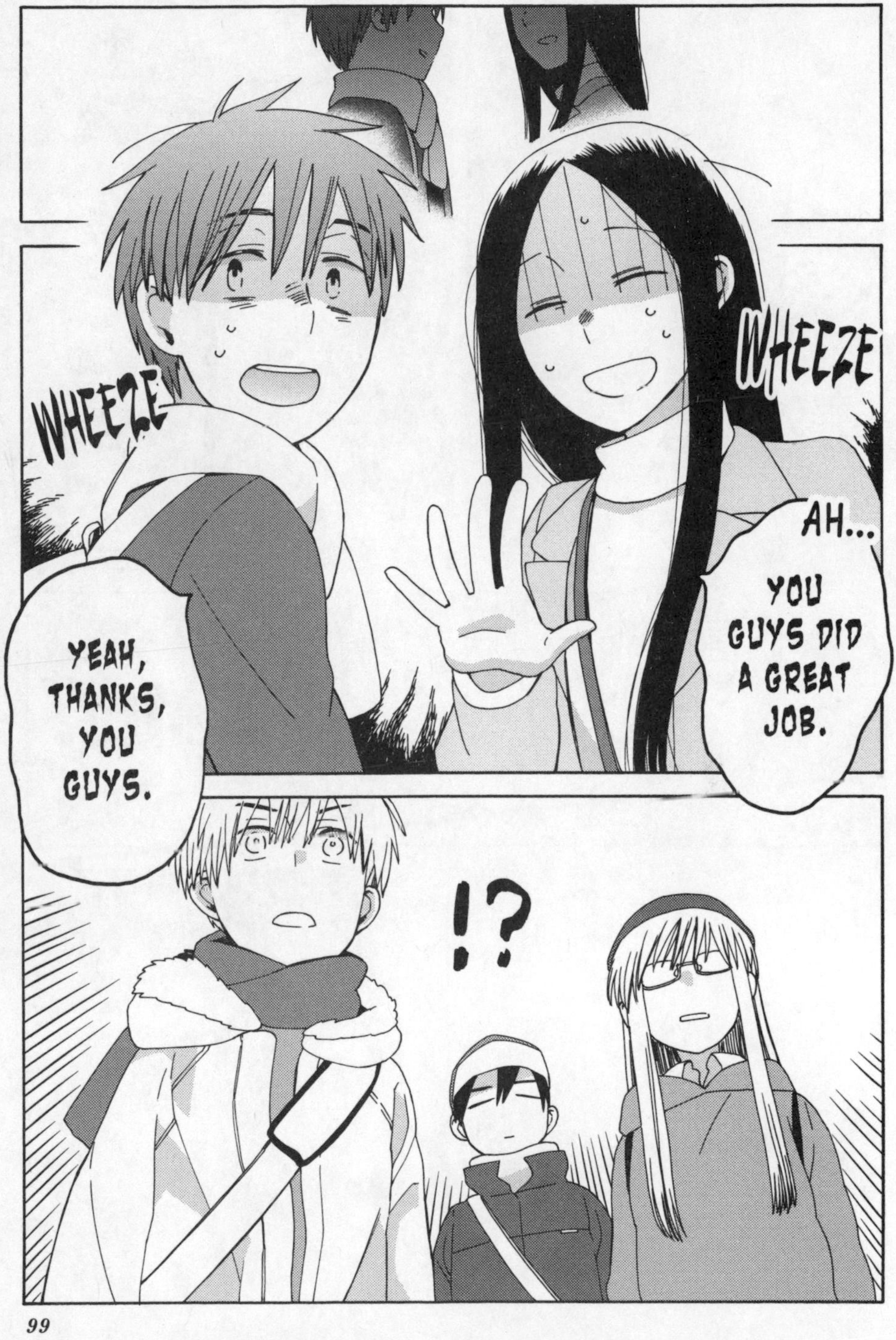
WHEEZE
AH... YOU GUYS DID A GREAT JOB.
WHEEZE
YEAH, THANKS, YOU GUYS.
!?

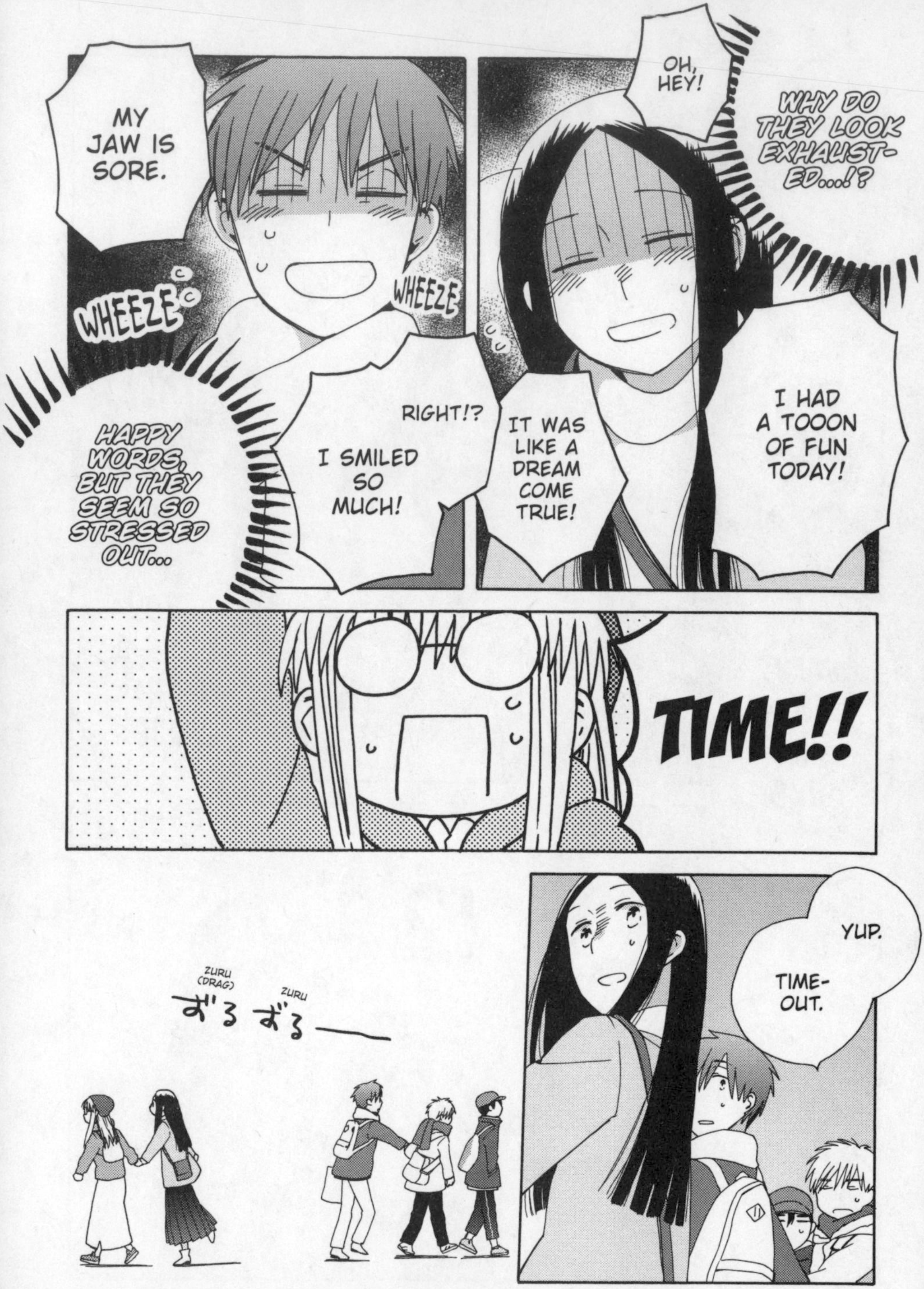
OH, HEY!
WHY DO THEY LOOK EXHAUST-ED...!?
I HAD A TOOON OF FUN TODAY!
IT WAS LIKE A DREAM COME TRUE!
MY JAW IS SORE.
WHEEZE
WHEEZE
RIGHT!? I SMILED SO MUCH!
HAPPY WORDS, BUT THEY SEEM SO STRESSED OUT...
TIME!!
YUP. TIME-OUT.
ZURU (DRAG) ZURU
ずるずるー

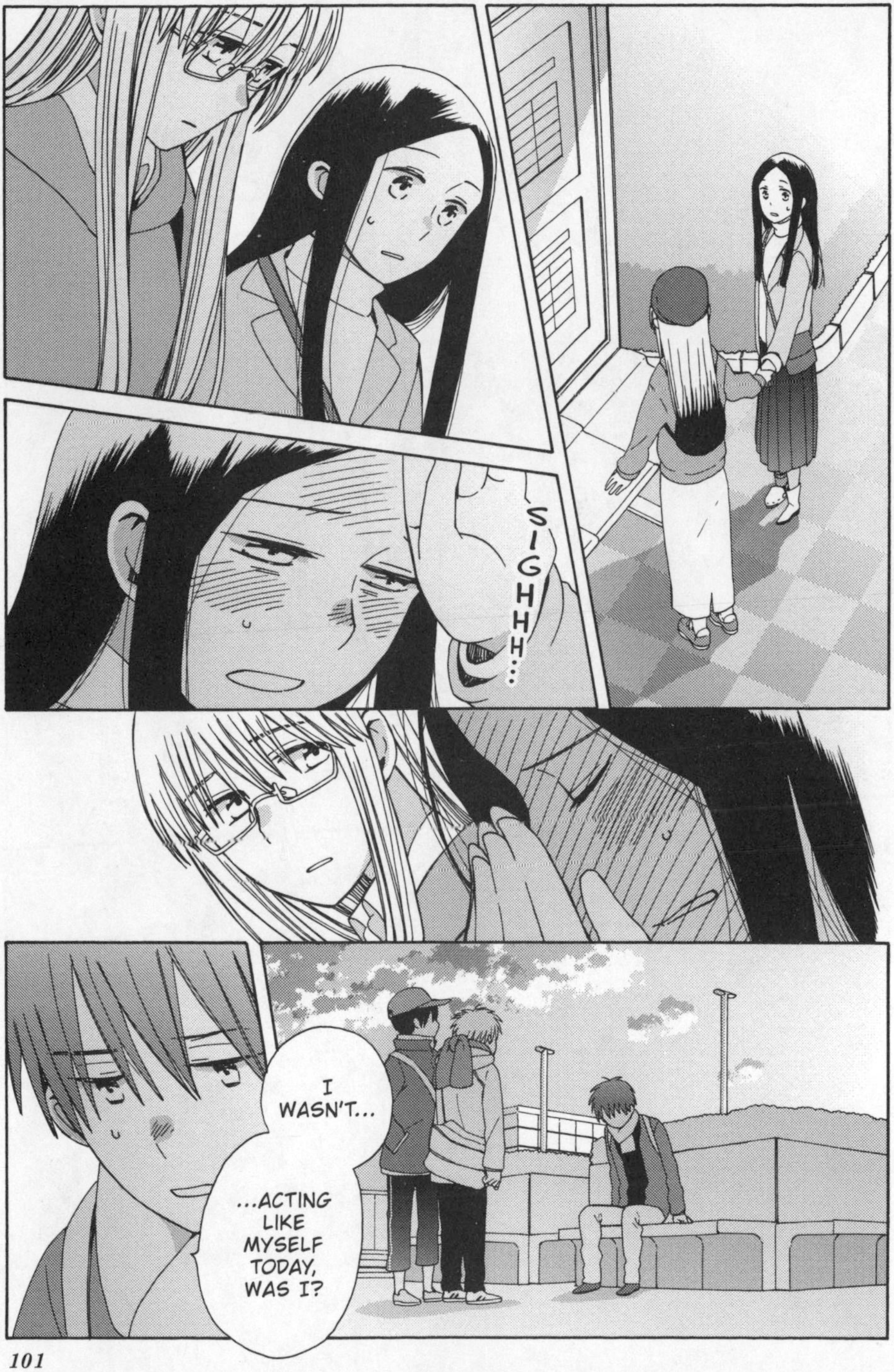
SIGHHH...
I WASN'T...
...ACTING LIKE MYSELF TODAY, WAS I?

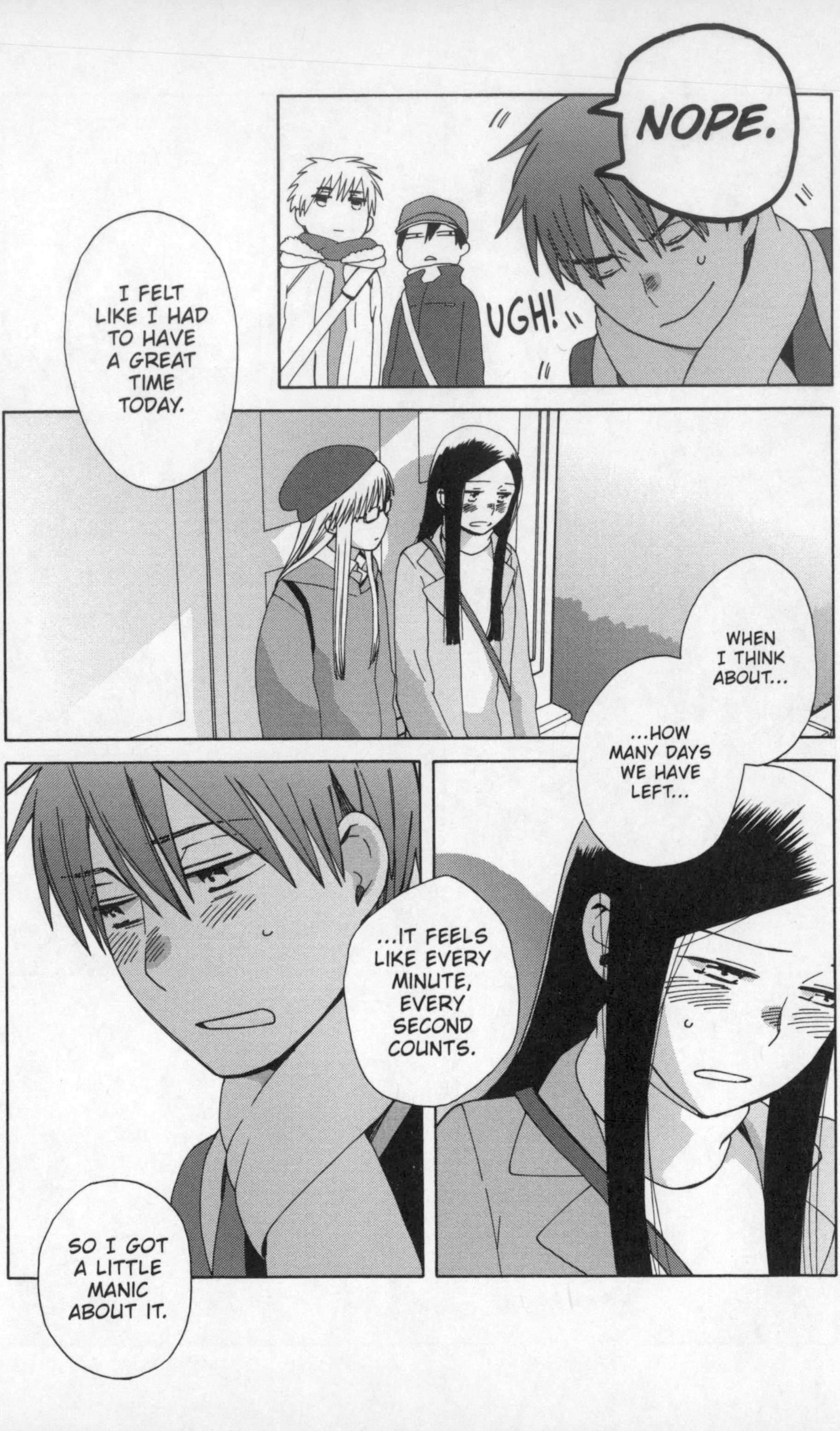
NOPE.
UGH!
I FELT LIKE I HAD TO HAVE A GREAT TIME TODAY.
WHEN I THINK ABOUT...
...HOW MANY DAYS WE HAVE LEFT...
...IT FEELS LIKE EVERY MINUTE, EVERY SECOND COUNTS.
SO I GOT A LITTLE MANIC ABOUT IT.

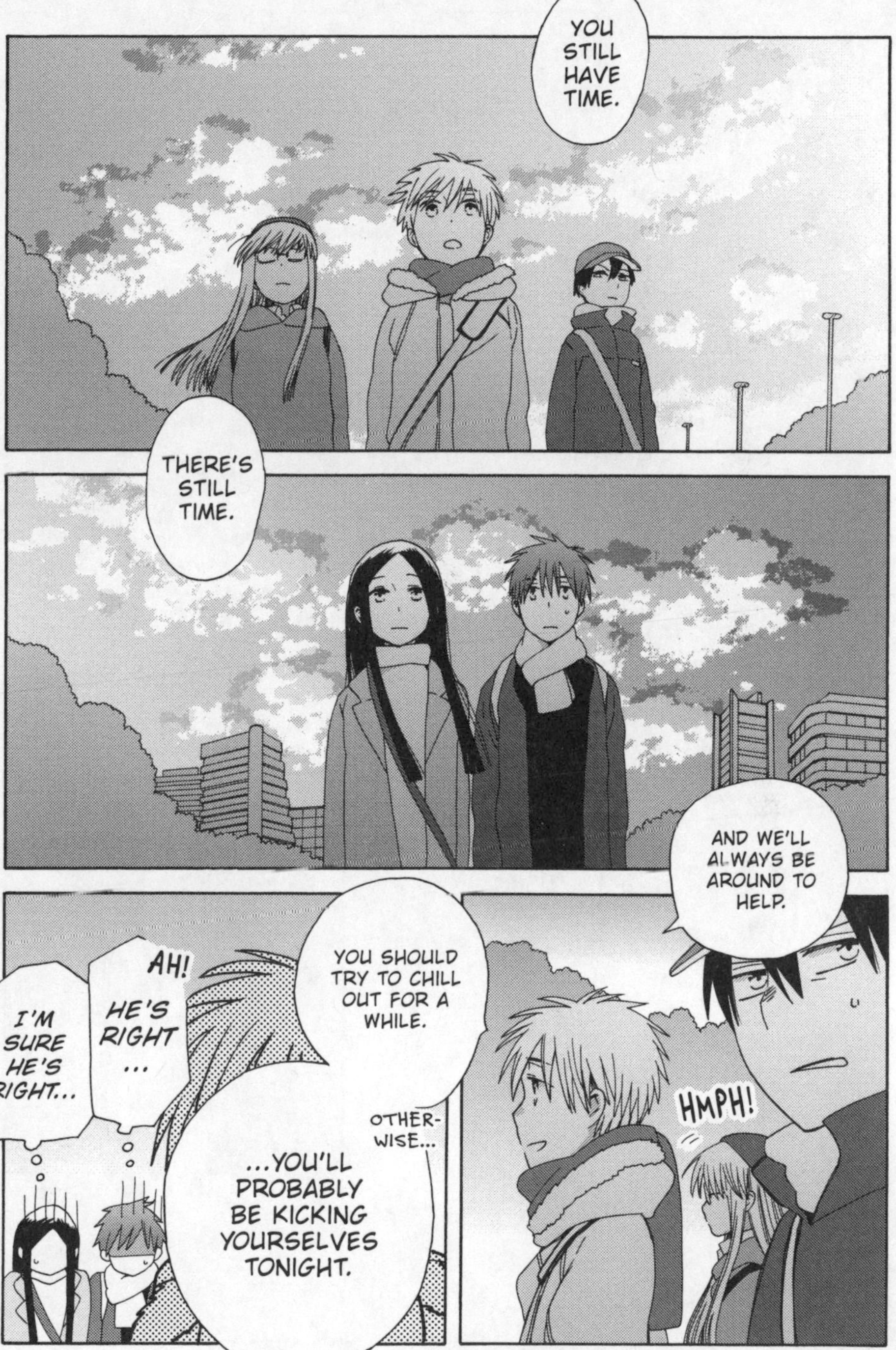
YOU STILL HAVE TIME.
THERE'S STILL TIME.
AND WE'LL ALWAYS BE AROUND TO HELP.
HMPH!
YOU SHOULD TRY TO CHILL OUT FOR A WHILE.
OTHER-WISE...
...YOU'LL PROBABLY BE KICKING YOURSELVES TONIGHT.
AH!
HE'S RIGHT...
I'M SURE HE'S RIGHT...

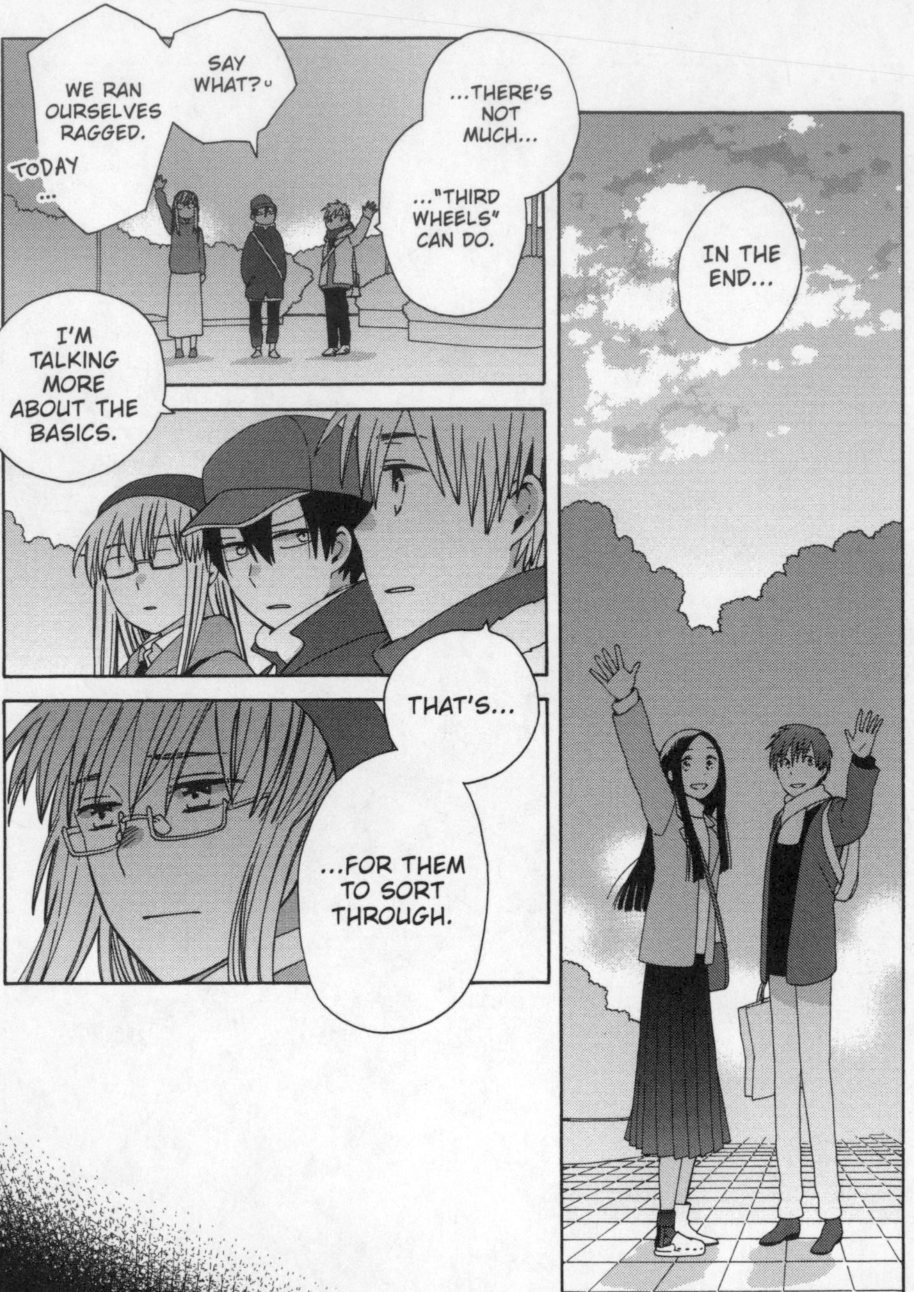
IN THE END...
...THERE'S NOT MUCH...
..."THIRD WHEELS" CAN DO.
SAY WHAT?
WE RAN OURSELVES RAGGED.
TODAY ...
I'M TALKING MORE ABOUT THE BASICS.
THAT'S...
...FOR THEM TO SORT THROUGH.

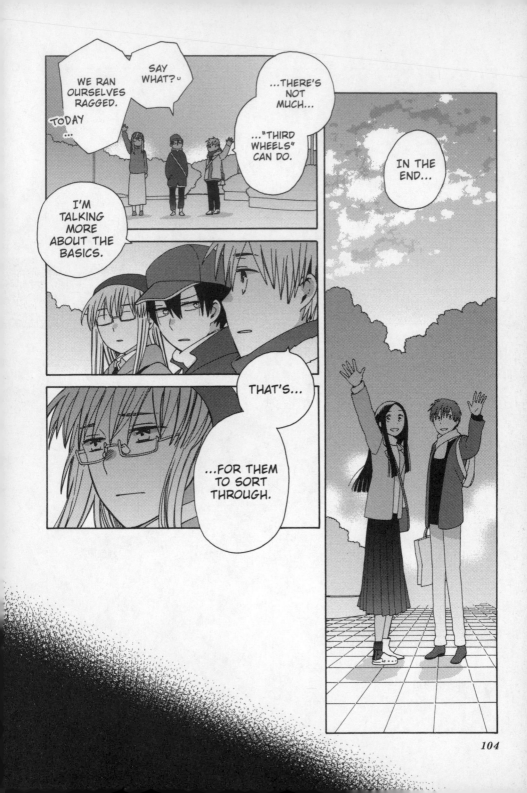

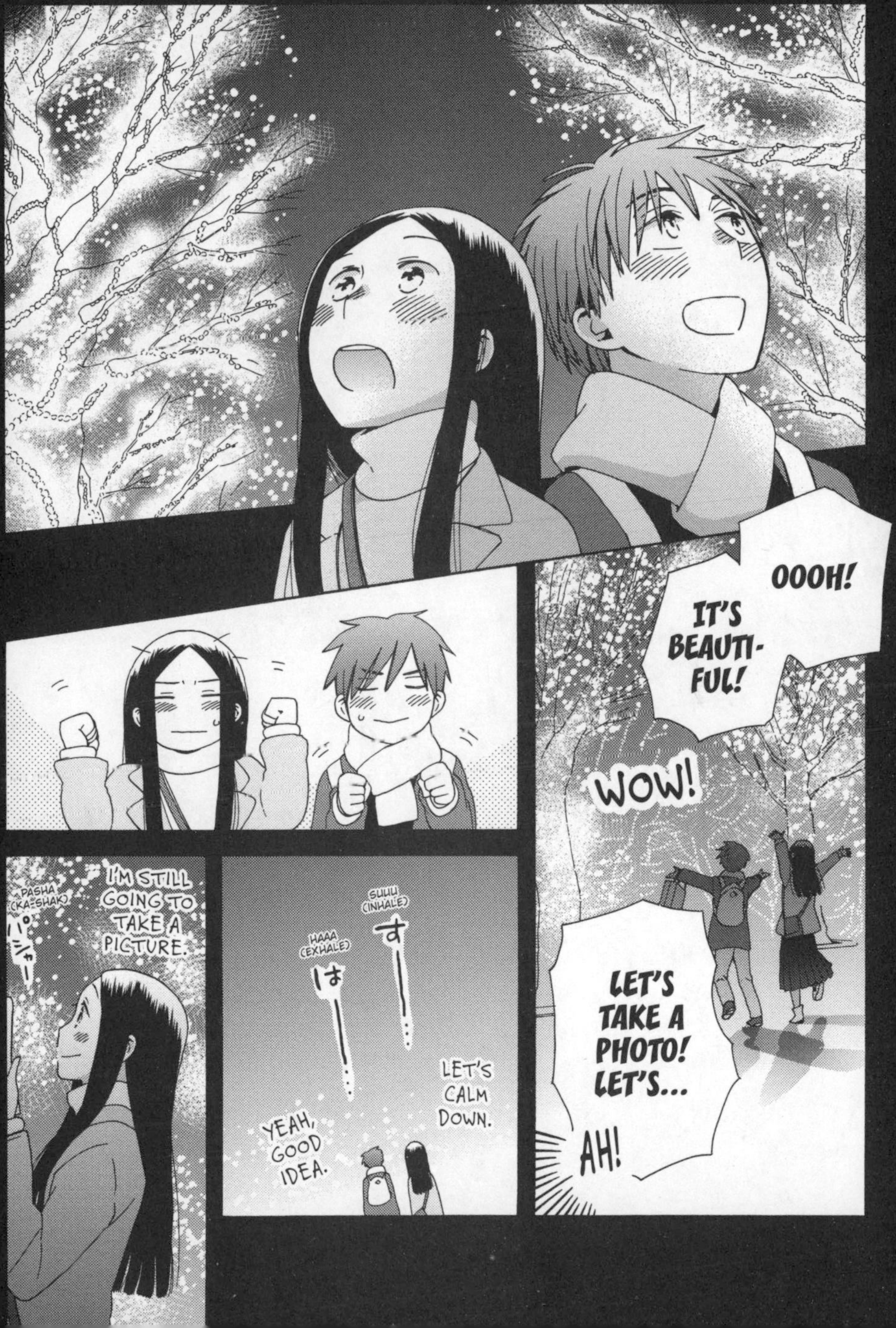
OOOH!
IT'S BEAUTI-FUL!
WOW!
LET'S TAKE A PHOTO! LET'S...
AH!
SUHU (INHALE) すー
HAAA (EXHALE) はー
LET'S CALM DOWN.
YEAH, GOOD IDEA.
I'M STILL GOING TO TAKE A PICTURE.
PASHA (KA-SHAK) パシャー

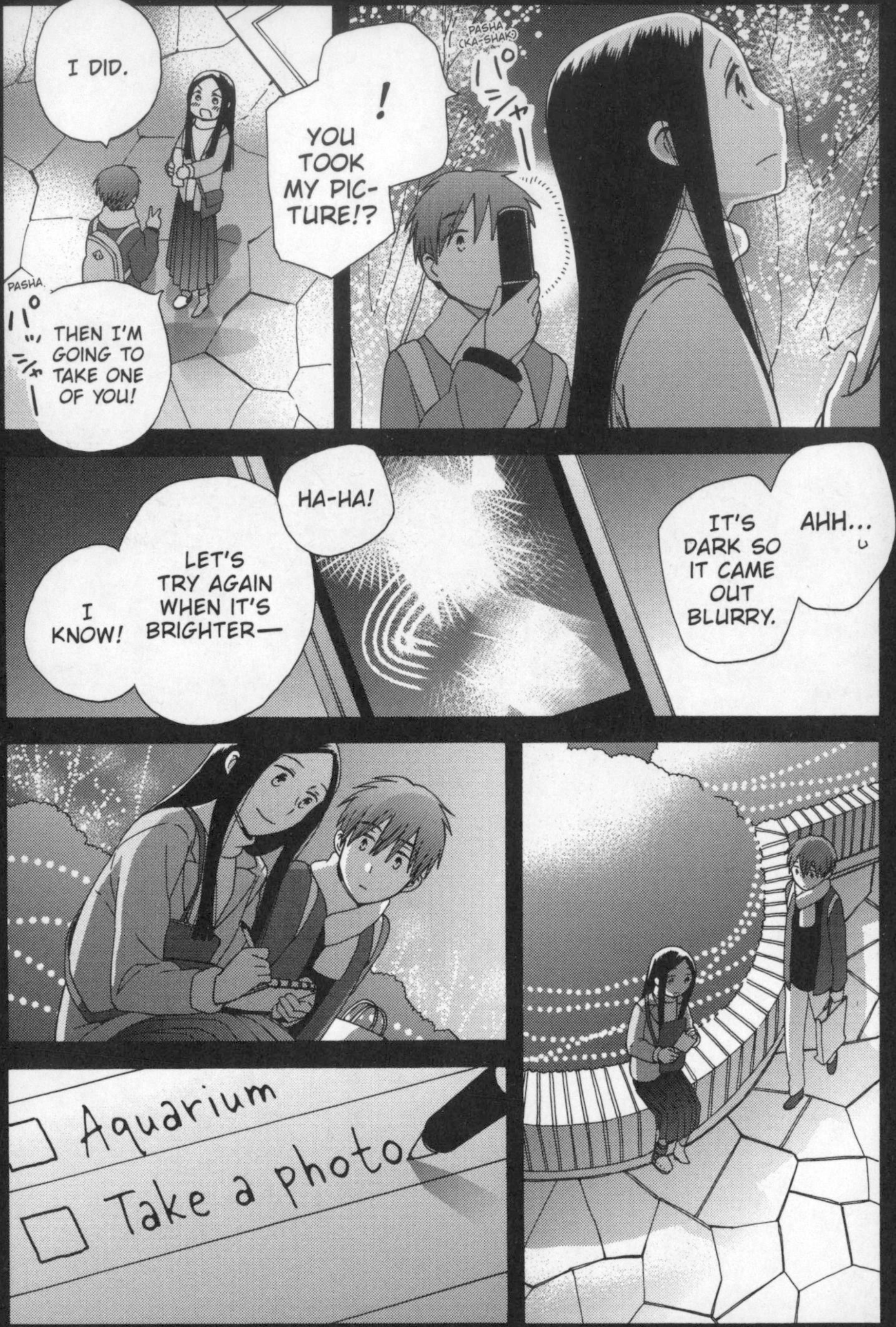
PASHA (KA-SHAK)
! YOU TOOK MY PICTURE!?
I DID.
PASHA
THEN I'M GOING TO TAKE ONE OF YOU!
AHH...
IT'S DARK SO IT CAME OUT BLURRY.
HA-HA!
LET'S TRY AGAIN WHEN IT'S BRIGHTER—
I KNOW!
Aquarium
Take a photo

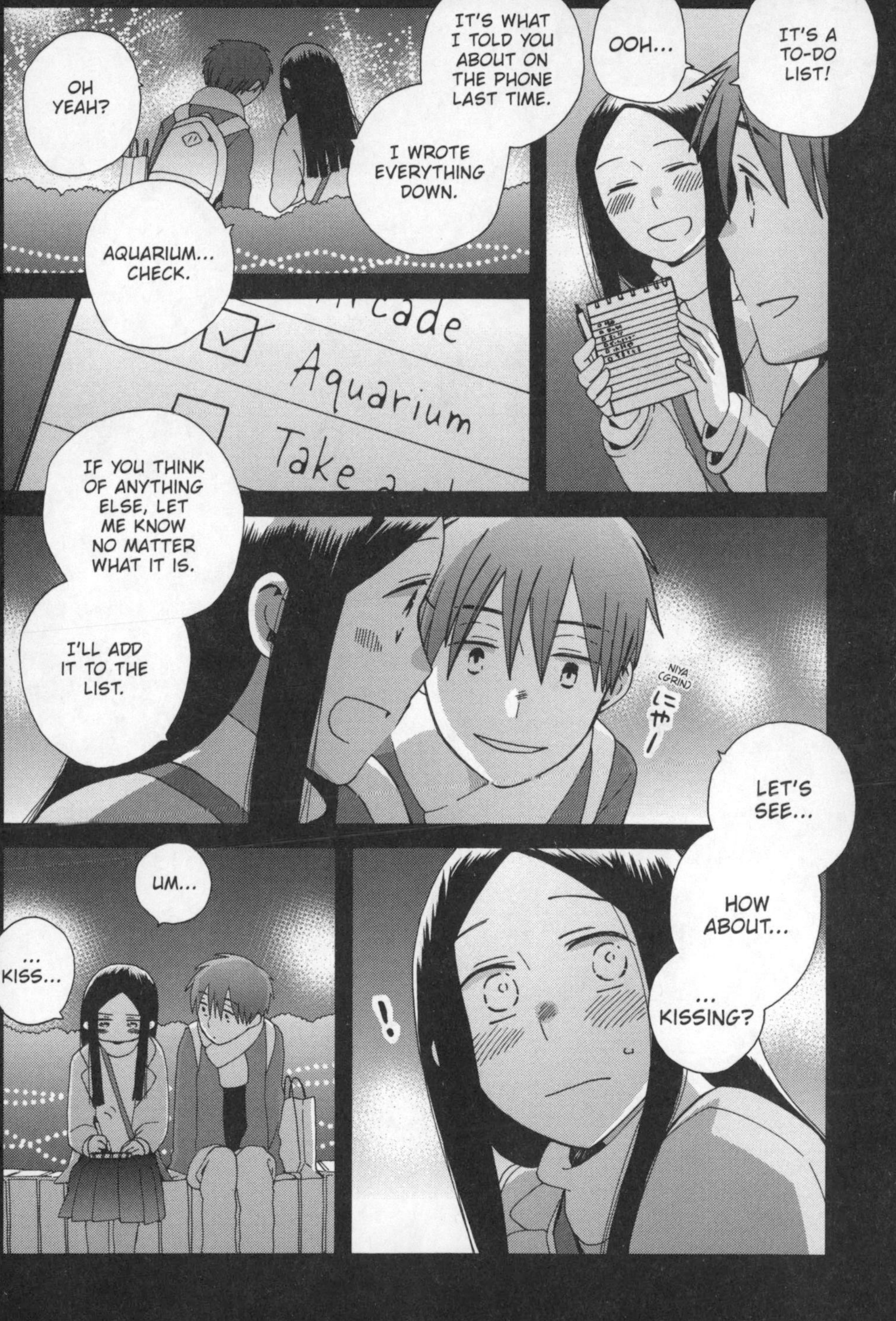
IT'S A TO-DO LIST!
OOH...
IT'S WHAT I TOLD YOU ABOUT ON THE PHONE LAST TIME.
I WROTE EVERYTHING DOWN.
OH YEAH?
AQUARIUM... CHECK.
Aquarium
Take
IF YOU THINK OF ANYTHING ELSE, LET ME KNOW NO MATTER WHAT IT IS.
I'LL ADD IT TO THE LIST.
NIYA (GRIN)
にやー
LET'S SEE...
HOW ABOUT...
... KISSING?
!
UM...
... KISS...

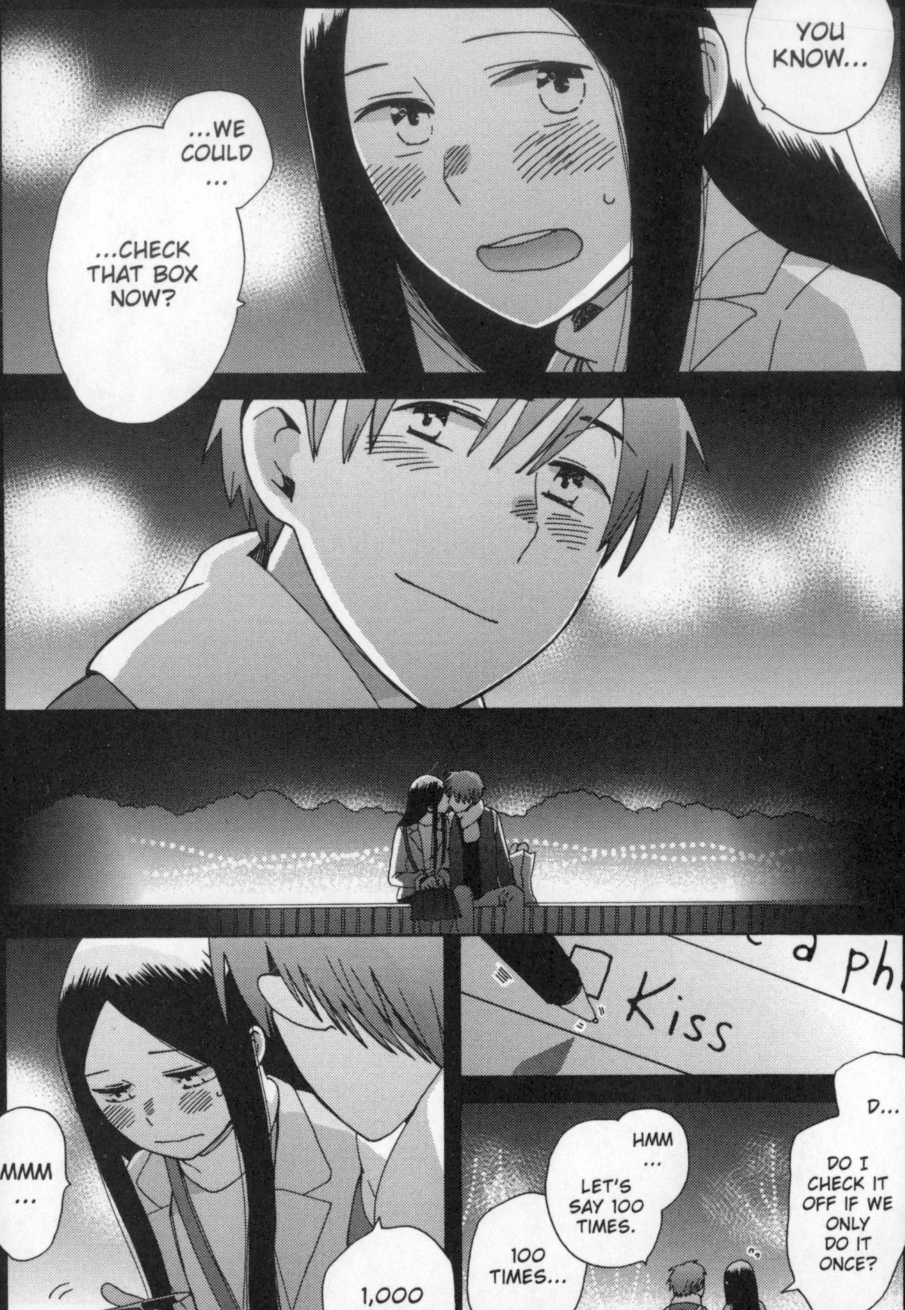
YOU KNOW...
...WE COULD ...
...CHECK THAT BOX NOW?
Kiss
D...
DO I CHECK IT OFF IF WE ONLY DO IT ONCE?
HMM ... LET'S SAY 100 TIMES.
100 TIMES...
1,000 TIMES?
MMM ...

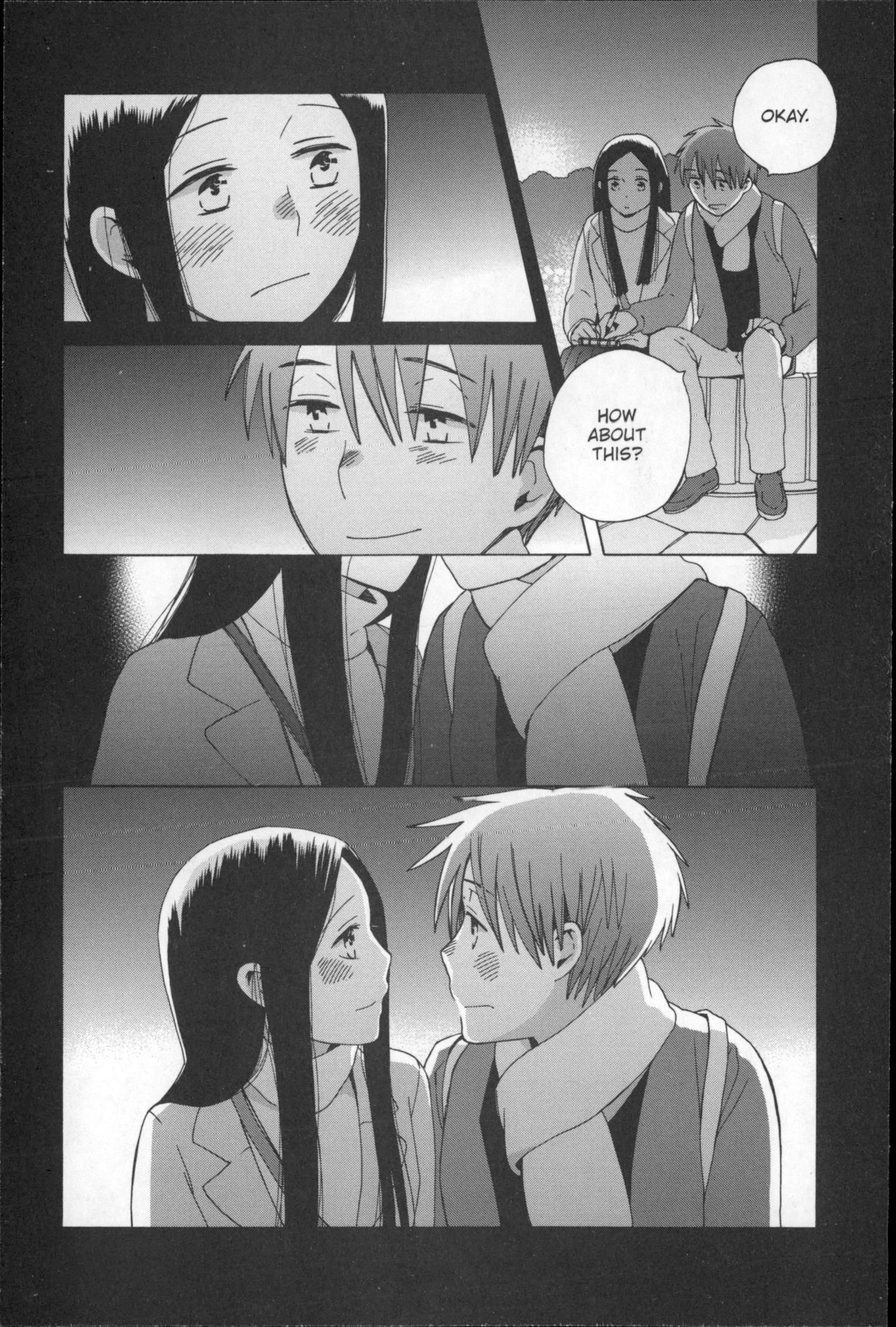
OKAY.
HOW ABOUT THIS?

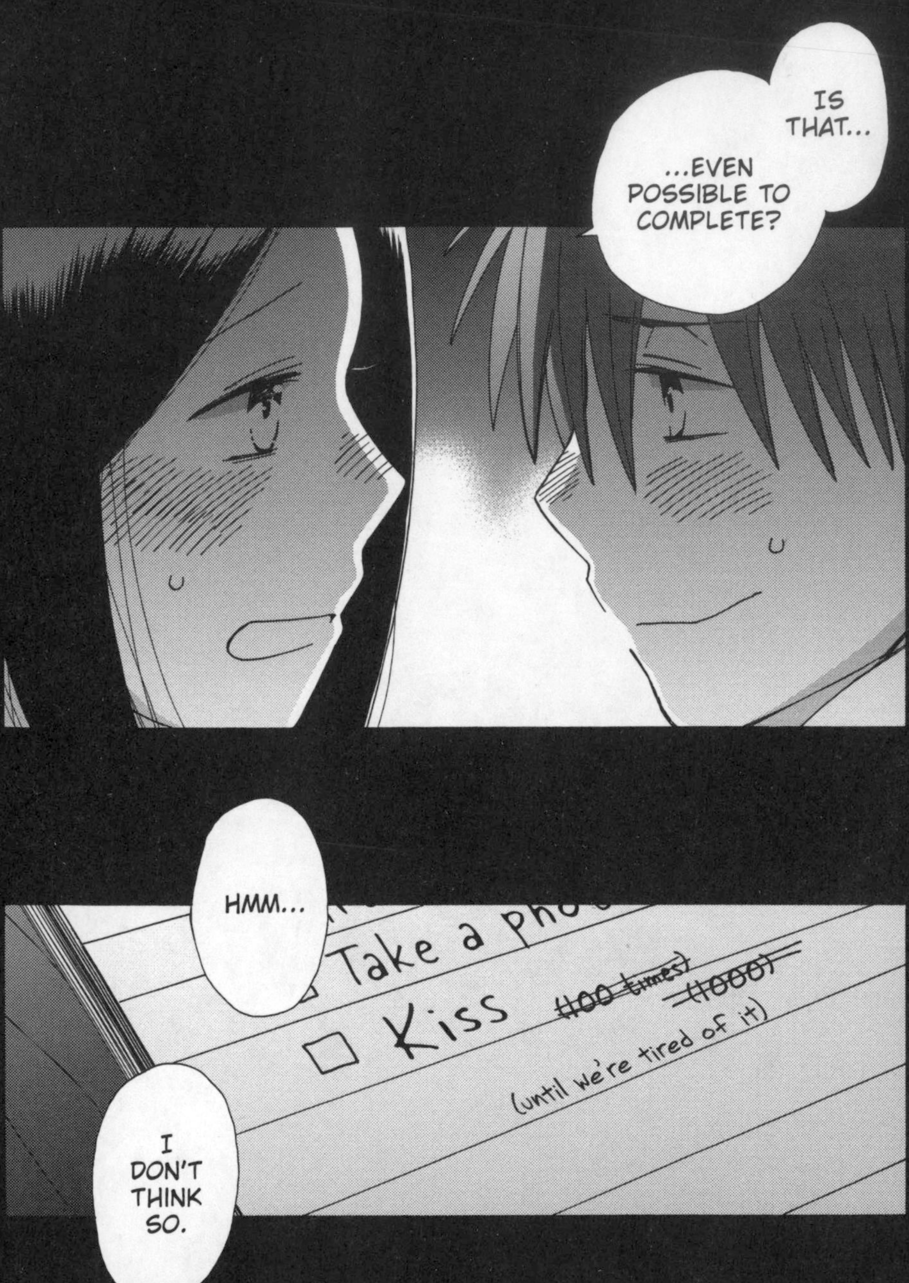
IS THAT... ...EVEN POSSIBLE TO COMPLETE?
HMM...
Take a pho
Kiss ~~(100 times)~~ ~~(1000)~~
(until we're tired of it)
I DON'T THINK SO.

Fin

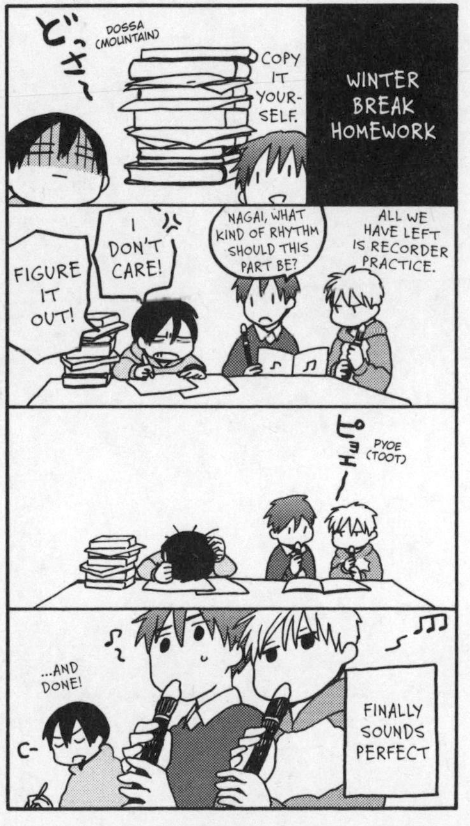
WINTER BREAK HOMEWORK
どっさ~
DOSSA (MOUNTAIN)
COPY IT YOURSELF.
ALL WE HAVE LEFT IS RECORDER PRACTICE.
NAGAI, WHAT KIND OF RHYTHM SHOULD THIS PART BE?
I DON'T CARE!
FIGURE IT OUT!
ピョエ~
PYOE (TOOT)
FINALLY SOUNDS PERFECT
...AND DONE!
C-

Love at Fourteen

Fuka Mizutani

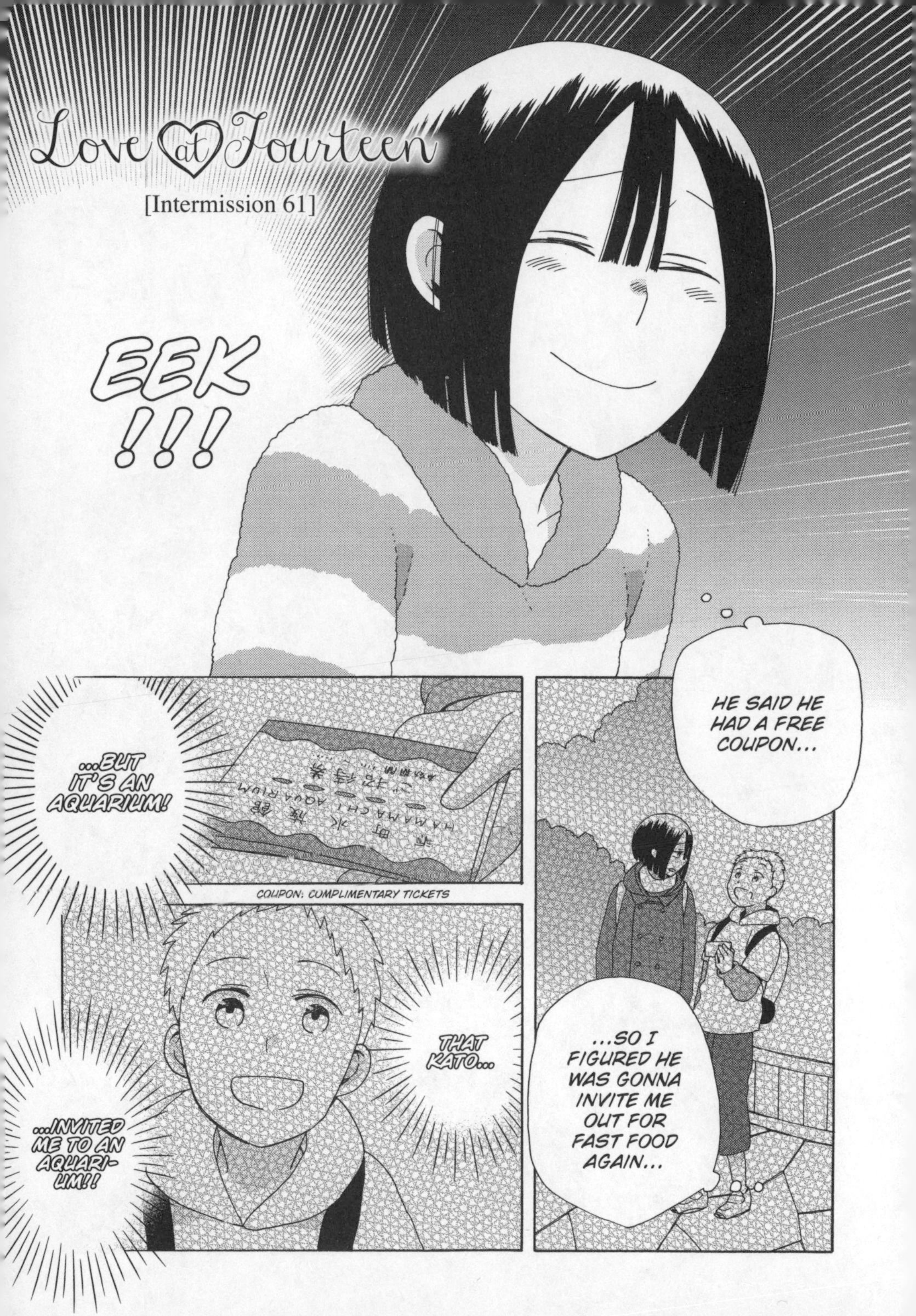

Love at Fourteen
[Intermission 61]
EEK !!!
HE SAID HE HAD A FREE COUPON...
...SO I FIGURED HE WAS GONNA INVITE ME OUT FOR FAST FOOD AGAIN...
...BUT IT'S AN AQUARIUM!
HAMAMACHI AQUARIUM
COUPON: COMPLIMENTARY TICKETS
THAT KATO...
...INVITED ME TO AN AQUARI-UM!!

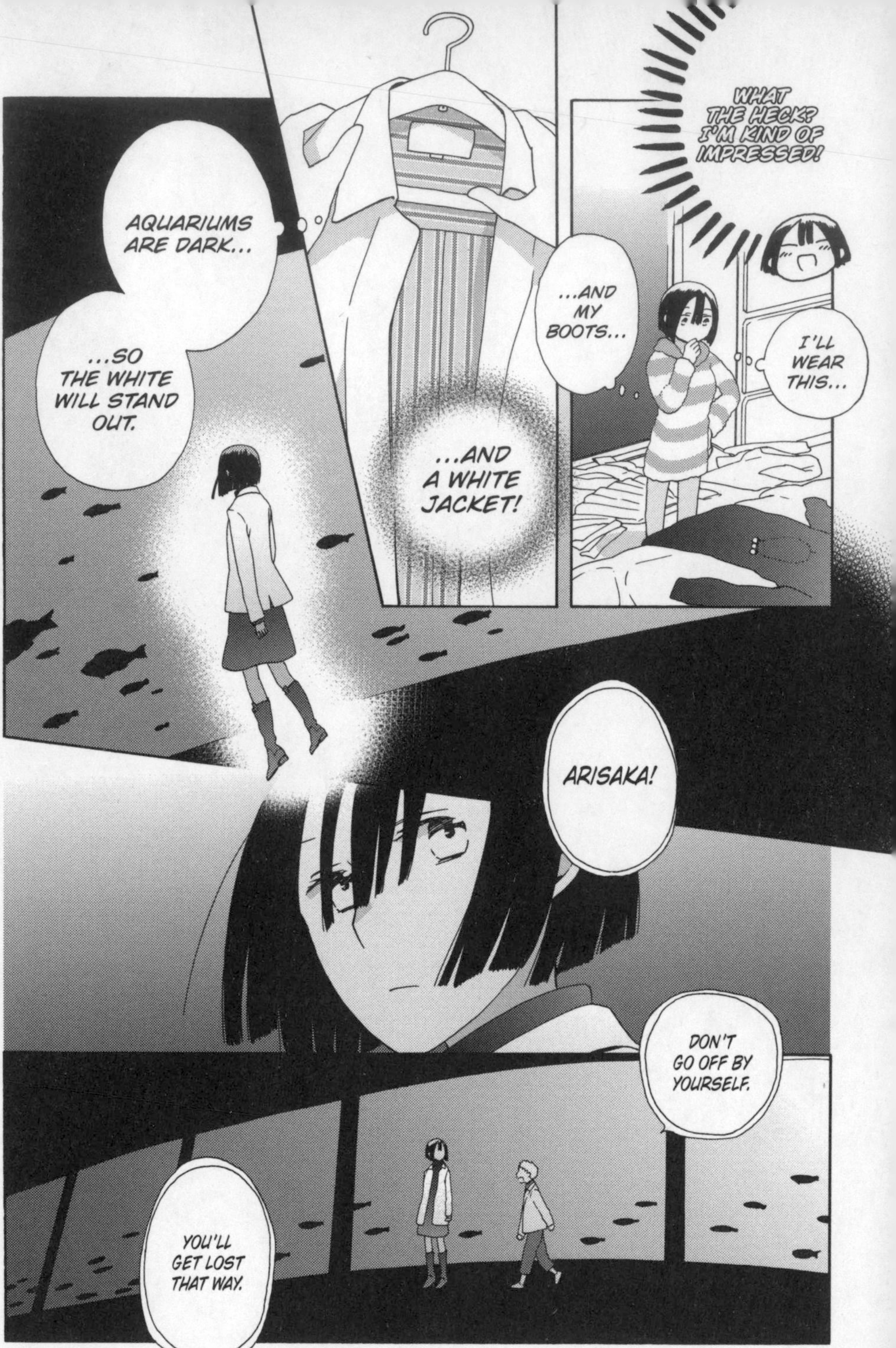
WHAT THE HECK? I'M KIND OF IMPRESSED!
I'LL WEAR THIS...
...AND MY BOOTS...
...AND A WHITE JACKET!
AQUARIUMS ARE DARK...
...SO THE WHITE WILL STAND OUT.
ARISAKA!
DON'T GO OFF BY YOURSELF.
YOU'LL GET LOST THAT WAY.

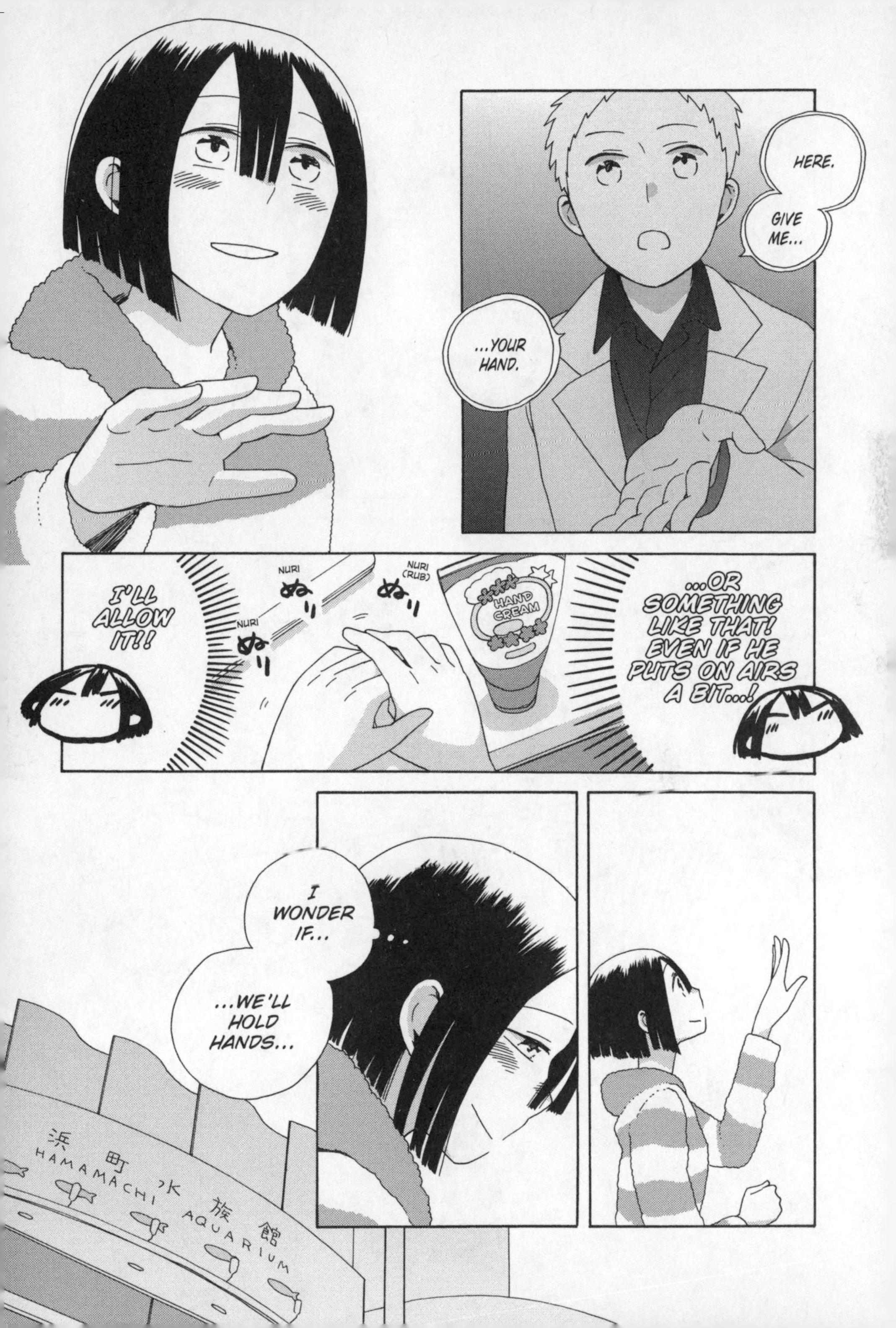
HERE.
GIVE ME...
...YOUR HAND.
...OR SOMETHING LIKE THAT! EVEN IF HE PUTS ON AIRS A BIT...!
NURI (RUB)
ぬり
NURI
ぬり
HAND CREAM
NURI
ぬり
I'LL ALLOW IT!!
I WONDER IF...
...WE'LL HOLD HANDS...
浜町水族館
HAMAMACHI AQUARIUM

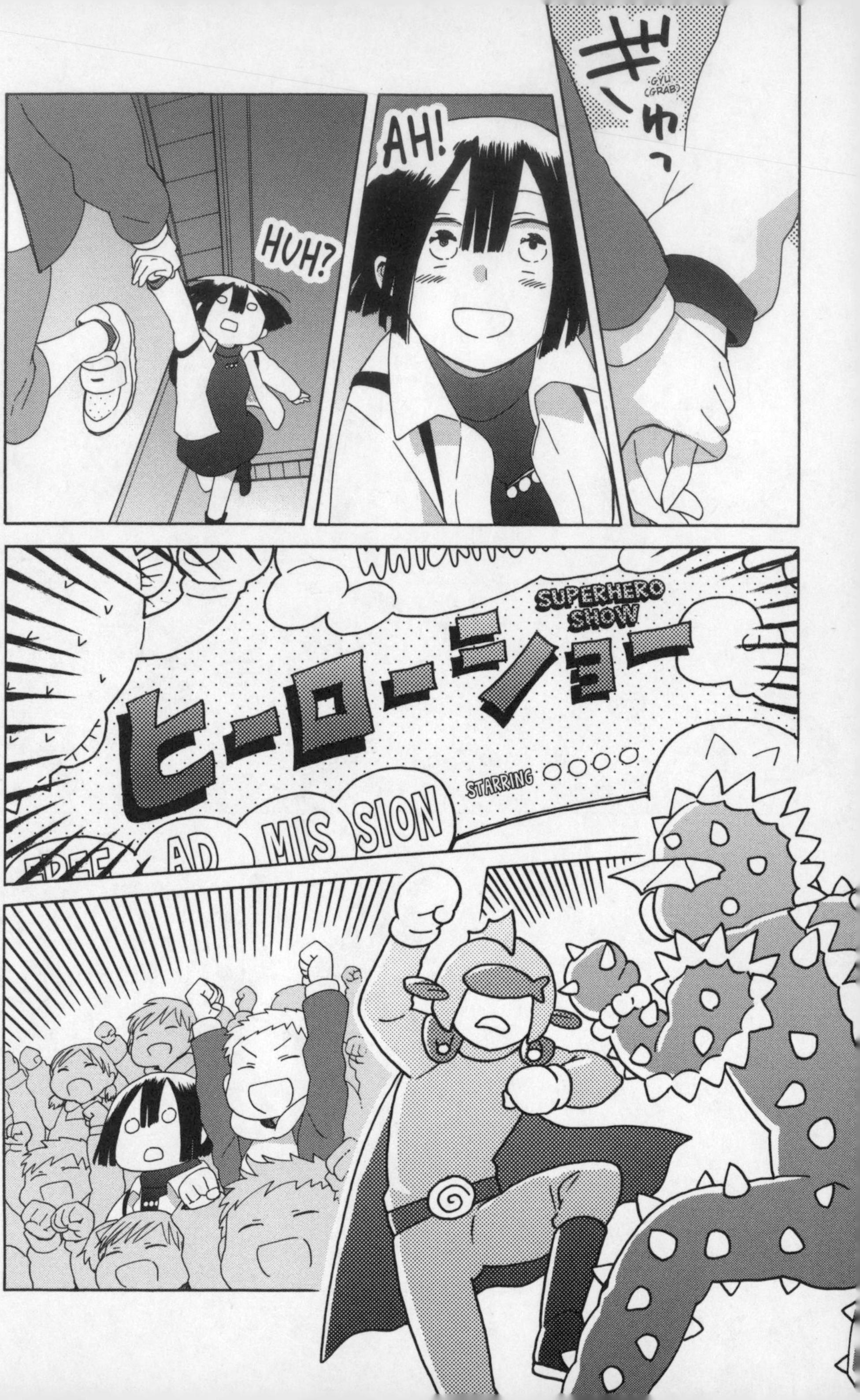

ぎゅっ
GYU (GRAB)
AH!
HUH?
SUPERHERO SHOW
ヒーローショー
STARRING ○○○○
AD MIS SION

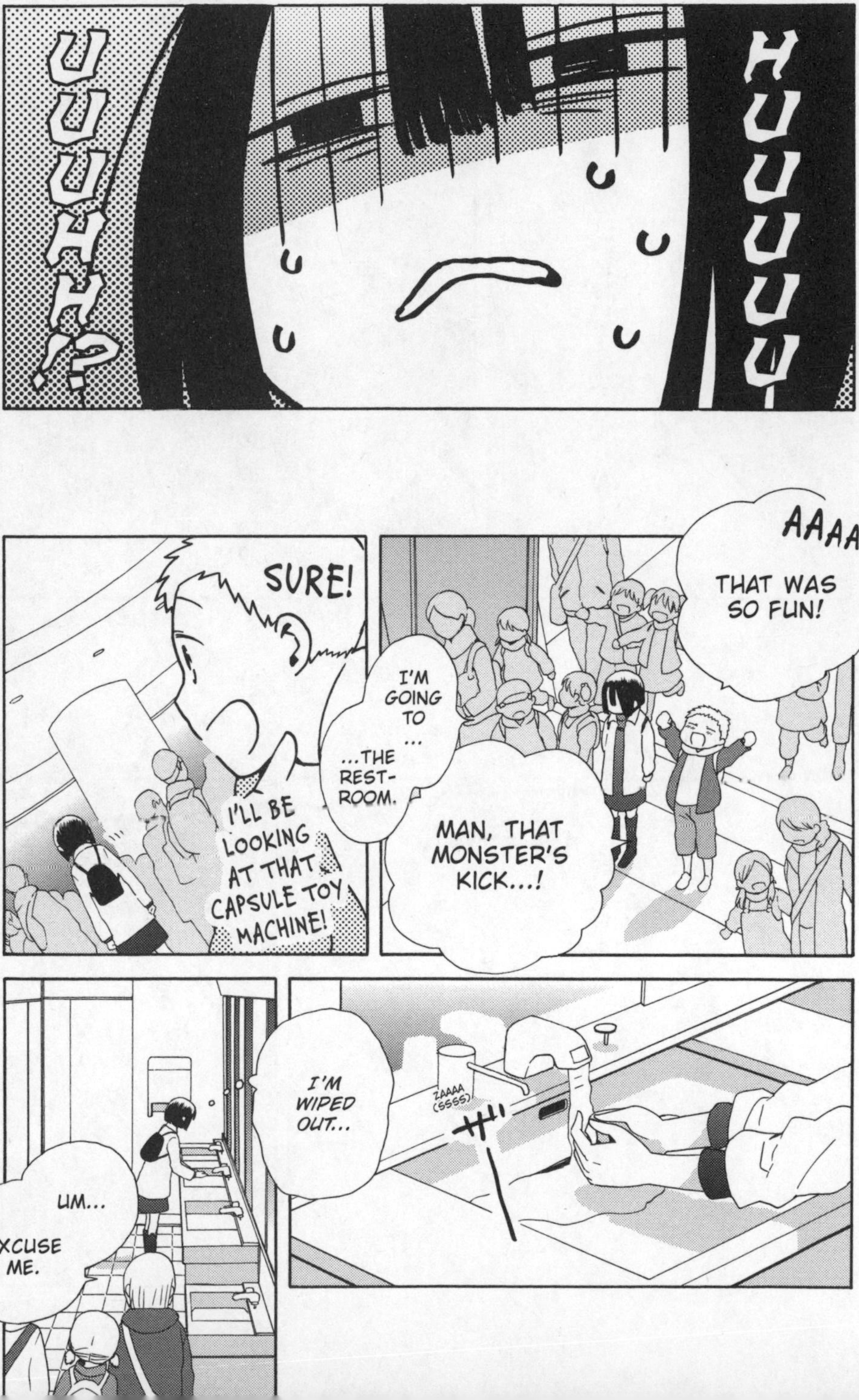
HUUUUUUU-
UUUH!?
AAAAH!
THAT WAS SO FUN!
MAN, THAT MONSTER'S KICK...!
I'M GOING TO ...
...THE REST-ROOM.
SURE!
I'LL BE LOOKING AT THAT CAPSULE TOY MACHINE!
I'M WIPED OUT...
ZAAAA (SSSS)
UM...
EXCUSE ME.

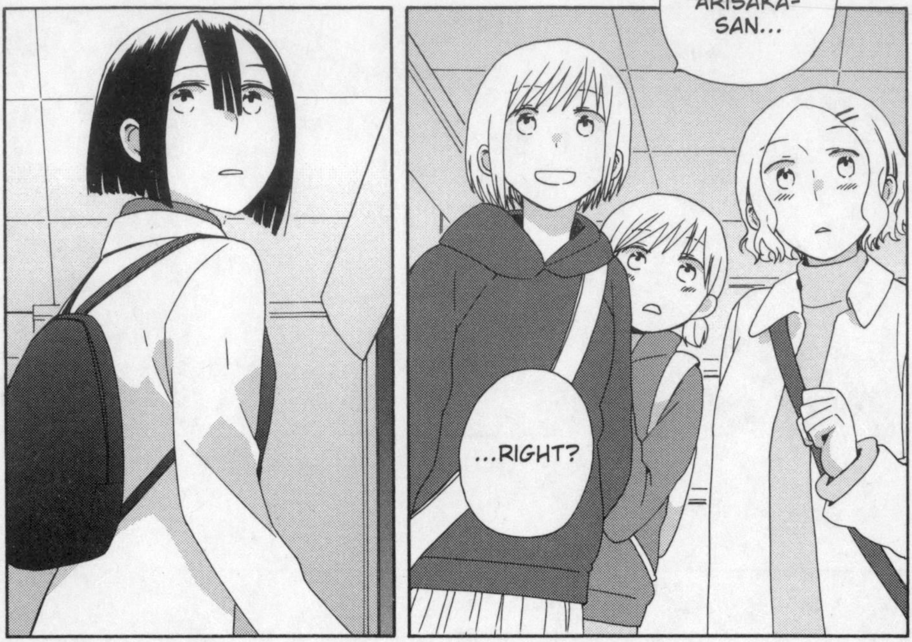
YOU'RE ARISAKA-SAN...
...RIGHT?

SIGN: CAPSULE TOY MECHA-FISH

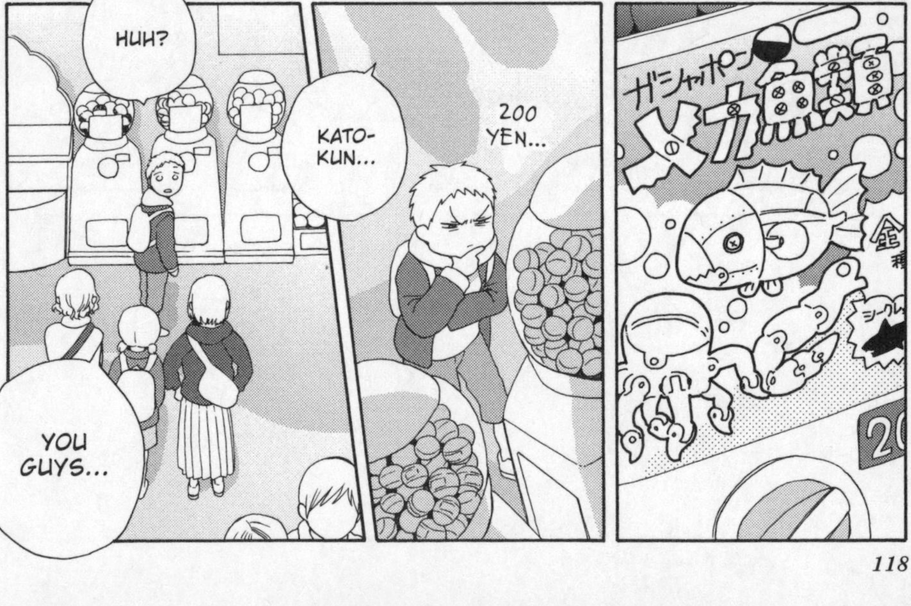
200 YEN...
KATO-KUN...
HUH?
YOU GUYS...

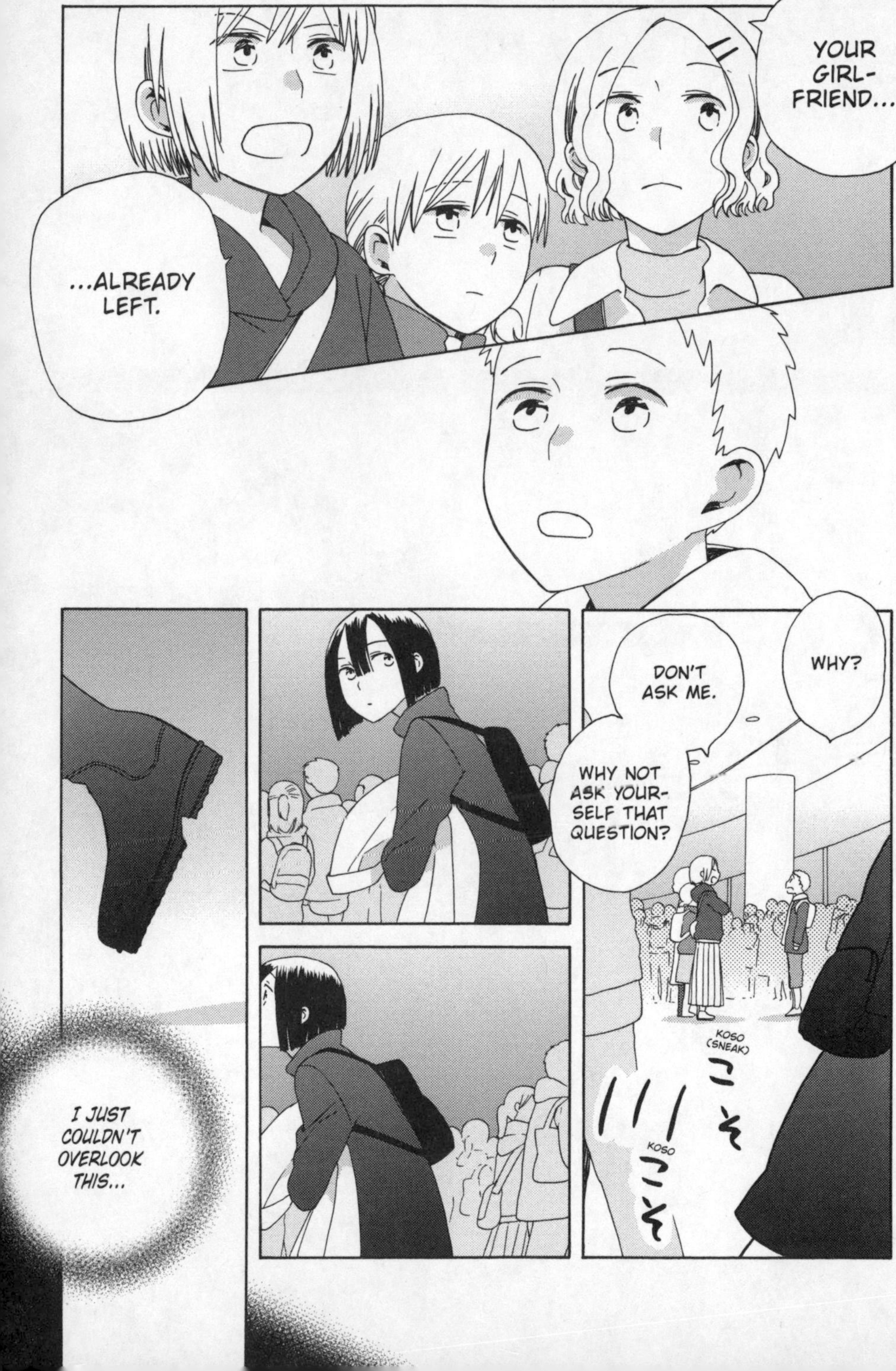
YOUR GIRL-FRIEND...
...ALREADY LEFT.
WHY?
DON'T ASK ME.
WHY NOT ASK YOUR-SELF THAT QUESTION?
KOSO (SNEAK) こそ
KOSO こそ
I JUST COULDN'T OVERLOOK THIS...

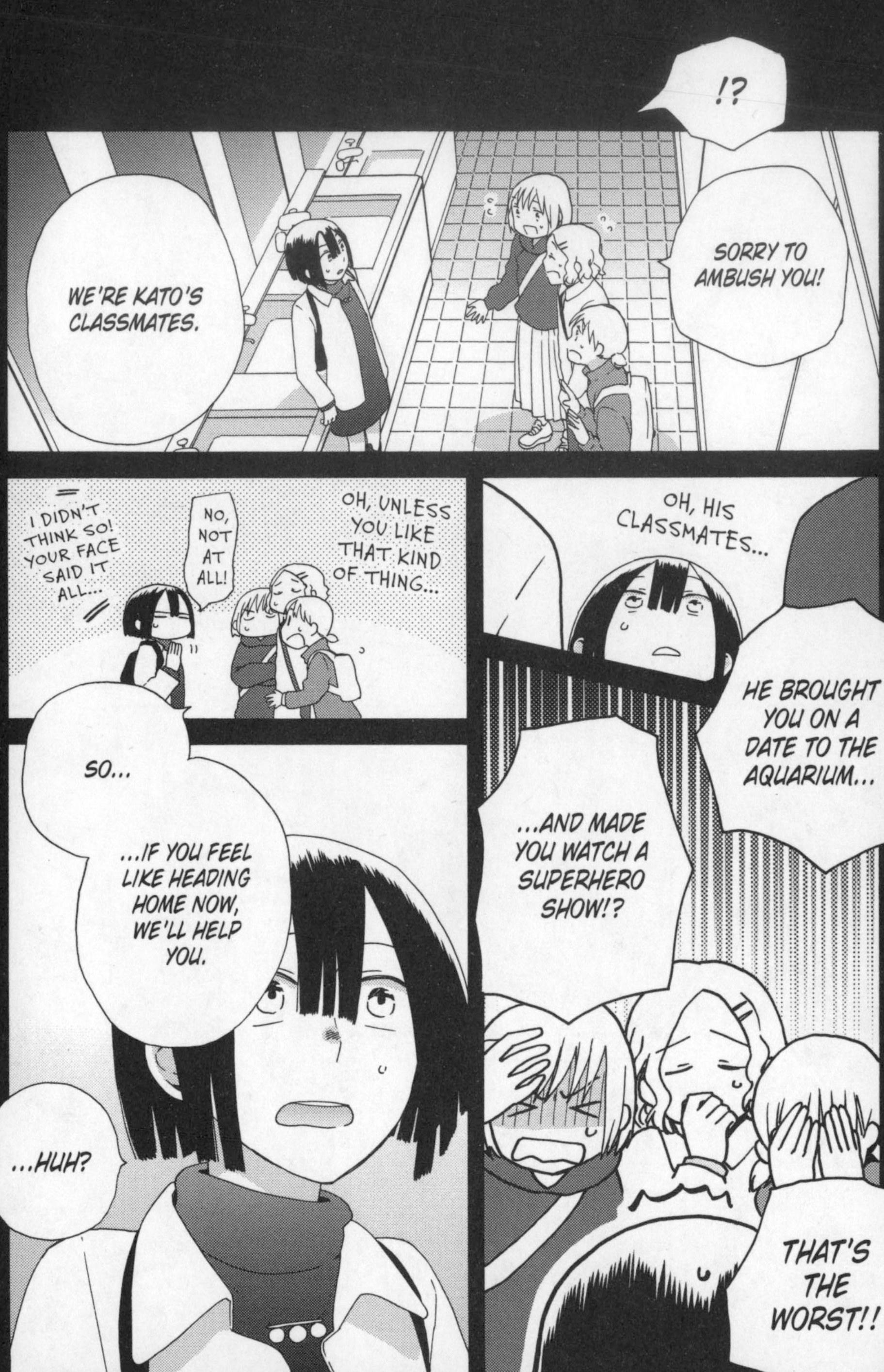
!?
SORRY TO AMBUSH YOU!
WE'RE KATO'S CLASSMATES.
OH, HIS CLASSMATES...
HE BROUGHT YOU ON A DATE TO THE AQUARIUM...
...AND MADE YOU WATCH A SUPERHERO SHOW!?
THAT'S THE WORST!!
OH, UNLESS YOU LIKE THAT KIND OF THING...
NO, NOT AT ALL!
I DIDN'T THINK SO! YOUR FACE SAID IT ALL...
SO...
...IF YOU FEEL LIKE HEADING HOME NOW, WE'LL HELP YOU.
...HUH?

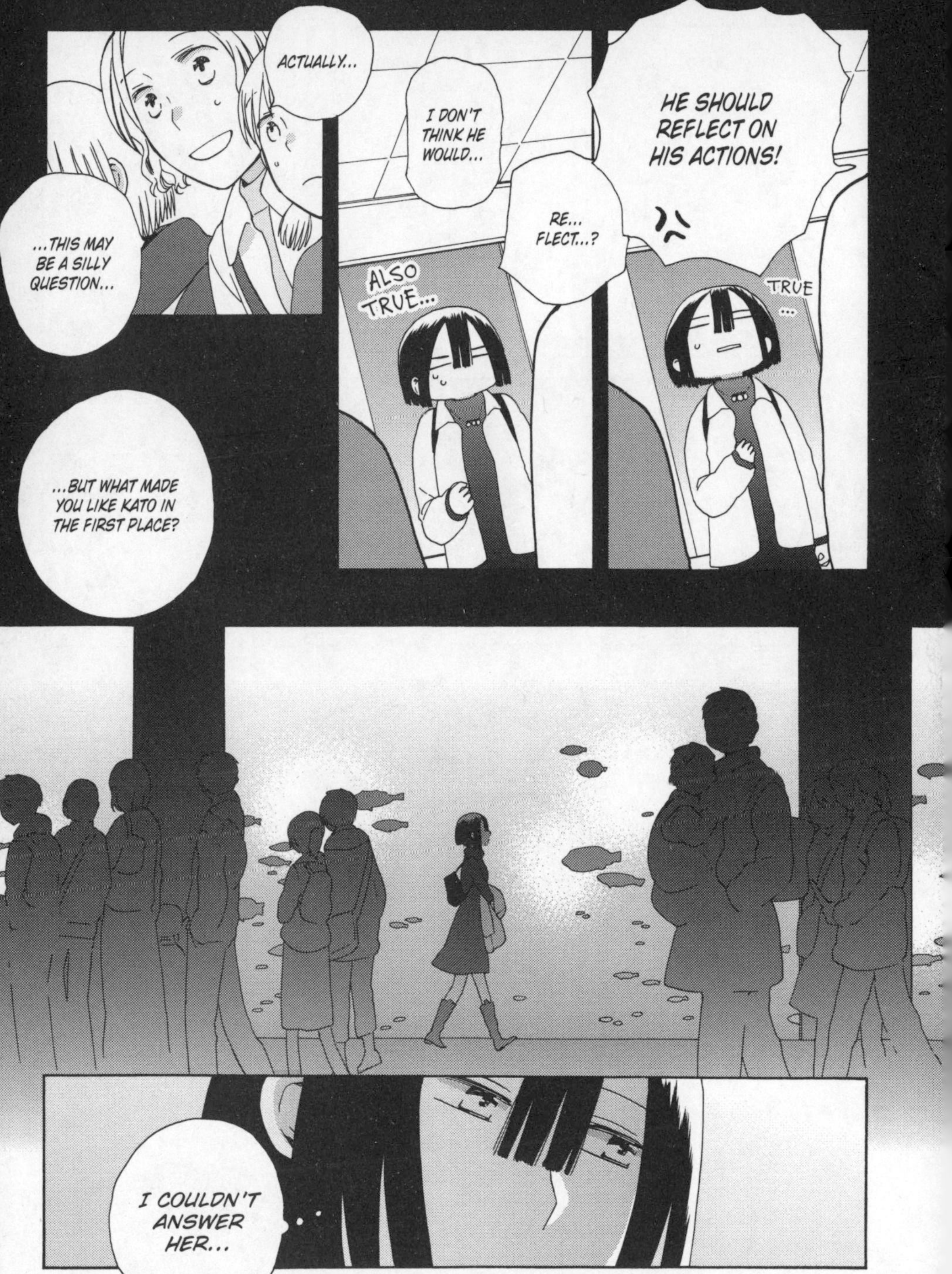
HE SHOULD REFLECT ON HIS ACTIONS!
TRUE...
I DON'T THINK HE WOULD...
RE... FLECT...?
ALSO TRUE...
ACTUALLY...
...THIS MAY BE A SILLY QUESTION...
...BUT WHAT MADE YOU LIKE KATO IN THE FIRST PLACE?
I COULDN'T ANSWER HER...

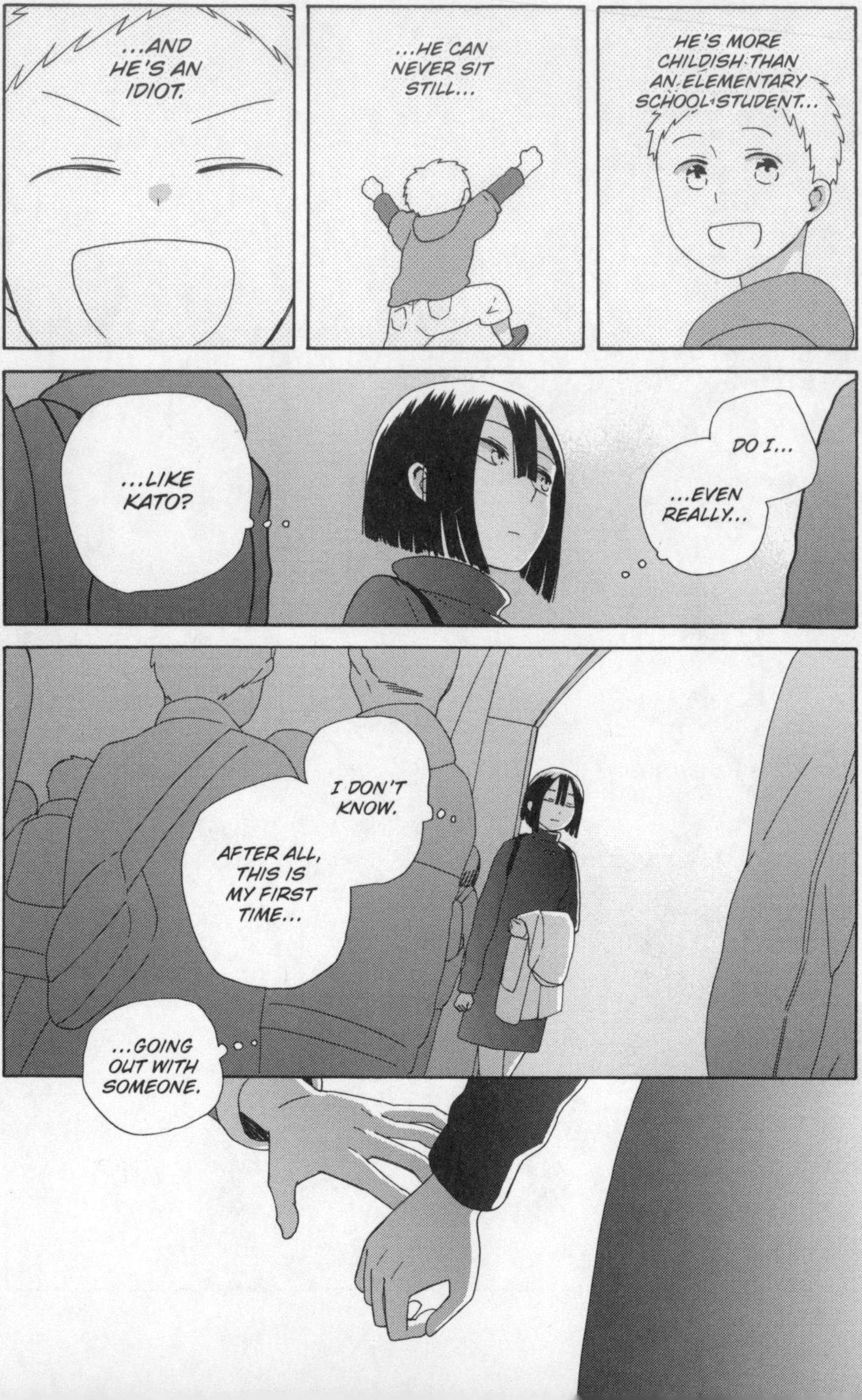
HE'S MORE CHILDISH THAN AN ELEMENTARY SCHOOL STUDENT...
...HE CAN NEVER SIT STILL...
...AND HE'S AN IDIOT.
DO I...
...EVEN REALLY...
...LIKE KATO?
I DON'T KNOW.
AFTER ALL, THIS IS MY FIRST TIME...
...GOING OUT WITH SOMEONE.

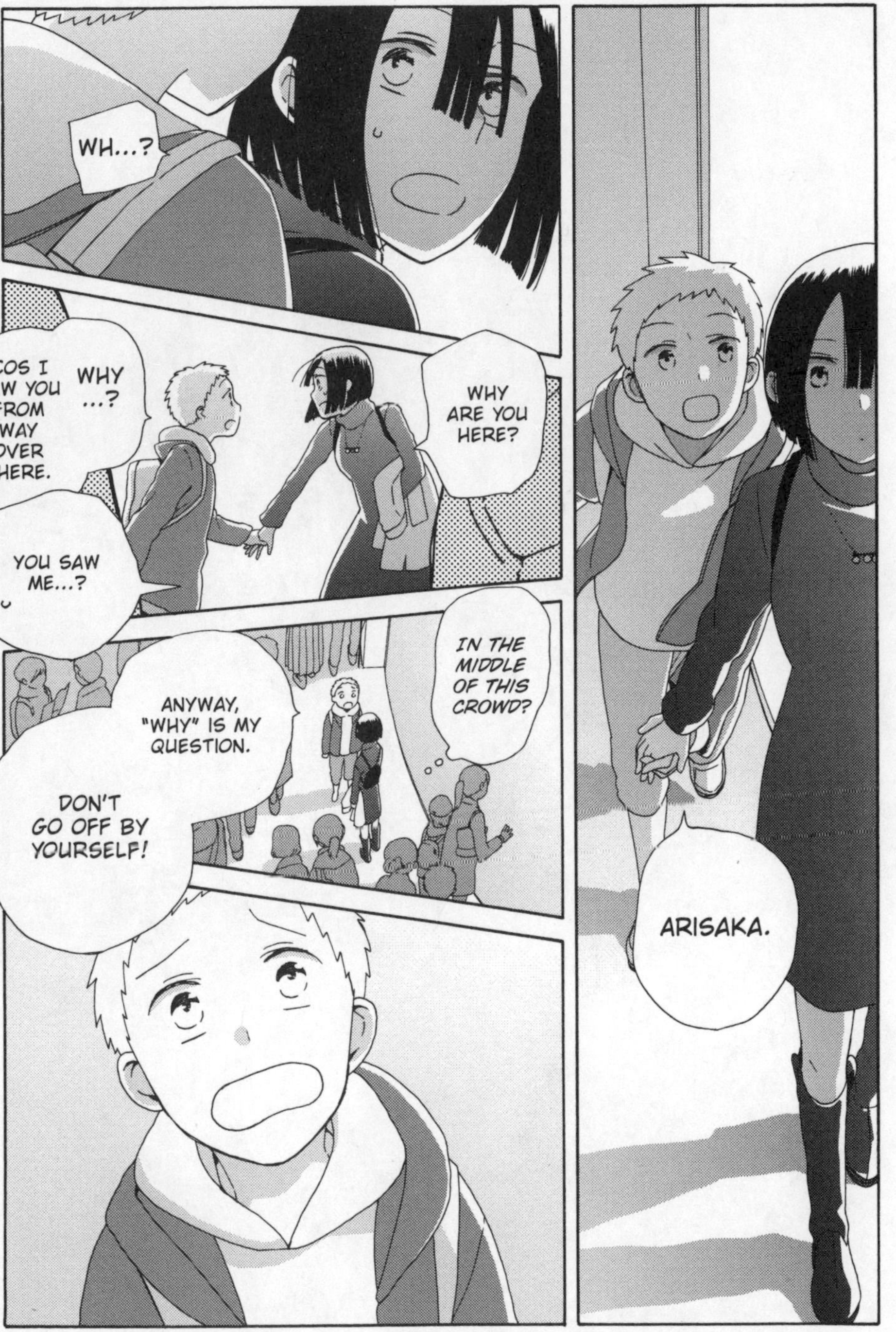
ARISAKA.
WH...?
WHY ARE YOU HERE?
WHY ...?
'COS I SAW YOU FROM WAY OVER THERE.
YOU SAW ME...?
IN THE MIDDLE OF THIS CROWD?
ANYWAY, "WHY" IS MY QUESTION.
DON'T GO OFF BY YOURSELF!

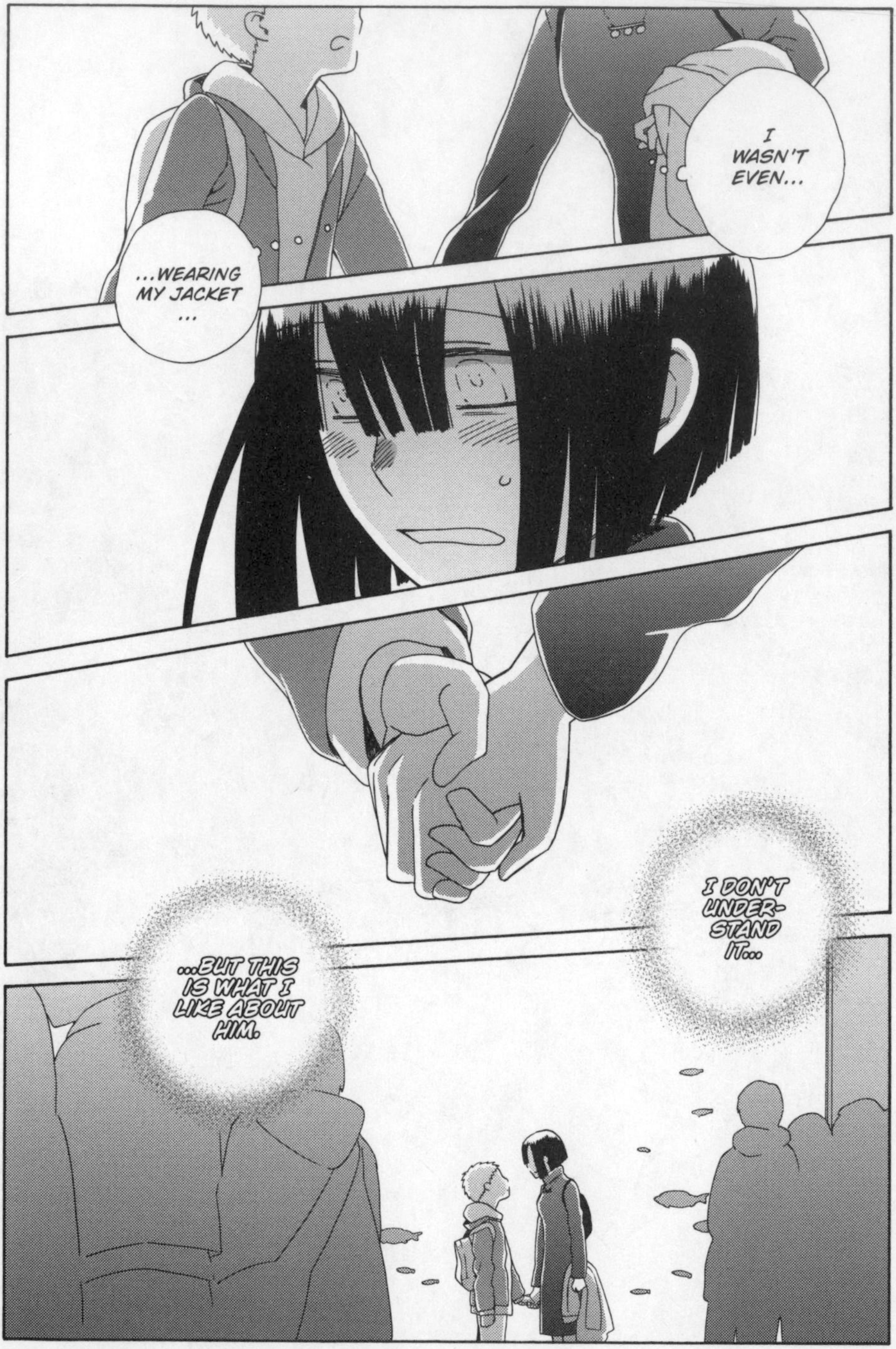
I WASN'T EVEN...
...WEARING MY JACKET ...
I DON'T UNDER-STAND IT...
...BUT THIS IS WHAT I LIKE ABOUT HIM.

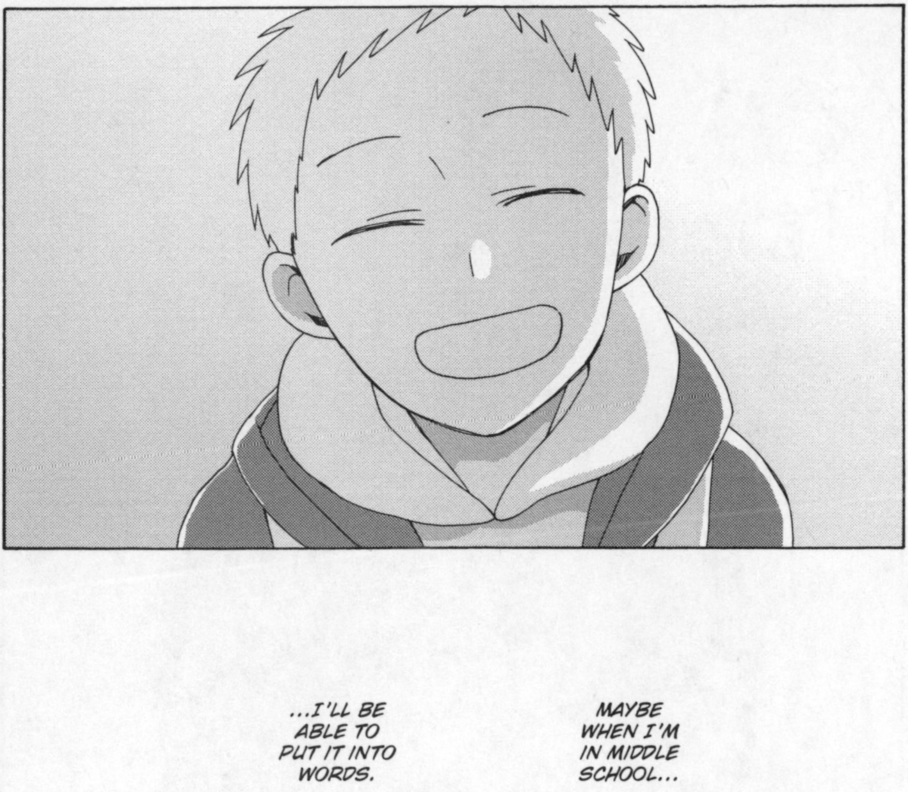
MAYBE WHEN I'M IN MIDDLE SCHOOL...
...I'LL BE ABLE TO PUT IT INTO WORDS.

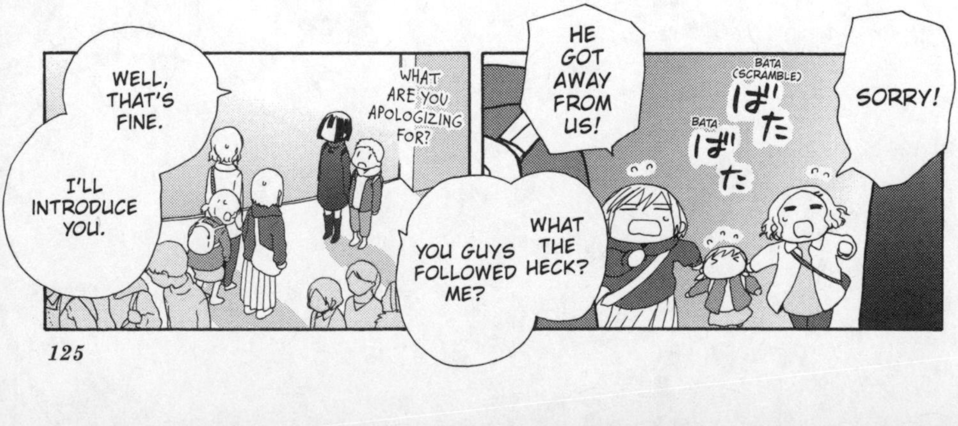
SORRY!
BATA (SCRAMBLE)
ばた
BATA
ばた
HE GOT AWAY FROM US!
WHAT THE HECK?
YOU GUYS FOLLOWED ME?
WHAT ARE YOU APOLOGIZING FOR?
WELL, THAT'S FINE.
I'LL INTRODUCE YOU.

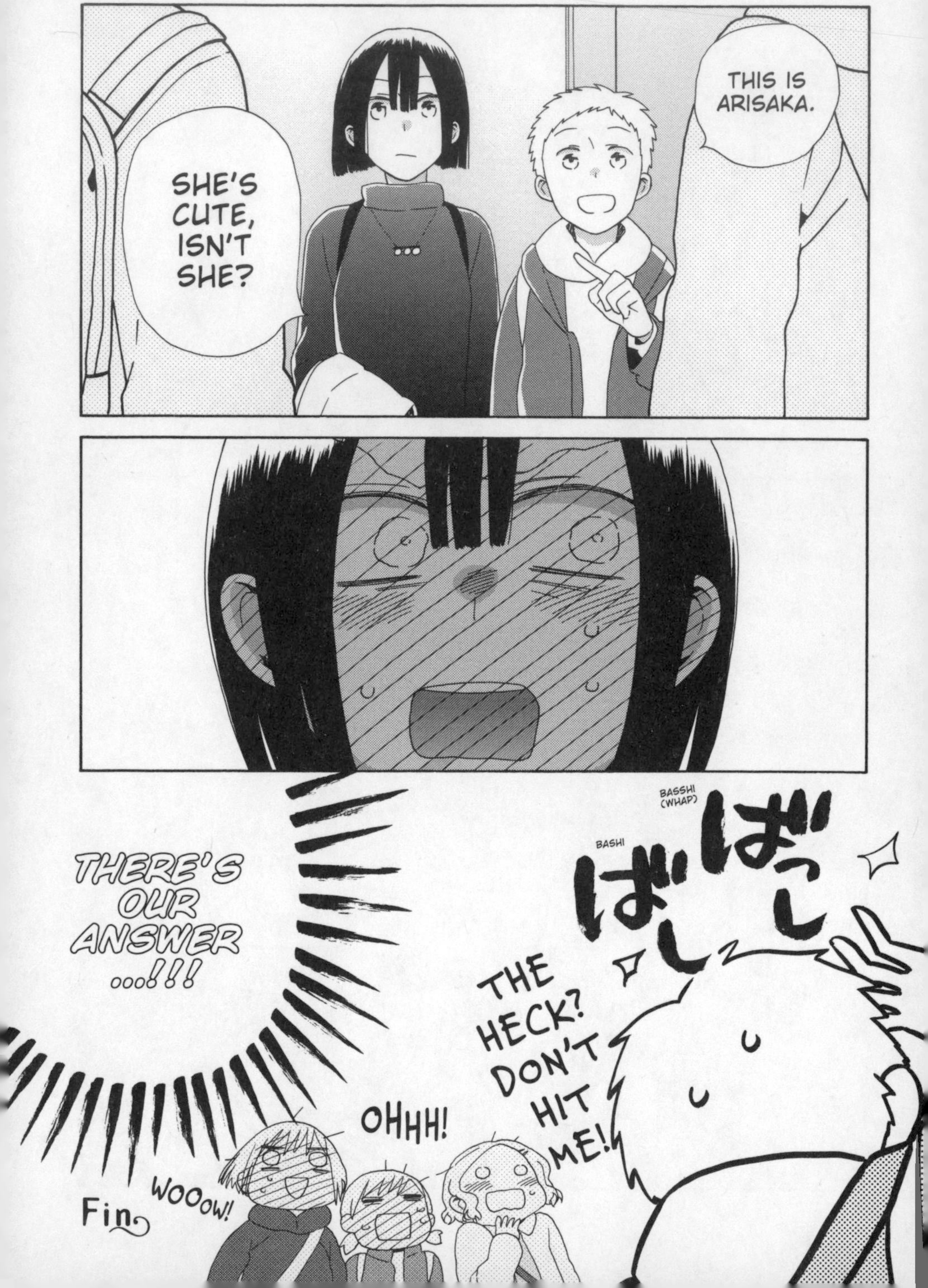
THIS IS ARISAKA.
SHE'S CUTE, ISN'T SHE?
BASSHI (WHAP)
ばっし
BASHI
ばし
THE HECK? DON'T HIT ME!
OHHH!
THERE'S OUR ANSWER ...!!!
WOOOW!
Fin

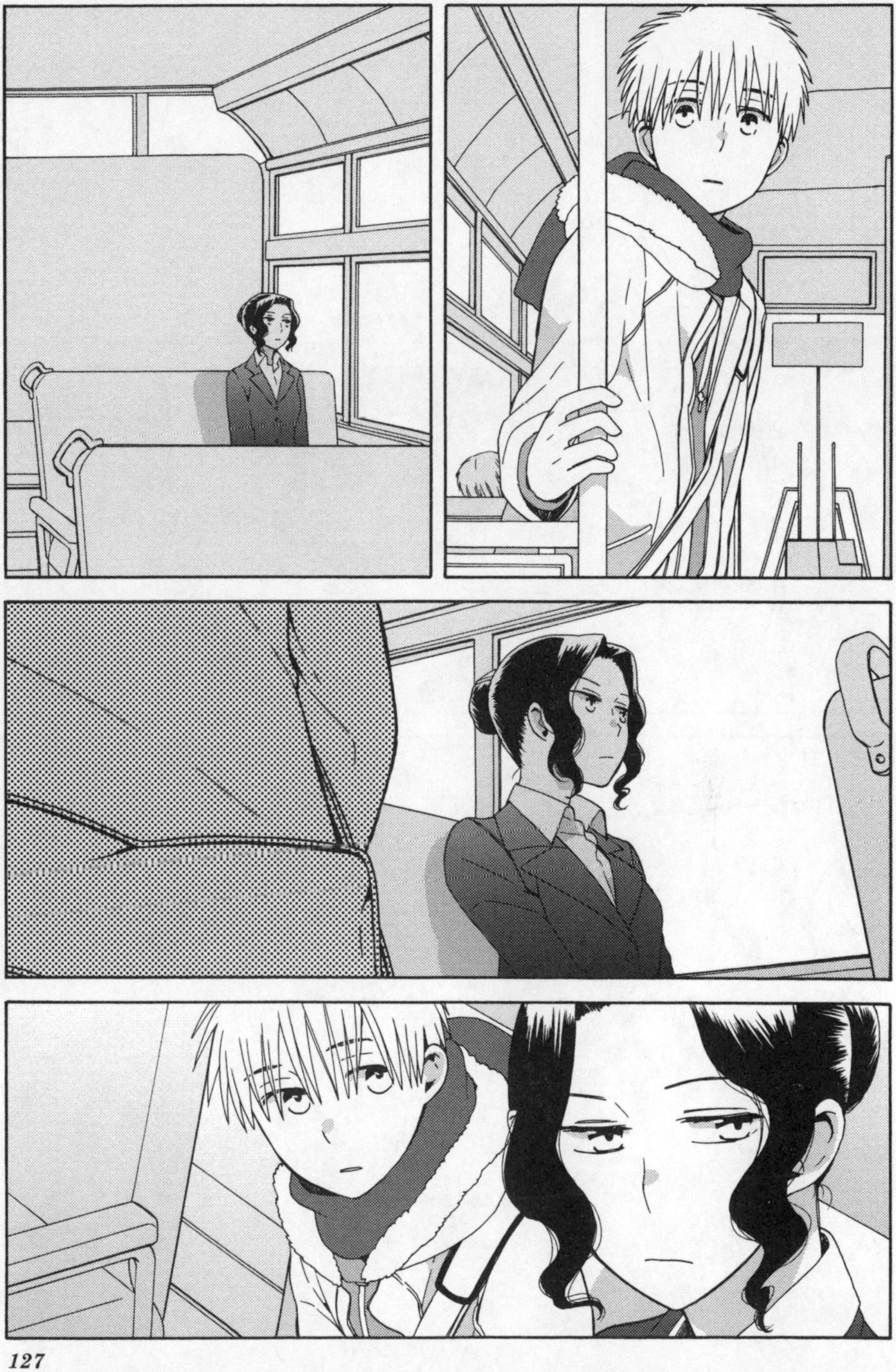

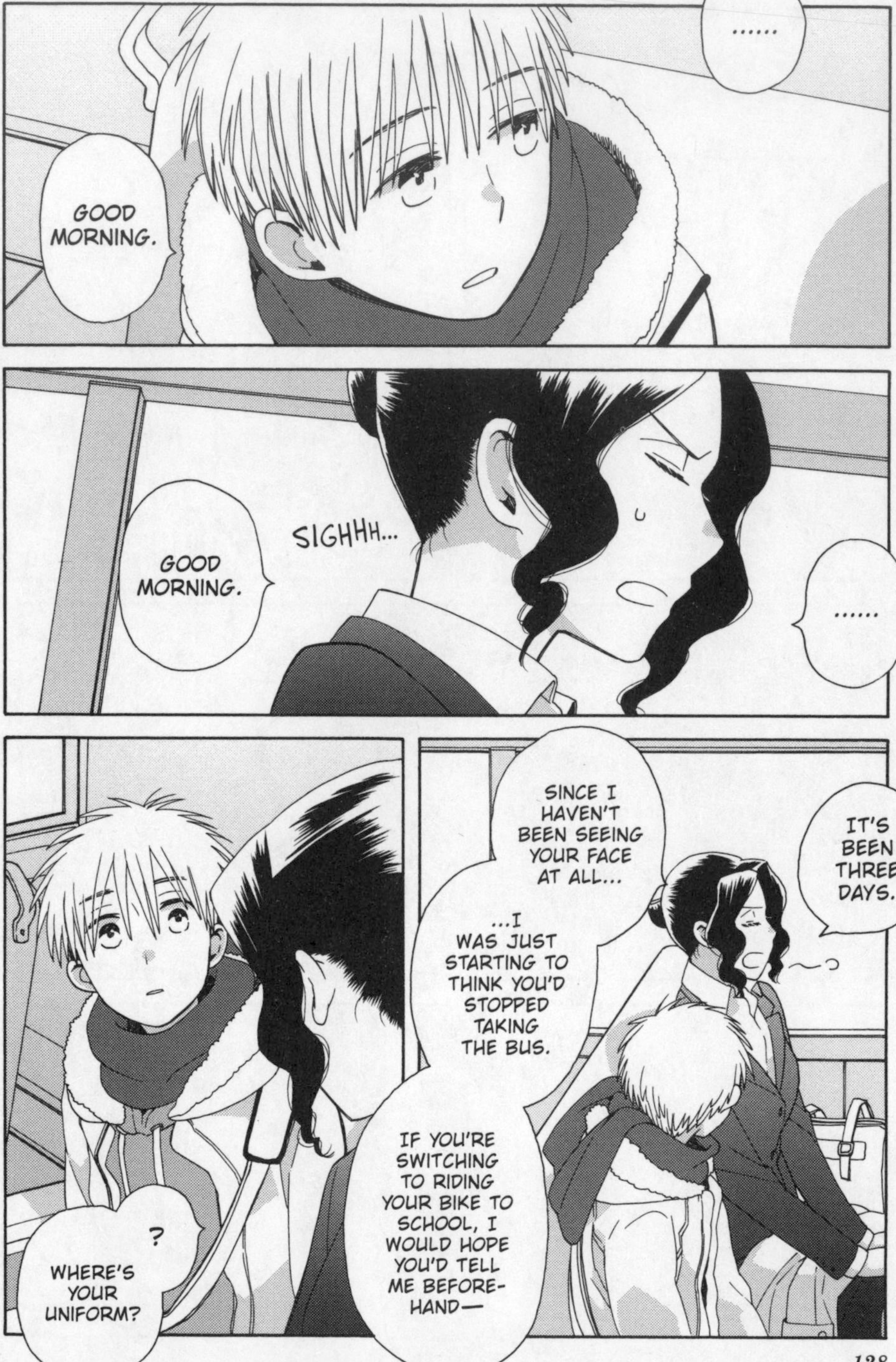
......
GOOD MORNING.
......
SIGHHH...
GOOD MORNING.
IT'S BEEN THREE DAYS.
SINCE I HAVEN'T BEEN SEEING YOUR FACE AT ALL...
...I WAS JUST STARTING TO THINK YOU'D STOPPED TAKING THE BUS.
IF YOU'RE SWITCHING TO RIDING YOUR BIKE TO SCHOOL, I WOULD HOPE YOU'D TELL ME BEFORE-HAND—
?
WHERE'S YOUR UNIFORM?

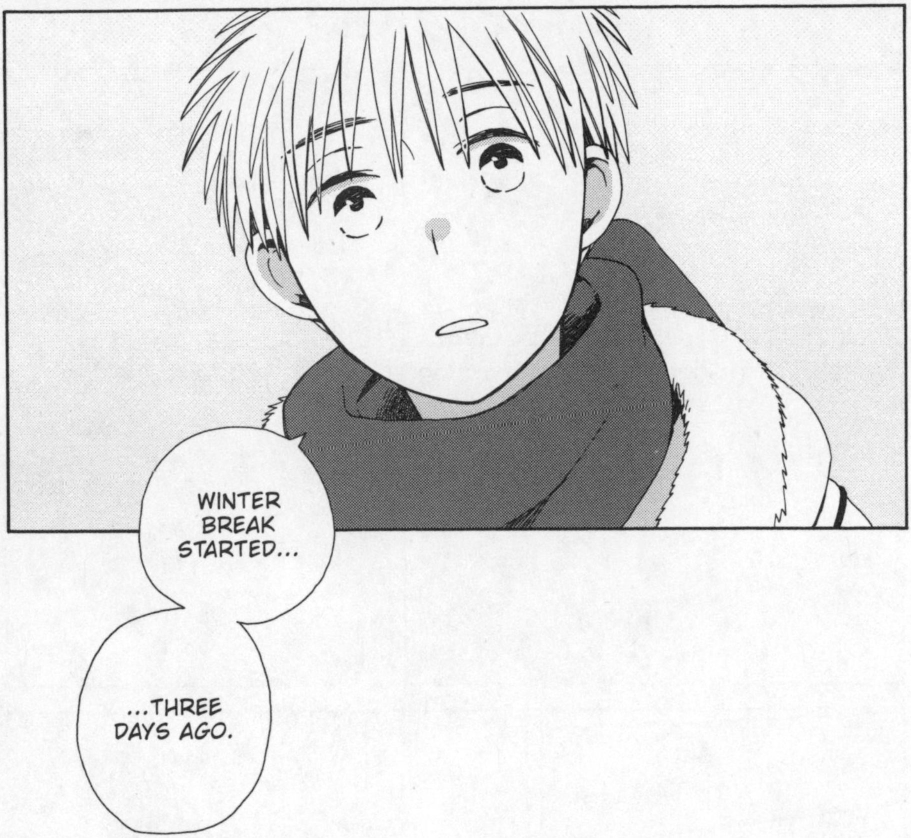
WINTER BREAK STARTED...
...THREE DAYS AGO.

Love at Fourteen

[Intermission 62]

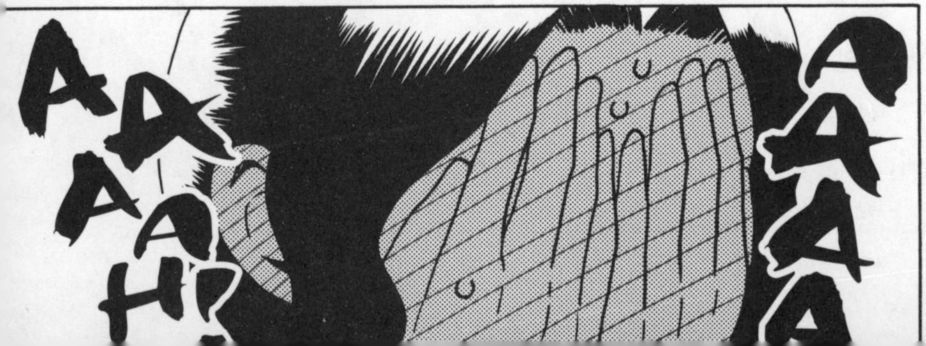
AAAA
AAAAH!?

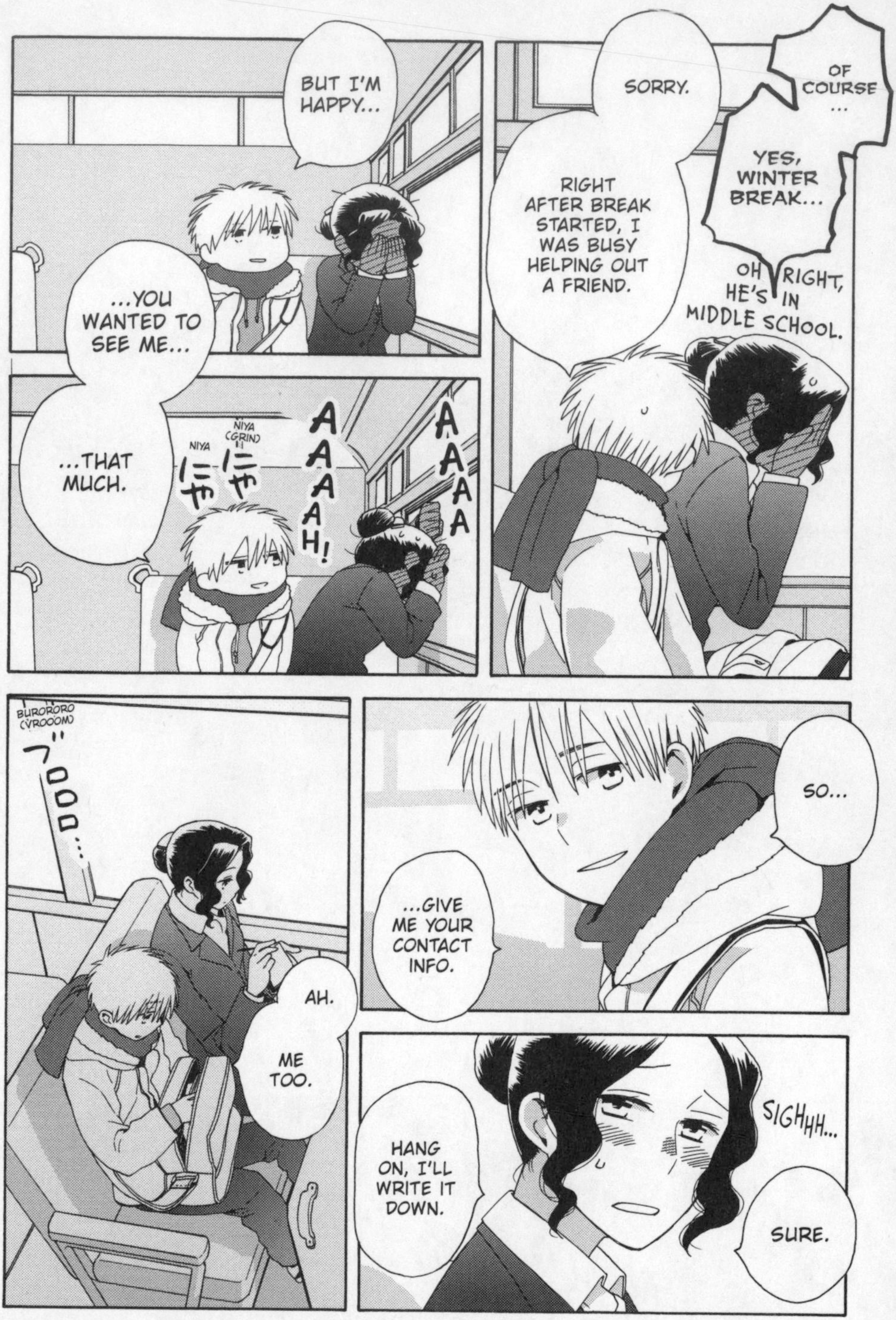
OF COURSE...
YES, WINTER BREAK...
SORRY.
RIGHT AFTER BREAK STARTED, I WAS BUSY HELPING OUT A FRIEND.
OH RIGHT, HE'S IN MIDDLE SCHOOL.
BUT I'M HAPPY...
...YOU WANTED TO SEE ME...
...THAT MUCH.
AAAAAH!
AAAAA
NIYA (GRIND)
にや
NIYA
にや
SO...
...GIVE ME YOUR CONTACT INFO.
SIGHHH...
SURE.
HANG ON, I'LL WRITE IT DOWN.
BURORORO (VROOOM)
ブロロロ...
AH.
ME TOO.

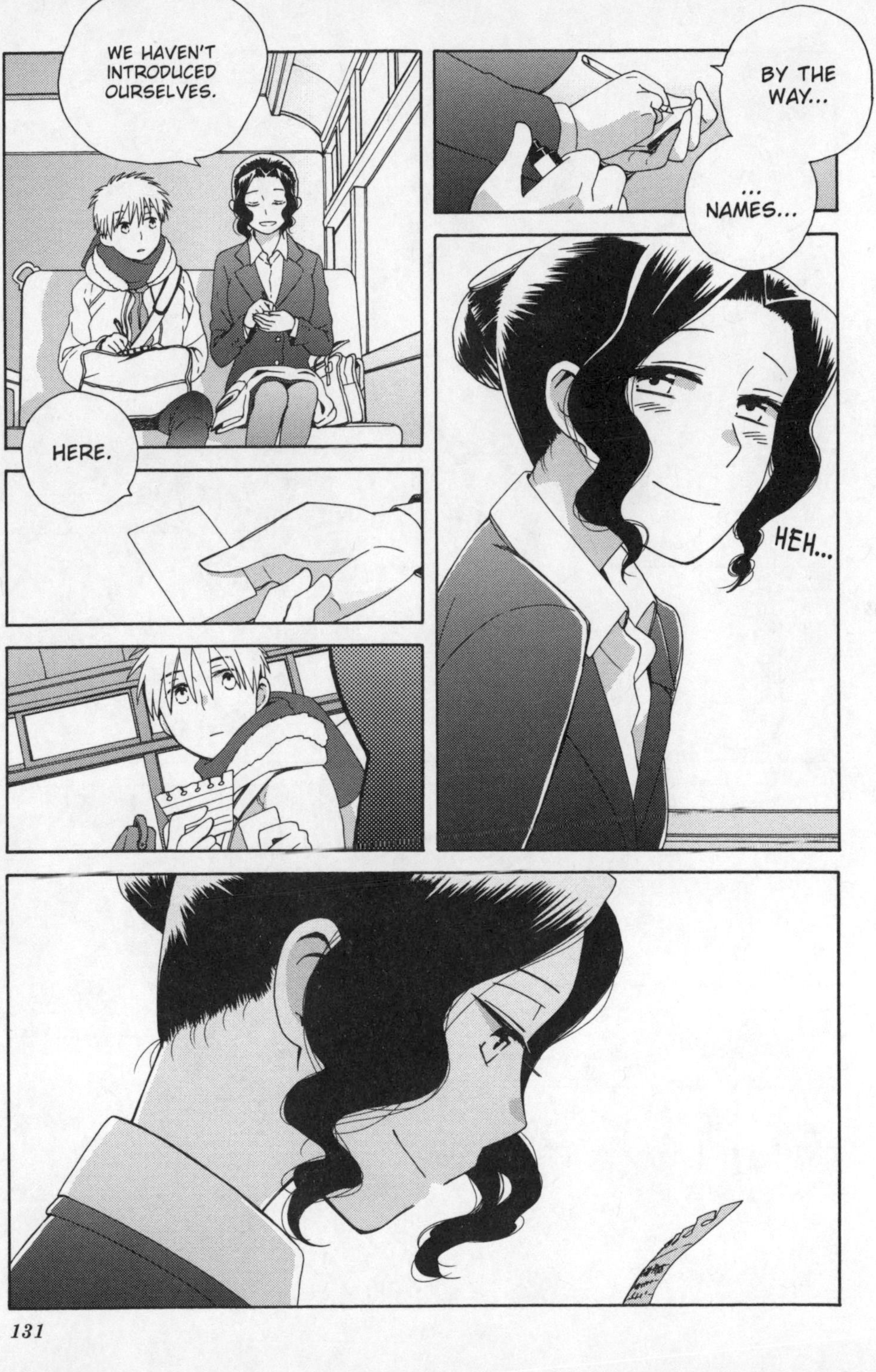
BY THE WAY...
... NAMES...
WE HAVEN'T INTRODUCED OURSELVES.
HERE.
HEH...

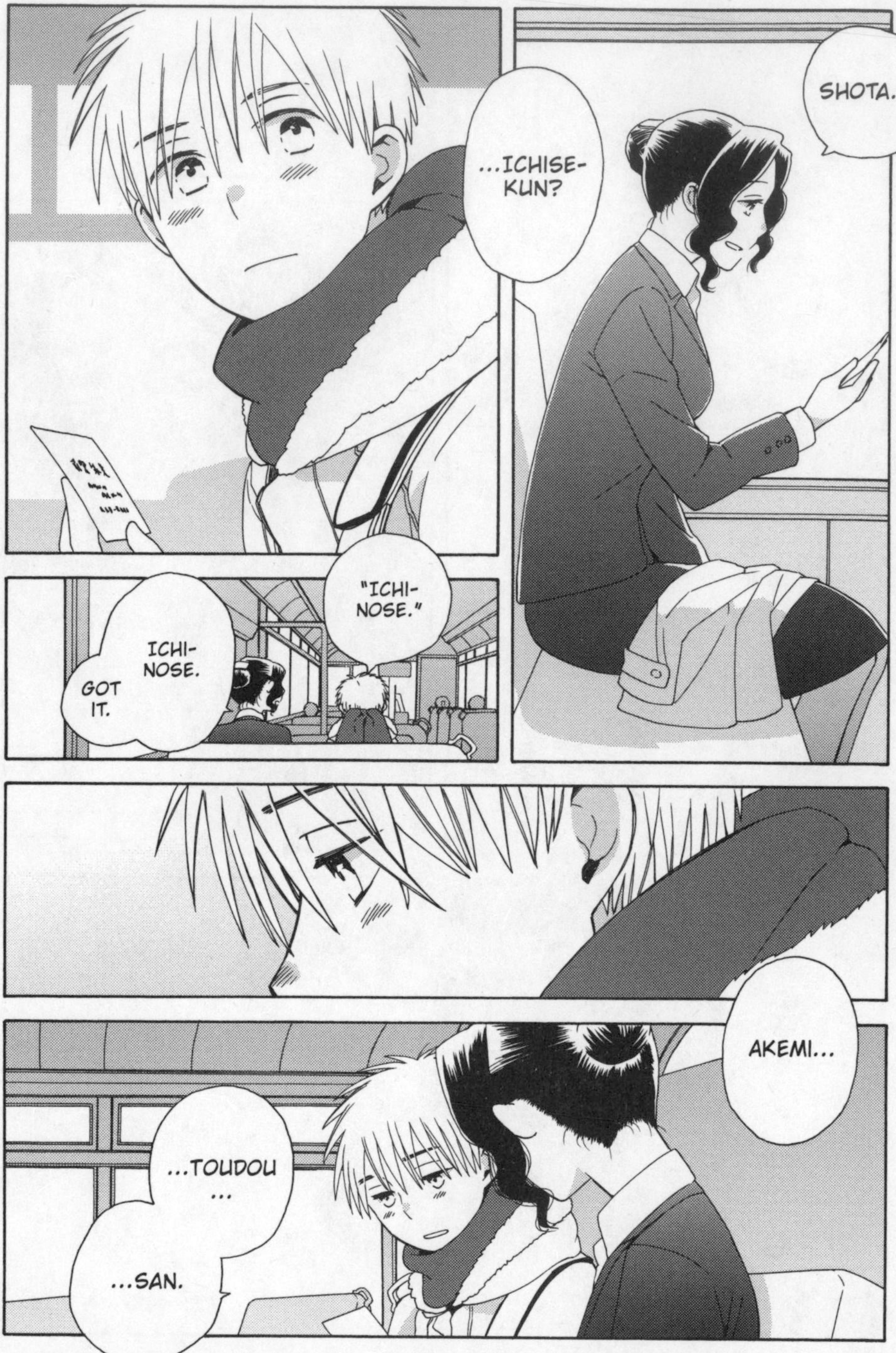
SHOTA...
...ICHISE-KUN?
"ICHI-NOSE."
ICHI-NOSE. GOT IT.
AKEMI...
...TOUDOU...
...SAN.

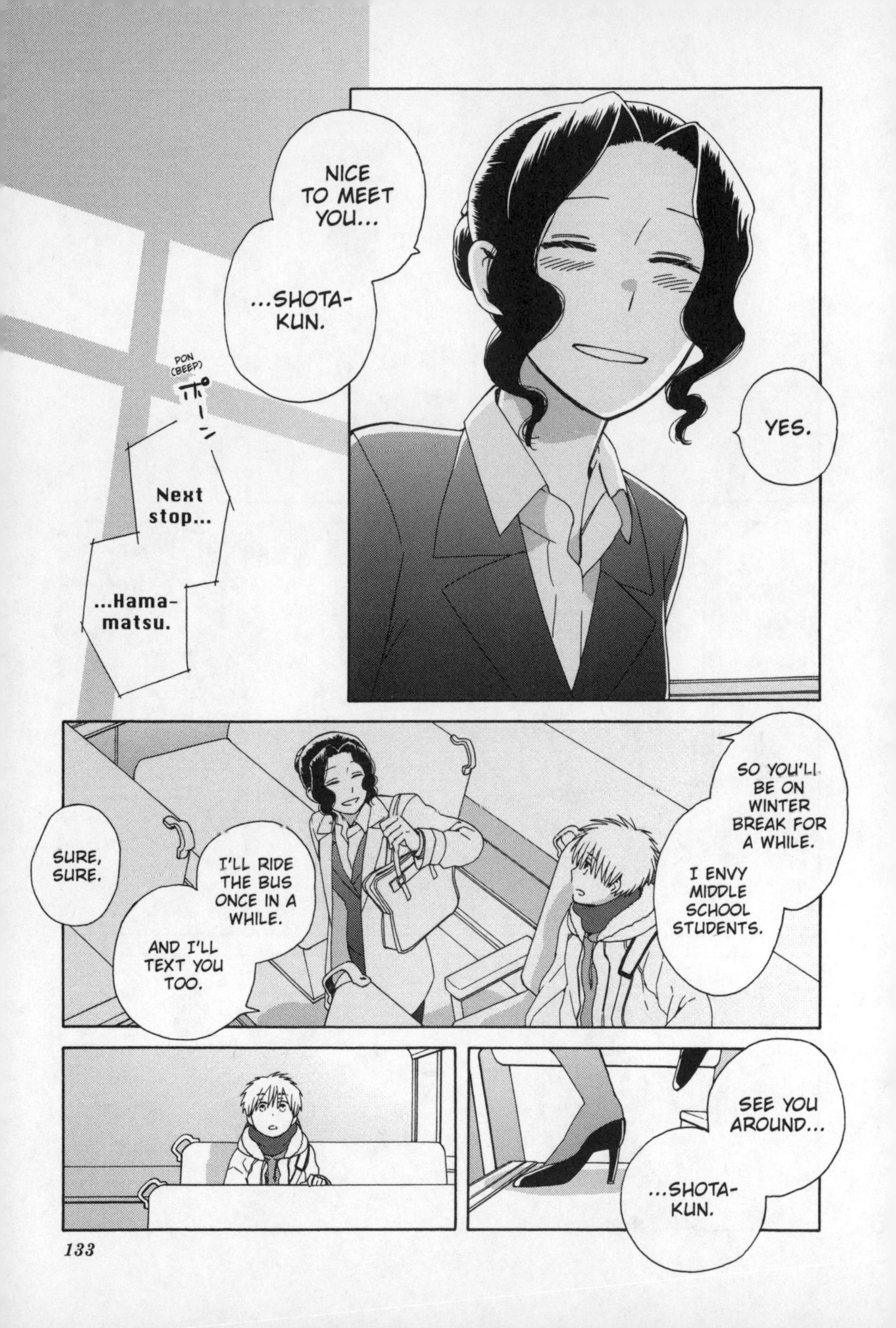
NICE TO MEET YOU...
...SHOTA-KUN.
YES.
PON (BEEP)
ポーン
Next stop...
...Hama-matsu.
SO YOU'LL BE ON WINTER BREAK FOR A WHILE.
I ENVY MIDDLE SCHOOL STUDENTS.
I'LL RIDE THE BUS ONCE IN A WHILE.
AND I'LL TEXT YOU TOO.
SURE, SURE.
SEE YOU AROUND...
...SHOTA-KUN.

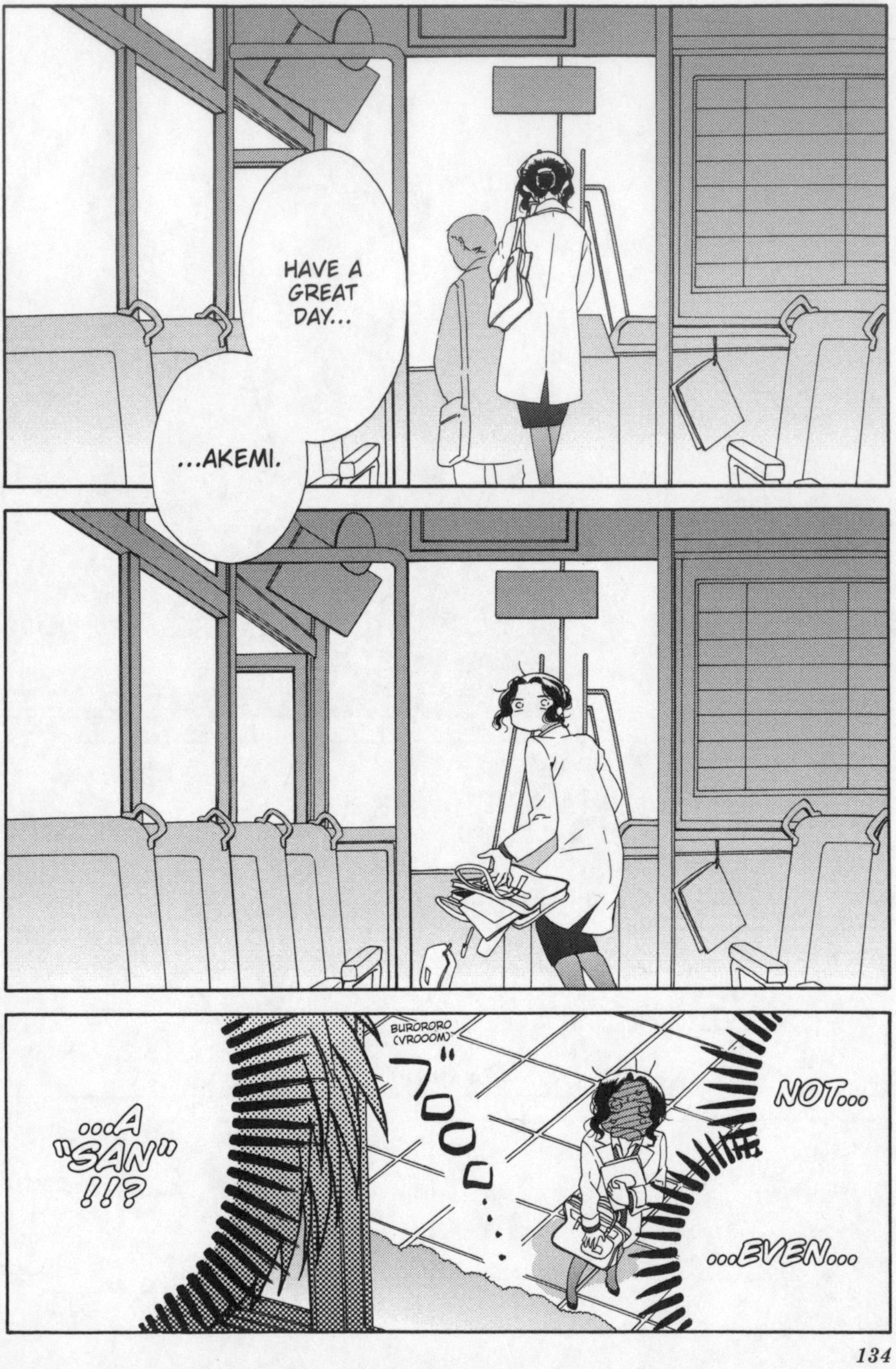
HAVE A GREAT DAY...
...AKEMI.
NOT...
...EVEN...
BURORORO (VROOOM)
...A "SAN" !!?

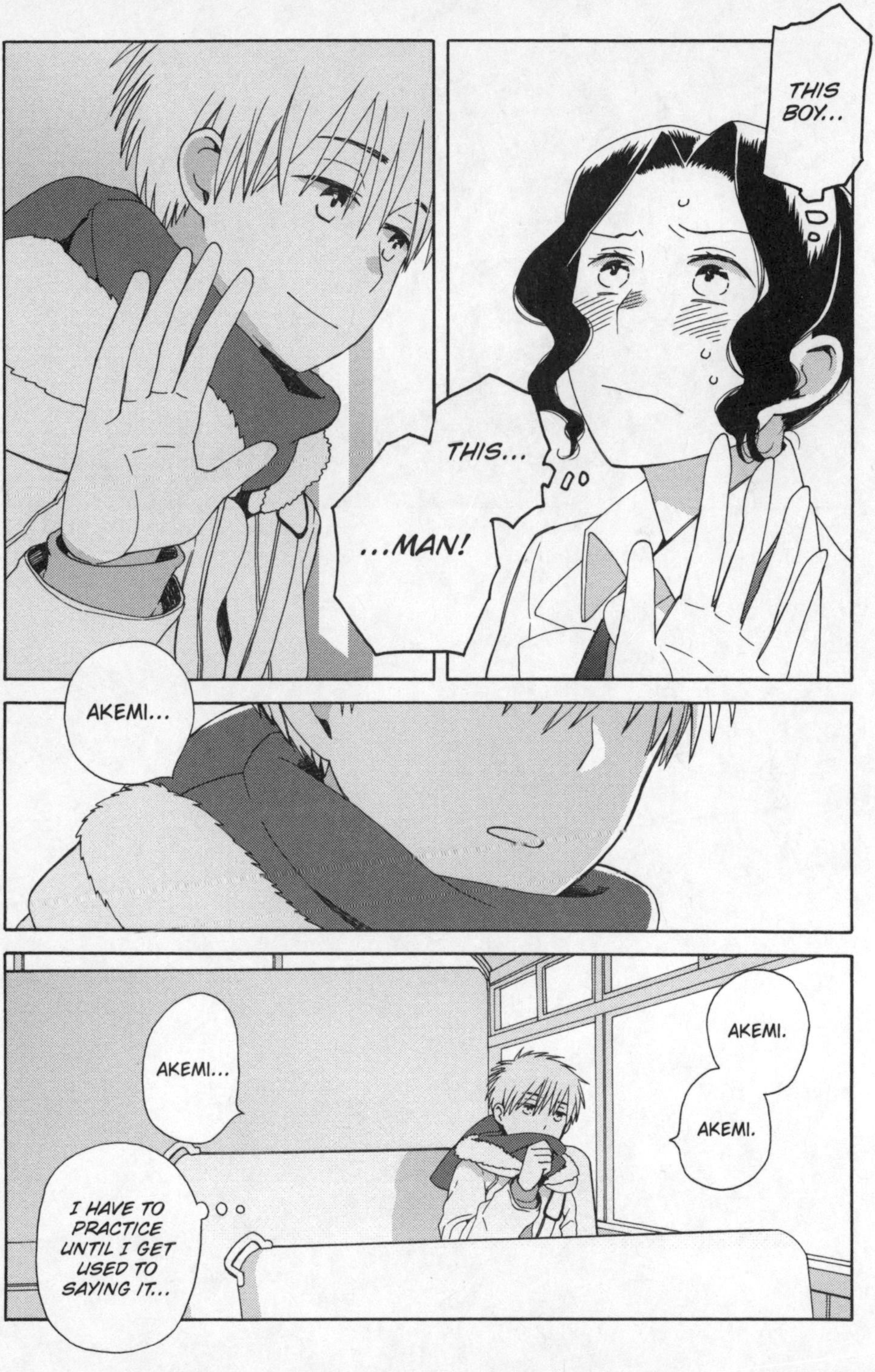
THIS BOY...
THIS...
...MAN!
AKEMI...
AKEMI.
AKEMI.
AKEMI...
I HAVE TO PRACTICE UNTIL I GET USED TO SAYING IT...

AKEMI
...

...HUH?

Fin

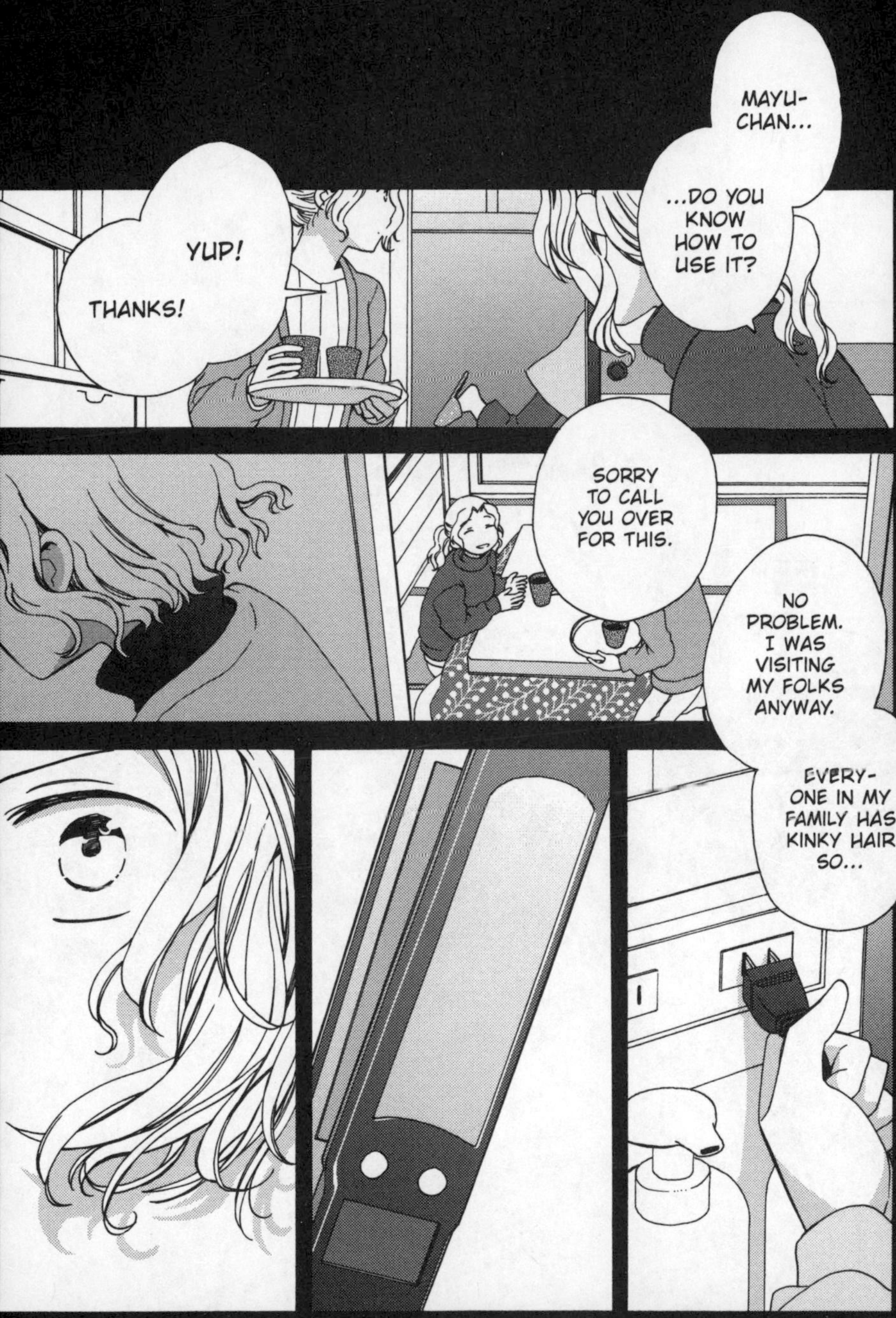
MAYU-CHAN...
...DO YOU KNOW HOW TO USE IT?
YUP!
THANKS!
SORRY TO CALL YOU OVER FOR THIS.
NO PROBLEM. I WAS VISITING MY FOLKS ANYWAY.
EVERY-ONE IN MY FAMILY HAS KINKY HAIR SO...

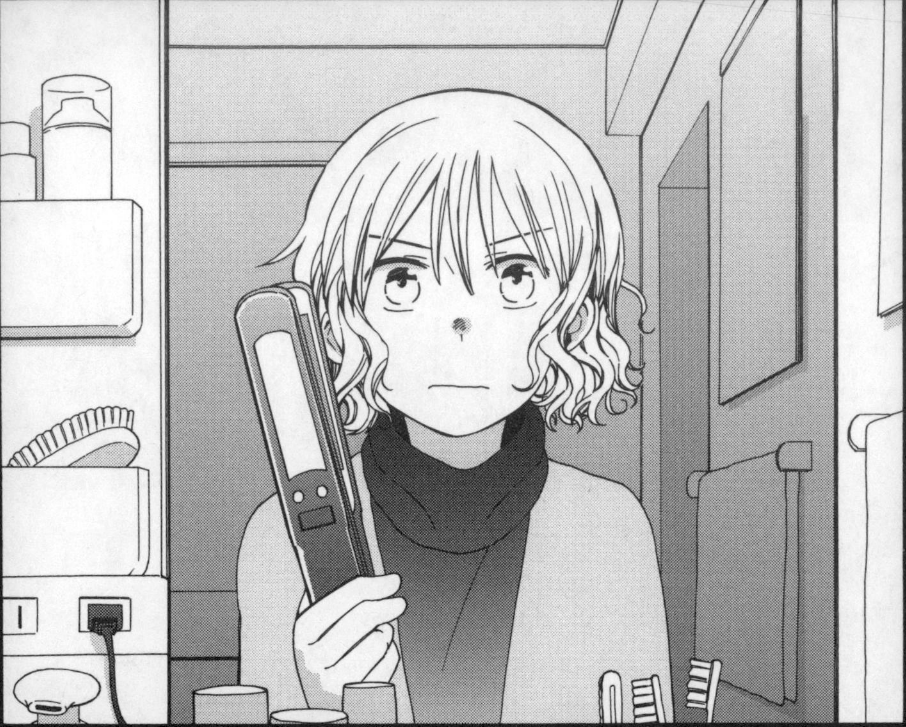

Love at Fourteen

[Intermission 63]

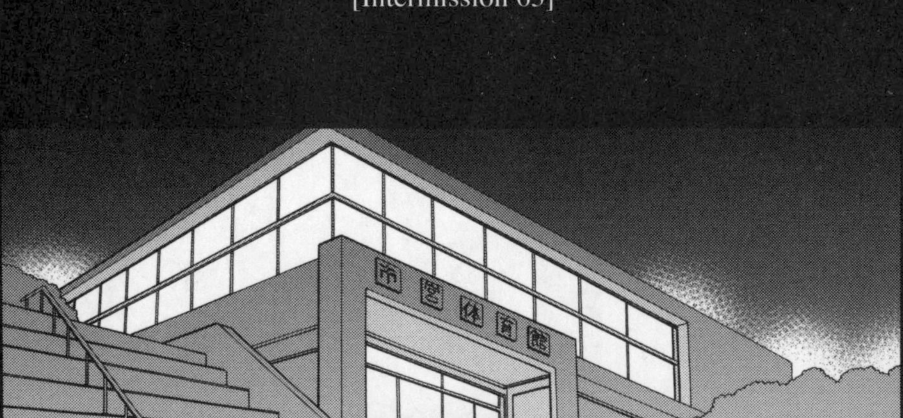
市営体育館

BUILDING: MUNICIPAL GYM

SIGN: STUDENT SPORTS, WEDNESDAY, FOR MIDDLE SCHOOL STUDENTS, BASKETBALL, SPECTATORS WELCOME

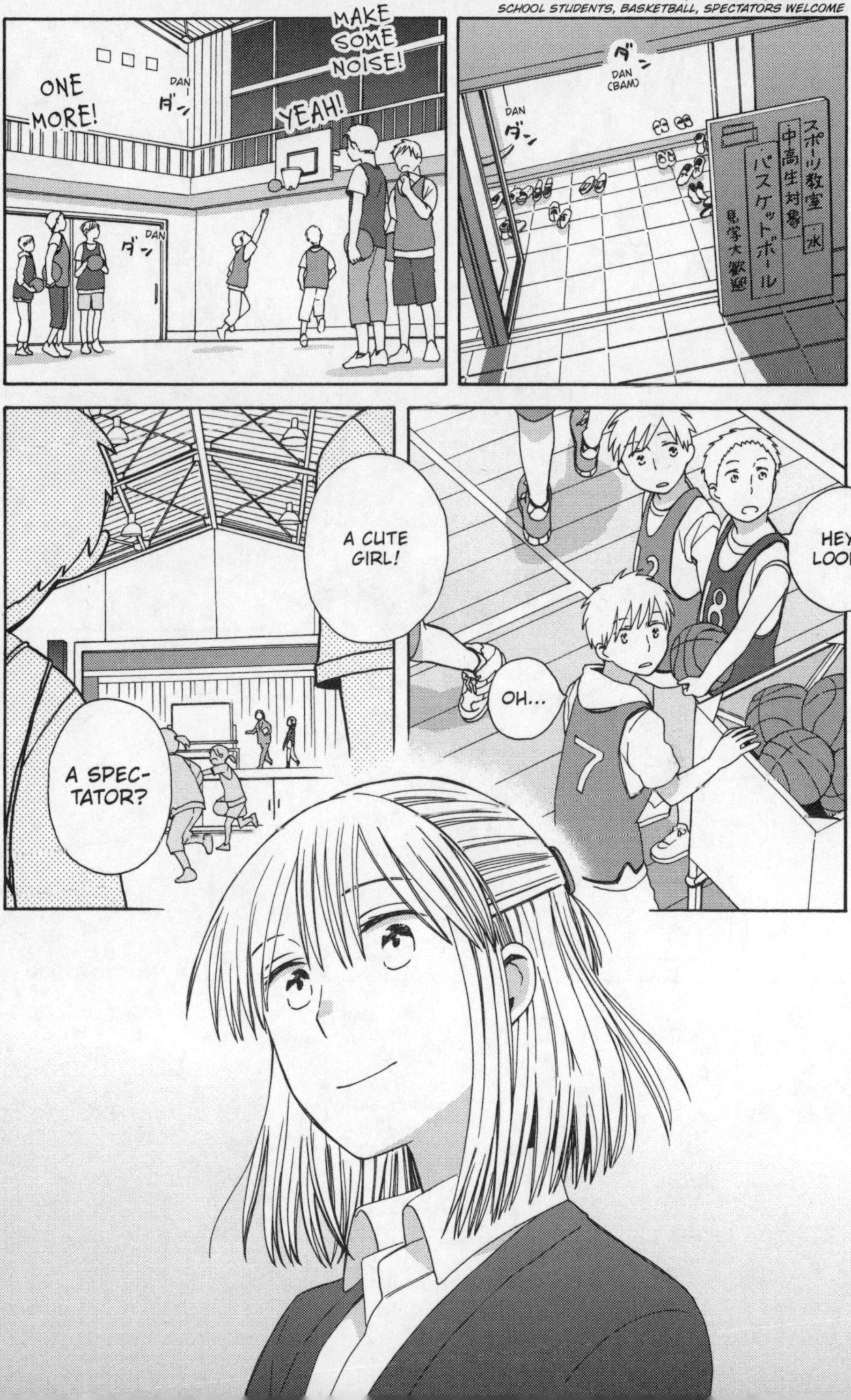

ダン
DAN (BAM)
DAN
ダン
スポーツ教室 水
中高生対象
バスケットボール
見学大歓迎
MAKE SOME NOISE!
YEAH!
DAN
ダン
ONE MORE!
DAN
ダン
HEY, LOOK.
OH...
A CUTE GIRL!
A SPECTATOR?

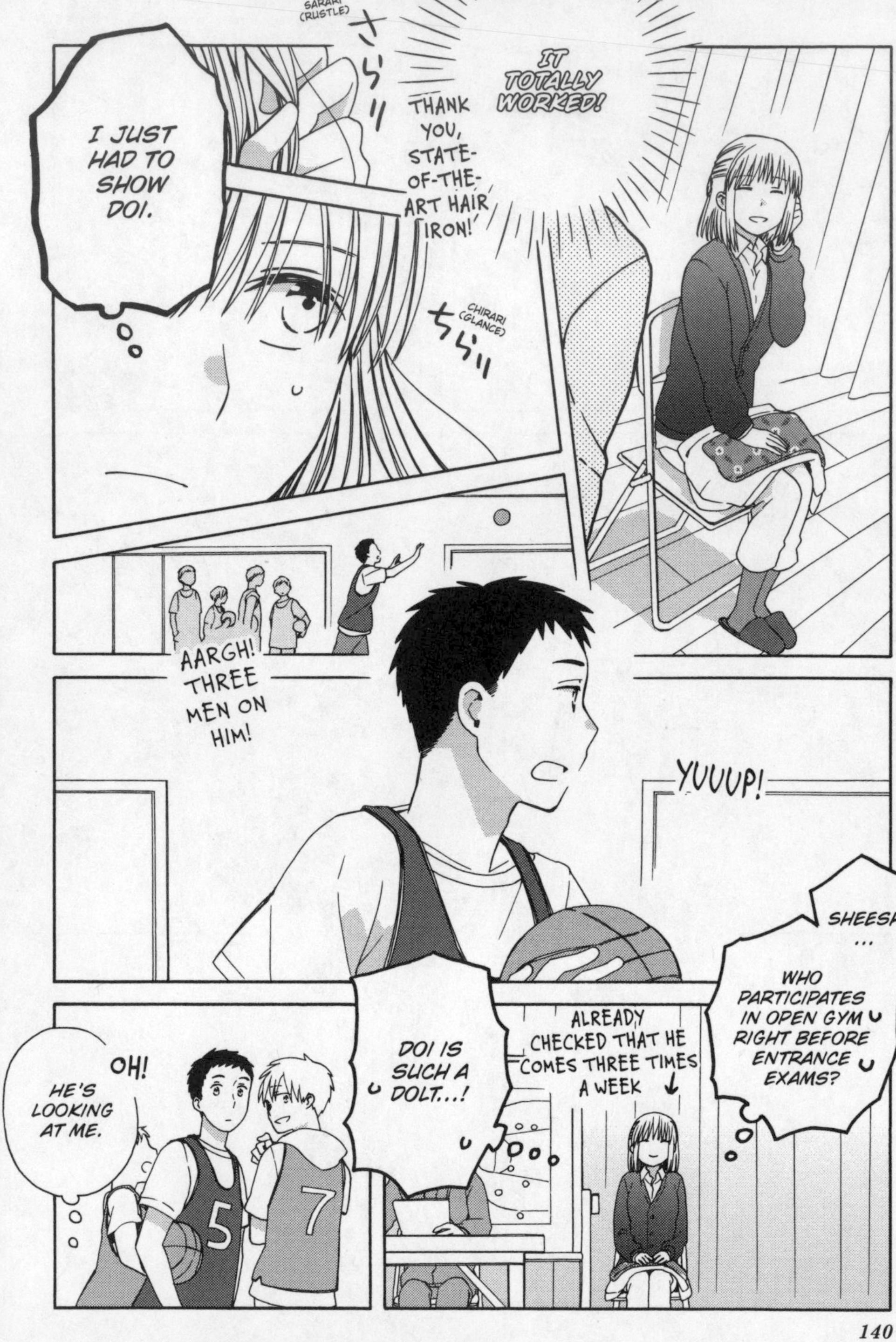

IT TOTALLY WORKED!
THANK YOU, STATE-OF-THE-ART HAIR IRON!
SARARI (RUSTLE)
I JUST HAD TO SHOW DOI.
CHIRARI (GLANCE)
AARGH! THREE MEN ON HIM!
YUUUP!
SHEESH... WHO PARTICIPATES IN OPEN GYM RIGHT BEFORE ENTRANCE EXAMS?
ALREADY CHECKED THAT HE COMES THREE TIMES A WEEK
DOI IS SUCH A DOLT...!
OH!
HE'S LOOKING AT ME.

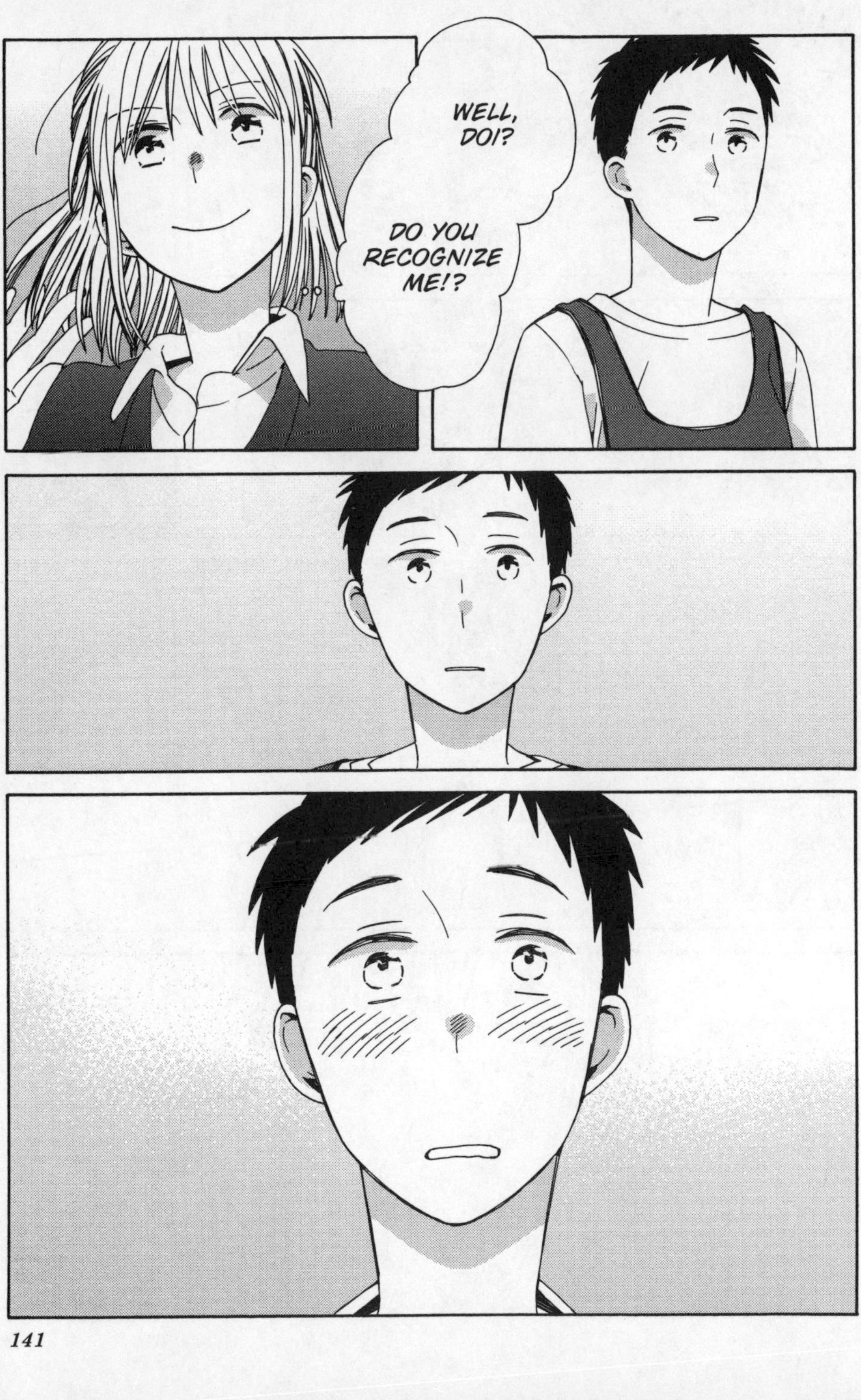
WELL, DOI?
DO YOU RECOGNIZE ME!?

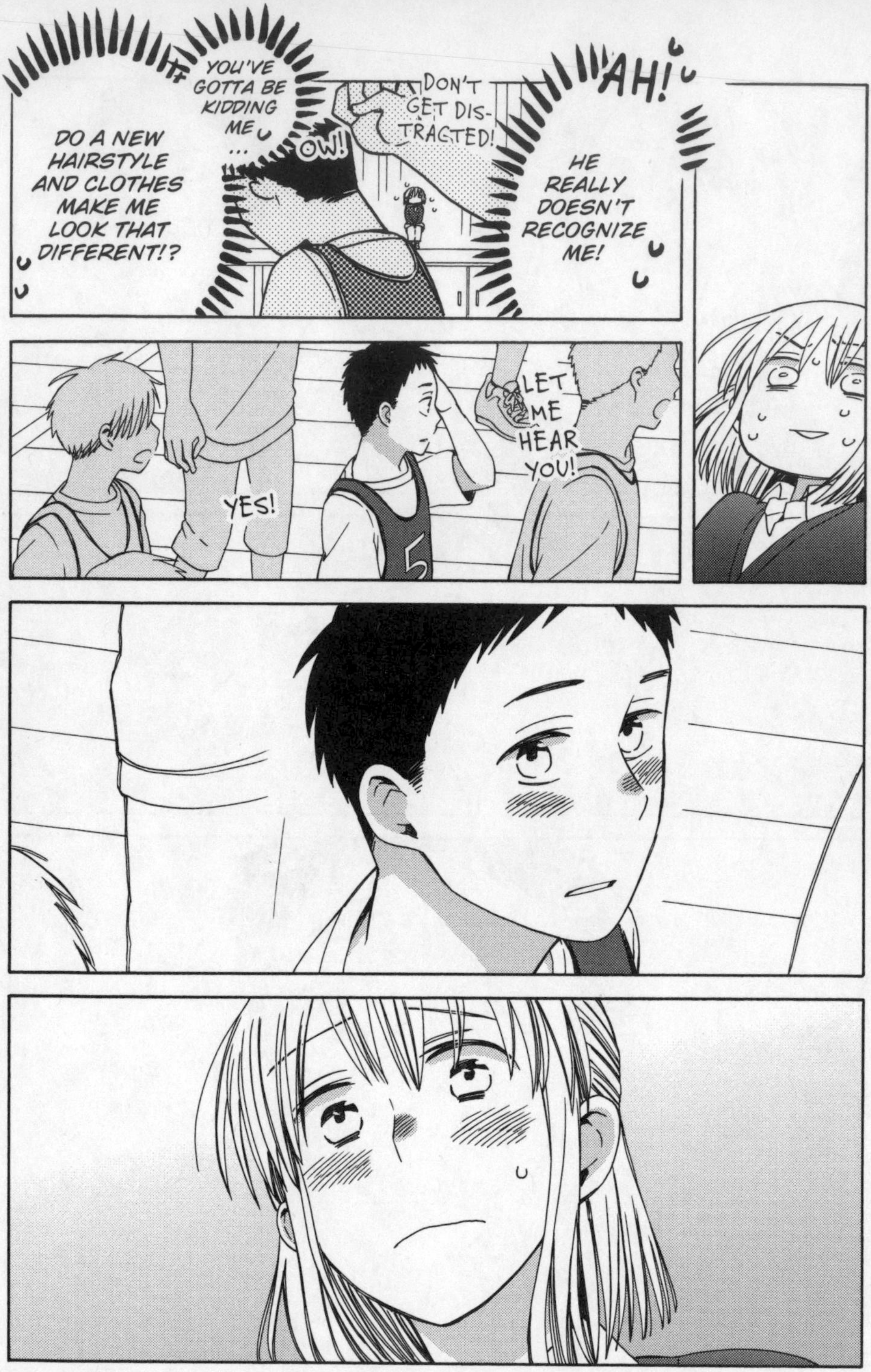
AH!
HE REALLY DOESN'T RECOGNIZE ME!
DON'T GET DIS-TRACTED!
OW!
YOU'VE GOTTA BE KIDDING ME ...
DO A NEW HAIRSTYLE AND CLOTHES MAKE ME LOOK THAT DIFFERENT!?
LET ME HEAR YOU!
YES!

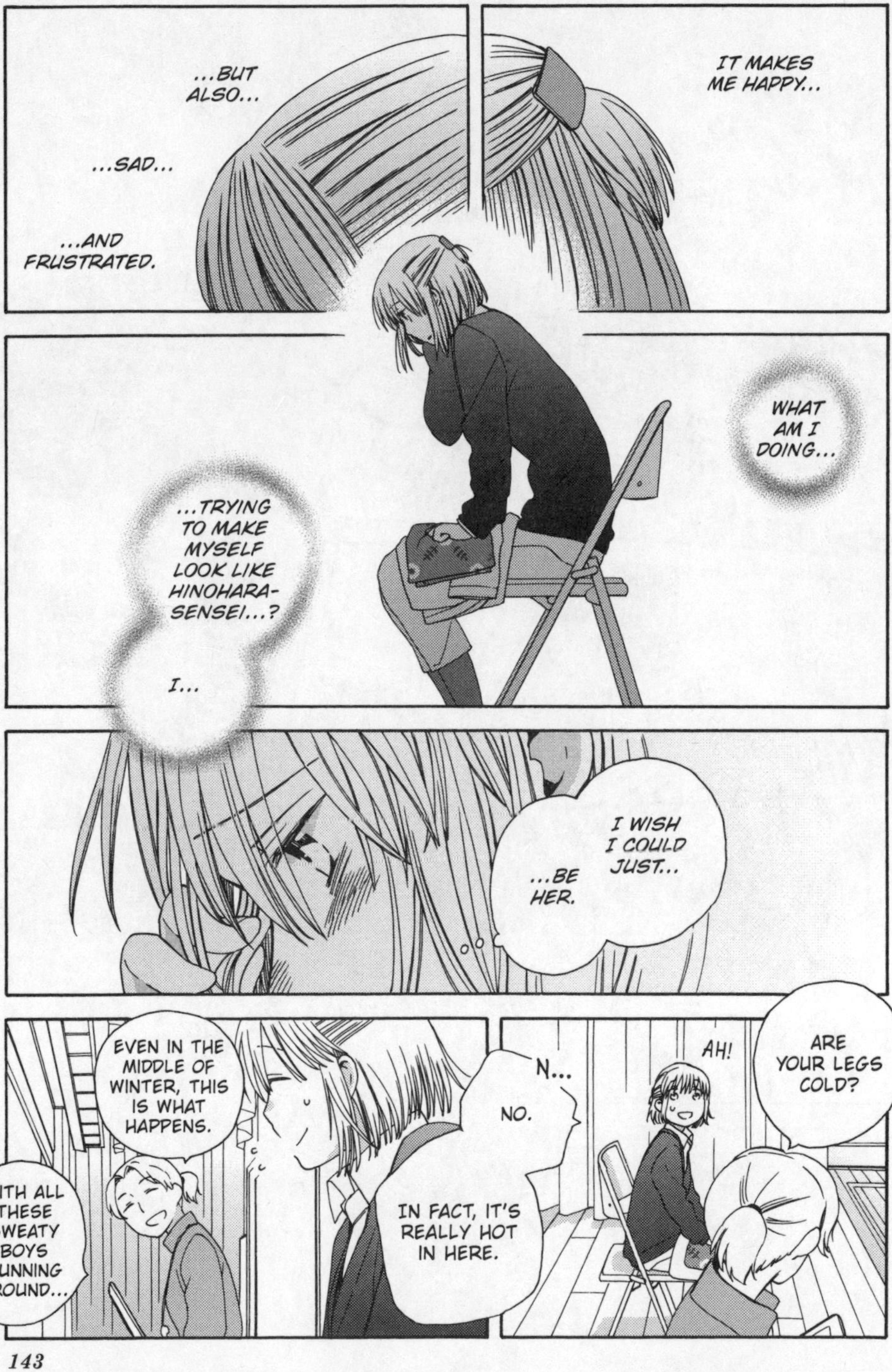
IT MAKES ME HAPPY...
...BUT ALSO...
...SAD...
...AND FRUSTRATED.
WHAT AM I DOING...
...TRYING TO MAKE MYSELF LOOK LIKE HINOHARA-SENSEI...?
I...
I WISH I COULD JUST...
...BE HER.
ARE YOUR LEGS COLD?
AH!
N...
NO.
IN FACT, IT'S REALLY HOT IN HERE.
EVEN IN THE MIDDLE OF WINTER, THIS IS WHAT HAPPENS.
WITH ALL THESE SWEATY BOYS RUNNING AROUND...

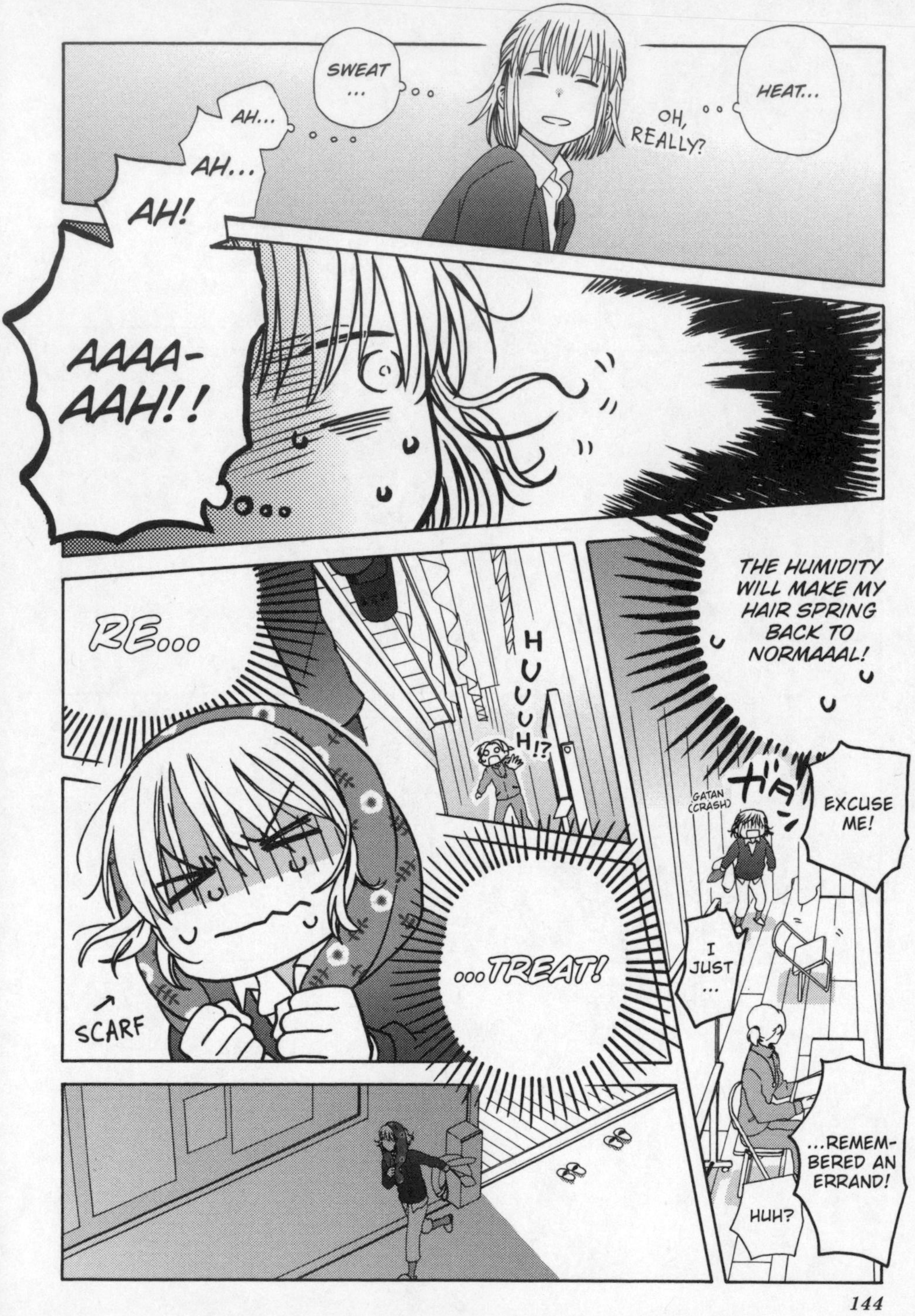
HEAT...
OH, REALLY?
SWEAT ...
AH...
AH...
AH!
AAAA-AAH!!
THE HUMIDITY WILL MAKE MY HAIR SPRING BACK TO NORMAAAL!
RE...
HUUUUH!?
...TREAT!
SCARF
GATAN (CRASH)
EXCUSE ME!
I JUST ...
...REMEMBERED AN ERRAND!
HUH?

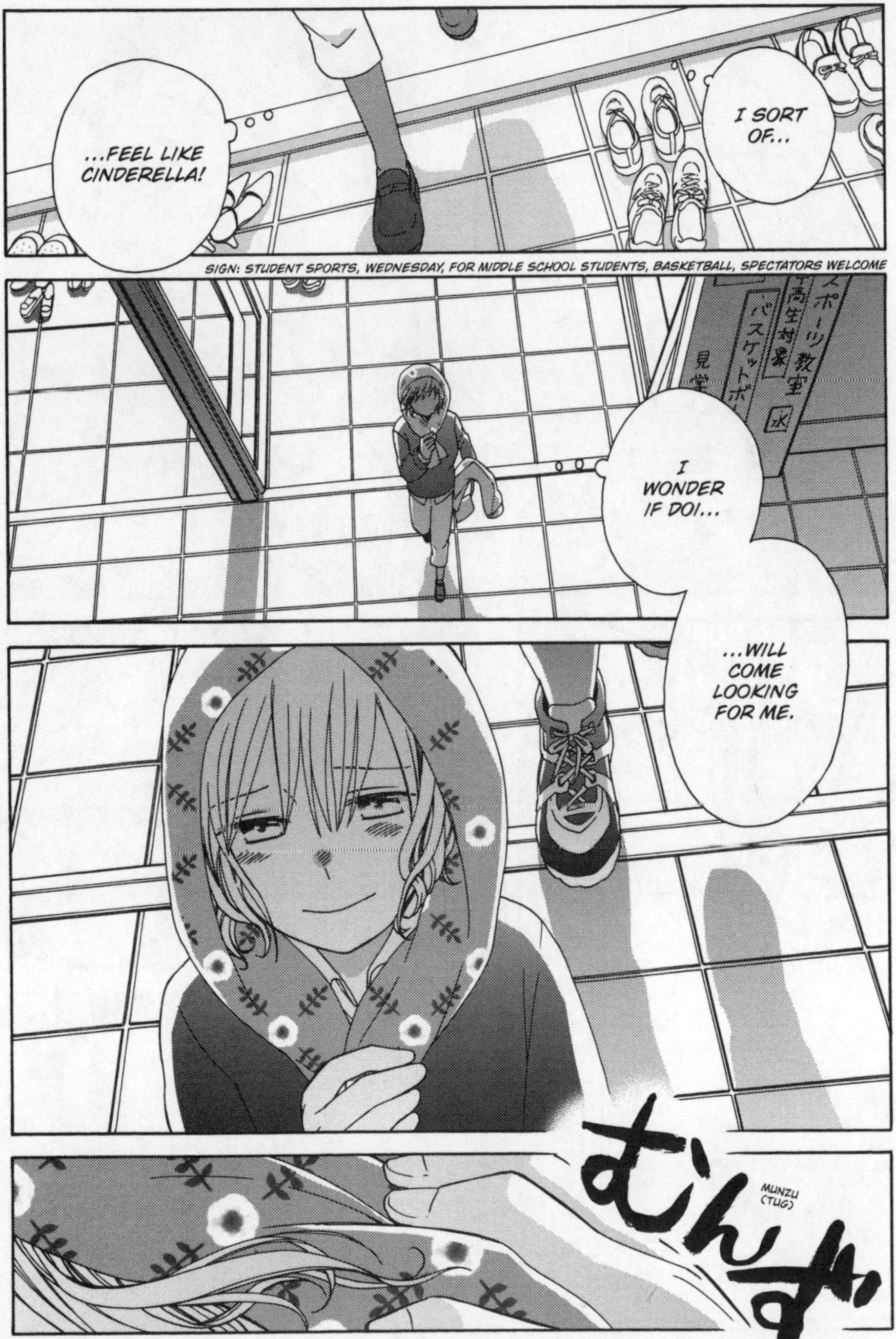
I SORT OF...
...FEEL LIKE CINDERELLA!
SIGN: STUDENT SPORTS, WEDNESDAY, FOR MIDDLE SCHOOL STUDENTS, BASKETBALL, SPECTATORS WELCOME
I WONDER IF DOI...
...WILL COME LOOKING FOR ME.
むんず
MUNZU (TUG)

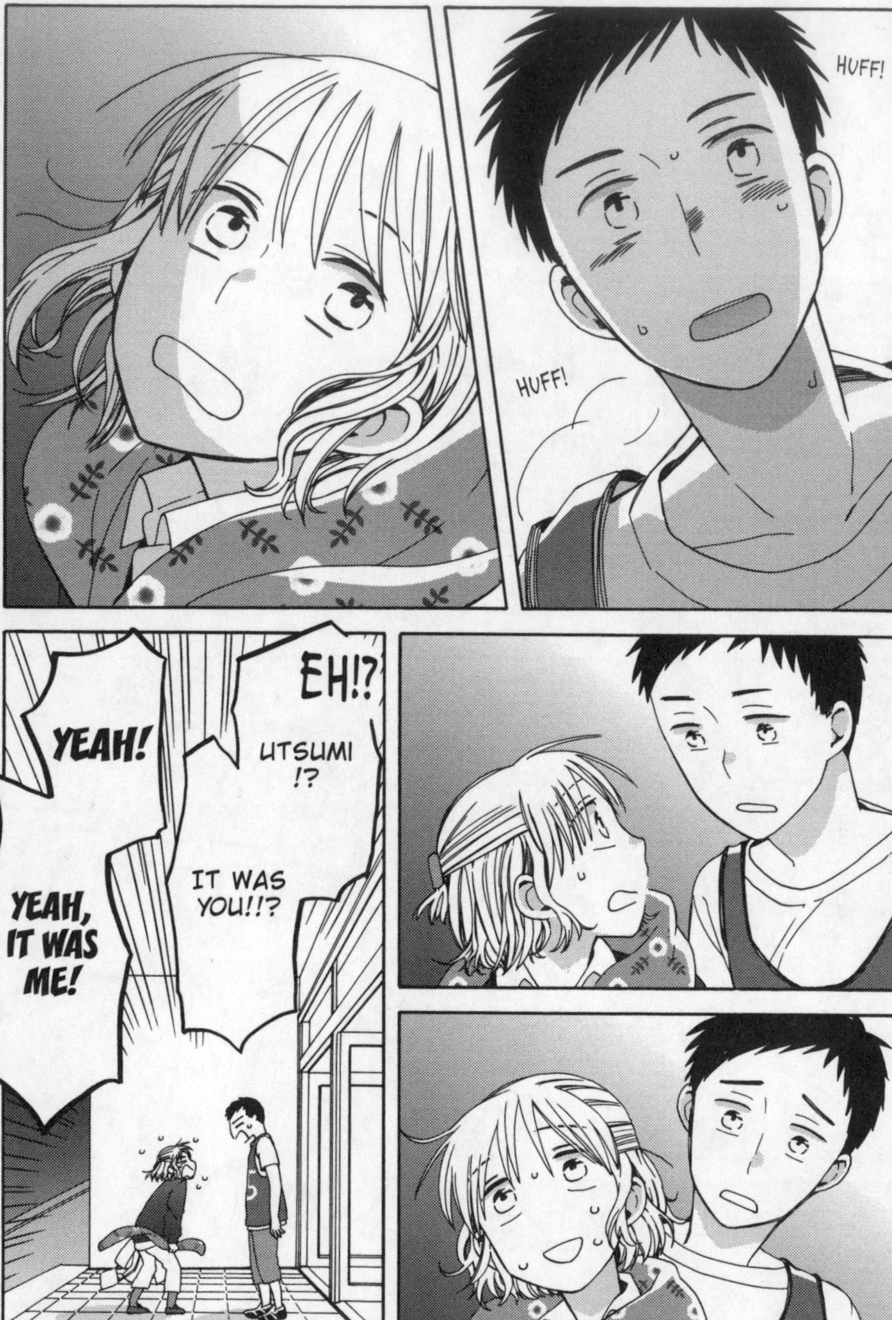
HUFF!
HUFF!
EH!?
UTSUMI !? IT WAS YOU!!?
YEAH! YEAH, IT WAS ME!

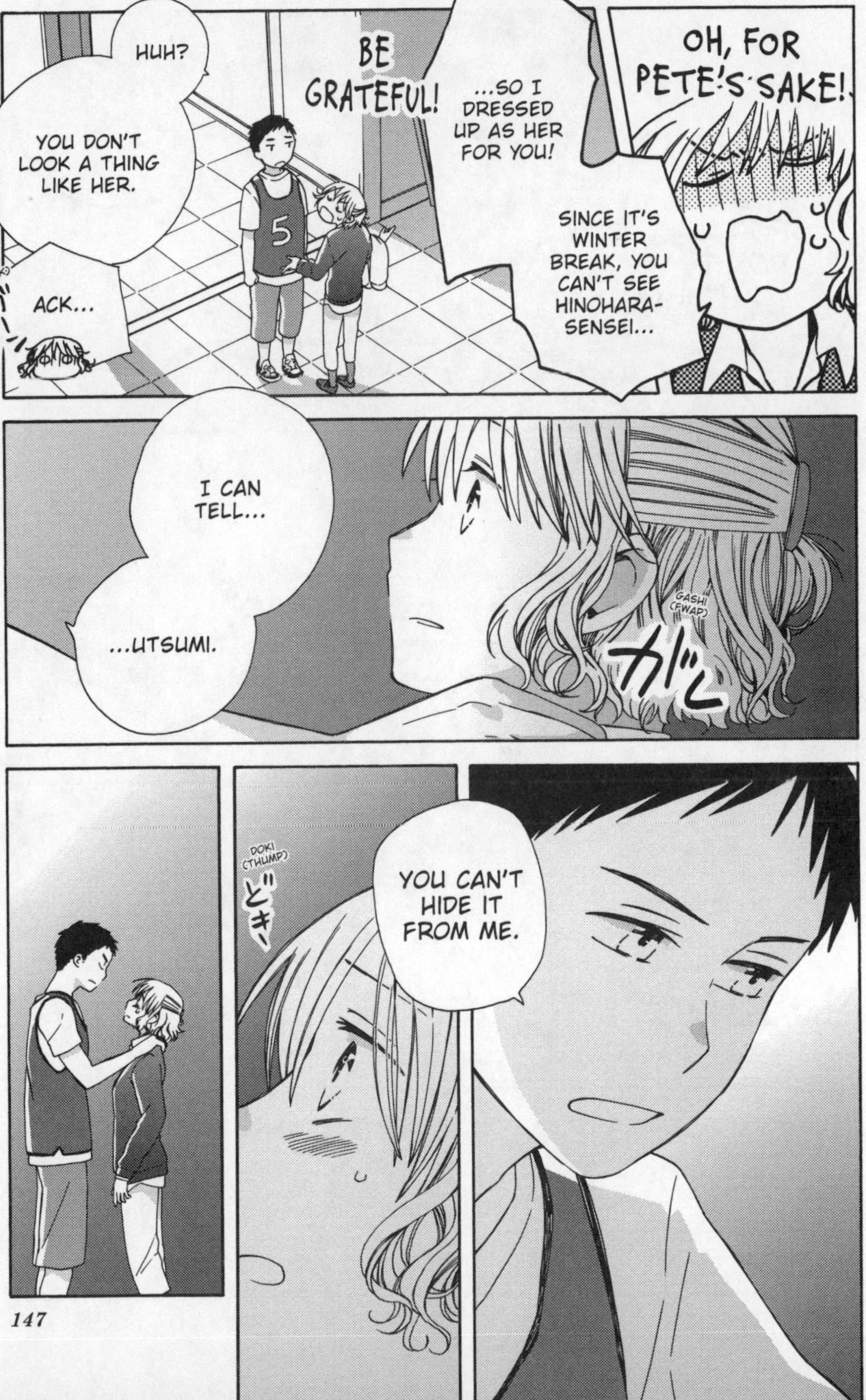
OH, FOR PETE'S SAKE!
SINCE IT'S WINTER BREAK, YOU CAN'T SEE HINOHARA-SENSEI...
...SO I DRESSED UP AS HER FOR YOU!
BE GRATEFUL!
HUH?
YOU DON'T LOOK A THING LIKE HER.
GAN (SHOCK)
ACK...
GASHI (FWAP)
I CAN TELL...
...UTSUMI.
YOU CAN'T HIDE IT FROM ME.
DOKI (THUMP)

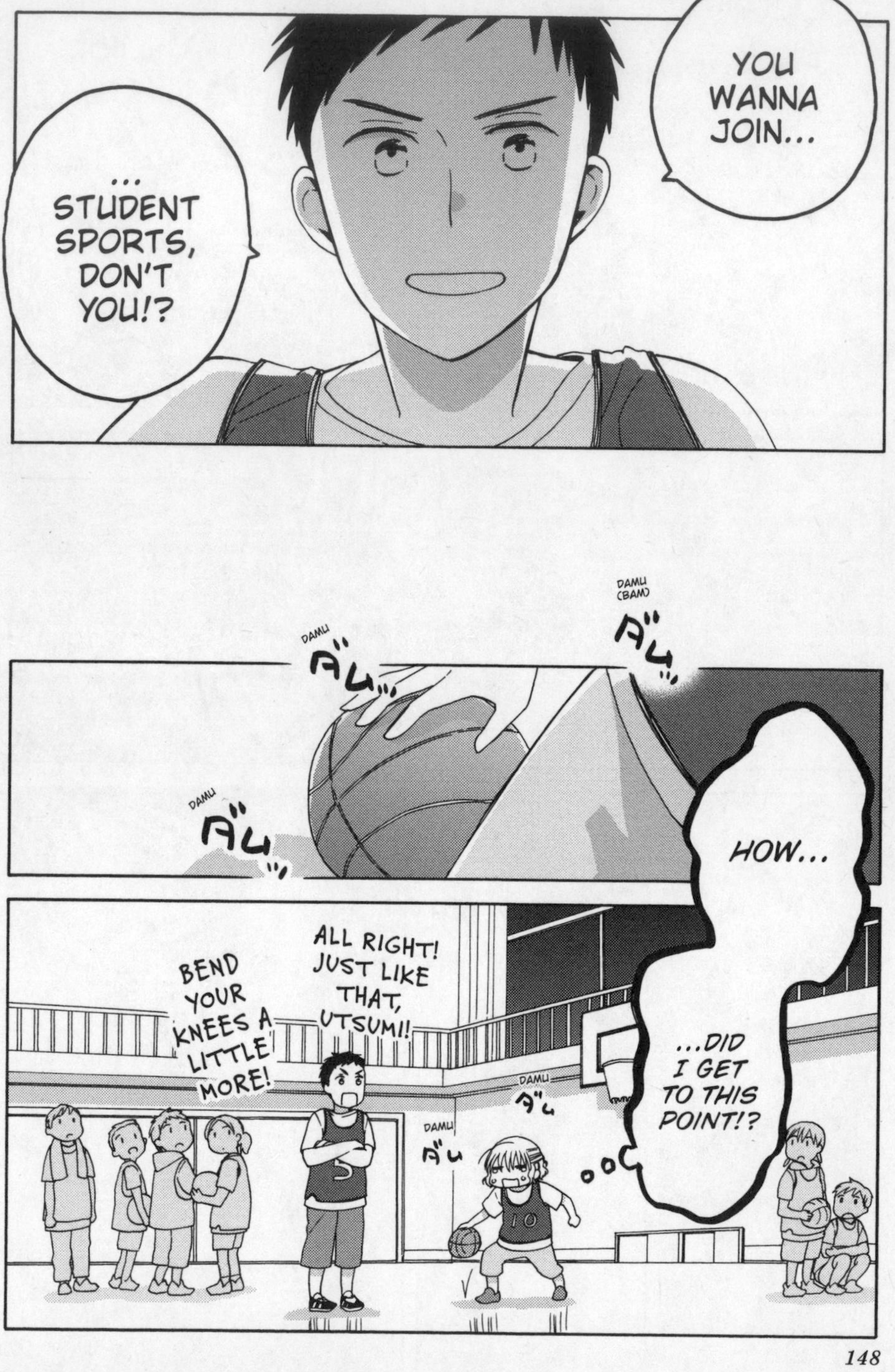
YOU WANNA JOIN...
...STUDENT SPORTS, DON'T YOU!?
DAMU (BAM)
ダム
DAMU
ダム
DAMU
ダム
HOW...
...DID I GET TO THIS POINT!?
ALL RIGHT! JUST LIKE THAT, UTSUMI!
BEND YOUR KNEES A LITTLE MORE!
DAMU
ダム
DAMU
ダム

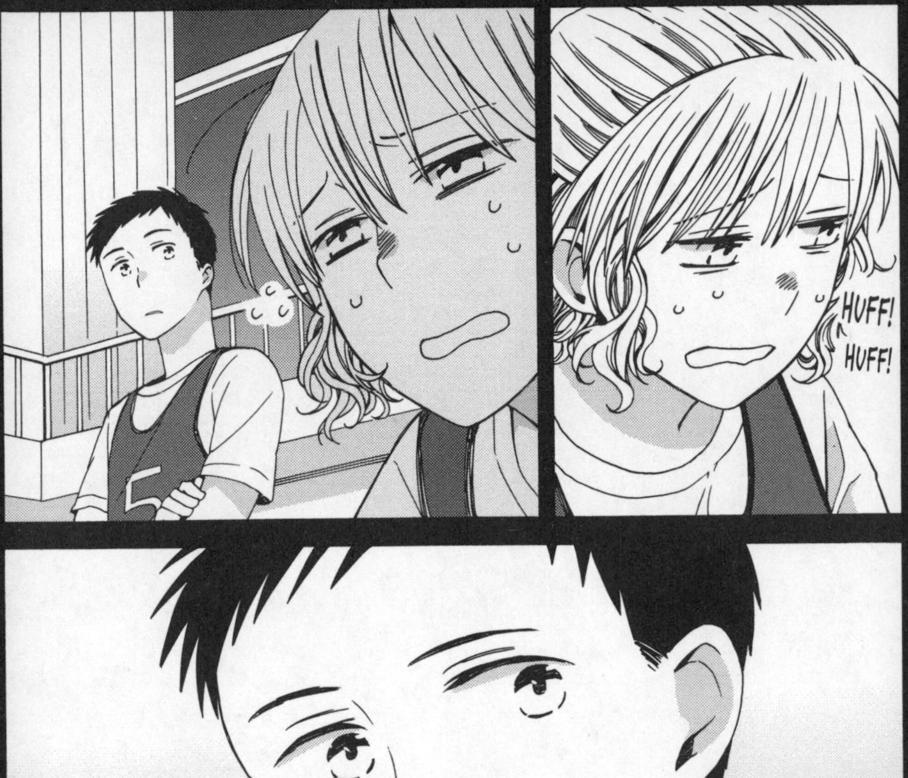
HUFF!
HUFF!

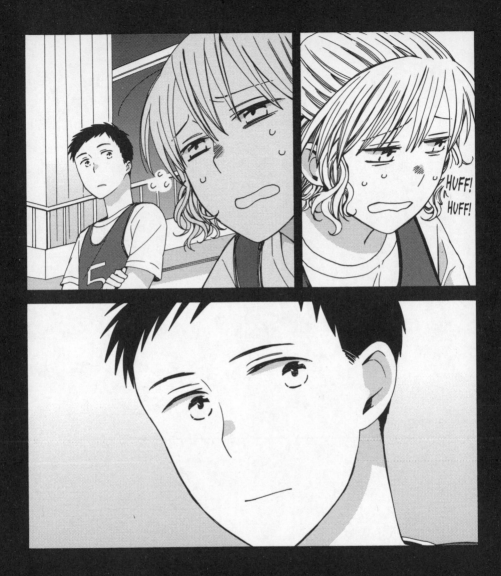

Fin

Love at Fourteen

Fuka Mizutani

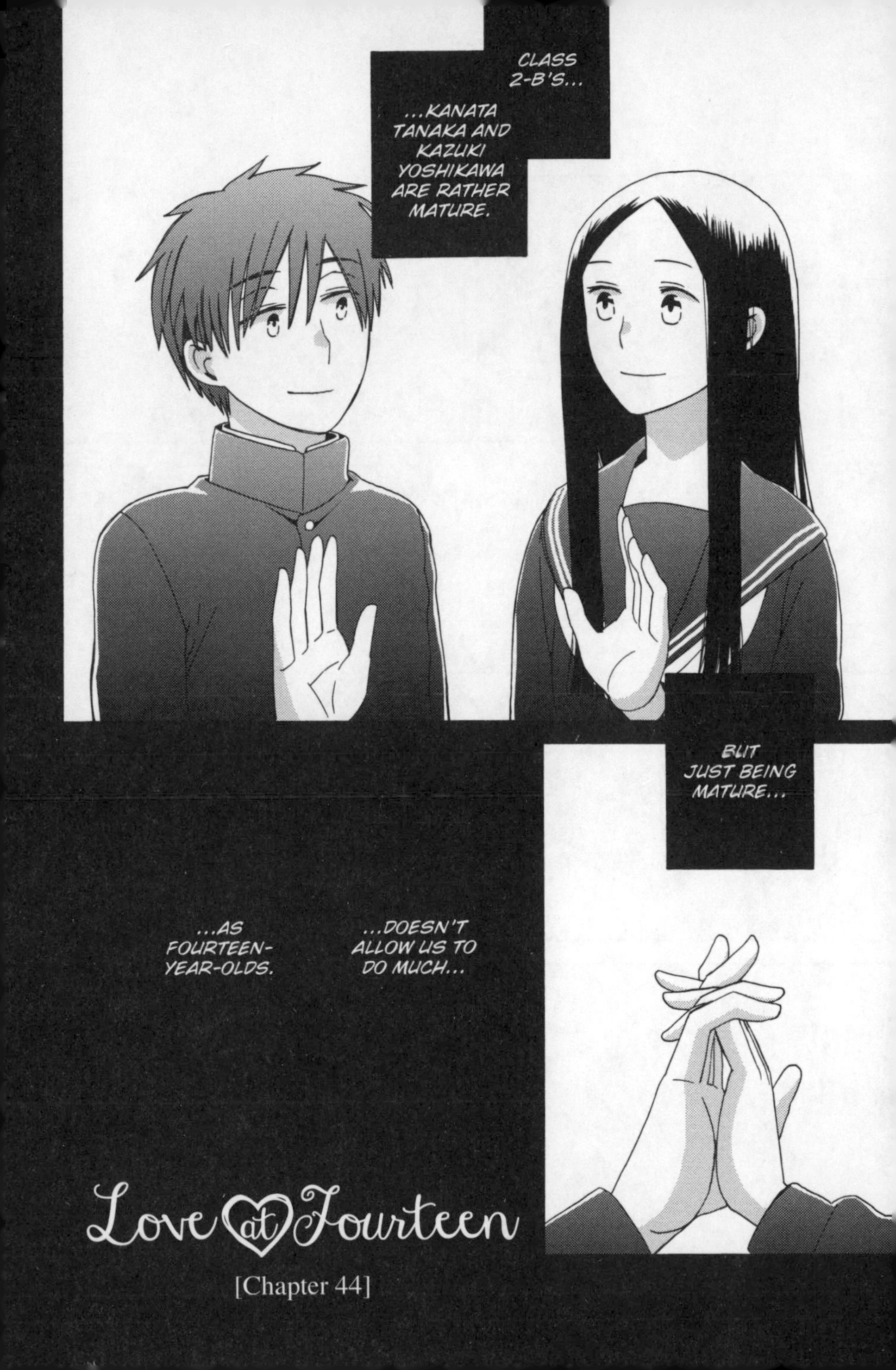
CLASS 2-B'S...
...KANATA TANAKA AND KAZUKI YOSHIKAWA ARE RATHER MATURE.
BUT JUST BEING MATURE...
...DOESN'T ALLOW US TO DO MUCH...
...AS FOURTEEN-YEAR-OLDS.
Love at Fourteen
[Chapter 44]

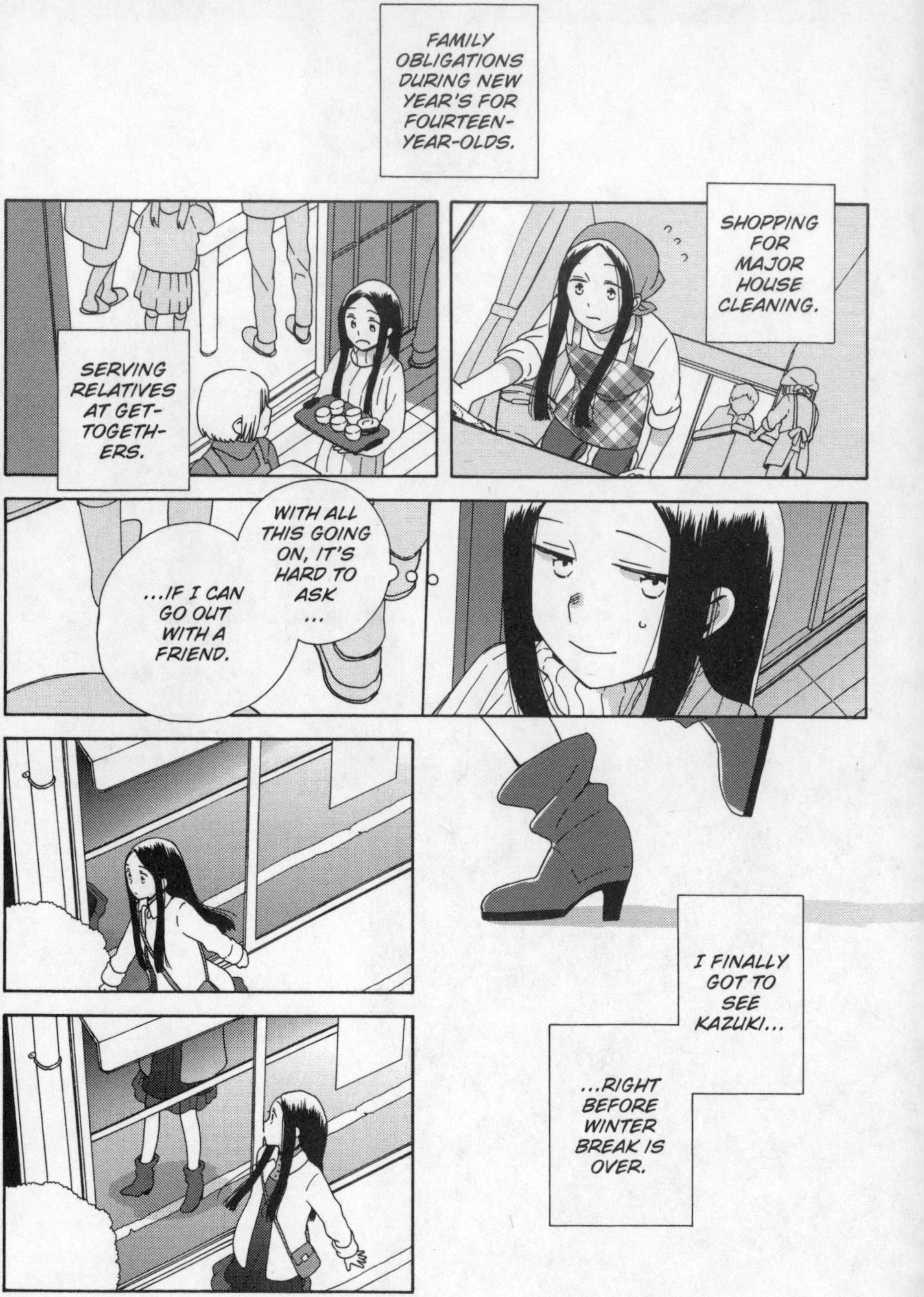
FAMILY OBLIGATIONS DURING NEW YEAR'S FOR FOURTEEN-YEAR-OLDS.
SHOPPING FOR MAJOR HOUSE CLEANING.
SERVING RELATIVES AT GET-TOGETHERS.
WITH ALL THIS GOING ON, IT'S HARD TO ASK ...
...IF I CAN GO OUT WITH A FRIEND.
I FINALLY GOT TO SEE KAZUKI...
...RIGHT BEFORE WINTER BREAK IS OVER.

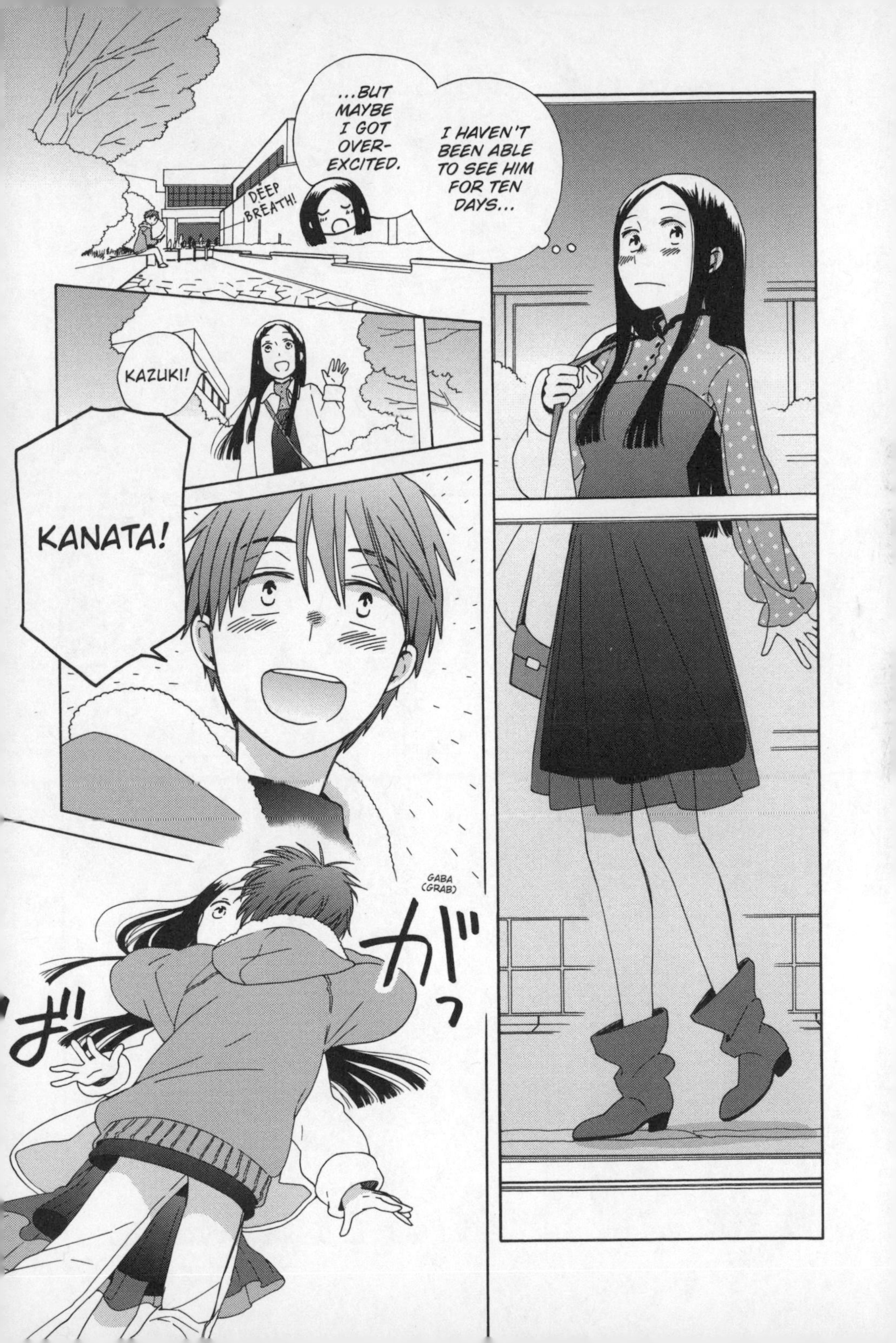
I HAVEN'T BEEN ABLE TO SEE HIM FOR TEN DAYS...
...BUT MAYBE I GOT OVER-EXCITED.
DEEP BREATH!
KAZUKI!
KANATA!
GABA (GRAB)
がっ

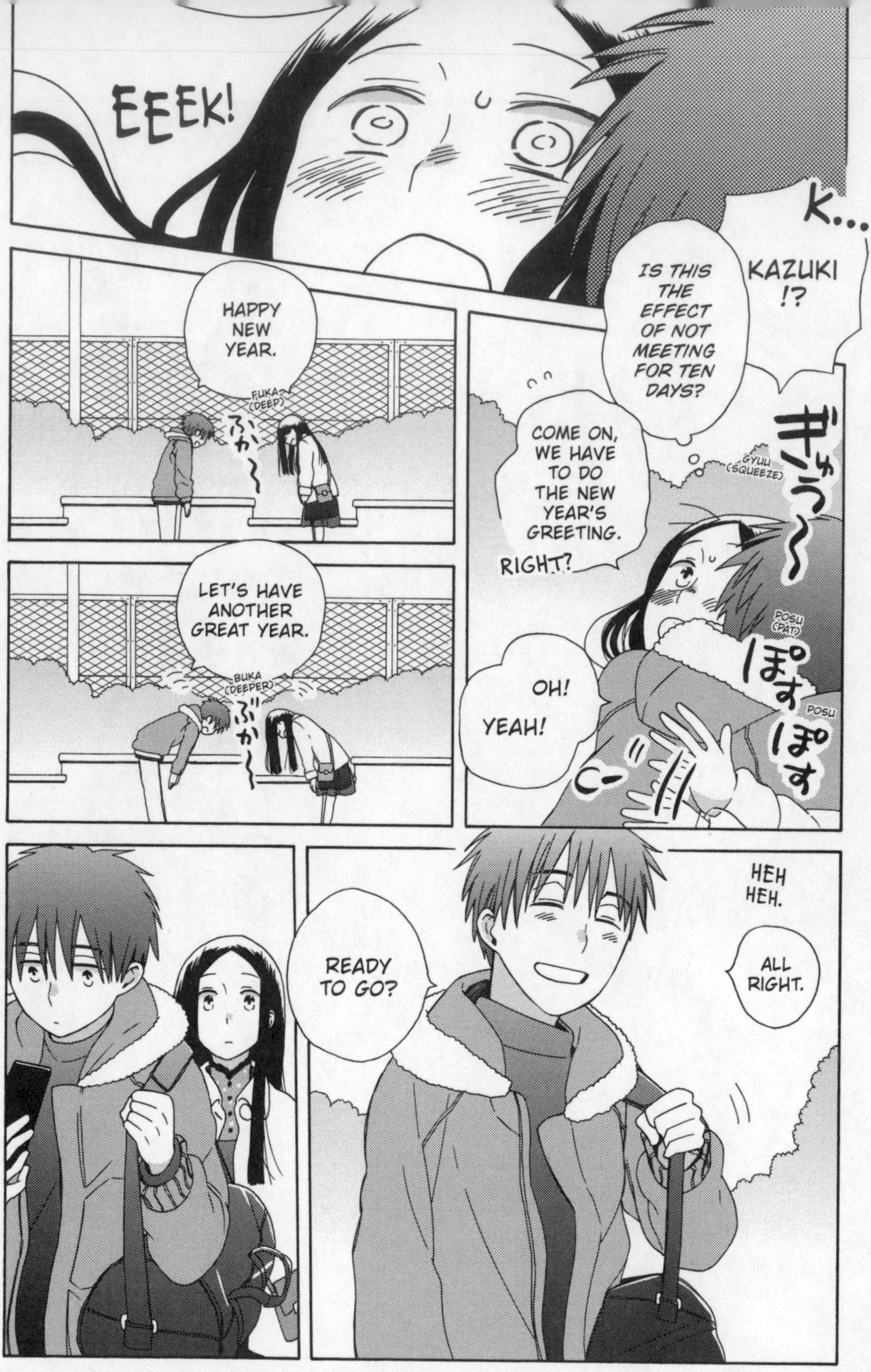
K...
EEEK!
KAZUKI !?
IS THIS THE EFFECT OF NOT MEETING FOR TEN DAYS?
COME ON, WE HAVE TO DO THE NEW YEAR'S GREETING.
RIGHT?
ぎゅう〜
GYUU (SQUEEZE)
ぽす
POSU (PAT)
OH!
YEAH!
ぽすぽす
POSU
HAPPY NEW YEAR.
ふか〜
FUKA (DEEP)
LET'S HAVE ANOTHER GREAT YEAR.
ぶか〜
BUKA (DEEPER)
HEH HEH.
ALL RIGHT.
READY TO GO?

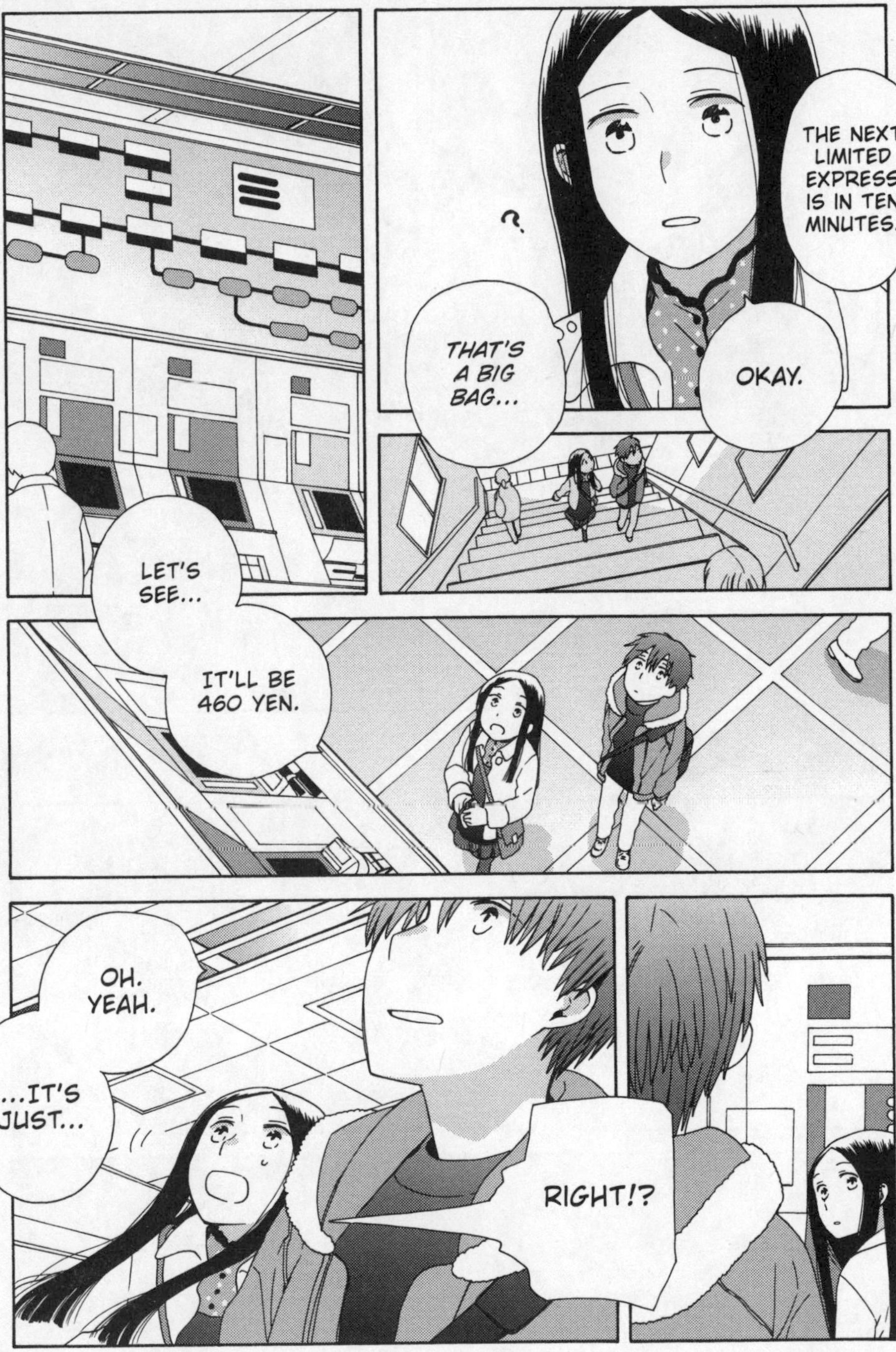
?
THE NEXT LIMITED EXPRESS IS IN TEN MINUTES.
OKAY.
THAT'S A BIG BAG...
LET'S SEE...
IT'LL BE 460 YEN.
OH. YEAH.
RIGHT!?
...IT'S JUST...

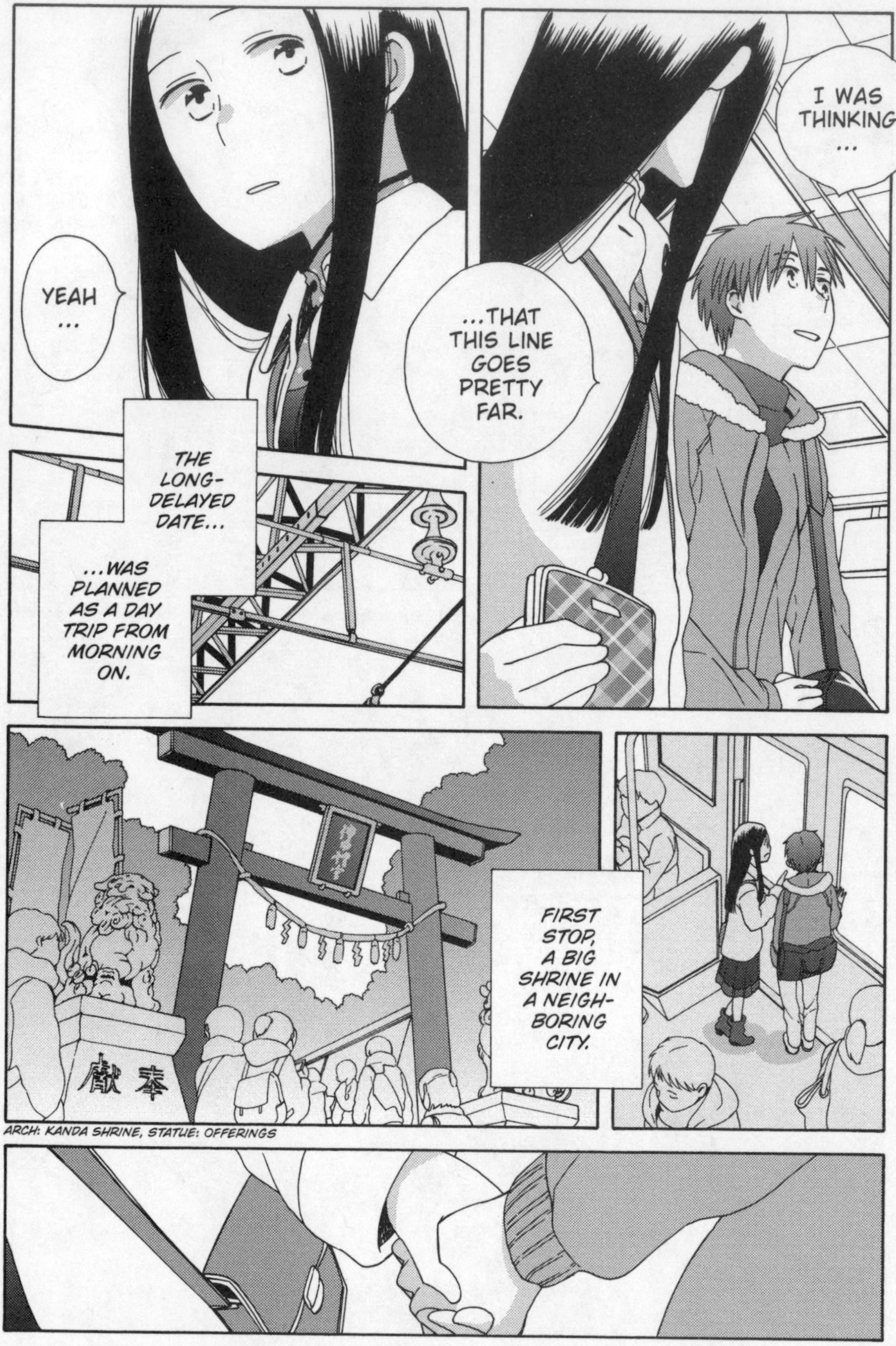
I WAS THINKING ...
...THAT THIS LINE GOES PRETTY FAR.
YEAH ...
THE LONG-DELAYED DATE...
...WAS PLANNED AS A DAY TRIP FROM MORNING ON.
FIRST STOP, A BIG SHRINE IN A NEIGHBORING CITY.
奉 獻
ARCH: KANDA SHRINE, STATUE: OFFERINGS

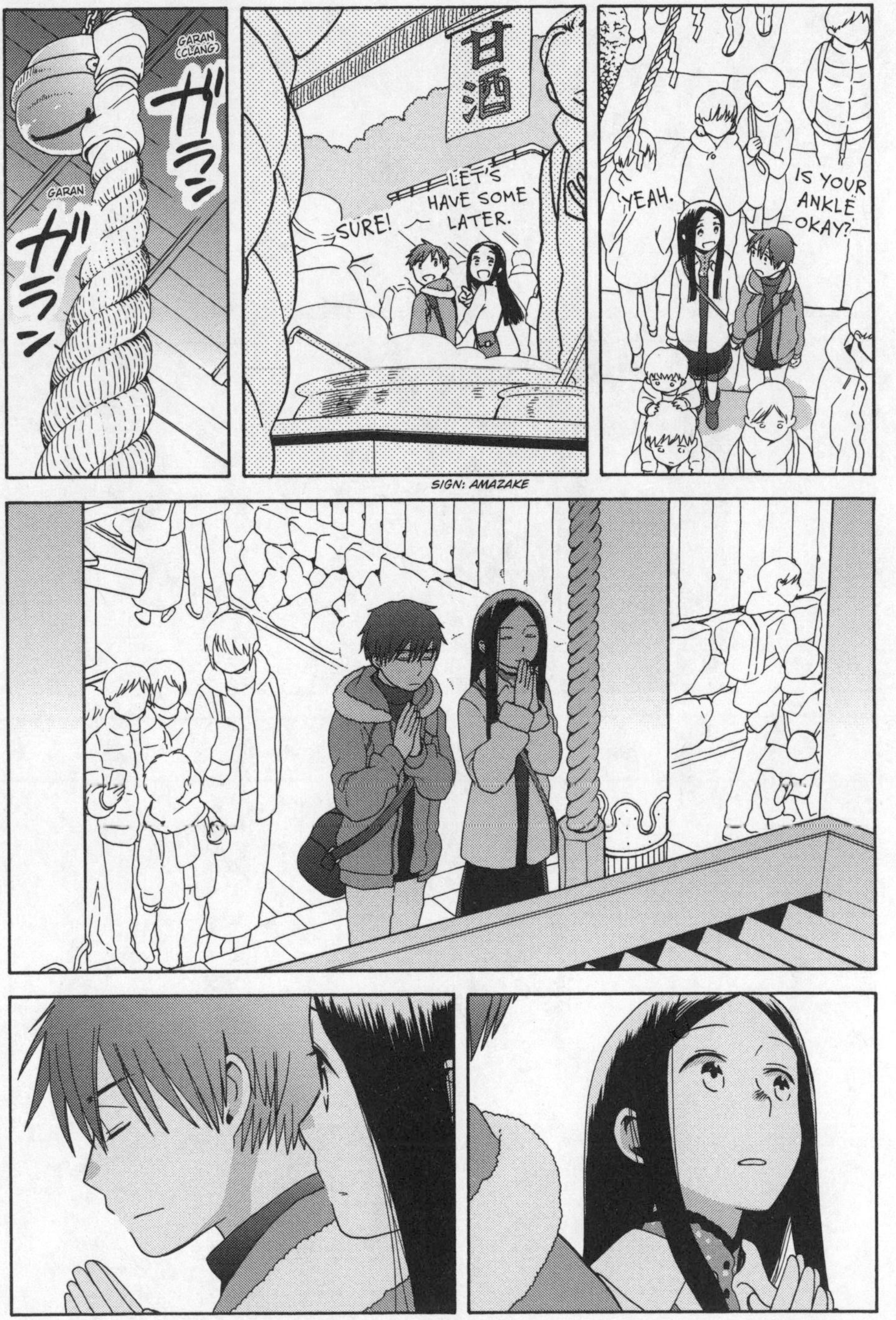
IS YOUR ANKLE OKAY?
YEAH.
甘酒
LET'S HAVE SOME LATER.
SURE!
SIGN: AMAZAKE
ガラン
GARAN (CLANG)
ガラン
GARAN

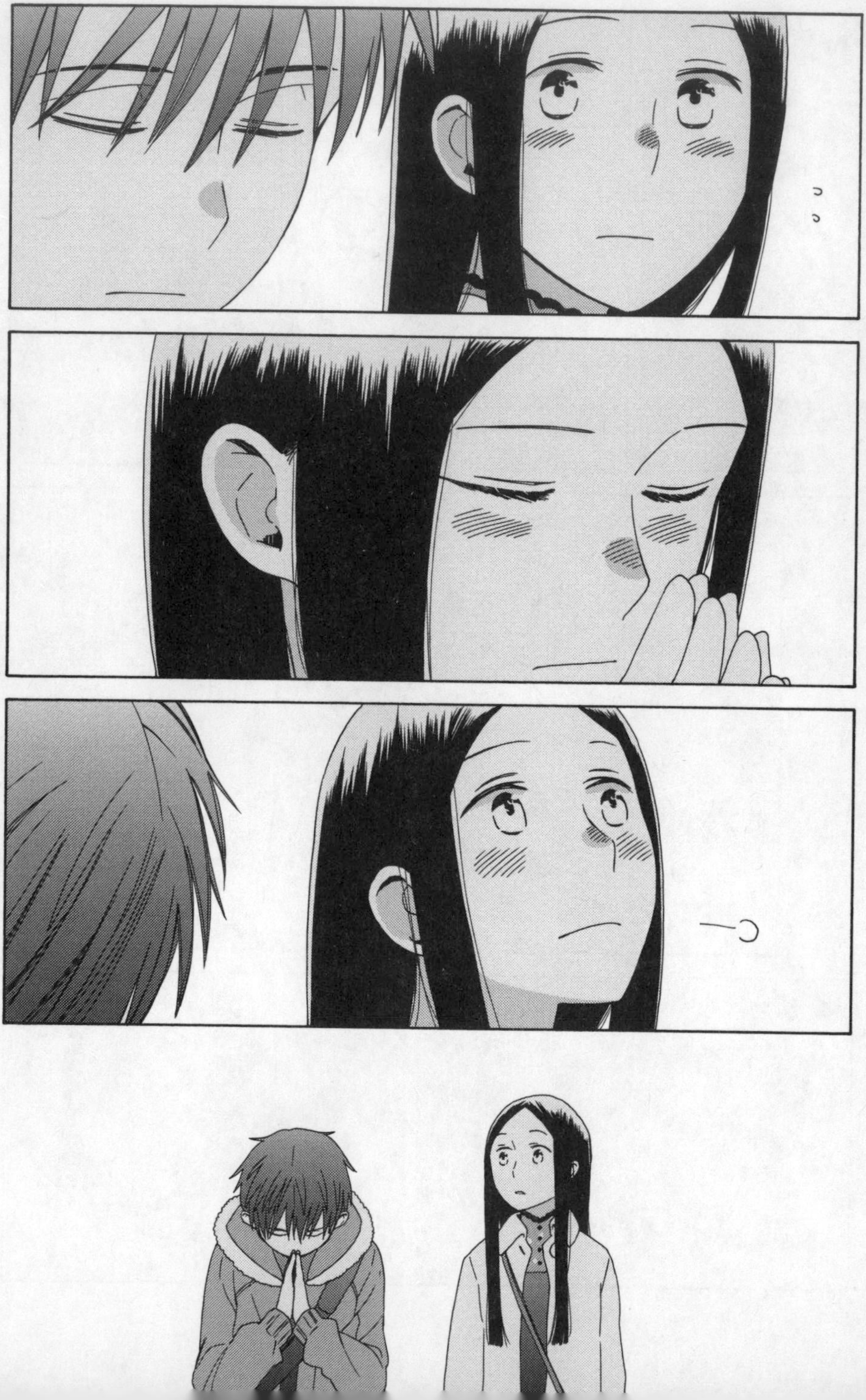

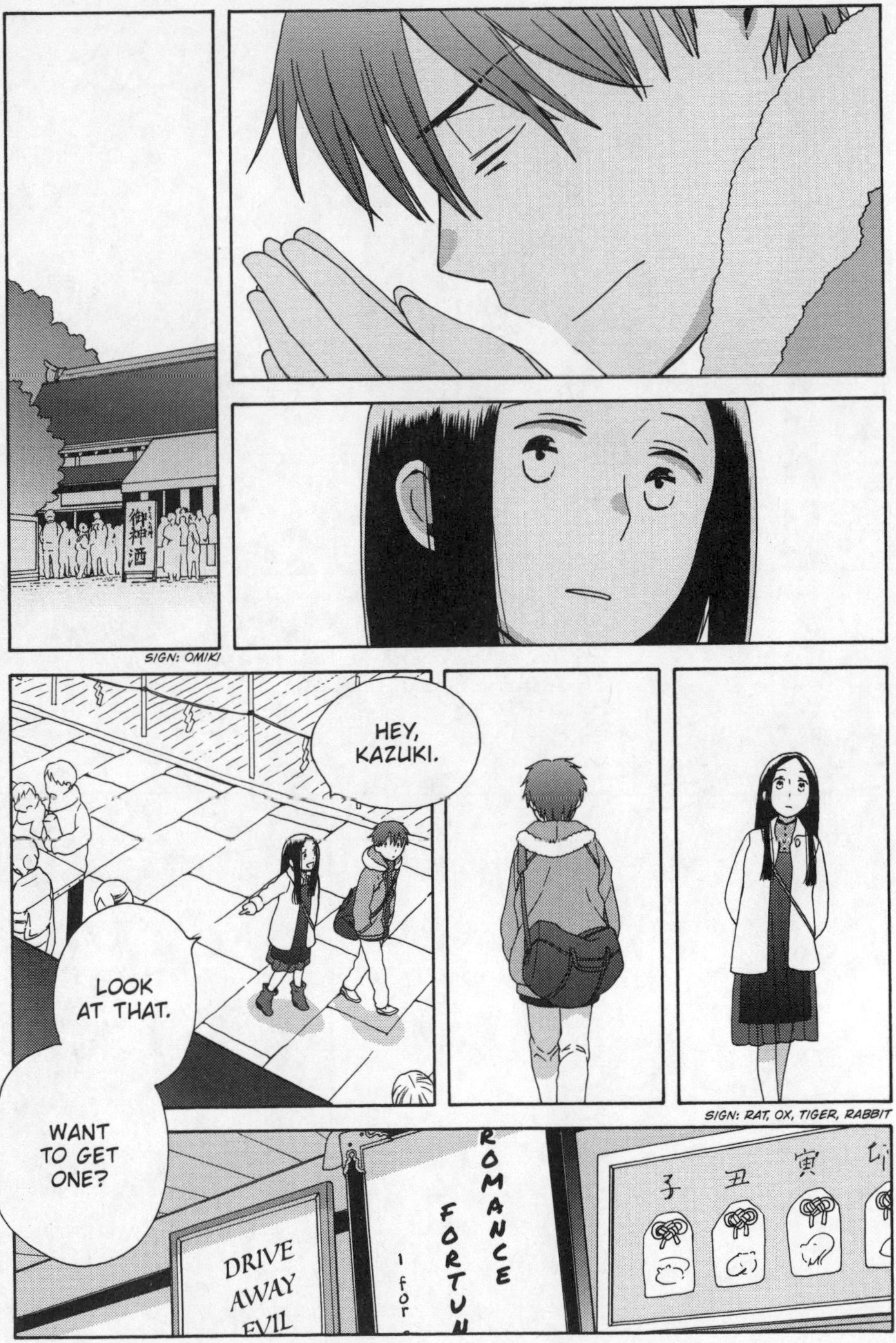
御神酒
SIGN: OMIKI
HEY, KAZUKI.
LOOK AT THAT.
WANT TO GET ONE?
SIGN: RAT, OX, TIGER, RABBIT
子 丑 寅
ROMANCE
FORTUN
1 for
DRIVE AWAY EVIL

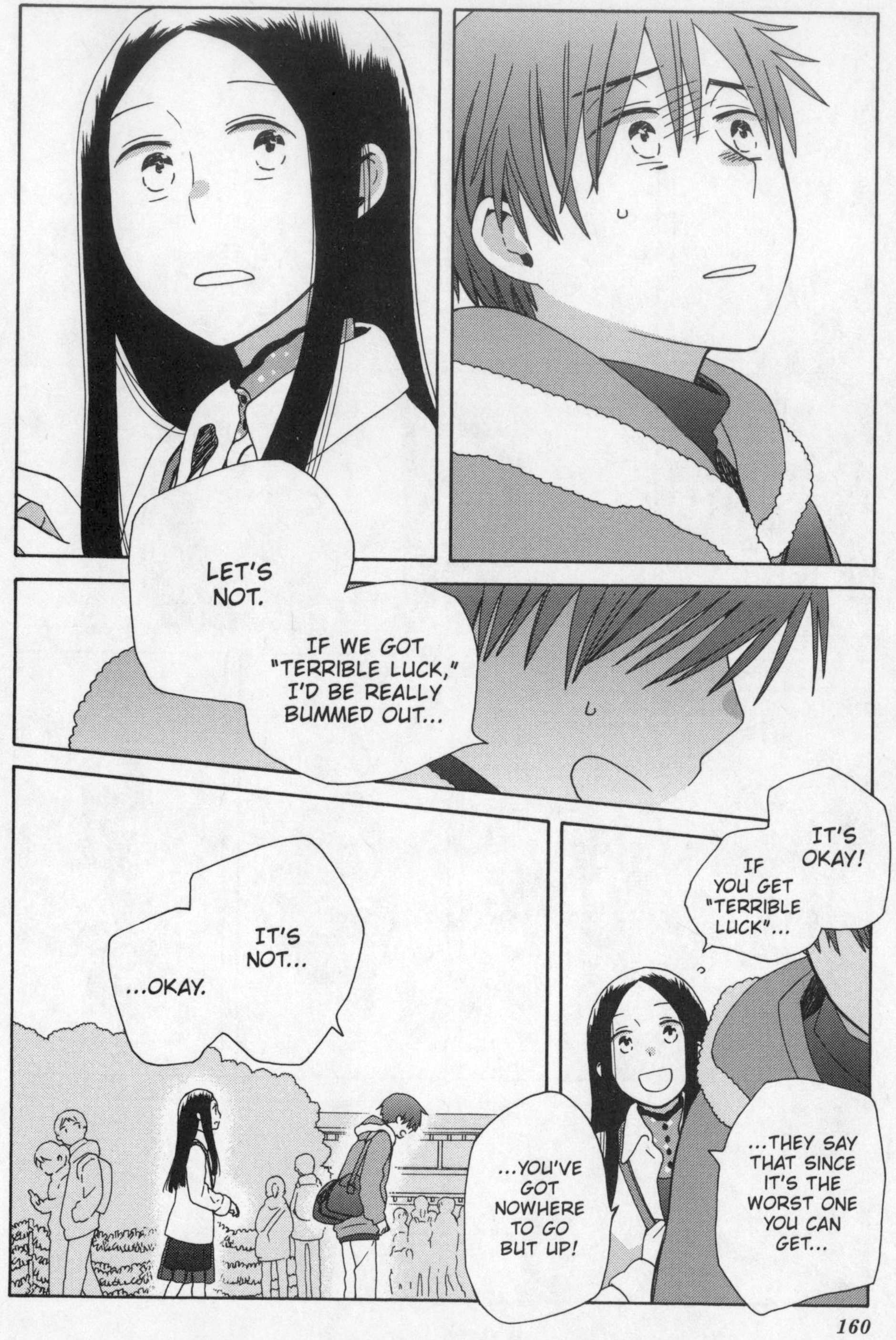
LET'S NOT.
IF WE GOT "TERRIBLE LUCK," I'D BE REALLY BUMMED OUT...
IT'S OKAY!
IF YOU GET "TERRIBLE LUCK"...
...THEY SAY THAT SINCE IT'S THE WORST ONE YOU CAN GET...
...YOU'VE GOT NOWHERE TO GO BUT UP!
IT'S NOT...
...OKAY.

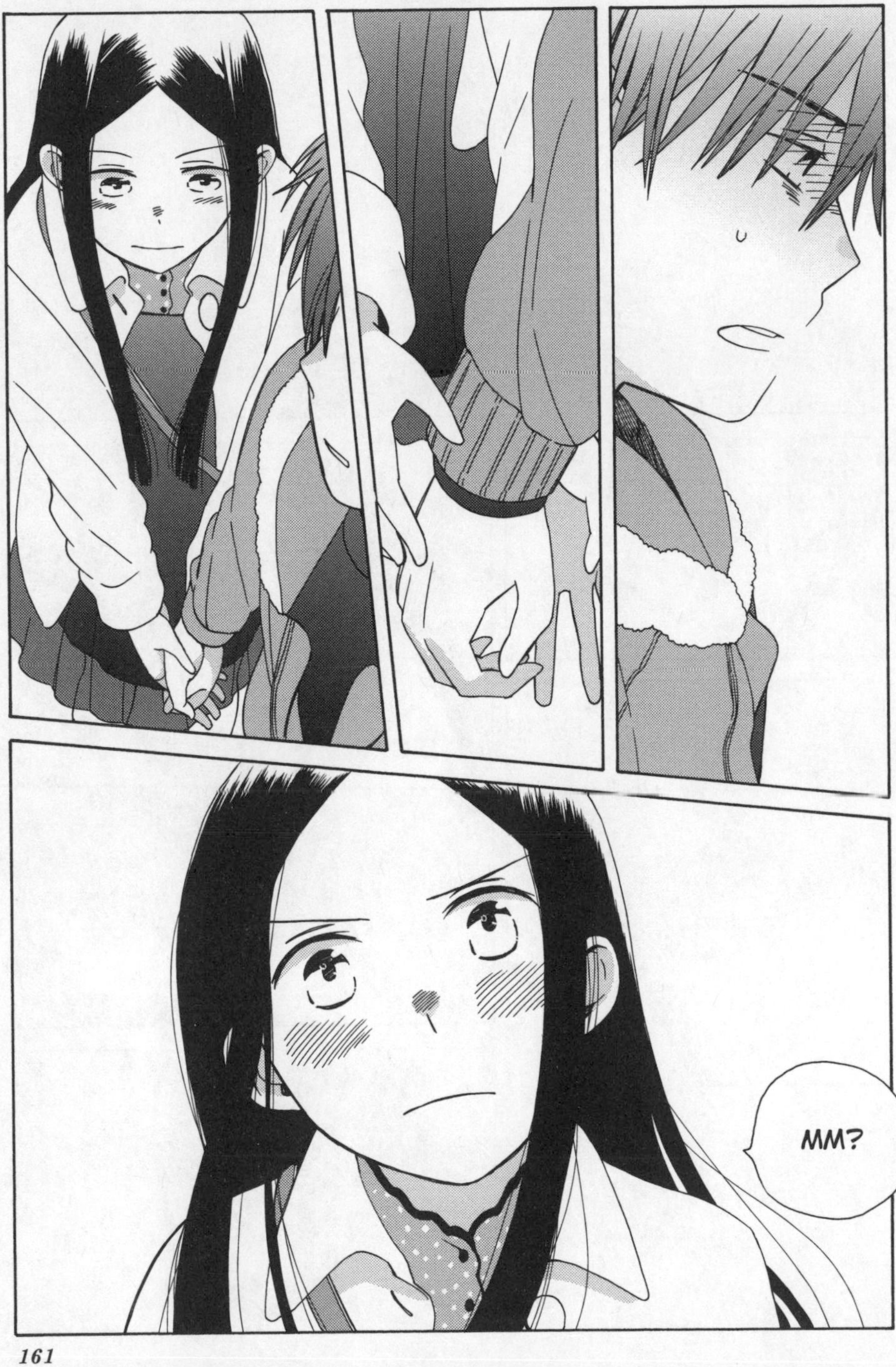
MM?

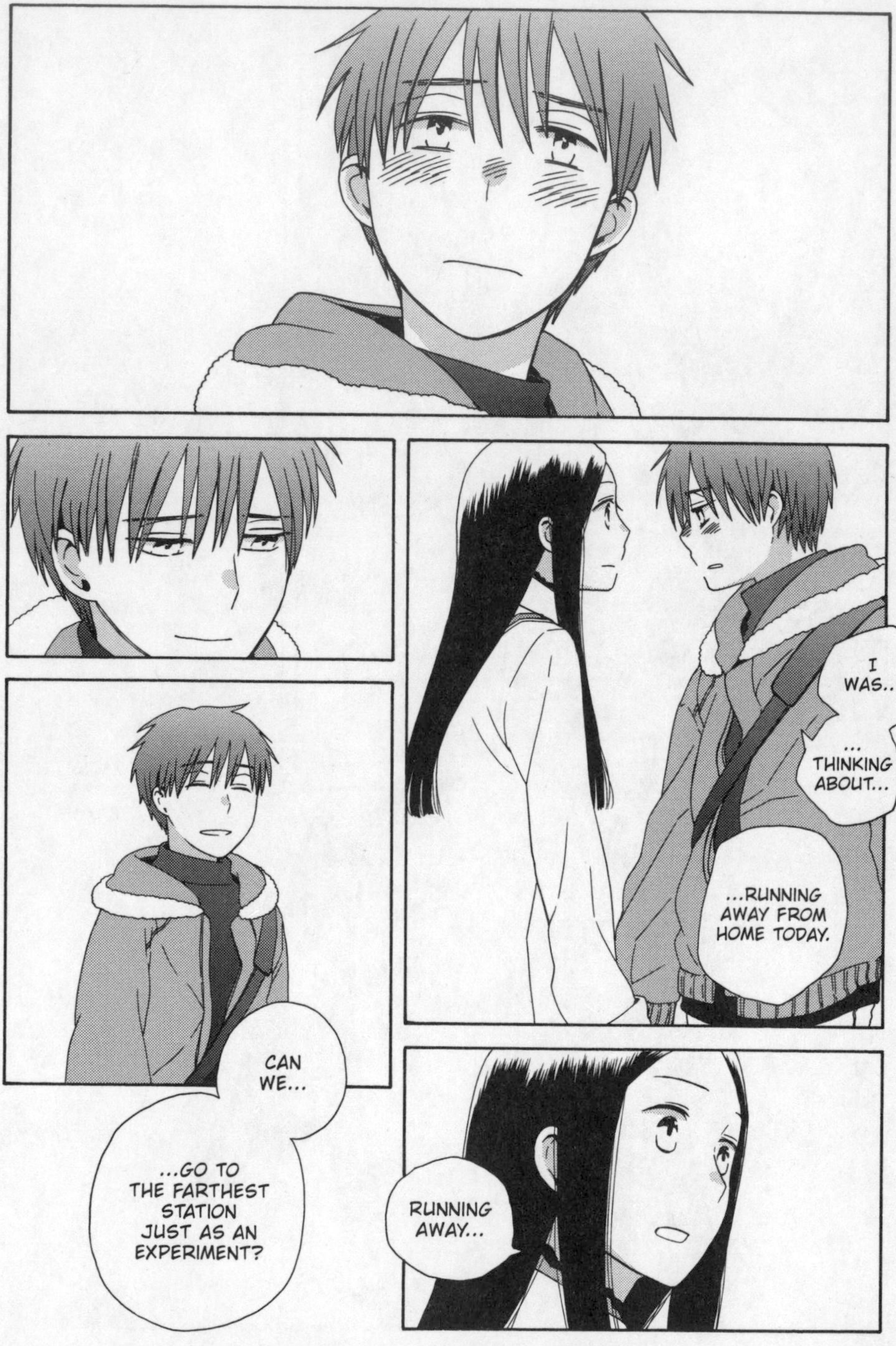
I WAS...
...THINKING ABOUT...
...RUNNING AWAY FROM HOME TODAY.
CAN WE...
...GO TO THE FARTHEST STATION JUST AS AN EXPERIMENT?
RUNNING AWAY...

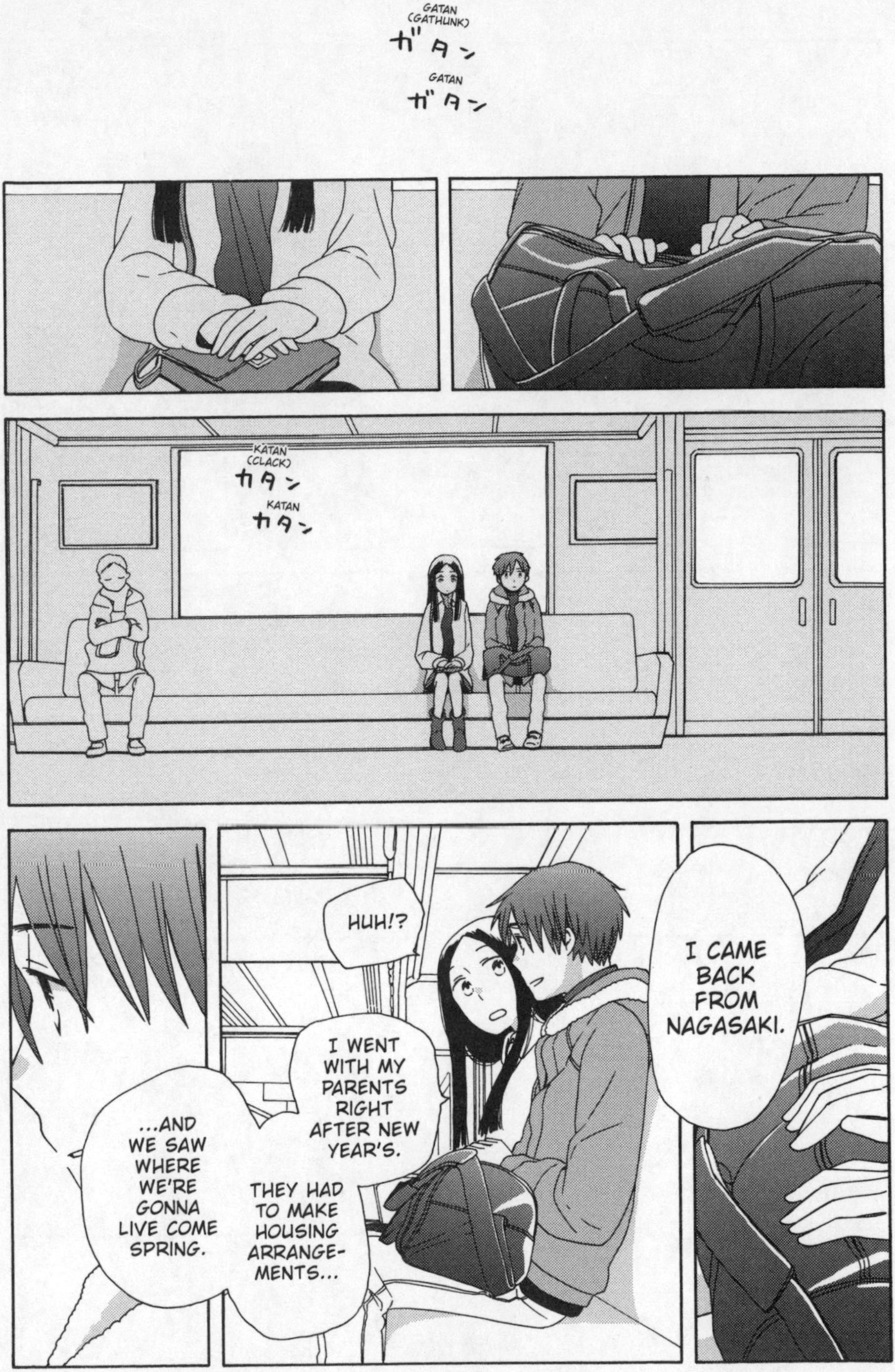
GATAN (GATHUNK)
ガタン
GATAN
ガタン
KATAN (CLACK)
カタン
KATAN
カタン
I CAME BACK FROM NAGASAKI.
HUH!?
I WENT WITH MY PARENTS RIGHT AFTER NEW YEAR'S.
THEY HAD TO MAKE HOUSING ARRANGE-MENTS...
...AND WE SAW WHERE WE'RE GONNA LIVE COME SPRING.

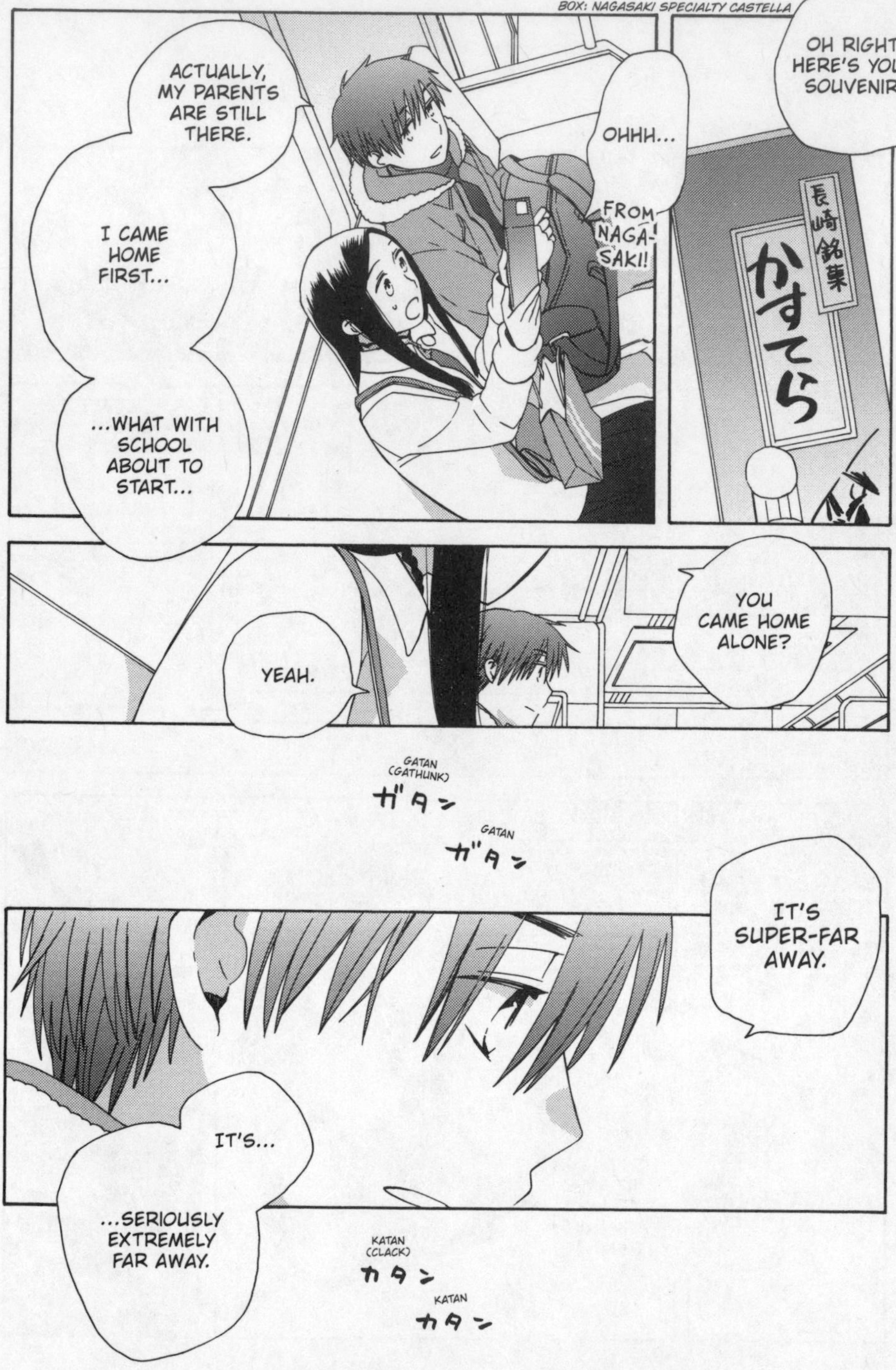
BOX: NAGASAKI SPECIALTY CASTELLA
OH RIGHT. HERE'S YOUR SOUVENIR.
長崎銘菓
かすてら
OHHH...
FROM NAGASAKI!
ACTUALLY, MY PARENTS ARE STILL THERE.
I CAME HOME FIRST...
...WHAT WITH SCHOOL ABOUT TO START...
YOU CAME HOME ALONE?
YEAH.
GATAN (GATHUNK)
ガタン
GATAN
ガタン
IT'S SUPER-FAR AWAY.
IT'S...
...SERIOUSLY EXTREMELY FAR AWAY.
KATAN (CLACK)
カタン
KATAN
カタン

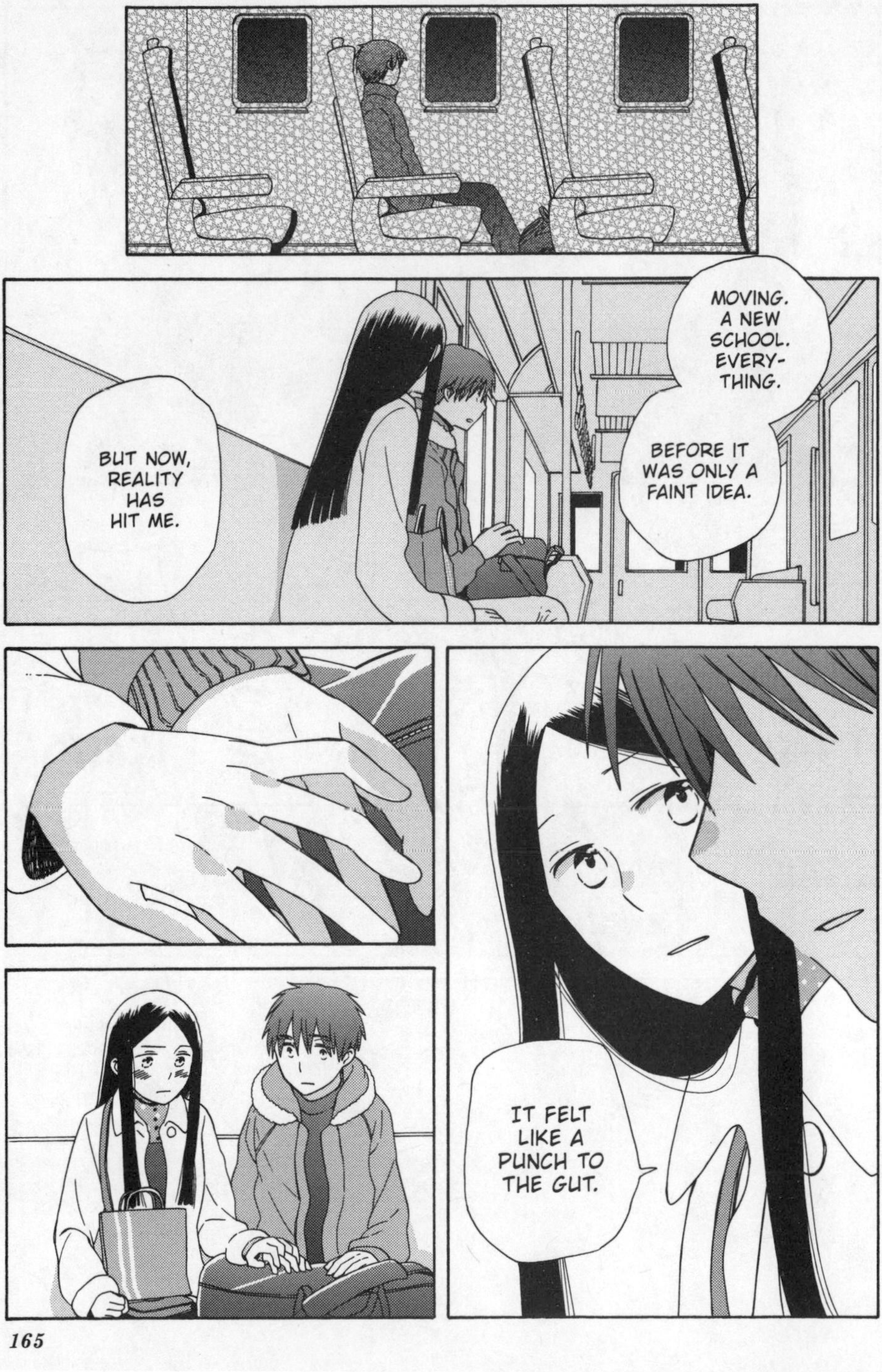
MOVING. A NEW SCHOOL. EVERY-THING.
BEFORE IT WAS ONLY A FAINT IDEA.
BUT NOW, REALITY HAS HIT ME.
IT FELT LIKE A PUNCH TO THE GUT.

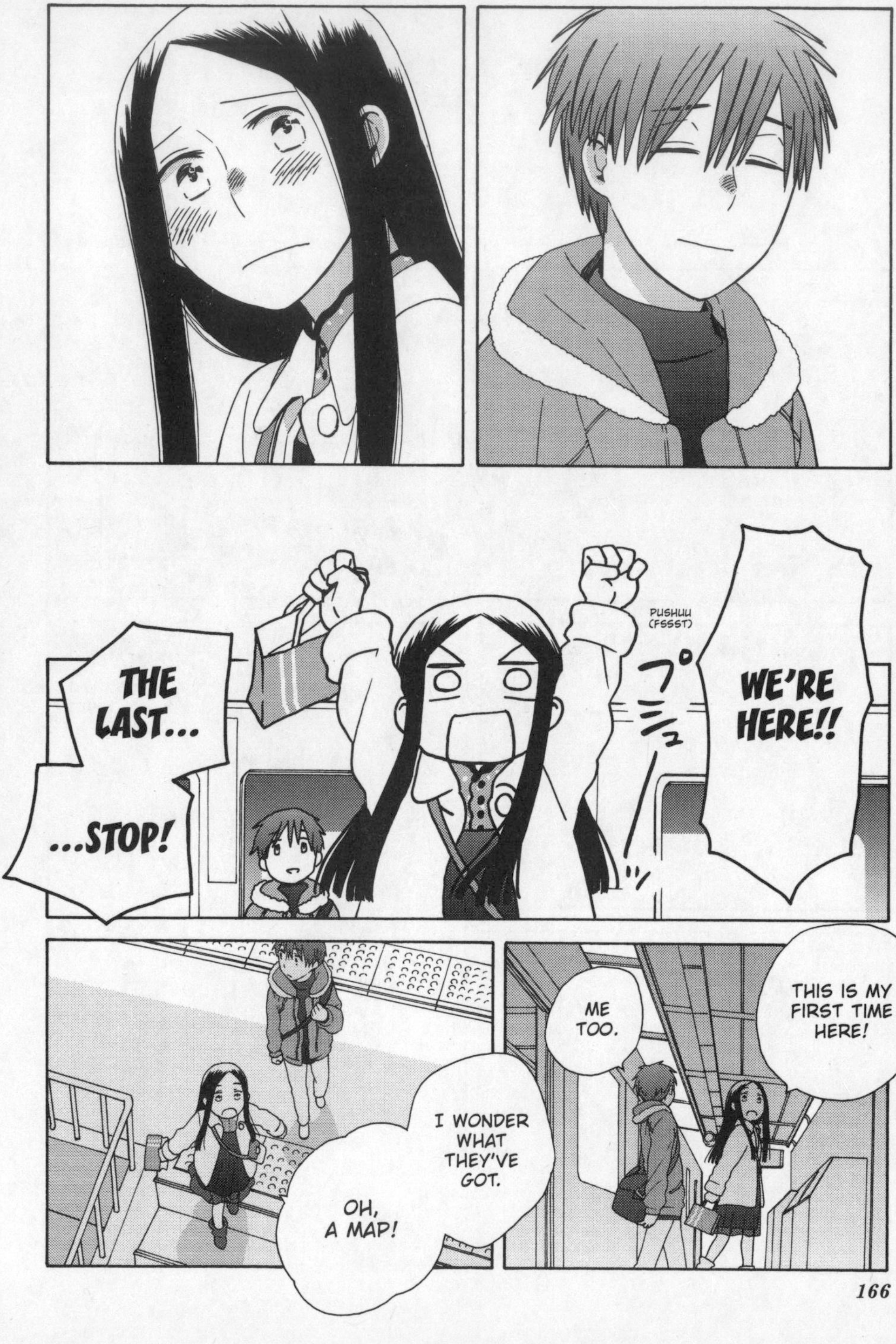
WE'RE HERE!!
PUSHUU (FSSST)
プシュ
THE LAST...
...STOP!
THIS IS MY FIRST TIME HERE!
ME TOO.
I WONDER WHAT THEY'VE GOT.
OH, A MAP!

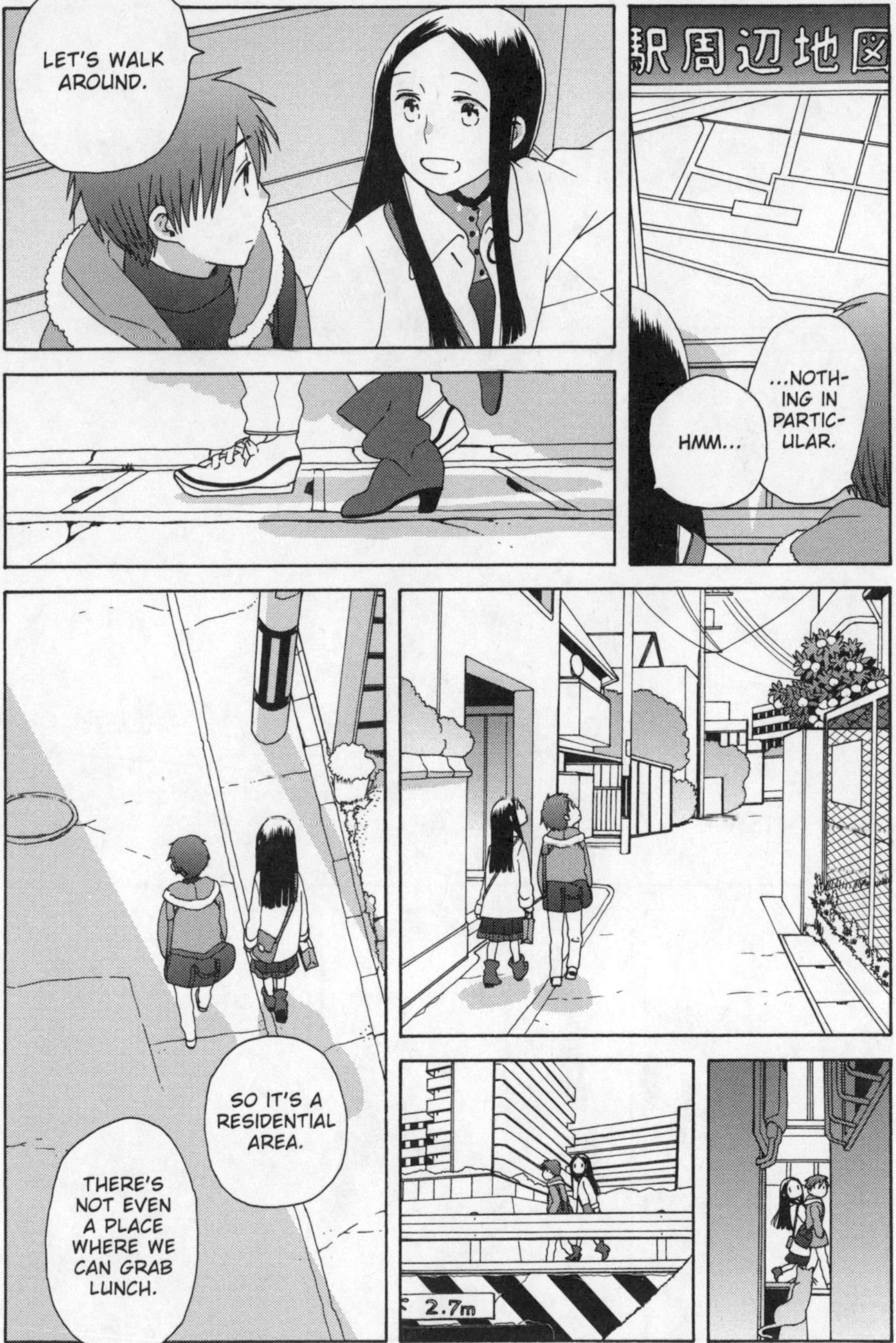
SIGN: MAP OF SURROUNDING AREA
駅周辺地図
...NOTHING IN PARTICULAR.
HMM...
LET'S WALK AROUND.
2.7m
SO IT'S A RESIDENTIAL AREA.
THERE'S NOT EVEN A PLACE WHERE WE CAN GRAB LUNCH.

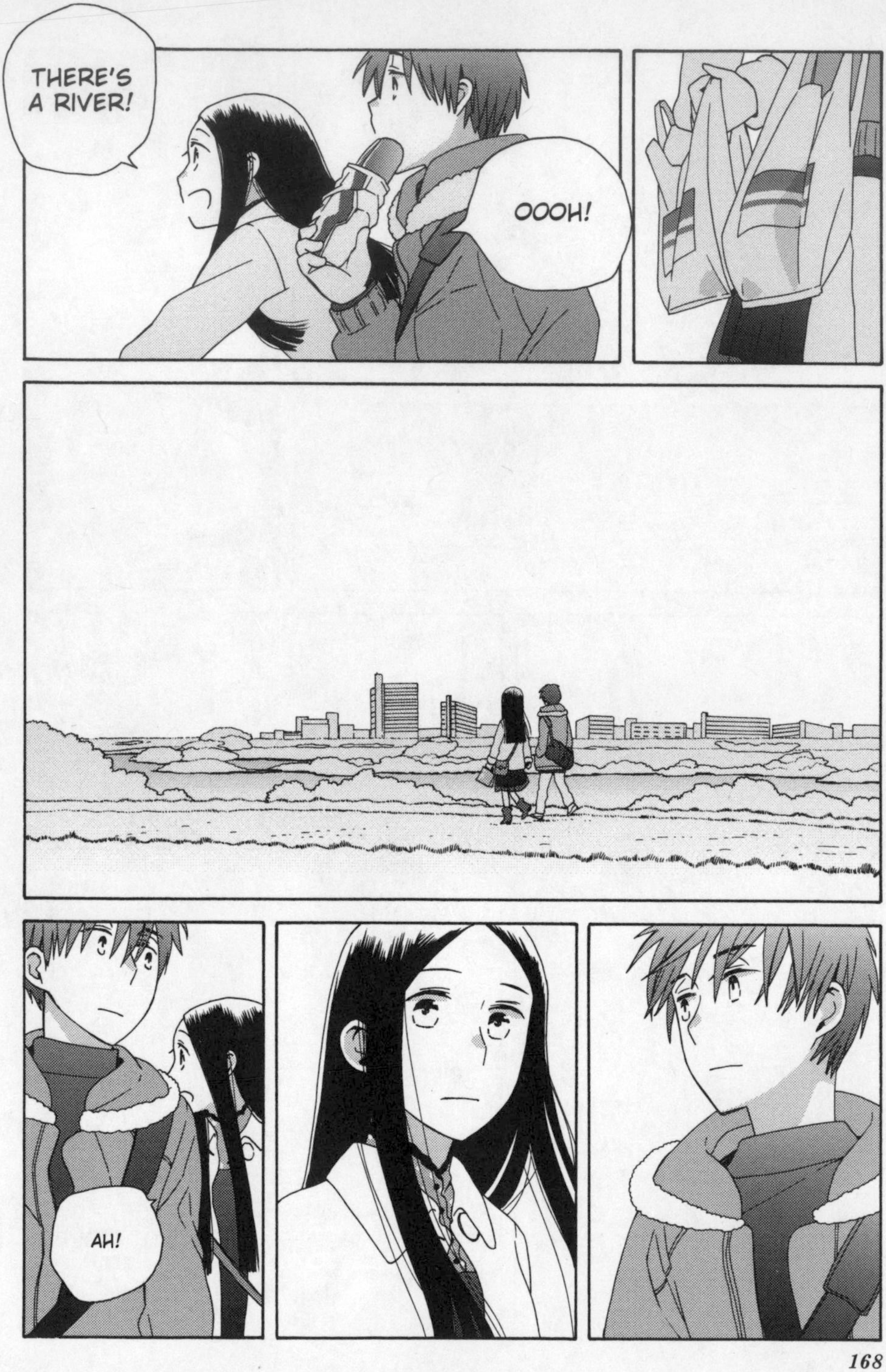
OOOH!
THERE'S A RIVER!
AH!

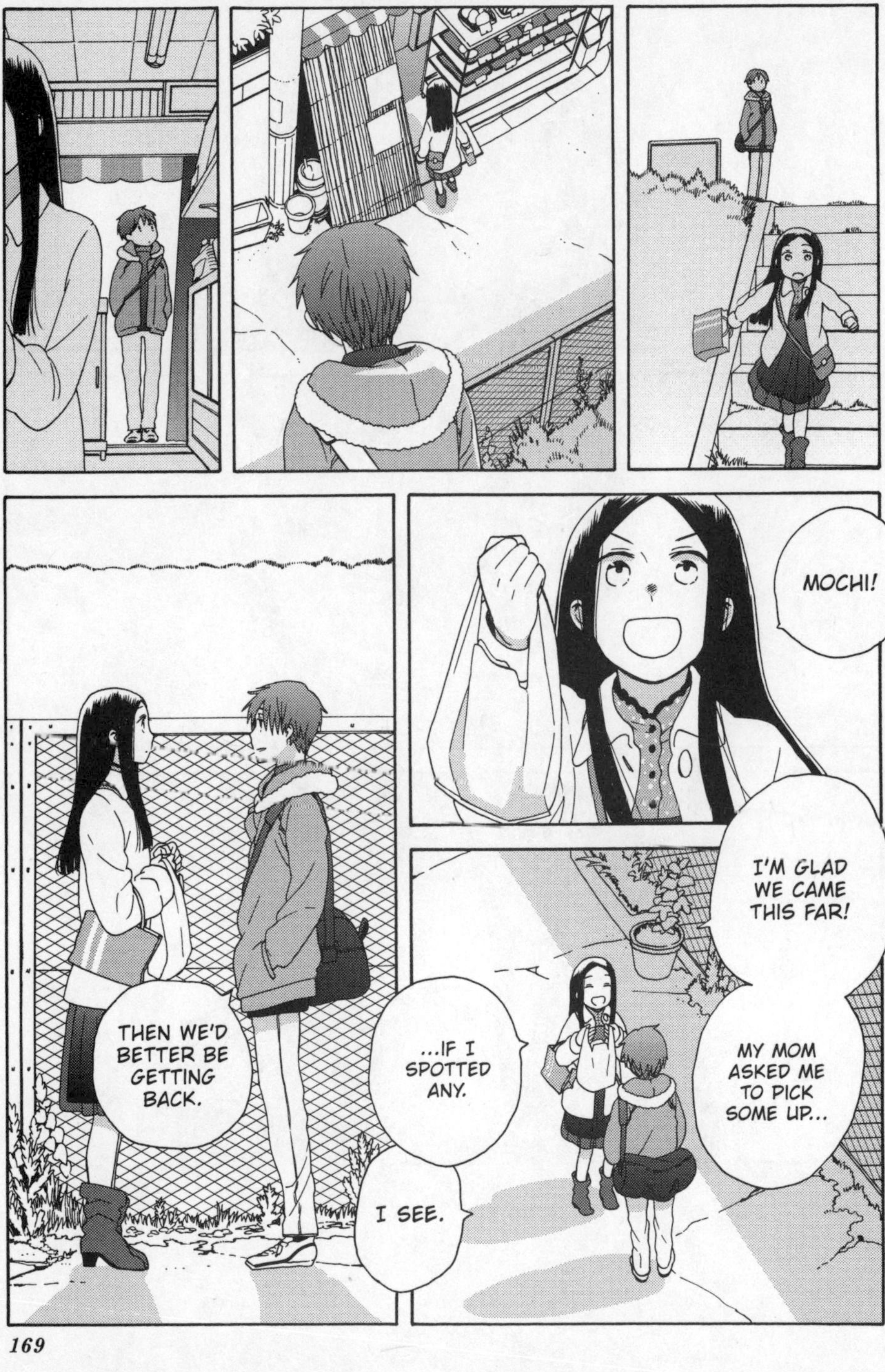
MOCHI!
I'M GLAD WE CAME THIS FAR!
MY MOM ASKED ME TO PICK SOME UP...
...IF I SPOTTED ANY.
I SEE.
THEN WE'D BETTER BE GETTING BACK.

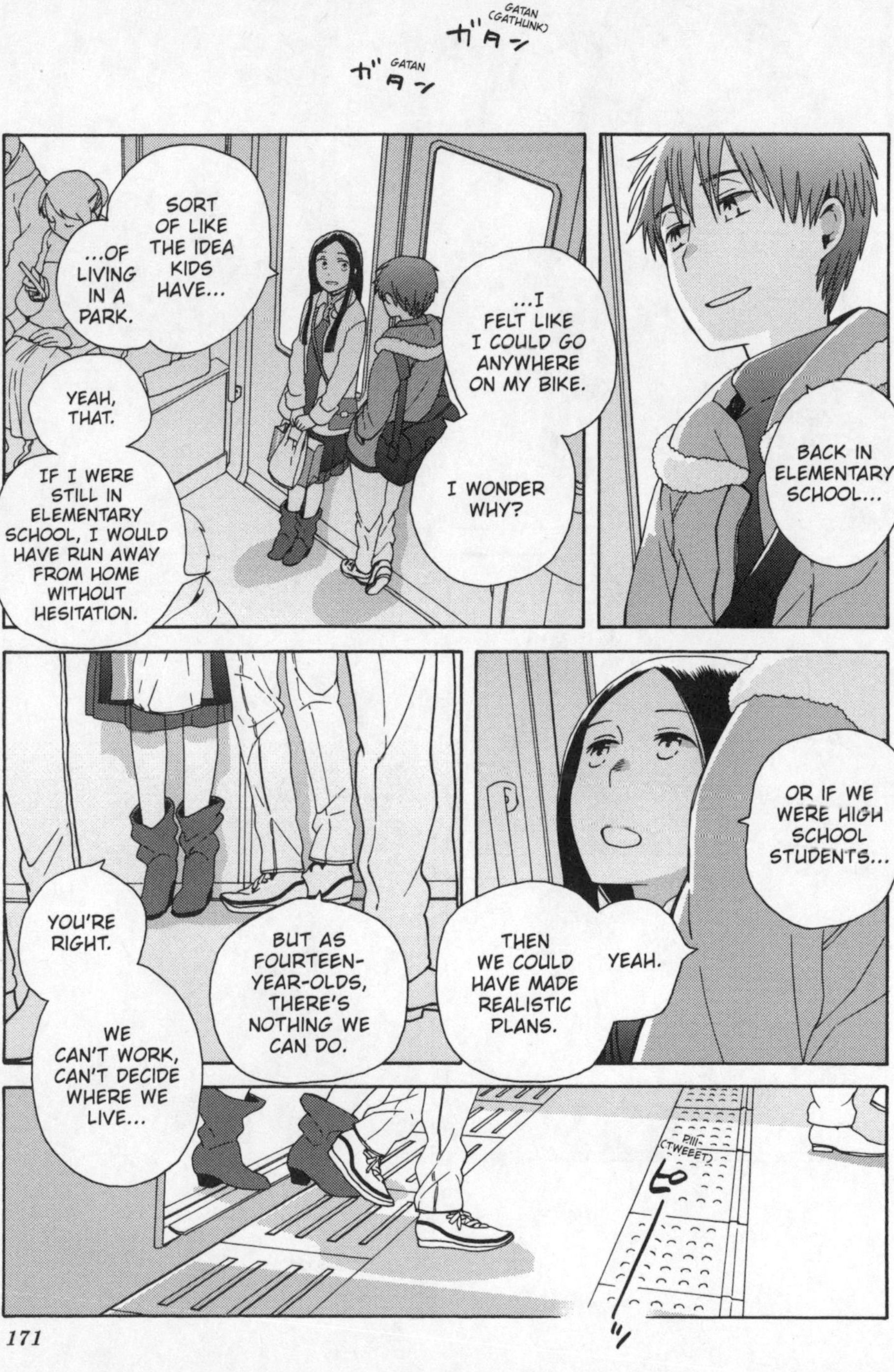
ガタン GATAN (GATHUNK)
ガタン GATAN
BACK IN ELEMENTARY SCHOOL...
...I FELT LIKE I COULD GO ANYWHERE ON MY BIKE.
I WONDER WHY?
SORT OF LIKE THE IDEA KIDS HAVE...
...OF LIVING IN A PARK.
YEAH, THAT.
IF I WERE STILL IN ELEMENTARY SCHOOL, I WOULD HAVE RUN AWAY FROM HOME WITHOUT HESITATION.
OR IF WE WERE HIGH SCHOOL STUDENTS...
YEAH.
THEN WE COULD HAVE MADE REALISTIC PLANS.
BUT AS FOURTEEN-YEAR-OLDS, THERE'S NOTHING WE CAN DO.
YOU'RE RIGHT.
WE CAN'T WORK, CAN'T DECIDE WHERE WE LIVE...
ピ PIII (TWEEET)

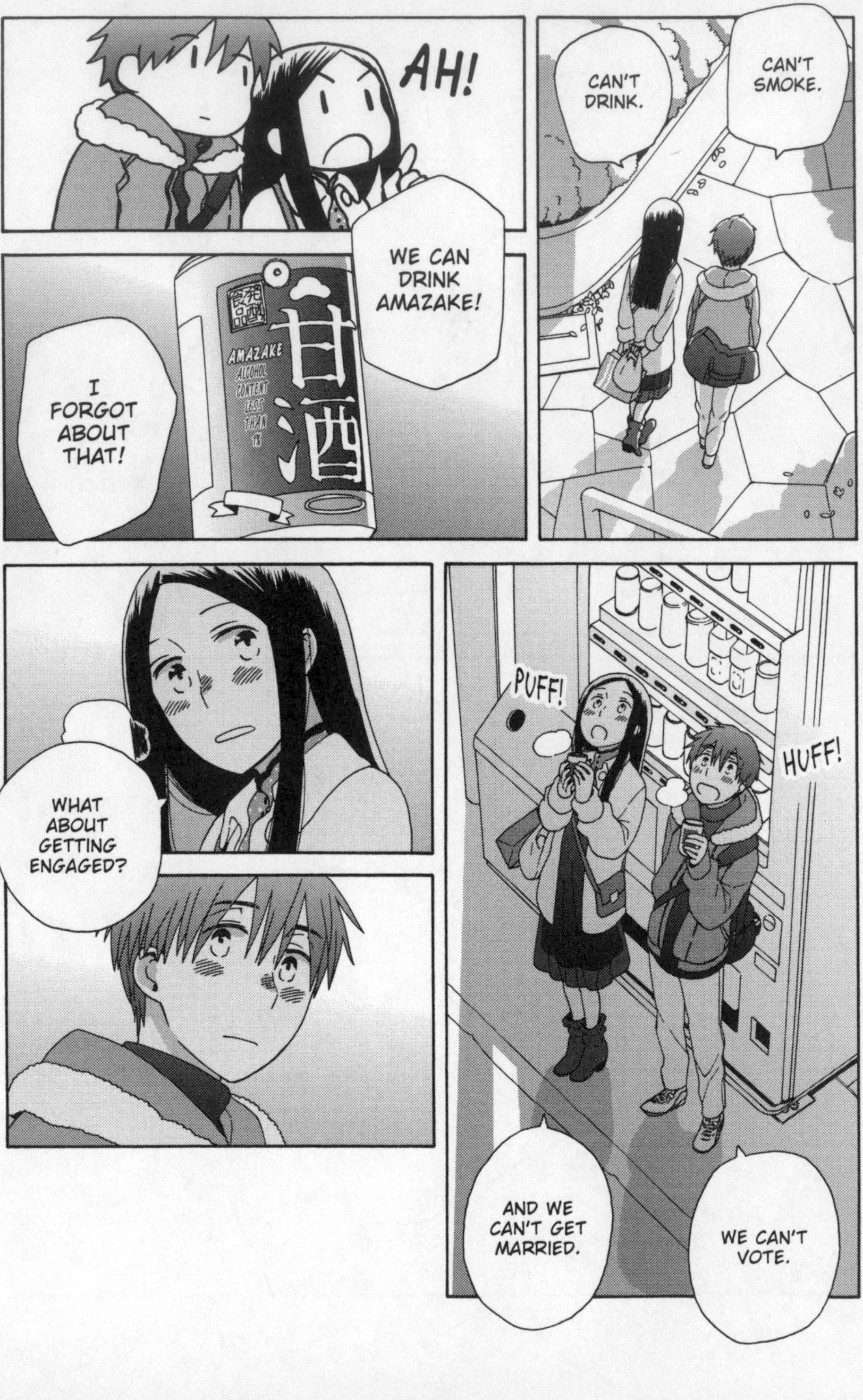
CAN'T SMOKE.
CAN'T DRINK.
AH!
WE CAN DRINK AMAZAKE!
甘酒
AMAZAKE ALCOHOL CONTENT LESS THAN 1%
I FORGOT ABOUT THAT!
HUFF!
PUFF!
WE CAN'T VOTE.
AND WE CAN'T GET MARRIED.
WHAT ABOUT GETTING ENGAGED?

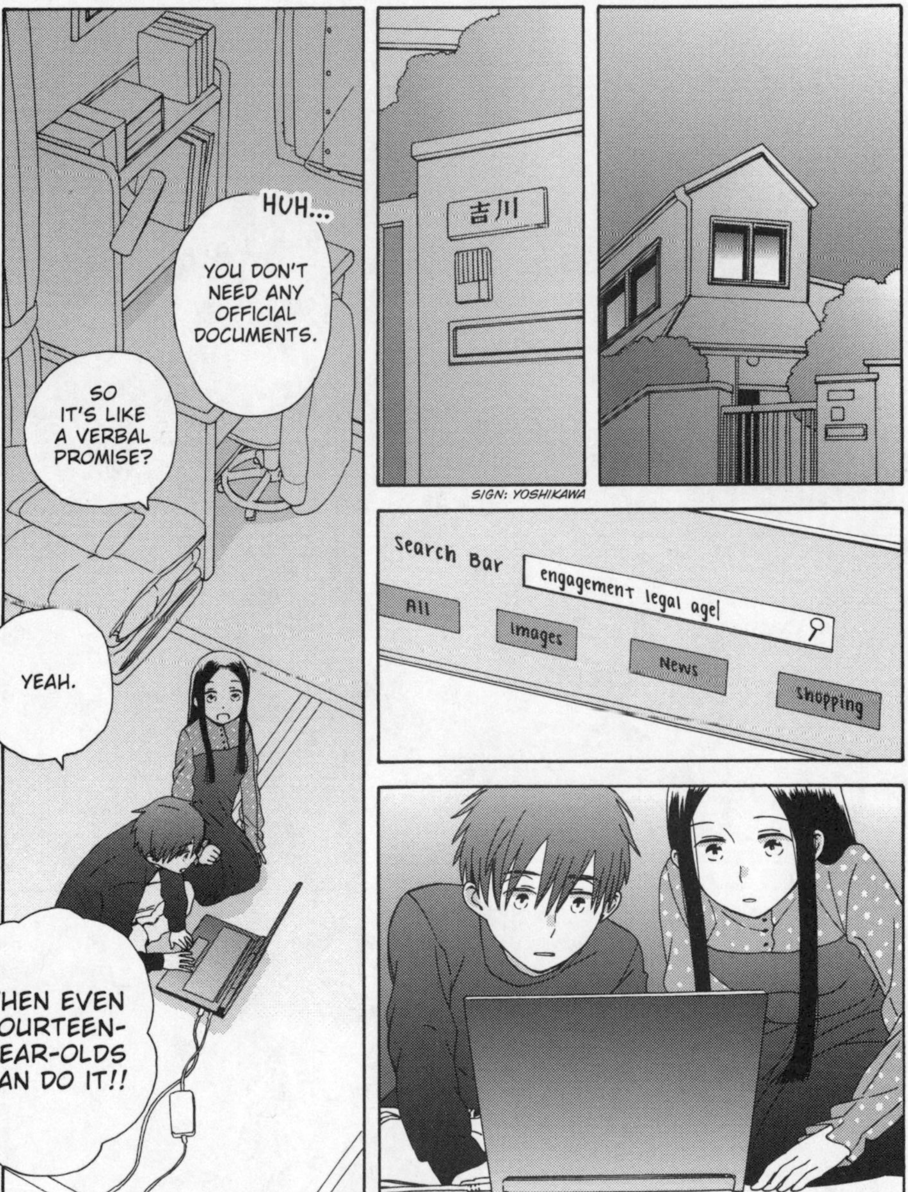
吉川
SIGN: YOSHIKAWA
Search Bar
engagement legal age
All
images
News
shopping
HUH...
YOU DON'T NEED ANY OFFICIAL DOCUMENTS.
SO IT'S LIKE A VERBAL PROMISE?
YEAH.
THEN EVEN FOURTEEN-YEAR-OLDS CAN DO IT!!

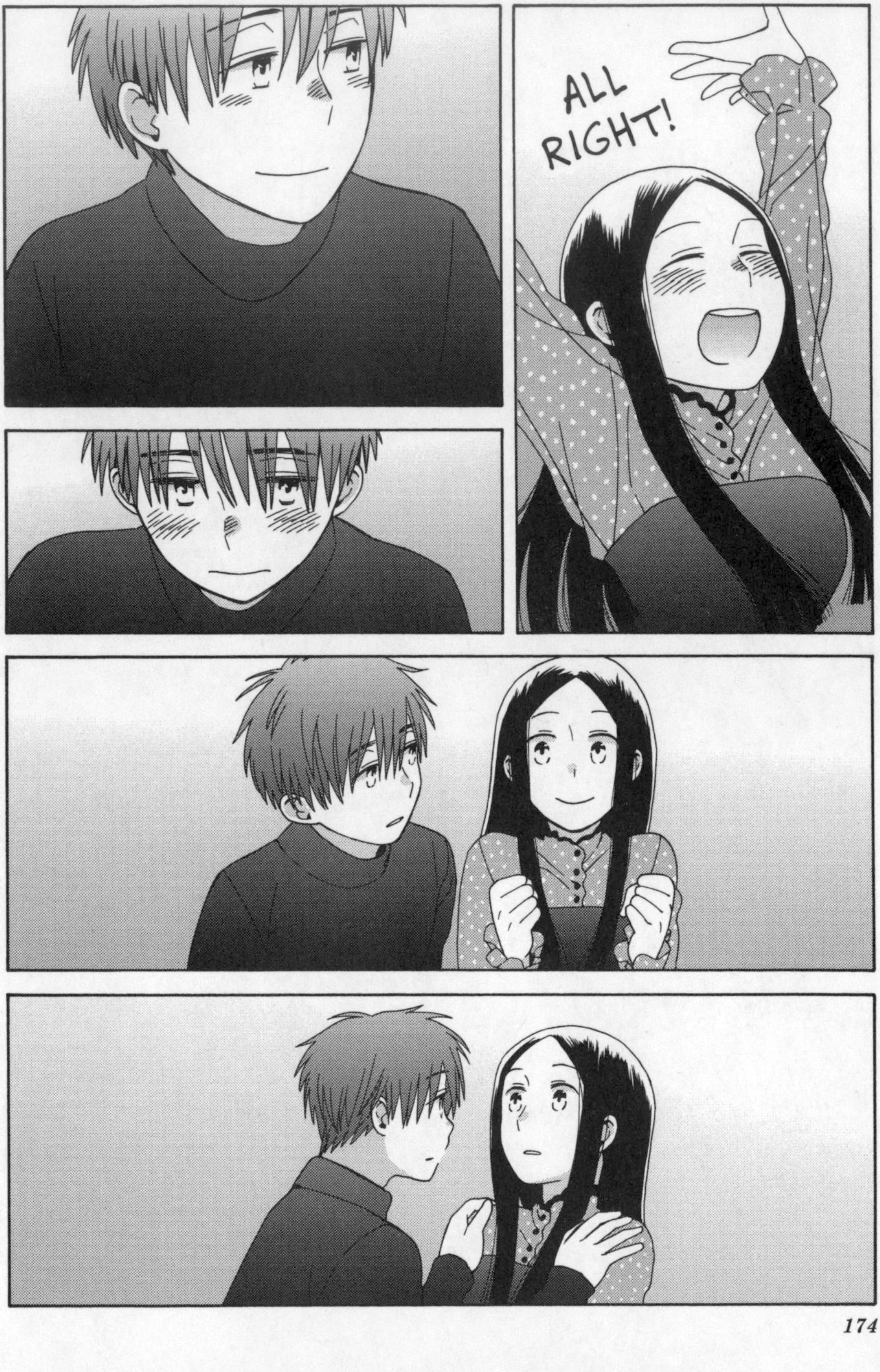
ALL RIGHT!

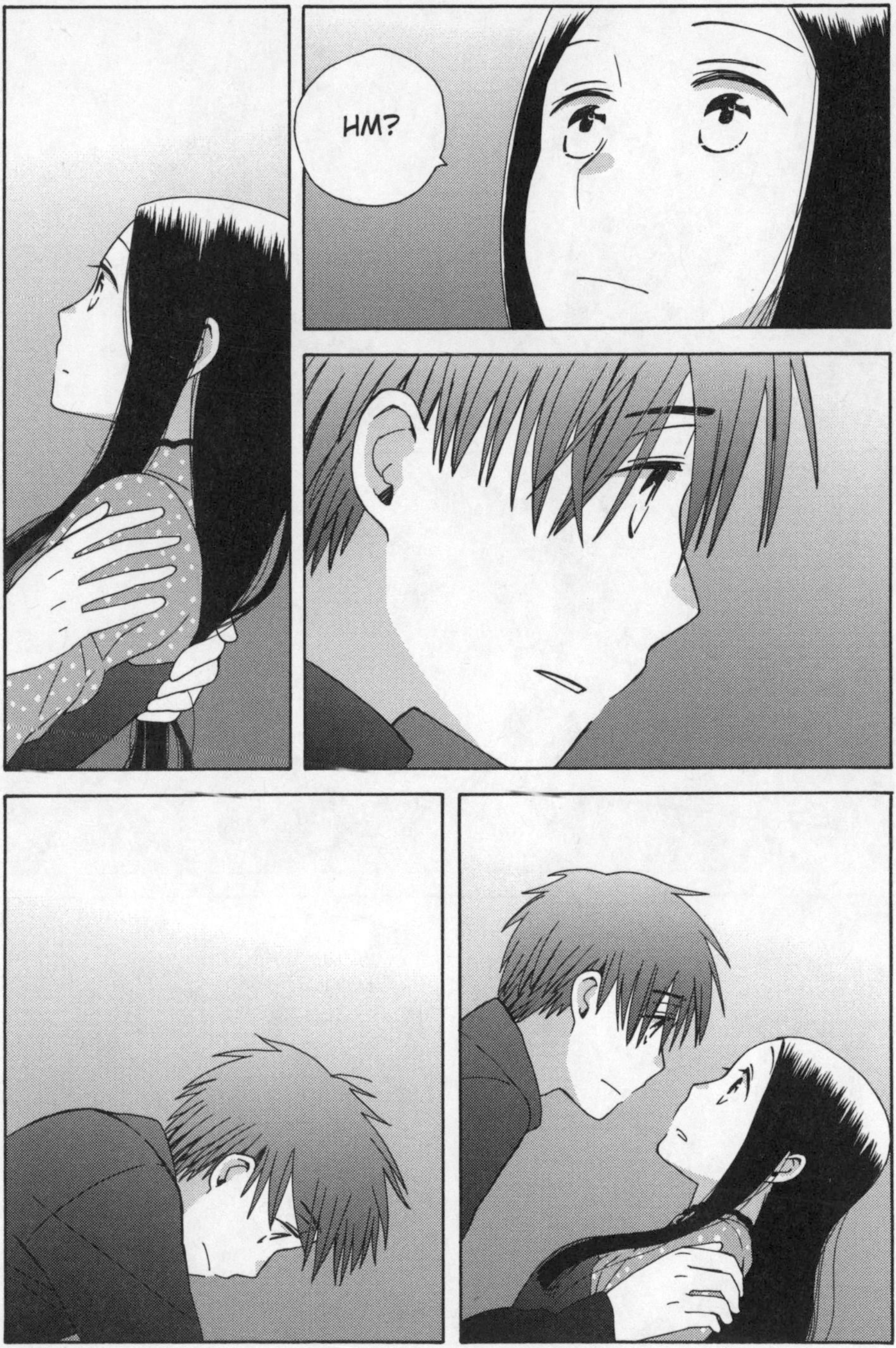
HM?

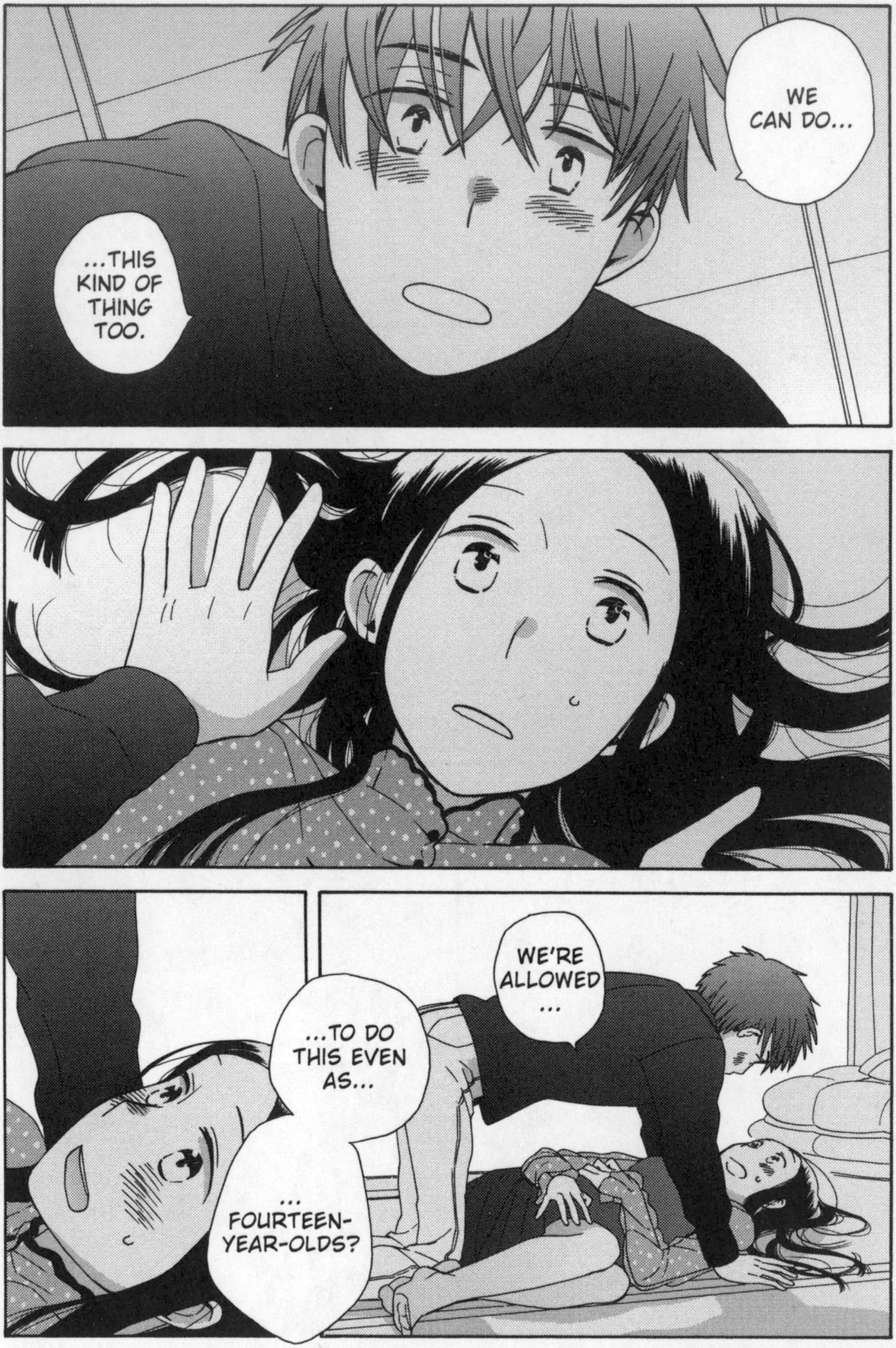
WE CAN DO...
...THIS KIND OF THING TOO.
WE'RE ALLOWED ...
...TO DO THIS EVEN AS...
... FOURTEEN-YEAR-OLDS?

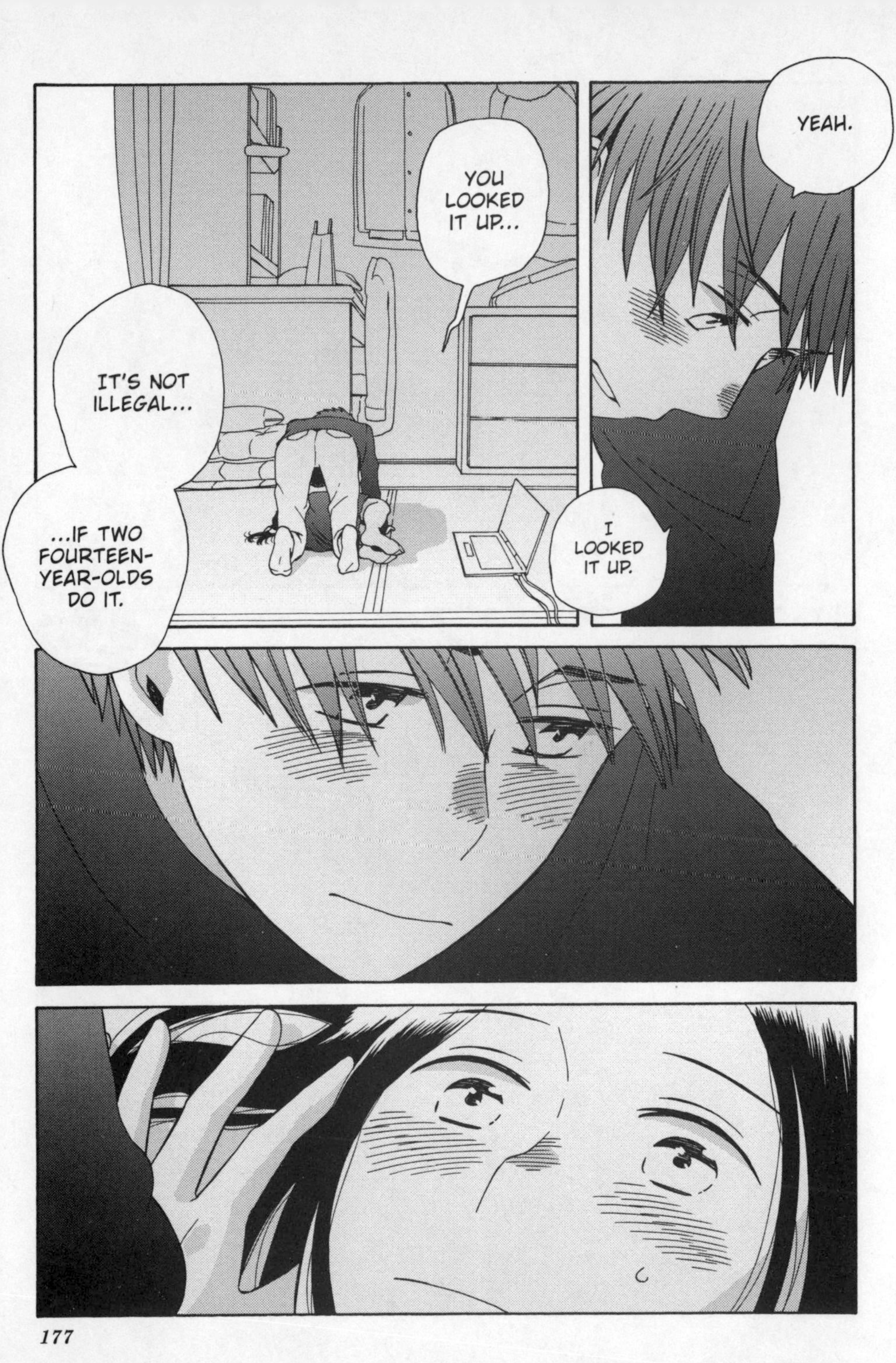
YEAH.
I LOOKED IT UP.
YOU LOOKED IT UP...
IT'S NOT ILLEGAL...
...IF TWO FOURTEEN-YEAR-OLDS DO IT.

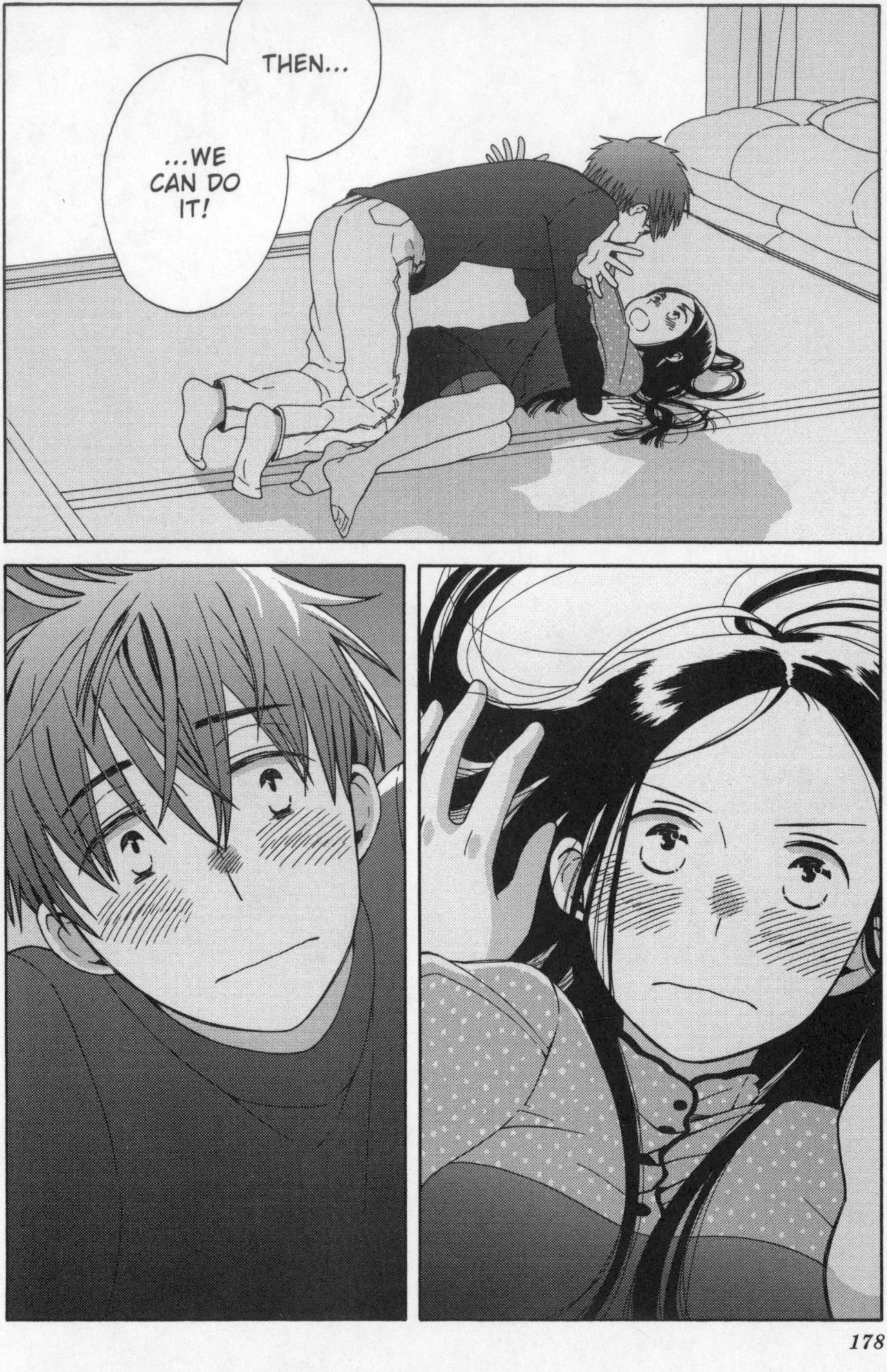
THEN...
...WE CAN DO IT!

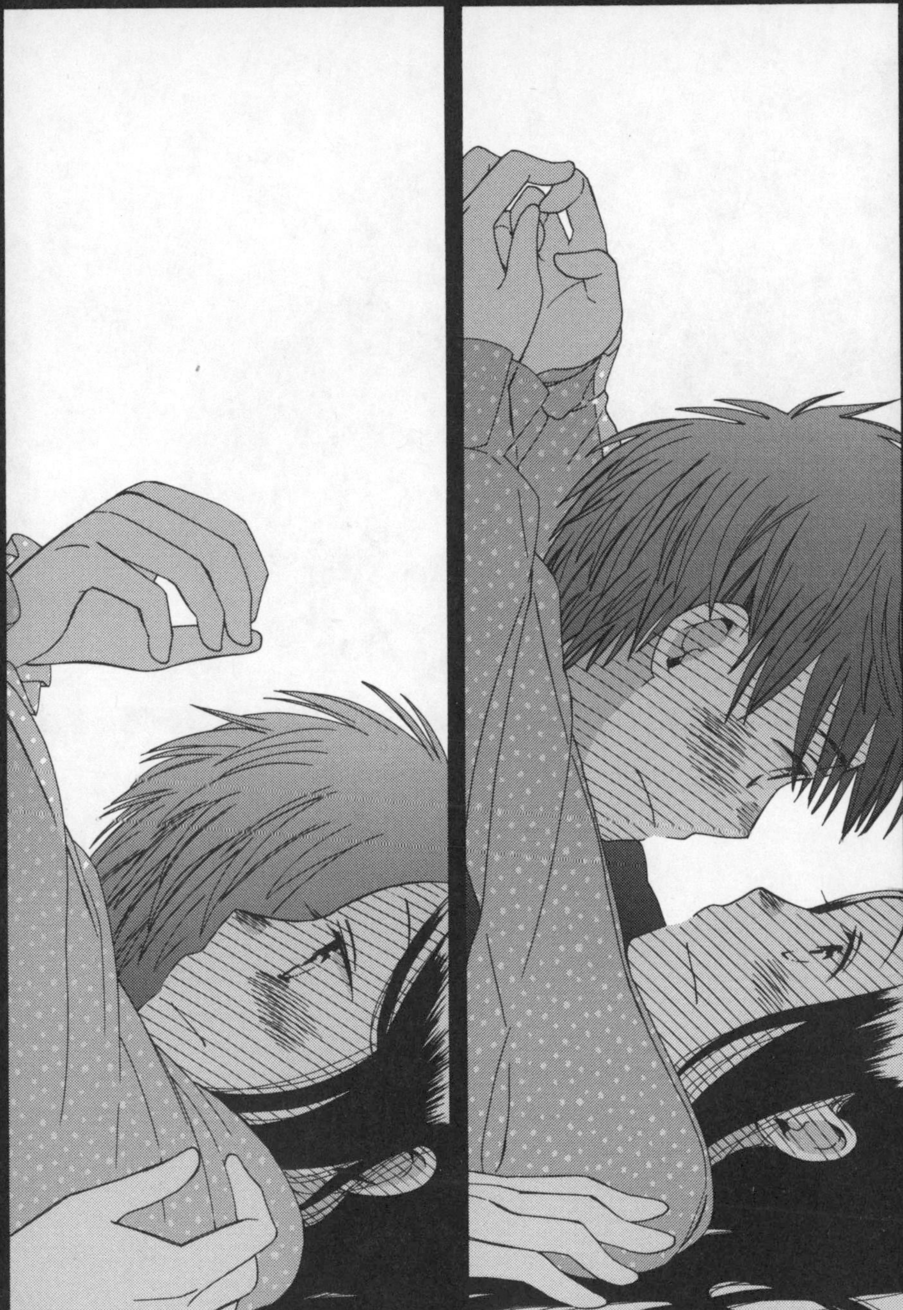

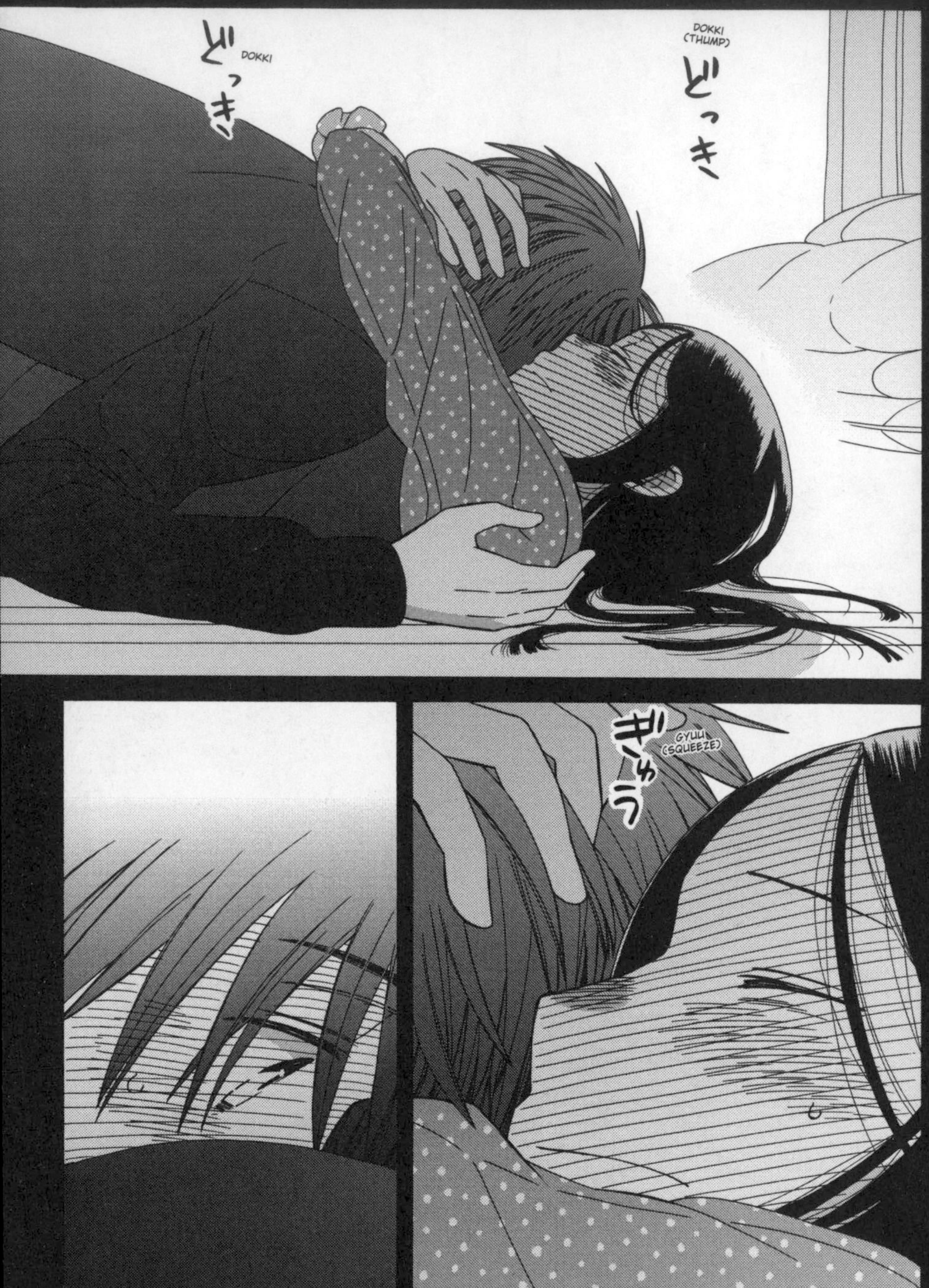

どっき
DOKKI (THUMP)
どっき
DOKKI
ぎゅう
GYUU (SQUEEZE)

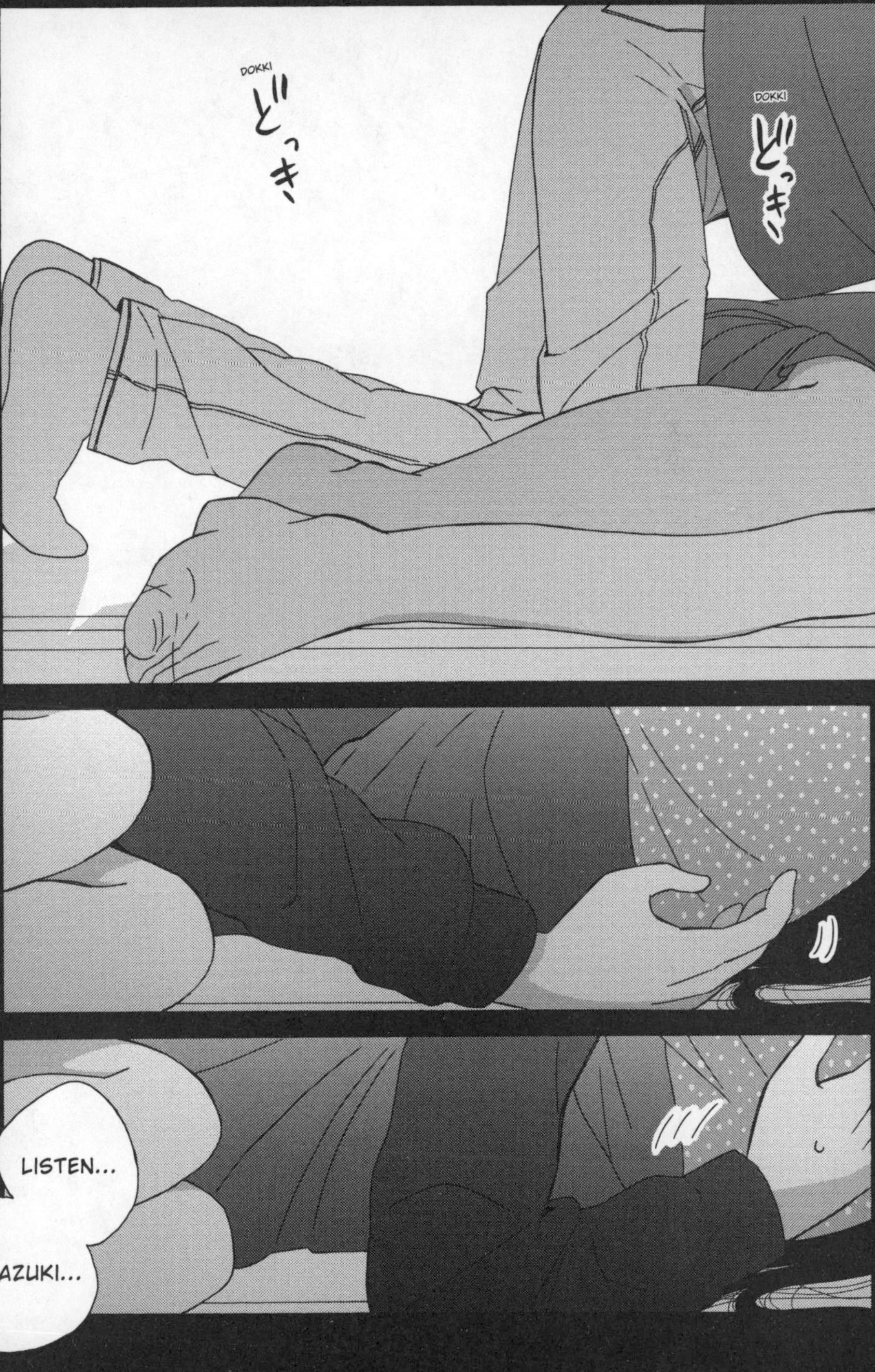
DOKKI
どっき
DOKKI
どっき
LISTEN...
...KAZUKI...

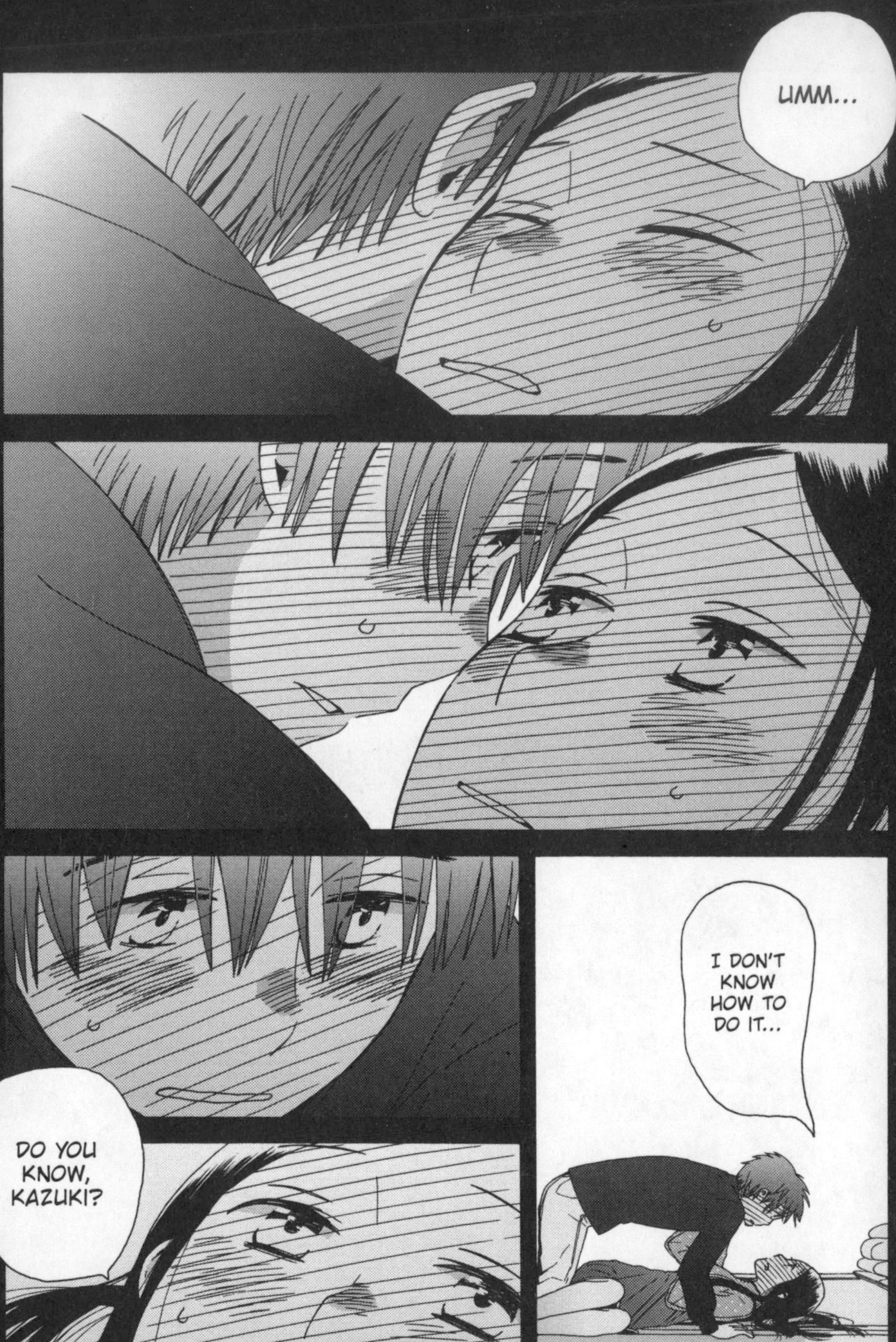
UMM...
I DON'T KNOW HOW TO DO IT...
DO YOU KNOW, KAZUKI?

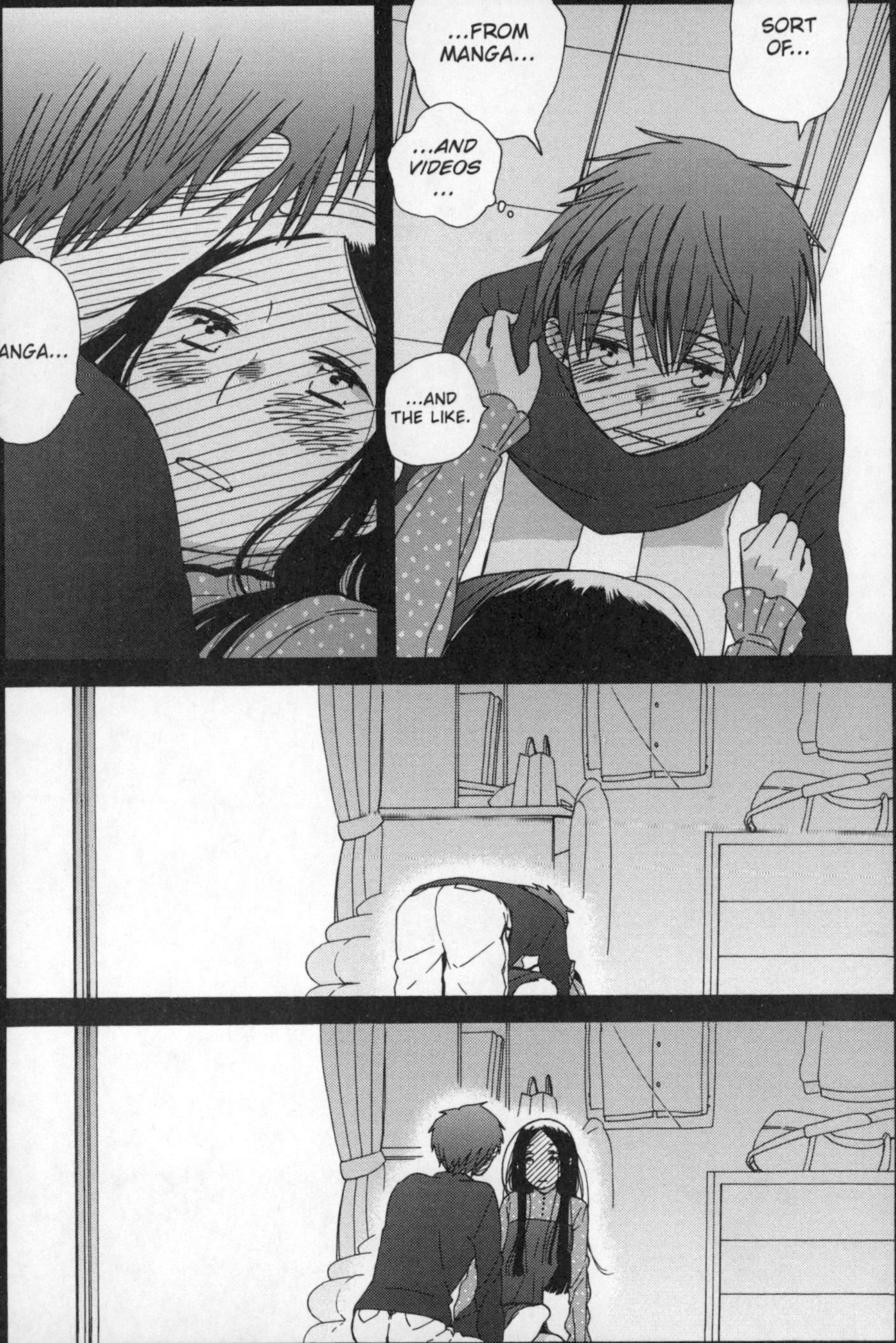
SORT OF...
...FROM MANGA...
...AND VIDEOS ...
...AND THE LIKE.
MANGA...

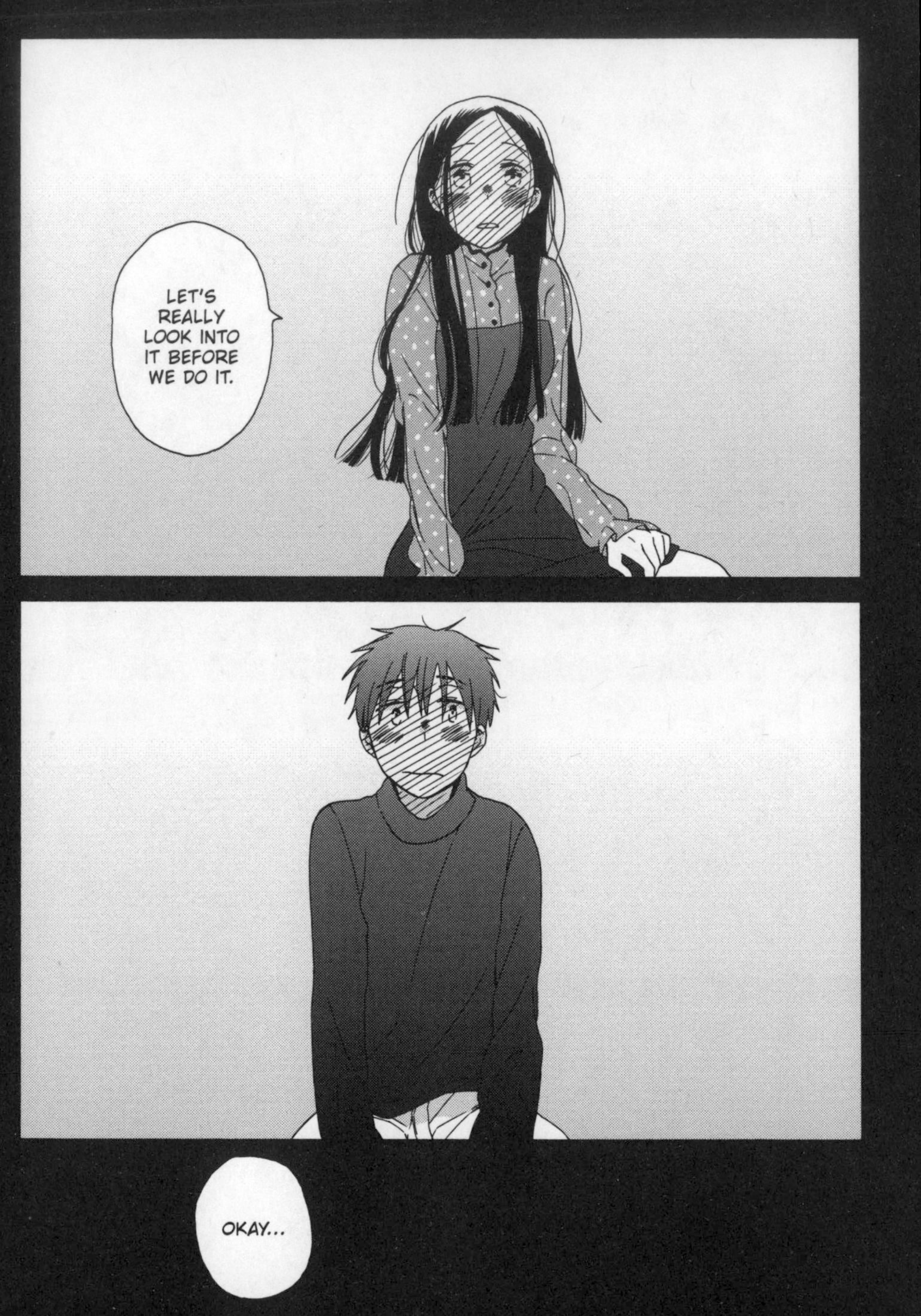
LET'S REALLY LOOK INTO IT BEFORE WE DO IT.
OKAY...

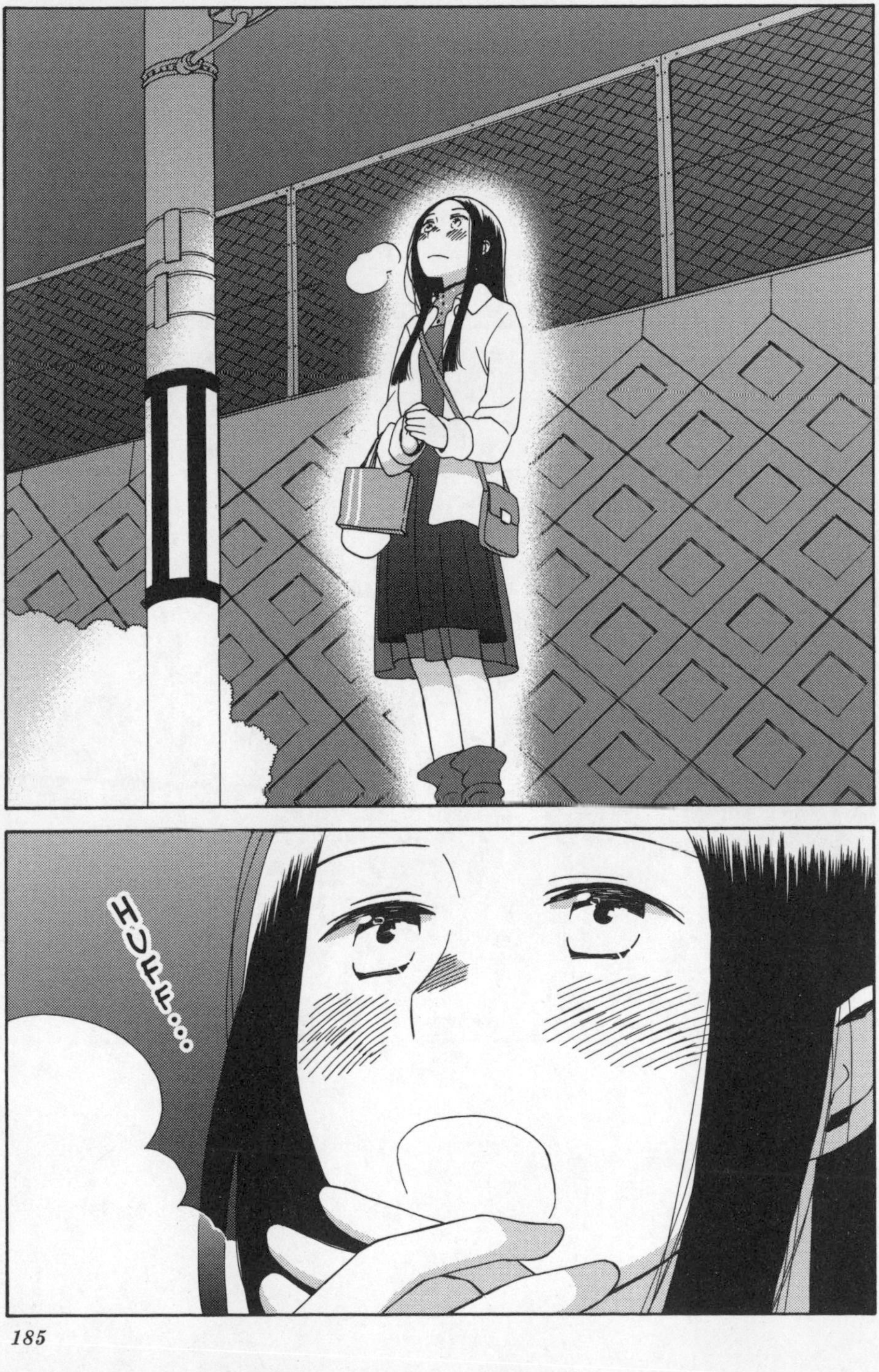
HUFF...

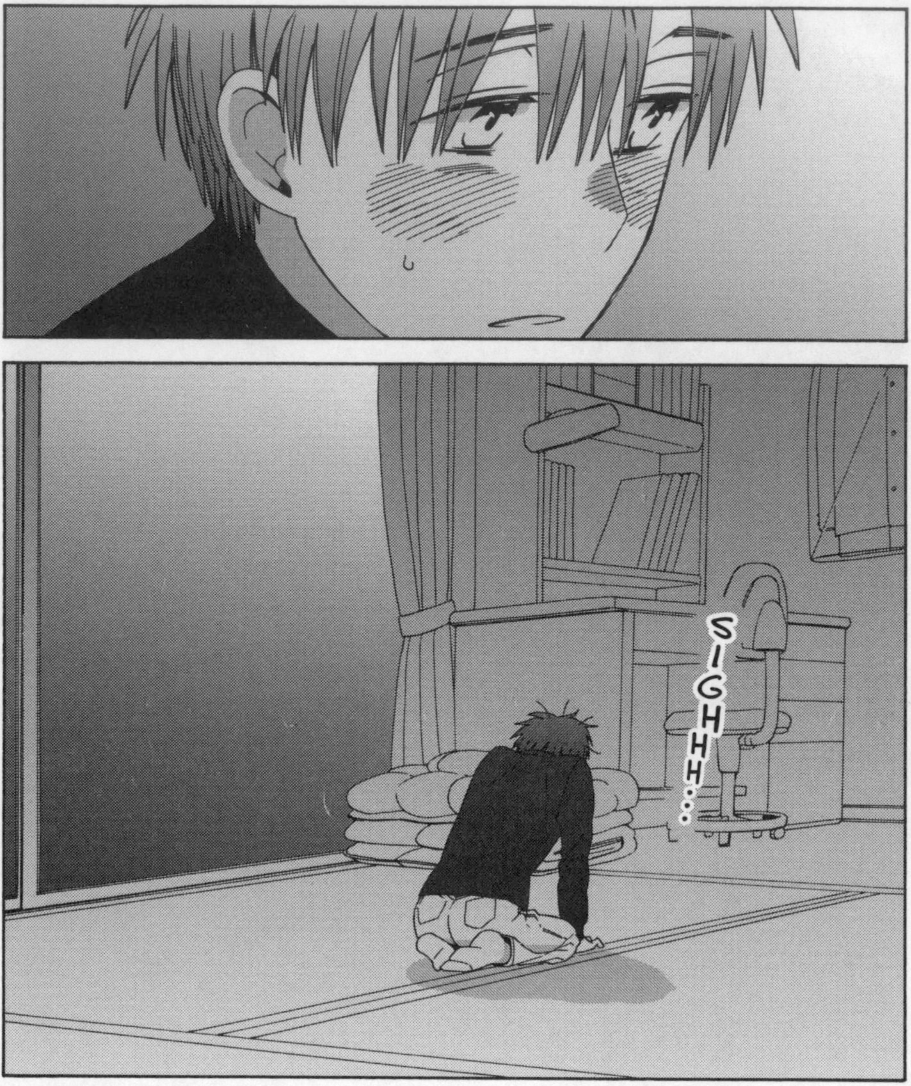
SIGHHH...

Fin

Love at Fourteen

Fuka Mizutani

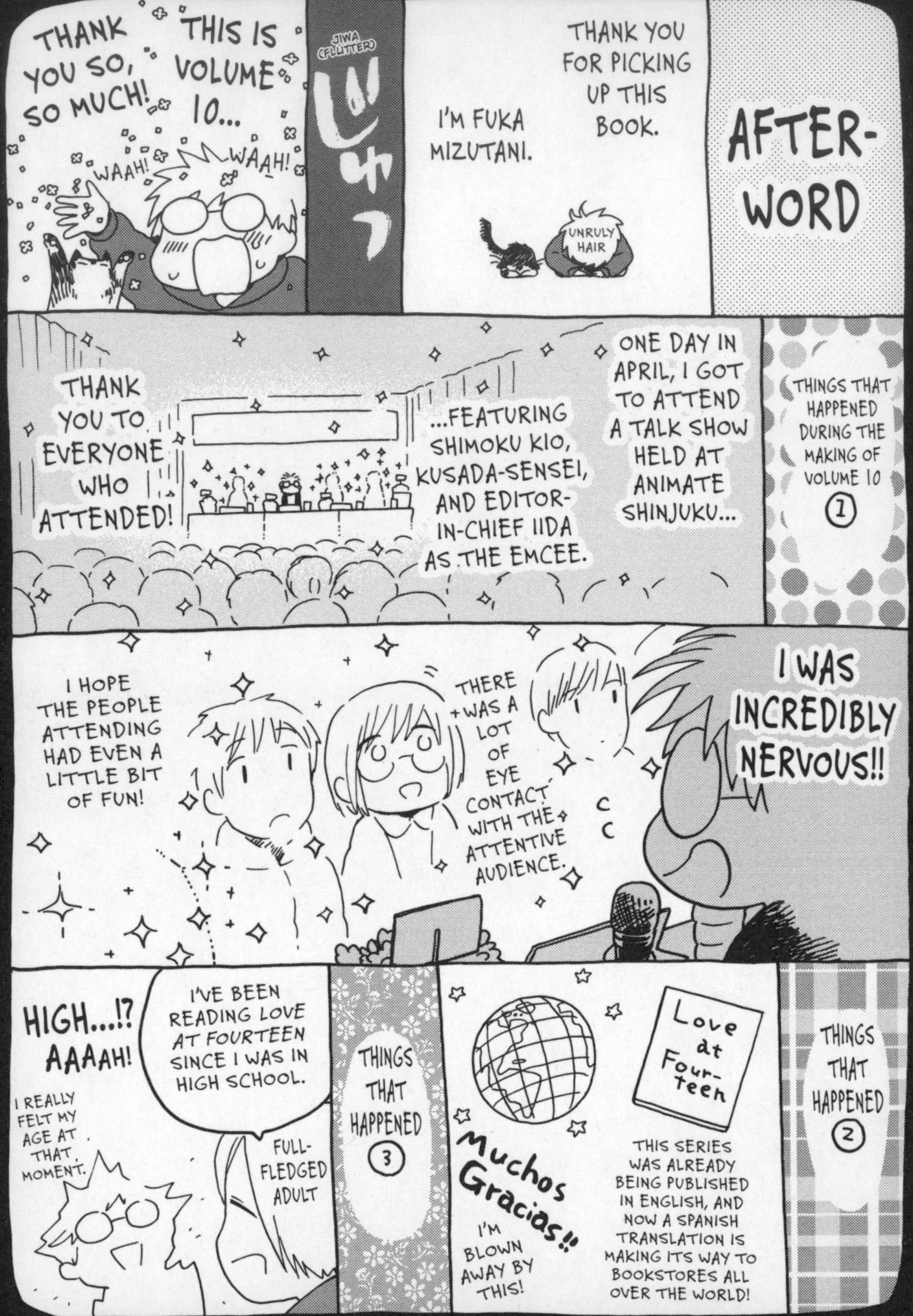
AFTER-WORD
THANK YOU FOR PICKING UP THIS BOOK.
I'M FUKA MIZUTANI.
UNRULY HAIR
JIWA (FLLITTER)
THIS IS VOLUME 10...
THANK YOU SO, SO MUCH!
WAAH!
WAAH!
THINGS THAT HAPPENED DURING THE MAKING OF VOLUME 10 ①
ONE DAY IN APRIL, I GOT TO ATTEND A TALK SHOW HELD AT ANIMATE SHINJUKU...
...FEATURING SHIMOKU KIO, KUSADA-SENSEI, AND EDITOR-IN-CHIEF IIDA AS THE EMCEE.
THANK YOU TO EVERYONE WHO ATTENDED!
I WAS INCREDIBLY NERVOUS!!
THERE WAS A LOT OF EYE CONTACT WITH THE ATTENTIVE AUDIENCE.
I HOPE THE PEOPLE ATTENDING HAD EVEN A LITTLE BIT OF FUN!
THINGS THAT HAPPENED ②
Love at Four-teen
THIS SERIES WAS ALREADY BEING PUBLISHED IN ENGLISH, AND NOW A SPANISH TRANSLATION IS MAKING ITS WAY TO BOOKSTORES ALL OVER THE WORLD!
Muchos Gracias!!
I'M BLOWN AWAY BY THIS!
THINGS THAT HAPPENED ③
I'VE BEEN READING LOVE AT FOURTEEN SINCE I WAS IN HIGH SCHOOL.
FULL-FLEDGED ADULT
HIGH...!? AAAAH!
I REALLY FELT MY AGE AT THAT MOMENT.

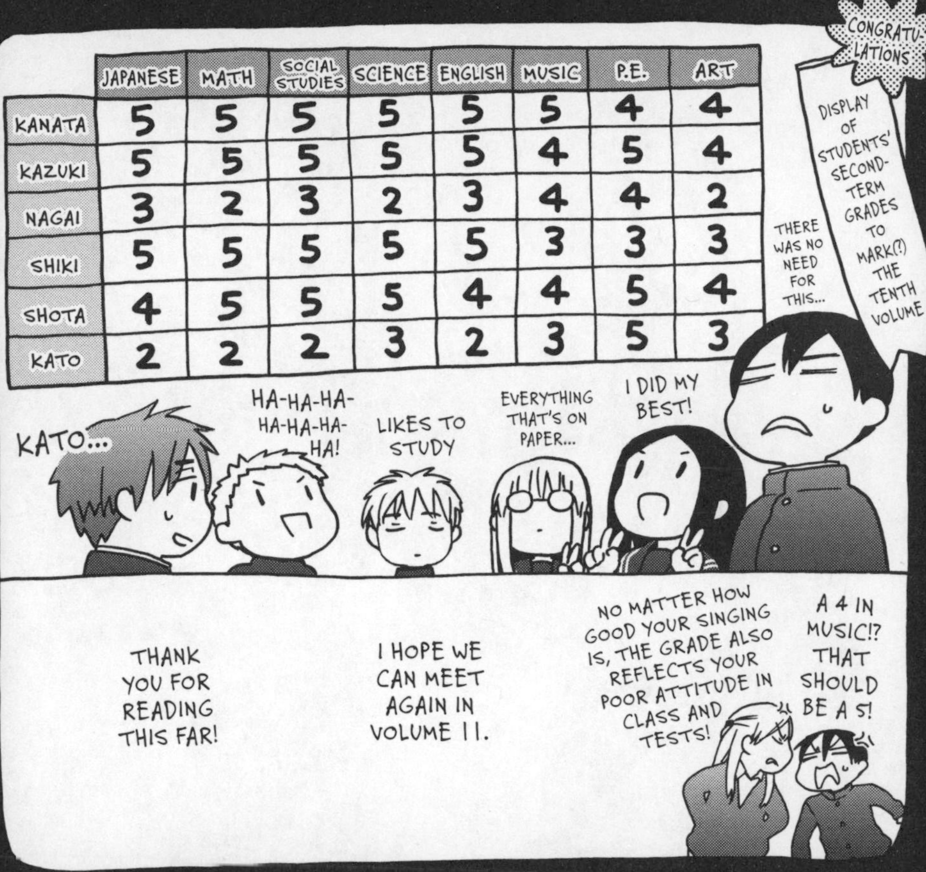
CONGRATULATIONS
DISPLAY OF STUDENTS' SECOND-TERM GRADES TO MARK(?) THE TENTH VOLUME
THERE WAS NO NEED FOR THIS...
I DID MY BEST!
EVERYTHING THAT'S ON PAPER...
LIKES TO STUDY
HA-HA-HA-HA-HA-HA-HA!
KATO...
A 4 IN MUSIC!? THAT SHOULD BE A 5!
NO MATTER HOW GOOD YOUR SINGING IS, THE GRADE ALSO REFLECTS YOUR POOR ATTITUDE IN CLASS AND TESTS!
I HOPE WE CAN MEET AGAIN IN VOLUME 11.
THANK YOU FOR READING THIS FAR!

	JAPANESE	MATH	SOCIAL STUDIES	SCIENCE	ENGLISH	MUSIC	P.E.	ART
KANATA	5	5	5	5	5	5	4	4
KAZUKI	5	5	5	5	5	4	5	4
NAGAI	3	2	3	2	3	4	4	2
SHIKI	5	5	5	5	5	3	3	3
SHOTA	4	5	5	5	4	4	5	4
KATO	2	2	2	3	2	3	5	3

Special Thanks

Hakusensha Iida-sama

Kohei Nawata DeSign

My family

My great friends

Digital Resouces Sangatsu-sama

Sayo Murata-chan

And all of you who are reading this now.

Winter 2019

水谷フーカ.
Fuka Mizutani

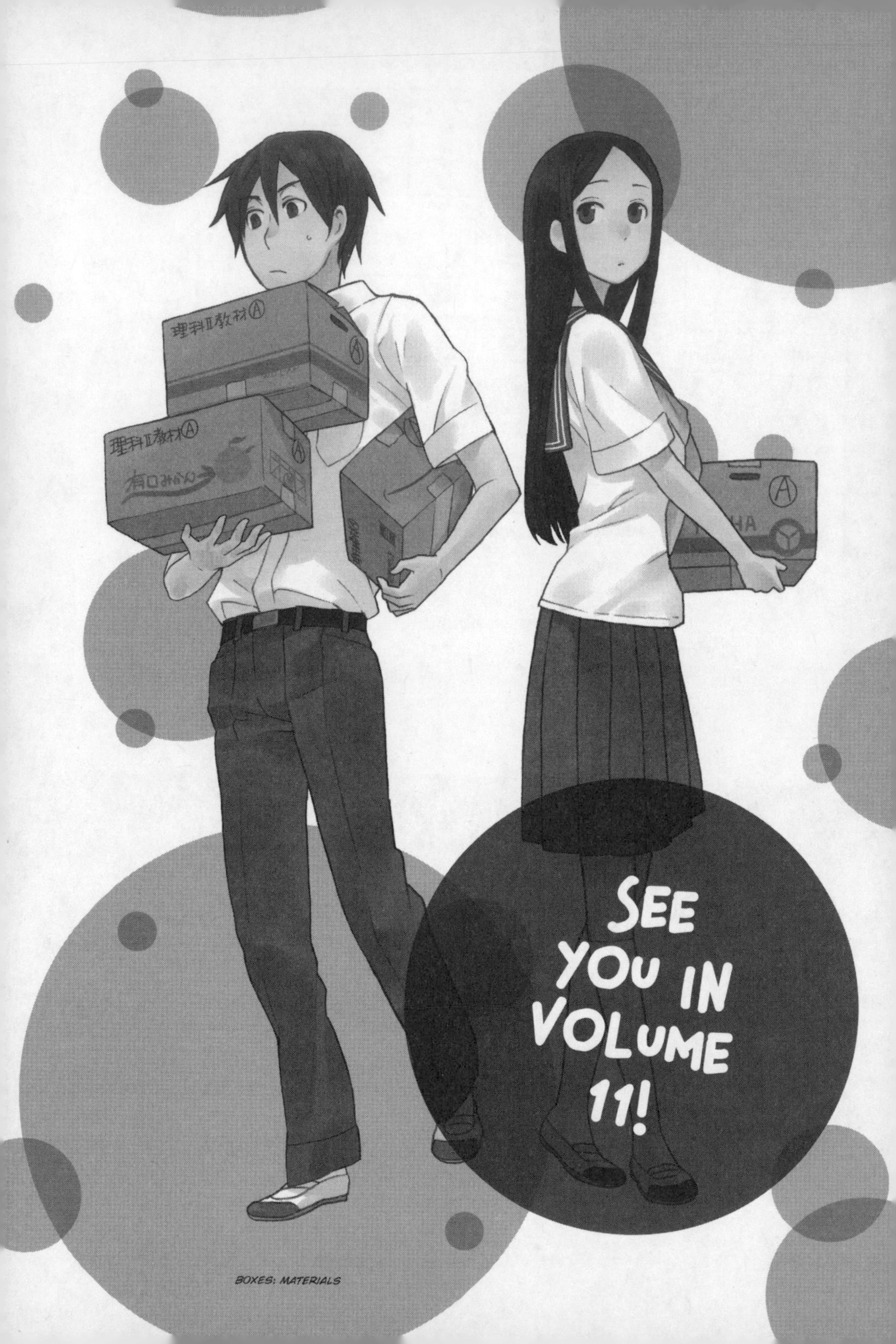
理科Ⅱ教材
理科Ⅱ教材
SEE YOU IN VOLUME 11!
BOXES: MATERIALS

TRANSLATION NOTES

COMMON HONORIFICS:

no honorific: Indicates familiarity or closeness; if used without permission or reason, addressing someone in this manner would constitute an insult.

-san: The Japanese equivalent of Mr./Mrs./Miss. If a situation calls for politeness, this is the fail-safe honorific.

-sama: Conveys great respect; may also indicate that the social status of the speaker is lower than that of the addressee.

-kun: Used most often when referring to boys, this indicates affection or familiarity. Occasionally used by older men among their peers, but it may also be used by anyone referring to a person of lower standing.

-chan: An affectionate honorific indicating familiarity used mostly in reference to girls; also used in reference to cute persons or animals of either gender.

-senpai: A suffix used to address upperclassmen or more experienced coworkers.

-sensei: A respectful term for teachers, artists, or high-level professionals.

PAGE 18

Kokkuri-san: Similar to ouija boards in how they work, kokkuri-san is usually played by school children and by setting up a piece of paper with the Japanese alphabet, "Yes," "No," and a torii drawn in the middle. Torii are gates found at the entrance or within Shinto shrines and mark a transition between the human and spiritual world. The actual rules for kokkuri-san differ between regions and even schools.

PAGE 24

Trimester: Most schools in Japan have three semesters as opposed to the two-semester system in America. It is usually broken into a spring, fall, and winter semester with extended breaks in the summer and winter. The Japanese school year starts in April and ends in March.

PAGE 86

Taiyaki: This is a kind of fish-shaped cake made out of regular pancake or waffle batter and is commonly filled with red bean paste but custard or chocolate are also popular fillings. In this case, the taiyaki is used in place of an ice-cream waffle cone.

PAGE 96

Superhero show: Stage shows are often held in places with many young children, such as amusement parks, department shows, and aquariums. They can feature superheroes from popular children's TV shows in choreographed battles against their enemies. The usual demographic is elementary school students.

PAGE 134

Dropping -san: When getting to know someone, Japanese people will usually address them by their family name with the honorific -san. Calling someone by their given name or dropping honorifics entirely is a sign that the two people are close, which is why Toudou is so shocked to hear Shota do both simultaneously.

PAGE 156

New Year's shrine visit: Going to a local shrine and praying for a good new year or something more specific is a common custom and can be done any time between midnight of New Year's Eve and early January, preferably before the winter holidays are over. During shrine vists, people also often get food from vendors, pull fortunes, and buy protective charms.

PAGE 157

Amazake: Traditional sweet drink made from fermented rice that is alcohol-free or contains such trace amounts that even teenagers are allowed to drink it. It can be served either chilled, warm, or hot but the latter is more popular in the winter months.

PAGE 159

Omiki: Sake offered to the deities at a shrine but may also be offered to adults who visit the shrine.

PAGE 164

Castella: Type of wagashi, or traditional Japanese sweet that is similar to a dense sponge cake and baked using a particular type of sugar syrup called mizuame. Originally introduced to Japan by Portugese merchants, it's now considered a specialty of Nagasaki prefecture.

PAGE 189

Grades: The Japanese grading system uses the numerals 1 to 5, with 5 being the equivalent to an A and 2 being a barely passing grade. Though a 1 is equivalent to an F, students in Japan don't retake courses that they fail.

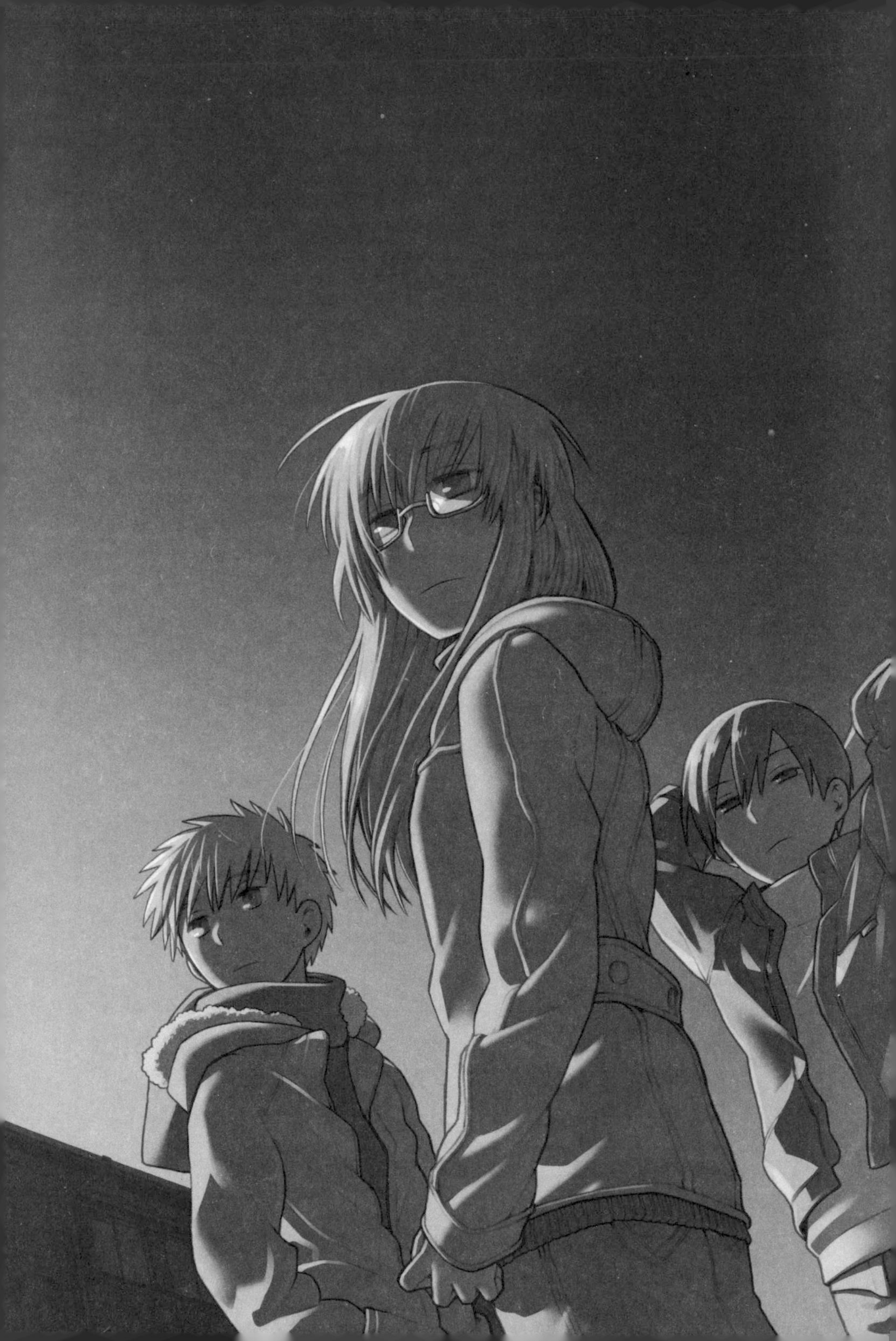

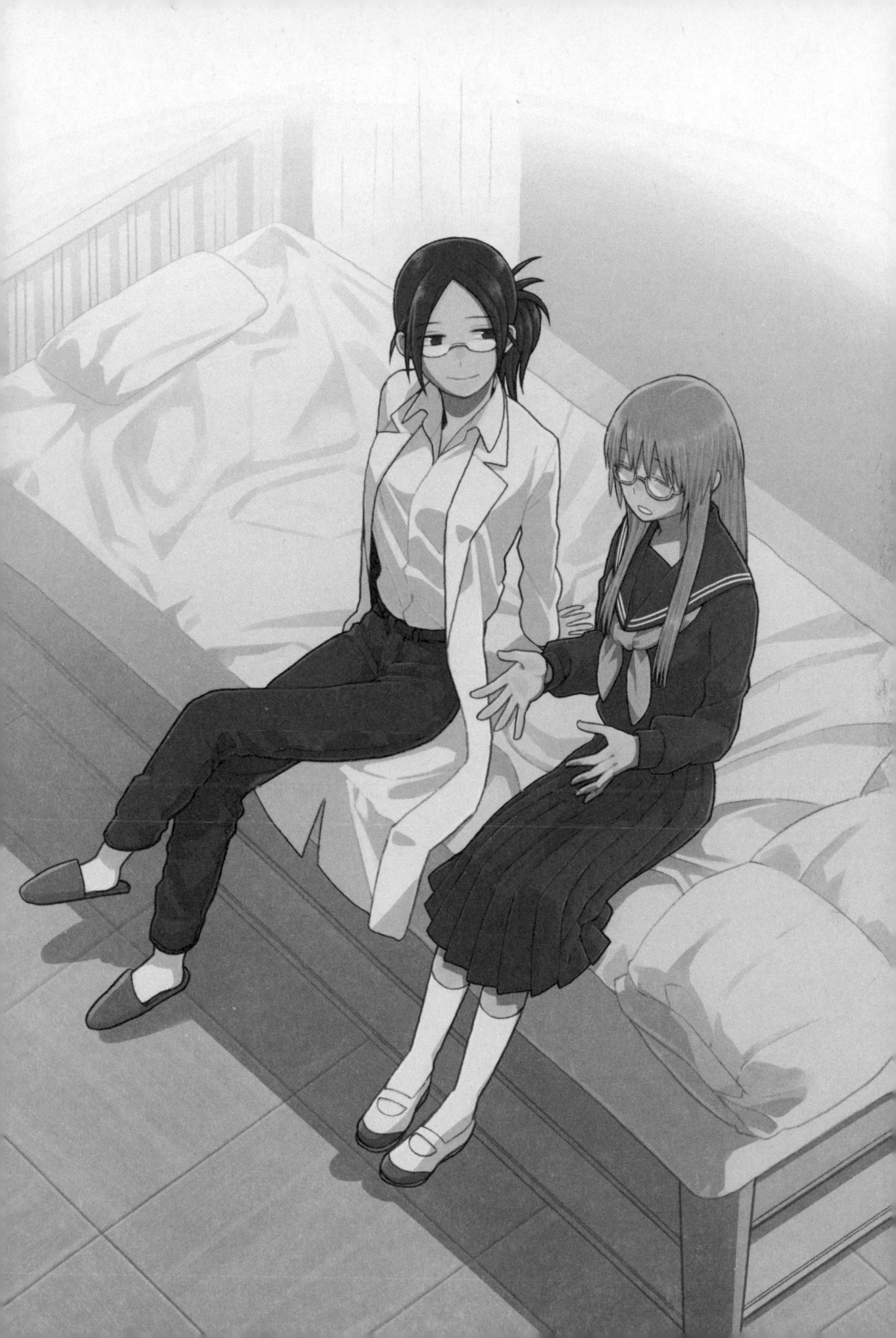

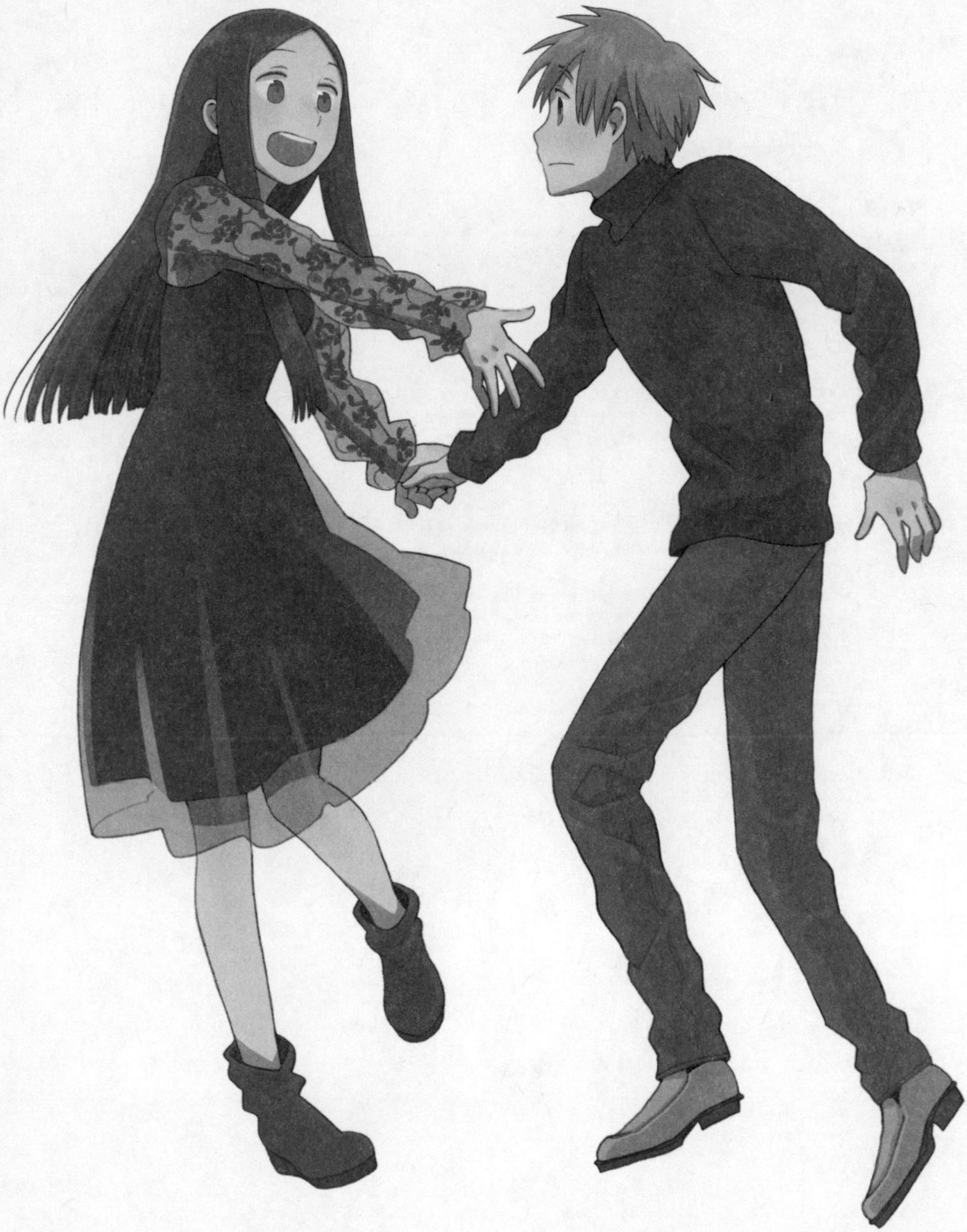

LOVE AT FOURTEEN ⑩

FUKA MIZUTANI

Translation: Sheldon Drzka

Lettering: Lys Blakeslee

JUYON-SAI NO KOI by Fuka Mizutani
© Fuka Mizutani 2019
All rights reserved.
First published in Japan in 2019 by HAKUSENSHA, INC., Tokyo.
English language translation rights in U.S.A., Canada and U.K. arranged with
HAKUSENSHA, INC., Tokyo through Tuttle-Mori Agency, Inc., Tokyo.

Yen Press
150 West 30th Street, 19th Floor
New York, NY 10001

Visit us at yenpress.com
facebook.com/yenpress
twitter.com/yenpress
yenpress.tumblr.com
instagram.com/yenpress

First Yen Press Edition: June 2021

Yen Press is an imprint of Yen Press, LLC.
The Yen Press name and logo are trademarks of Yen Press, LLC.

The publisher is not responsible for websites (or their content) that are not owned by the publisher.

Library of Congress Control Number: 2016297684

ISBNs: 978-1-9753-1685-3 (paperback)
        978-1-9753-1686-0 (ebook)

10 9 8 7 6 5 4 3 2 1

WOR

Printed in the United States of America